Child Language

2nd Edition

acquisition and development

Matthew Saxton

SAGE

Los Angeles | London | New Delhi
Singapore | Washington DC | Melbourne

Los Angeles | London | New Delhi
Singapore | Washington DC | Melbourne

SAGE Publications Ltd
1 Oliver's Yard
55 City Road
London EC1Y 1SP

SAGE Publications Inc.
2455 Teller Road
Thousand Oaks, California 91320

SAGE Publications India Pvt Ltd
B 1/I 1 Mohan Cooperative Industrial Area
Mathura Road
New Delhi 110 044

SAGE Publications Asia-Pacific Pte Ltd
3 Church Street
#10-04 Samsung Hub
Singapore 049483

Editor: Luke Block
Editorial assistant: Lucy Dang
Production editor: Imogen Roome
Copyeditor: Sarah Bury
Proofreader: Christine Bitten
Indexer: Martin Hargreaves
Marketing manager: Lucia Sweet
Cover design: Wendy Scott
Typeset by: C&M Digitals (P) Ltd, Chennai, India
Printed in the UK

© Matthew Saxton 2017

First published 2010
Reprinted 2010, 2011, 2012, 2015, 2016

Library of Congress Control Number: 2016962661

British Library Cataloguing in Publication data

A catalogue record for this book is available from
the British Library

ISBN 978-1-4462-9561-8
ISBN 978-1-4462-9562-5 (pbk)

For Gary, Sue and Alex

Drawing of Alex Saxton by Colin Saxton

Contents

Contents

Acknowledgements

I have had much help and encouragement in the writing – and updating – of this book from family, friends and former colleagues in academia. It has also been gratifying to receive help from colleagues further afield, in the wider world of child language research, many of whom I have yet to meet, but all of whom responded to my queries with considerable generosity of spirit. In particular, I should like to thank Ayhan Aksu-Koç, Shanley Allen, Ben Ambridge, Misha Becker, Heike Behrens, Ruth Berman, Raymond Bertram, Joan Bybee, Robin Campbell, Shula Chiat, Anne Christophe, Alex Clark, Eve Clark, Gina Conti-Ramsden, Annick de Houwer, Holly Garwood, Jonathan Ginzburg, Roberta Golinkoff, Marisa Teresa Guasti, Bart Guerts, Margaret Harris, Maya Hickmann, Josephine Howard, Christine Howe, Dick Hudson, Jane Hurry, Evan Kidd, Sarah King, Mike Kirkman, Shalom Lappin, Elena Lieven, Brian MacWhinney, Michael Maratsos, Theo Marinis, Chloe Marshall, Cecile McKee, Evelyne Mercure, David Messer, Gary Morgan, Vicki Murphy, Letitia Naigles, Keith Nelson, David Olson, Mitsuhiko Ota, Anna Papafragou, Lisa Pearl, Colin Phillips, Li Ping, Dorit Ravid, Maritza Rivera Gaxiola, Stuart Rosen, Caroline Rowland, Jenny Saffran, Colin Saxton, Susan Sciama, Yasuhiro Shirai, Melanie Soderstrom, Morag Stuart, Mike Swan, Michael Tomasello, Michael Ullman, Angelika van Hout, Athena Vouloumanos, Catherine Walter, Dan Weiss and Charles Yang.

Beyond the professional, there is the personal. My husband, Gary Yershon, is constant in his support. My son, Alex – a grown man now – features throughout the book with examples from a diary study I did with him during my doctoral studies. In the field of child language, it is not enough simply to breed one's own data. One needs also a son with a generous spirit who is happy to share his early ventures into language with the wider world. My father, Colin Saxton, drew the picture of Alex as a newborn which features as the frontispiece. And my mother, Josephine Howard, created the painting which has been used for the book cover. Finally, friends, family and colleagues make numerous appearances in these pages, embedded in the examples of linguistic structures. To them all, I offer my heartfelt thanks.

Publisher's Acknowledgements

The author and publisher wish to thank the following for the permission to use copyright material:

We thank APA for granting us permission to reproduce:

Baillargeon, R. (1987). Object permanence in 3½-month-old and 4½-month-old infants. *Developmental Psychology*, *23(5)*, 655–664. Fig. 1, p. 656.

Ganger, J. & Brent, M.R. (2004). Reexamining the vocabulary spurt. *Developmental Psychology*, *40(4)*, 621–632. Fig. 1. A spurtlike function (logistic) superimposed on slightly modified data from Child 041B (p. 623). Fig. 2. A nonspurtlike curve (quadratic) superimposed on the same data shown in Figure 1, p. 623.

We thank Cambridge University Press for granting us permission to reproduce:

Gershkoff-Stowe, L., Connell, B. & Smith, L. (2006). Priming overgeneralizations in two- and four-year-old children. *Journal of Child Language*, *33(3)*, 461–486. Figure 1, p. 464. Levels of processing and lexical competition involved in naming a perceived object.

Dromi, E. (1987). *Early lexical development.* Cambridge: Cambridge University Press. Figure 1, p. 111. Keren's cumulative lexicon at the one-word stage.

Bates, E. & Goodman, J.C. (1997, p. 517, Fig. 2) in E. Bates, I. Bretherton & L. Snyder (1988). *From first words to grammar: Individual differences and dissociable mechanisms.* New York: Cambridge University Press.

Smith, L.B. (2001). How domain-general processes may create domain-specific biases. In M. Bowerman & S.C. Levinson (Eds.), *Language acquisition and conceptual development* (pp. 101–131). Cambridge: Cambridge University Press. Figure 4.1. Sample stimuli from Landau, Smith & Jones (1988). All stimuli were three-dimensional objects made of wood, wire, or sponge.

We thank Elsevier for granting us permission to reproduce:

A figure from Johnson, J.S. & Newport, E.L. (1989). Critical period effects in second language learning: The influence of maturational state on the acquisition of English as a second language. *Cognitive Psychology*, *21(1)*, 60–99.

Nicoladis, E. (2003). What compound nouns mean to preschool children. *Brain and Language, 84(1)*, 38–49. Fig. 2. 'Sun bag' target for comprehension, p. 43.

Benasich, A.A., Choudhury, N., Friedman, J.T., Realpe-Bonilla, T., Chojnowska, C. & Gou, Z.K. (2006). The infant as a prelinguistic model for language learning impairments: Predicting from event-related potentials to behavior. *Neuropsychologia, 44(3)*, 396–411. Fig. 1. Photograph of a 6-month-old child seated on his mother's lap during an ERP testing session using a dense array Geodesic Sensor Net system (Electric Geodesic, Inc., Eugene, Oregon, USA), p. 399.

We thank the Linguistic Society of America for granting us permission to reproduce Brooks, P.J. & Tomasello, M. (1999). How children constrain their argument structure constructions. *Language, 75(4)*, 720–738. Figure 1. Novel 'directed motion' and 'manner of motion' verbs, p. 724.

We thank MIT Press for granting us permission to reproduce Hirsh-Pasek, K. & Golinkoff, R.M. (1996). *The origins of grammar: Evidence from early language comprehension*, Figure 6.1, © 1996 Massachusetts Institute of Technology, by permission of the MIT Press.

We thank Wiley-Blackwell for granting us permission to reproduce:

Gertner, Y., Fisher, C. & Eisengart, J. (2006). Learning words and rules: Abstract knowledge of word order in early sentence comprehension. *Psychological Science, 17(8)*, 684–691. Figure 1, p. 686.

Saffran, J.R. (2003). Statistical language learning: Mechanisms and constraints. *Current Directions in Psychological Science, 12(4)*, 110–114. Figure 1, p. 111.

Fenson, L., Dale, P.S., Reznick, J.S., Bates, E., Thal, D.J. & Pethick, S.J. (1994). Variability in early communicative development. *Monographs of the Society for Research in Child Development, 59(5)*. Figure 1, p. 35 and Figure 2, p. 38.

Notes on the Organization of this Book

This text is aimed principally at students of psychology with an interest in child language. It is suitable for use at undergraduate level, and also at postgraduate level, in cases where the field is new. In both cases, I am keenly aware that most psychology students have no prior training in linguistic theory. In fact, if you're like me – the member of a lost generation – you may not even have learnt very much at all about language at school. For this reason, I have tried to take nothing for granted as far as linguistic terminology is concerned, not even with common items like *noun* or *verb*. Of course, you can always skip over the linguistic interludes, if it's all old hat, and stick with the main event. Either way, the aim of this book is to equip you to appreciate more fully the arguments and evidence advanced in the study of child language. The following menu of pedagogic features should sustain you on the journey ahead.

- Glossary of linguistic terms

  Linguistic terms are highlighted in **bold** to indicate their appearance in the glossary, towards the end of the book. There you will find definitions of all things linguistic. You can test your knowledge of terminology via the related website, where you will find eFlashcards to help you.

- Pronunciation guide: English phonemes

  A list of the special symbols used to represent the consonant and vowel sounds of English. And yes, the terms *phoneme*, *consonant* and *vowel* all feature in the glossary.

- Boxes

  Boxes have been used for two kinds of diversion from the main text: (1) to expand on essential terminology from linguistic theory; and (2) to provide extra information on key background concepts.

- References and further reading

  As well as the list of references at the end of the book, I have ended each chapter with a few suggestions for further reading. These latter are annotated with potted reviews and notes.

- Website addresses

  The internet makes life easy for students in all kinds of ways. But with regard to reading material, articles found on the internet can be intrinsically unreliable. The crux of the matter is this: one cannot always tell, with any certainty, who wrote a given internet article. Nor can one always be sure if the claims made in internet sources are reasonable, valid, and backed up by reference to genuine and appropriate research. That said, many sources are perfectly respectable – as testified by the burgeoning number of electronic journals now available. I have been as careful as I can in my listing of websites, but approach with caution. I have included the academic web pages of some key child language researchers, and these should be pretty reliable. In particular, many academics now post downloadable versions of research articles on their university homepages.

- Discussion points

  Discussion points are sprinkled throughout the book wherever they seem like a Good Thing. They can be used in seminars or in student self-study groups (never tried the latter? – give them a go). For some of the Discussion points, you should equip yourself by reading the relevant chapter in advance and/or reading an item from the Further Reading section.

- Exercises on linguistic concepts (with answers)

  Like cod liver oil, linguistic exercises are unpalatable, but very good for you. The idea is to limber up with some practice on unfamiliar concepts, before tackling the literature. Model answers are provided at the end of the book.

- PowerPoint slides

  These slides are intended for use by your lecturers. They fillet the main points from each chapter, allowing room to expand on the main points in classroom teaching sessions. But they could also quite easily be used for private study, as the basis for identifying key points for revision and reflection.

- Multiple choice questions

  You will find a set of MCQs for each chapter on the companion website. They will help sharpen your understanding of key concepts. Or maybe they'll just reveal how lucky you are.

- Author index

  Find your favourite authors, as mentioned in the text, and source their work in the list of references. Then challenge yourself to find other work, especially *recent* research, by the same authors (your university library will help if you're new to the sport of Reference Hunting).

- Subject index

  Separate from the author index, because it makes life a little less cluttered. Relevant topics from each chapter are included to enhance the sum total of your learning happiness.

Companion Website page

The second edition of *Child Language* is supported by a wealth of online resources for both students and lecturers to aid study and support teaching, which are available at **https://study. sagepub.com/saxton2e.**

For students

Multiple choice questions to test your knowledge of key concepts and make sure you have retained the most important parts of each chapter.

Weblinks direct you to relevant resources to broaden your understanding of chapter topics and link to real conversations about social research.

Flashcard glossary so you can test yourself on all the key terms from the book and check your understanding.

For lecturers

PowerPoint slides featuring figures, tables, and key topics from the book can be downloaded and customized for use in your own presentations.

1

Prelude: Landmarks in the Landscape of Child Language

CONTENTS

OVERVIEW

By the end of this chapter you should have some appreciation of the challenges facing the newborn infant in the acquisition of language. Major landmarks in language development are presented at each of the following four levels of linguistic analysis:

- phonology (the sound system)
- vocabulary
- morphology (parts of words, especially those parts used for grammar)
- grammar

We will consider some of the philosophical problems facing the child (for example, how does the child know what a word is, or what it might refer to?). And we will introduce the nature–nurture problem: to what extent do genetic factors determine the development of language? To set the child's language learning achievements in context, an overview is provided of the child's achievements in other developmental domains (cognitive, perceptual–motor and social), before sketching out the contents of the chapters that follow.

From burping to grammar in the pre-school years

Have you ever had a chat with a toddler? A rather precocious two-year-old, known as Eve, came out with the following one day, while in conversation with her mother:

(1) Eve aged two years (Brown, 1973):
he go asleep
want more grape juice
putting sand in the pail
I have get my crayons
where other baby?

We can see straight away that Eve is fairly savvy about a number of different topics. But however impressed we are by Eve's knowledge of crayons, sand and juice, it is clear that not one of the sentences would pass muster if they were uttered by an adult in the same setting. If nothing else, this reminds us that language *develops*.

As we shall discover in this book, though, Eve has already come a long way by the age of two years. A typical newborn is capable, vocally, of no more than reflexive crying and fussing, plus a small repertoire of vegetative sounds, principally, burping, spitting up and swallowing (Stark, 1986). This repertoire is lent some charm at about eight weeks, with the emergence of cooing and laughter. But if we fast forward to the typical five-year-old, then we suddenly find ourselves in the company of a linguistic sophisticate, someone with an extensive vocabulary who is able to put words together in interesting, complex sentences that, for the most part, are perfectly well formed.

(2) Ross aged 5;1 (MacWhinney, 2000):
   I had the worst dream of my life
   I wish I could let you in here, but there's no room
   You thought he couldn't go to school because we didn't have the medicine

---

BOX 1.1   NOTATION FOR THE CHILD'S AGE

There is a standard convention for denoting a child's age in the child language literature. A child aged two years, three months would be recorded as 2;3. The child of four years, six months appears as 4;6, and so on. Note the use of the semi-colon to separate years from months. When even more fine-grained analyses are required, we can also add the number of days after a period (.) For example, 1;9.10 is read as one year, nine months and ten days.

   This shorthand, in which we note months as well as years, is very useful. Things can move fast in child language and important distinctions might otherwise be lost. For example, take two children, both aged one year. The first child, aged 1;0, might not yet have produced her first word, whereas the second child, aged 1;10, might already be stringing multi-word utterances together.

   Eve aged 1;10 (Brown, 1973):

Sue make some
oh my Graham cracker broke
here Fraser briefcase
have to drink grape juice first

The acquisition of language is a staggering feat. It is all too easy to overlook the monumental nature of this achievement, because language learning seems to come so easily to all typically developing children. Perhaps we take the miracle of language learning for granted because, as adults, we typically take the *possession* of language itself for granted. Every cognisant reader of this book has an extensive, complex, rich knowledge of language. But this knowledge is such universal currency – so very much part of everyday life – that we often fail to notice or appreciate the great gift it affords the human species. Exercise 1.1 (below) throws a spotlight on the position of language in human society.

EXERCISE 1.1

Imagine a world *without* language. Consider the world we live in and consider the ways in which we depend on language. In some ways, this is an incredibly easy task. In others, it is quite overwhelming. Once you begin, there seems to be no end to the ways in which we rely, either directly or indirectly, on our ability to communicate with language. Write down two or three topics that characterize some aspect of the human experience (I provide a few suggestions below, but don't feel restricted by these). Consider the ways in which they depend on language for their existence.

- bridges
- governments
- a family meal
- travelling from London to Paris
- football
- laws
- taking a shower
- gardens

Levels of language

In this section, we will try to get a sense of the magnitude of the task facing the newborn child. The first thing to note is that the child is battling on several different fronts at once. Language has different components, or levels, each of which must be tackled.

The Big Four levels of language:

phonology:	concerned with the sounds of speech
vocabulary:	the storehouse of meaning (words)
morphology:	bits of meaning encoded in the grammar, like the plural ending, *-s* in *dogs*
grammar:	the rules dictating how words are put together into sentences

By way of hors d'oeuvre, the current chapter will sample from each of these key areas of language, to get some flavour of how the child tackles them.

Our division of language into four levels stems from **linguistics**, the study of language. In academia there are typically many different ways to dissect an issue in analysis. It all depends on one's theoretical perspective. For example, we could add **pragmatics** to the list above, if we believe that the way language is *used* is especially important (see Chapter 4 for more on this). Or we might reduce our list to just two factors: meaning and sound. We know that language is used to communicate meanings. And we know that, typically, the human vocal apparatus is used to transmit those meanings via sound. The study of language (and also child language) could thus be reduced to working out how meaning and sound are connected (Chomsky, 1995). From the perspective of child language, our problem is not just one of deciding how to cut up language into its component parts (see Chapter 2). It is also one of working out how they interconnect and influence each other.

Highlighting different aspects of language is useful. At the same time, though, there are times when the divisions seem artificial, especially if we focus on one level at the expense of another. For example, we could examine the development of phonology in isolation. How does the infant come to distinguish one sound from another in the torrent of speech assailing their ears? This is a big question. But if we concentrated solely on the problem of phonology, we would fail to notice that the child is also learning something about words, and even grammar, in the first year of life, long before they ever produce speech of their own (see Chapter 5). Unfortunately, research has tended to consider each level of language independently, as though the child had a series of different boxes to tick off in a particular order. Traditionally, this has been seen as phonology first, followed by words and then morphology and finally, grammar (Bates & Goodman, 1997). We can still examine each level of language in its own right (and the chapters in this book follow that general pattern), but we will be mindful that the levels of language do not comprise the rungs of a ladder for the child to ascend. Simultaneous development and mutual influence are more characteristic of language acquisition.

Listen in mother

Imagine what it is like to hear language for the first time. No, really: imagine.

Did you picture yourself in a crib listening to your mother? Understandable, but think again. We hear language before we are even born. As you will know from those noisy neighbours who drive you mad, sound passes through solid barriers – not just the walls of houses but also through the wall of the womb. And it has long been known that the human ear begins to function several weeks before birth, in the third trimester (or third) of pregnancy at about seven months (Sontag & Wallace, 1936). The foetus can respond to the sound of bells, and can even discriminate between different tones. But sensitivity to sound is not the same as sensitivity to language. Can the foetus distinguish noises, like a power drill or the banging of a door (those neighbours again), from the sound of their own mother's voice? Remarkably, the answer is 'yes'. Moreover, the foetus has already begun to recognize the distinctive properties of their native language (May, Byers-Heinlein, Gervain & Werker, 2011). The brain responses of newborn infants (0–3 days old) differ when they hear a foreign language (in this case, Tagalog from the Philippines) versus the language heard in the womb (English). Even more remarkable, the unborn baby can learn to recognize the telling of a particular story.

The cat in the hat in the womb

In an ingenious experiment, DeCasper & Spence (1986) asked women in the later stages of pregnancy (7½ months) to make recordings of three different children's stories. One was the first part of the classic 1958 Dr Seuss story, *The cat in the hat*. The second story, *The dog in the fog*, was created by adapting the last part of *The cat in the hat*, including, as you can see from the title, some changes to vocabulary. The third story, meanwhile, *The king, the mice and the cheese*, was unrelated to the first two, but all three stories were of very similar length, with equal-sized vocabularies. Even a good proportion of the actual words in all three stories was shared (about 60–80 per cent of the total, depending on which two stories are compared). But note, *The dog in the fog* shared the rhythmic properties of *The cat in the hat*, while *The king...* story did not. The influence of rhythm was thus controlled for in a study that, in many ways, provides an excellent model of well-designed research.

The pregnant women were asked to read just one of the three stories out loud twice a day which meant that, on average, they recited their particular story 67 times prior to giving birth. At just three days old, these neonates displayed a clear preference for the particular story they had heard in the womb. You might wonder how a newborn baby tells you which story they want to hear. Infant interest was measured via their sucking behaviour on a nipple, with high rates of sucking being taken as a sign of increased attention (see Box 5.1, Chapter 5). For example, babies exposed in the womb to *The cat in the hat* sucked more fervently when they heard this story played to them than when either of the other two stories were played. The same result was found irrespective of the story: newborns prefer the particular story they have already heard in the womb. This finding is remarkable, but what can we conclude about the linguistic abilities of the foetus? No-one would claim that these infants knew anything about the characters in the story or the development of the plot. But clearly, something rather specific about the story was familiar to them.

Infant preference was unlikely to be influenced by either the length of the story, or its rhythmic qualities, or the particular vocabulary used. As noted above, these factors were controlled for. We can also rule out voice quality as the source of infant interest. As you will know, one human voice is distinct from another. The unique qualities of each person's voice allows us to recognize family, friends, or even celebrities' voices (Philippon, Cherryman, Bull & Vrij, 2007). Given this ability, it is conceivable that the infant's display of interest (high amplitude sucking) is driven by preference for the mother's voice (not the story). As it happens, infants do prefer to listen to their own mother's voice (Mehler, Bertoncini, Barrière & Jassik-Gerschenfeld, 1978), but that was not the critical factor here. We know this because every story heard by every infant in every condition was read to them in their own mother's voice. So their marked preference for one story over the others was not based on voice quality or recognition of the mother. Instead, we are left with **intonation** as the critical factor. One might think of intonation as the 'music' of speech. Modulations in pitch, up and down, during the course of an utterance provide speech with its melody. It turns out that the unborn child can perceive and later recall very specific information from the intonation contours produced in the telling of each story.

A further point of interest is that foetal sensitivities to speech intonation seem to be confined to low-frequency sounds (think bass guitar). This restriction might point to an immature hearing system in the foetus. But the more likely explanation is that the quality of sound that the foetus hears through the barrier of maternal body tissue (including the womb wall) is degraded. In particular, high-frequency sounds (think school recorder) do not penetrate the womb very well. We know this from a further study by Spence & DeCasper (1987). They found that newborns prefer to hear a low-frequency version of their mother's voice. This special version was created by filtering out high-frequency sounds to simulate what the baby would have heard in the womb. This latter study thus refines the discovery that children can tune into language and form memories of their experience even before birth. The prenatal experience of the mother can also have an impact on the child's language development. A recent study on a large cohort (>34,000) mothers in Norway reveals that prenatal distress in the mother is associated with negative language outcomes for the child at three years of age (Ribeiro, Zachrisson, Gustavson & Schjølberg, 2016). Fortunately, though, this effect is not very large.

Some conclusions on sound

So far, we can make at least four interesting observations about language development. First, it starts before the child is born. Second, the foetal brain is well equipped to process human speech sounds. Third, whatever specialization or 'mental equipment' the child is endowed with, specific experiences have a large impact on learning and memory, again, before the child is born. We can see this both in the preference for the mother's voice and also in the preference for a particular story. Fourth, DeCasper & Spence's study provides a really good demonstration that, when it comes to unlocking the secrets of child language acquisition, considerable ingenuity is required. Psychology, in general, faces the fundamental problem of understanding what goes on inside someone's head. Even if we cracked open the skull for a close look at the brain, it would not get us very far in understanding how the mind works or develops. In child language research, we have the added frustration that we lack one of the most obvious tools for investigating the mind: language. In adult psychology, I might ask you directly about your attitudes or personality. But we cannot use language to ask the foetus or the newborn or even a toddler to use language themselves, to tell us anything about how they *acquire* language. Thinking *about* language, so-called **metalinguistic skill**, does not emerge in any sophisticated way until the child is about five years old (Gombert, 1992). Ironically, then, language is not a tool we can use to examine language learning in the young child. This raises the bar very high for empirical study. But happily, you will discover that there are numerous examples of both great ingenuity and good science that overcome this problem.

Word learning: From 0 to 14,000 in five years

Say 'mama'

One of the great landmarks in a baby's life happens around the time of their first birthday: the moment when they produce their first word. Parents are typically captivated on this occasion and make a great fuss over what is, indeed, a major achievement. As you might guess, the first word is very often the name for 'mother' or 'father' (including *mummy, mama, daddy, papa*). A word like *mama* is relatively easy for the 12-month-old to pronounce. In fact, it often arises spontaneously in the child's babbling some time before its appearance as a word. This may happen because *mama* is composed of simple sounds, arranged into repetitive strings of simple syllables

(Goldman, 2001). Parents are quick to ascribe meaning to the baby's vocal productions and will be very easily convinced that *mama* means 'mother'. Although some version of 'mother' is a common first word, it should be pointed out that children differ. Some children produce their first word a little earlier than 12 months: an acquaintance of mine, Arthur, started saying *bye* at the age of 10 months. Many other children, meanwhile, do not speak until some time later. As we see from Arthur, the child's first word is not inevitably some version of 'mother' or 'father'. My own son, Alex, produced his first word, *juice*, at the age of 15 months. His second word only appeared three months later, at Christmas time, when he joined us in saying *cheers*. He was still on the juice, by the way: there's no point wasting good champagne on toddlers. The idea that children differ with respect to language learning is an important one. Accordingly, we will pick up the theme of individual differences, where appropriate, as we proceed.

Once the child has cracked the problem of the first word, many other words follow. At first, new words are acquired at a fairly gentle rate, something like one per week on average. But then things speed up, once the child has passed another, somewhat more intriguing milestone: the accumulation of roughly 50 words. For many children, a step-change in the rate of word learning takes place at this point, with words being added to the total store at the rate of one or two per day (Tamis-LeMonda, Bornstein, Kahana-Kalman, Baumwell & Cyphers, 1998). Between the ages of two and six years, many children then step on the gas again, with something like 10 new words per day being learned (Clark, 1993). This huge increase in rate of word learning is often described as the *vocabulary spurt*. As we shall see in Chapter 6, there are individual differences among children in both the rate and pattern of word learning (Bloom, 2000). But the notion of a vocabulary spurt enjoys widespread currency as a general feature of child language. Ten words per day is a lot. Think of the last adult evening class you attended where you tried to learn a new foreign language (or why not give it a go, if you've never tried). Think how hard you would find it to acquire 10 new words every single day for four years. And when I say 'acquire', I mean learn, remember, retrieve at will and use with facility and accuracy in a range of settings. Seen in this light, the child's word learning prowess in the early years is deeply impressive, resulting in a vocabulary somewhere between 10,000 (Bloom & Markson, 1998) and 14,000 (Clark, 1993) by the age of six.

Estimating vocabulary size

10,000 or 14,000 words? The wide discrepancy in these two estimates hints at a tricky empirical problem: how does one begin to estimate the number of words in someone's head? To get some idea of the problem, open a dictionary at random and scan the words on the page. My guess is that the words which catch your eye will be the new or unfamiliar words. But I would also guess that you do, in fact, know a good many words on any given page, at least to some degree. Given that dictionaries often contain thousands of pages, on each of which you will know many words, you can begin to calculate the extent of your vocabulary (see the website listed at the end of this chapter for information on a more rigorous method). Arriving at this estimate is not straightforward. Among many factors that have to be entertained, there is the fundamental question: what constitutes a word? In a dictionary, the verb *cogitate* will typically appear under its own heading.

It is unlikely, though, you will find related forms like *cogitates*, *cogitating* or *cogitated*. But each one of these versions looks like a separate word. Whichever way we decide to count, it should be clear that your vocabulary is enormous (Kučera, 1992). At birth, your vocabulary was zero. By the time you left school it was more like 50,000 (Nagy & Anderson, 1984). Individual differences aside, we all make quite a leap. In Chapters 5 and 6, we will consider how the child manages the feat of word learning. But first, we will consider an even deeper mystery. How does the child ever manage to work out the meaning of even a single word?

The *gavagai* problem

We have seen that it is no straightforward matter to define what a word is. Equally vexing is the issue of what words mean. Take *rabbit*. In pronouncing this word, rabbit is a sequence of sounds that comes out of my mouth. Its special status as a word derives from my ability to use this sound-string symbolically. The sounds are used to 'stand for' an object in the world. In this way, words provide the vehicle for pairing sound with meaning. Critically, the pairing we have made between the sound string and the object is arbitrary: there is no intrinsic or necessary relationship between the particular sounds and the particular object denoted (de Saussure, 1916/1974). This becomes obvious when you consider that, in languages other than English, reference to the object would be made using different combinations of speech sounds (for example, *lapin* in French, *krolik* in Russian, and so on). So far, our definition of *word* comprises a simple pairing between a sound pattern and an object (or referent). But maybe it is not quite that simple. W.V.O. Quine, an American philosopher, complicated matters (as philosophers are wont to do), when he conjured up the image of an intrepid linguist who comes across a culture whose language is entirely foreign to him. The linguist tries to learn all he can about this new language. Then one day …

> a rabbit scurries by, the native says '*Gavagai*', and the linguist notes down the sentence 'Rabbit' (or 'Lo, a rabbit') as tentative translation. (Quine, 1960: 29)

But how good is this translation? Quine demonstrated that we cannot take the linguist's translation for granted. Conceivably, the 'native' was using *gavagai* in a predictable way, to mean the type of animal that scurried by. But *gavagai* might equally well refer exclusively to white rabbits (not grey), or it might mean rodent or even a special sub-class of rodents (important to the native's culture) comprising only rabbits, gerbils and coypu. *Gavagai* might conceivably refer to the rabbit's eyes, or to the rabbit's feet. *Gavagai* might refer to the rabbit as it appears in a particular light (sunshine rather than shade, say). *Gavagai* might be confined to a rabbit in mid-scurry, not when it is stationary. And so on, *ad infinitum*. From Quine's discussion of the translation problem, we learn something important about word learning. How does the infant work out what an adult means when they use a particular word? Does *mummy* refer exclusively to the woman who gave birth to the infant? Or to both parents? Or does it mean the hair on a particular woman's head? Or the hair plus her left ear, viewed in the autumn light? Or …? As you see, the infant faces the *gavagai* problem. We have no good grounds, in advance, for assuming that the child will ascribe the same meaning to a word that we would.

Quine's *gavagai* raises several more fundamental challenges in the study of child language (Bloom, 2000). First, how does the child know that a word such as *rabbit* is the name for something? Without prior information about what a word is, one might simply assume that the speaker was making a random noise or expressing emotion. If we ignore that problem for a moment, a second issue is to identify individual words. How does the child come to know (without prior knowledge or help) that *rabbit* is one word and not two (*rab* and *it*, perhaps)? This second issue is an example of the **segmentation problem**: we need to explain how the child cuts up a continuous stream of speech into appropriate linguistic units (see Chapter 6). Third, Quine's *gavagai* is untypical because it is a single-word utterance. Although perfectly possible, words are not generally used in isolation. We are much more likely to string words together into phrases and sentences. We need to consider, therefore, how the child extracts each new word and its meaning from running discourse. We must also deal with the issue of *generalization*. You may have noticed, above, that my notion of a typical meaning for *gavagai* was not confined to the particular rabbit that scurried past. It embraced the type of animal, that is, all rabbits. In other words, I would normally expect to extend (or generalize) my use of *gavagai* to refer to different rabbits that might crop up in the future. What about the infant? Even if the child is able to extend the use of *gavagai*, how do they know what to extend it to? Again, there is an infinity of possibilities. The word could extend to just white rabbits, or rabbit ears, or rabbits with eating disorders, and so on. All in all, words and their meanings seem to present the child with a massively daunting learning problem.

Are the problems of word-learning insurmountable? Evidently not. Every typical child solves the *gavagai* problem with alacrity. We can assume this from the simple observation that children acquire words quickly and easily, once they get started (though see Chapter 8 on what might count as 'quick' in language learning). Put another way, if children acquired word meanings in ways that, according to Quine, are logically possible, then we would expect linguistic chaos to break out. For example, the child who decided that *rabbit* is confined exclusively to 'the pet we keep in a hutch in the garden' would soon find themselves incredibly restricted in their ability to use that word. *Rabbit* would not be much use when watching Bugs Bunny, to name but one limitation. At the same time, the child would presumably hear people using the word, but in different (conventional) ways that would not make any sense to the child. Communication would be impossible. As noted, though, we can be pretty confident that this kind of chaos does not break out. We must conclude, therefore, that something clearly prevents the child from entertaining wild hypotheses about word meaning, even though they are logically possible. What is it that constrains the child's word learning? We will explore this issue in Chapter 6.

Morphology: Bits and pieces

Words seem like neat, self-contained linguistic bundles. In speech, I can pronounce any word in isolation (even if, as we'll see in Chapter 5, this is quite rare). On the page, each word is surrounded, and therefore demarcated, by white space on either side. Hence it would be easy to mistake words as the smallest meaningful units of language. In fact, though, we can dig deeper. Words can often be subdivided into separate parts, known as **morphemes**, and it is the morpheme that constitutes the smallest unit of meaning in a language.

As the examples in Table 1.1 show, some morphemes can stand alone as single words (*tree* or *flower*). But others cannot exist independently and must be attached (or bound) to a lexical stem. An example of a bound morpheme is the *-s* that can be added to *tree* to make *trees*, where the *-s* morpheme denotes a plural meaning. The existence of morphemes is one reason why the concept of word is so difficult to define. If you recall, we cited above the example of *cogitates, cogitating* and *cogitated*, wondering, in the process, if we were dealing with three words or just one. One solution is to recognize that there is one lexeme (*cogitate*), and three word forms, each one inflected with a different morpheme (see Figure 1.1). In each case, the inflection serves a different grammatical function, specifying more precisely the meaning to be conveyed (see **inflectional morpheme** for more on this).

Even from this very brief sketch, we can see that morphology complicates matters. For the language-learning child, it is not enough to learn a verb like *jump*. The child must also be able to distinguish between the different meanings and uses of different forms of the verb (*jump, jumps, jumping, jumped*). In English, this is difficult enough. But some languages have far more complex systems of inflectional morphology than English. Russian, for example, would make

Table 1.1 Analysis of words into constituent morphemes

Number of morphemes	Word	Morphemes
1	fool	fool
	tree	tree
	flower	flower
2	foolish	fool + ish
	trees	tree + s
	flowering	flower + ing
	sticky	stick + y
3	foolishness	fool + ish + ness
	happiness	happ + i + ness
	unsystematic	un + system + atic
7	antidisestablishmentarianism	anti + dis + establish + ment + ari + an + ism

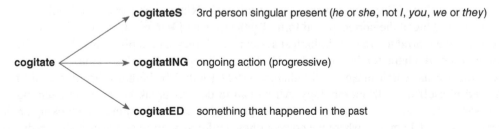

Figure 1.1 The meaning of three inflectional morphemes in English

11

your eyes water (Wade, 1992, will really make the tears flow). Russian **nouns** can be marked in a bewildering number of ways, because, to start with, there are at least six **cases: nominative, accusative, genitive**, dative, prepositional and **instrumental**. These different noun forms each fulfil a different grammatical function, like **subject** or **object**. Beyond case, nouns select from two forms for number (singular or plural) and three forms for gender (masculine, feminine and neuter). And then there are different markings for **adjectives** and **verbs**, too. We do not need to dwell on the grammar of Russian nouns (sighs of relief all round), but we can at least pause to consider the monumental task facing some of the world's children. Do children really have to learn all these different morphemes? Well, maybe not. Conceivably, each inflected form could be learnt as a separate word, together with its specific meaning. Provided the child learns the difference in meaning between *jumps* and *jumping*, for example, then internal analysis of each word might not be necessary. Of course, there is a lot of redundancy in this approach. It would mean learning a huge number of separate word forms, especially in a language like Russian. But then again, a huge capacity for word-learning is something we possess, both as children and as adults. What do children do? Are they whole-word learners? Or can they dissect words into their constituent parts and extract the separate morphemes?

Jean Berko Gleason addressed this question some sixty years ago in what is probably the first experiment in child language research (Berko, 1958). Berko reasoned that, in the ordinary run of things, we cannot tell if a child has acquired inflectional morphemes or not. We have seen that, in English, we can mark the third **person** singular of a verb by adding -*s* (*jumps*). We can also add -*s* to the end of a noun, this time to denote plurality (*one apple* versus *seven apples*). How do children learn to mark plurality? They could assemble the word by applying a rule: *apple* + *s* → *apples*. Or they could learn *apples* as a single, indivisible unit. To distinguish between these two possibilities, Berko devised a series of novel creatures, depicted in line drawings, each with a novel name, like *wug* or *niz* (for more on nonsense words see Box 4.2). The child is first shown a picture of a single creature and hears: *This is a wug*. Next the child sees a picture of two creatures and hears the following: *Now there is another one. There are two of them. There are two _*. The child is thus invited to complete the sentence. Observe that the child has only ever heard the uninflected form *wug* (and then only once). Because the experimenter is controlling the input to the child, at no point does the child hear the plural form, *wugs*. In consequence, if the child can complete the test sentence successfully, then they must be compiling the correct plural form, *wugs*, online, that is, at the time of production.

The child cannot have simply dragged *wugs* out of memory as a single, unanalysed chunk of language, if only because it cannot have entered memory in the first place. In the event, Berko found that children were very good at this task. Ninety-one per cent of children aged 4–7 years produced the correct plural form. By the time children reach school, therefore, they seem to have a productive morphological system which they can apply to words never before encountered. A character in James Joyce's *Ulysses*, Stephen Dedalus, remarks that 'I fear those big words which make us so unhappy' (1922/1960: 37). Perhaps Dedalus could have cheered himself up with morphology. All he had to do was break down those daunting big words into their separate morphemes. We will guarantee our own happiness by picking up this theme again in Chapter 7, where we consider how children acquire and access the productive power promised by morphology.

Syntax: Putting it all together

Words by themselves, even without the aid of morphology, have considerable expressive power. But consider what happens when we start putting them together. At 1;6, the little girl we met at the start of this chapter, Eve, produced the following utterances:

One word	Two words	Three words
baby	Eve writing	doll eat celery
there	block broke	Eve find it
coffee	Fraser water	read the puzzle
eye	more cookie	man have it
hat	that radio	man no spoon

Notice how Eve can be much more precise in her meaning when she combines even just two or three words. In contrast, the single word utterance, *baby*, is extremely vague. It might be taken to mean *I'm a baby* or *The baby's on the loose* or *Do you think they'll ever give babies the vote?* and so on. Without being in the room with Eve, it's difficult to discern her intention. But with two or three words, the picture is much clearer and contextual support is less vital for working out Eve's meaning. *Eve writing* probably means *Eve is writing*, while *Eve find it* might well be glossed as *Eve can find it*. Putting words together into utterances is therefore useful for communicating specific ideas. It is no wonder, then, that 'the words of the world want to make sentences' (Bachelard, 1960/1971: 188). And to make sentences, we need **syntax**, the set of principles or rules which dictate how words can combine. See Box 1.2 on syntactic categories, and then take a breather with Exercise 1.2 below.

BOX 1.2   SYNTACTIC CATEGORIES

The words of a language belong to different syntactic categories, like **verb**, **noun**, **adjective** and **preposition** (explained individually in the Glossary). One way of distinguishing these different categories is to think about the kinds of meanings each one conveys. Thus, verbs like <u>run</u>, <u>fly</u> and <u>chase</u> might be thought of as 'action words,' while nouns are often associated with objects (<u>tree</u>, <u>book</u>, <u>house</u>). But this only gets us so far. The category of verb also includes words like <u>anticipate</u> and <u>procrastinate</u>, which are not easily described as actions. Similarly, <u>purity</u> and <u>truth</u> are classed as nouns, though they do not denote concrete objects.

To get round this problem, linguists rely on two further criteria for identifying syntactic categories: (1) possible word forms; and (2) behaviour in phrases. Word form (an aspect

(Continued)

---

of **morphology**) refers to the way we can change the shape of words in particular ways. Each syntactic category permits its own set of characteristic endings (**inflections**). The verb shout can appear as <u>shout*ed*</u> or <u>shout*ing*</u>; a noun like <u>table</u> can also occur as <u>tables</u>; and an adjective like <u>red</u> can appear as <u>red*der*</u> or <u>red*dest*</u>. We cannot just add any inflection to any category (for example, <u>shout*est*</u>).

We can also determine which category a word belongs to by looking at its behaviour in phrases, that is, the combinations that are allowed with other words. Words that can substitute for one another in the same slot within a sentence belong to the same syntactic category.

Hanadi does nothing but _____

The empty slot calls for a verb, so I could insert <u>complain</u>, <u>belch</u>, or <u>procrastinate</u> and come up with a grammatical sentence. The outcome would not be grammatical if I tried inserting a noun instead (e.g., *Hanadi does nothing but <u>tree</u>*). We can take this observation one step further by considering whole phrases, that is, groups of words that can function as a single unit, and which therefore constitute syntactic categories themselves. For example, a Noun Phrase constitutes a group of words with a noun as the key constituent (or head), for example, <u>a tiger</u> or <u>the old dark house</u>. Like our single-word categories, noun phrases can only occupy certain slots within sentences.

Ben wants to buy _____

Both of our noun phrases, <u>a tiger</u> and <u>the old dark house</u>, could happily fill the empty position in this sentence frame. But other syntactic categories, like verb, would fare less well (for example, *Ben wants to buy <u>think</u>*).

EXERCISE 1.2
GRAMMATICAL CATEGORIES

You may want to start by checking the Glossary to make sure you're up to speed with the following four terms: **noun; verb; adjective; preposition**. Then use these four categories to sort the following words. If you have trouble, try using the tests of category membership described in Box 1.2. Answers at the back of the book.

dog	in	eat	hot
by	happiness	Somerset	from
inculcate	divorce	pusillanimous	happy
acceptance	complete	up	charming

Back to Eve. The imperfections in her utterances are due, in part, to missing morphemes. Compare *doll eat celery* with *The doll is eating celery* (more on this in Chapter 7). One thing Eve does seem to be getting right, though, is the grammatical feature of word order. We cannot just put words together in any old order. Think back to Example (2). Instead of saying *I had the worst dream of my life*, Ross might have thrown the words together at random: *The of dream life had worst I my*. (The asterisk (*) is used to denote an ungrammatical sequence.) Word order is especially important in English, as we can see from the study illustrated in Figure 1.2.

If I was two years old, I'd be terrified by these characters. They look like something out of a bank heist movie. Happily, though, the two-year-olds doing this study were unfazed. Observe that we have another novel word, the verb *gorp*. If I were to tell you: *The duck is gorping the bunny*, which picture would you choose as most appropriate? I'm guessing the one on the right. But why? The answer is to do with agency. On the right, the duck seems to be actively doing something to the rabbit (gorping, in fact). But on the left, it is the rabbit who seems to be the **agent** (the doer) of the action (notice how the meaning of *gorp* is different in each case). For *The duck is gorping the bunny*, we choose the right-hand picture because the default in English syntax dictates that the agent of the verb comes first in the sentence. So we look for a picture where the duck is the agent. Children as young as 2;1 do the same thing, provided they are presented with typical, default sentences (Hirsh-Pasek & Golinkoff, 1996; Gertner et al., 2006; Dittmar,

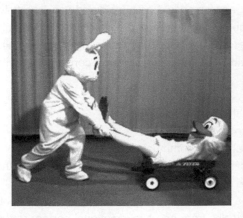

Figure 1.2 'The duck is gorping the bunny' (adapted from Gertner, Fisher & Eisengart, 2006)

Abbot-Smith, Lieven & Tomasello, 2011). Consider what happens if we change our test sentence to *The rabbit is gorping the duck*. Suddenly, the left-hand picture becomes the appropriate illustration. All we have done is switch *duck* and *rabbit* around in the sentence. But see what a profound effect this change in word order has on the meaning. How do children acquire this knowledge of syntax so early in life? We will explore this question further in Chapters 8 and 9.

Language in context: Perceptual, cognitive and social development

How do millions of typically developing children get to the point where they can produce and understand an infinite number of different sentences? Let's find out. But before we get started, have a glance at Table 1.2, where you will find some of the key milestones in child development over the first few years of life. This table allows you to compare progress in physical, cognitive, social and linguistic development. The first thing to say is that these are not separate streams in development, running in parallel. There are numerous overlaps along the way. To take just one example, it

---

EXERCISE 1.3

I began this chapter by asking if you had ever chatted with a toddler. Even if you have, it would be a good idea to repeat the experience, this time focusing on the child's language. There is no substitute for real data and talking to a young child will bring the subject to life in a way that no textbook can. But you need to take seriously the sensitivities of this task. Consult established guidelines for research (e.g., the *Code of Ethics and Conduct* published by the British Psychological Society, www.beta.bps.org.uk). Unless you enjoy the luxury of being parent to a young child, access should be considered very carefully, even if you are related to the child in question. The mother (or primary caregiver) should be present at all times for fairly obvious reasons, but also to better ensure that the child feels sufficiently comfortable to talk freely with you. If you can secure a conversation with a toddler, consider the following:

- What kinds of words and phrases does the child know?
- How easy is it to make yourself understood?
- What limitations are there in the child's ability to communicate?
- Are there any differences in the quality of interaction between mother and child, on the one hand, and between yourself and the child, on the other?
- Now compare the way you talk with the child with the way you talk with the parent. How does the interaction differ, linguistically, from one conversational partner to the other?

Table 1.2 Developmental milestones in the first five years

Age (months)	Perceptuo-Motor	Cognitive	Social	Linguistic
0	reflexes (e.g., grasping, sucking)	imitation of tongue protrusion	two emotions: positive (contentment) and negative (distress)	preference for own mother's voice can distinguish different speech sounds (phonemes) can distinguish own language from a foreign language
4	voluntary control over movements physical coordination: can hold head up and roll over onto side	cross-modal perception: can integrate sight, sound, feel of an object categorization: can perceive a variety of objects as members of a single category	co-ordinated interaction with mother emotion: can express anger, surprise, sadness	can recognize own name sensitive to the serial order of words in sentences
7	can sit unsupported can stand while holding on to something	memory of new experience lasts 14 days object permanence displayed in actions: knows that an object continues to exist when out of sight	wary of strangers attachment to mother (upset when separated)	early babbling can understand first words (e.g., mummy)
12	can walk unaided can roll a ball and throw it awkwardly	deferred imitation: ability to recall and imitate behaviours seen on a previous occasion	communicate emotions to others showing gradations of feeling explore environment, using parent as a secure base	jargoning: babbling with the stress and intonation of actual speech produces first word
18	can build a tower of two blocks can walk up steps	symbolic play: can pretend that one object is another (e.g., a stick used as a sword)	emotion: can express contempt and guilt self: recognize self in mirror	understand about 50 words produce two-word utterances
24	can jump up and down can use a spoon to feed themselves	categorization: can sort objects into two categories digit span of two (immediate recall of two numbers)	secondary emotions: pride, envy, shame, guilt	multi-word utterances with basic grammatical features
60	can bounce and catch a ball fine motor co-ordination: can string 10 beads	theory of mind: realize other people have a different point of view with thoughts and feelings of their own	friendship: can make friends, often with children of same sex can interpret others' emotions	6,000-word vocabulary grammar: can produce and understand complex sentences acquiring literacy

has been shown recently that once the child starts walking, their language development takes off, much like the child (Walle & Campos, 2014). Table 1.2 might give the impression that the child's achievements in language are especially impressive. For example, at the age of four years, the average child has a digit span of just four (Kail, 1990). That is, they can reliably repeat back a random list of four single-digit numbers, for example, $6 - 2 - 3 - 9$. But if we added just one more digit, the same four-year-old would struggle to repeat them back correctly. Our average four-year-old also assumes, erroneously, that other people share their own perspective on the world. They believe that other people see (and know) the same things that they see, from the same vantage point (Happé, 1994). In some rather fundamental sense, therefore, the child's cognitive representation of the world is qualitatively different from that of an adult. In linguistic terms, though, the four-year-old is much closer to an adult. The differences are more a matter of degree than kind. For example, an obvious difference between child and adult is vocabulary size. In terms of grammar (both syntax and morphology), there is perhaps less to distinguish a four-year-old child and an adult.

The examples raised here make the child look linguistically fast, but cognitively slow. But this is partly because of the examples that have been chosen. Consider, instead, object permanence. Object permanence is the knowledge that an object remains the same object when viewed from different angles or under different lighting conditions, and that an object continues to exist even when out of sight. Many authors argue that infants attain an understanding of object permanence much earlier than the seven months suggested in Table 1.2 (for example, Rochat, 2001). But I have been cautious, because seven months is the earliest point at which the infant can *demonstrate* their knowledge of object permanence in their own actions. But even with this caution, it is apparent that the infant has a sophisticated understanding of an object's physical properties long before they utter their first word. Now, all of a sudden, the child's linguistic development looks comparatively slow. Evidently, it is no easy matter deciding how rapid and easy child development is, in *any* domain, be it linguistic, perceptual, cognitive or social. We return to this theme in Chapter 8.

The study of child language

The overview of child language sketched out in this chapter sets the scene for the rest of the book. Before we plunge into detail, though, it is worth remarking on how far the *study* of language acquisition has come over the years. Perhaps the first published study on child language was by a German biologist, Tiedemann, in 1787 (see Murchison & Langer, 1927, and Appendix 1). But until the late 1950s, it is fair to say that child language research was not especially systematic or scientific in its approach. Research was often confined to fairly informal observations (for example, Lukens, 1894) or diary studies, conducted by researchers on their own children (for example, Taine, 1877; Marsden, 1902). And the total output of research on child language was rather limited. Leopold (1952) compiled a bibliography of child language studies, comprising every possible source he could find, including work on several different languages (not just English). But the total number of studies from more than a century of endeavour amounted to just 746 published works. This figure has now been dwarfed, owing to a seismic shift that occurred in the late 1950s, presaged by two academics – Roger Brown and Noam Chomsky – both based in Boston in the USA. Roger Brown introduced a fresh rigour and thoroughness in the collection of child language data that remains an excellent role model and inspiration decades later. Brown and his students also generated a wealth of theoretical ideas and insights that, again, continue to resonate to the present day (see Kessel, 1988). Incidentally, the child known as Eve, quoted in (1) above, was one of Brown's early research participants, recorded on a regular basis for nine months between the ages of 1;6 and 2;3. If you want to mull over the full set of transcripts of these sessions for yourself, it is now possible online (see Box 1.3).

BOX 1.3 THE CHILD LANGUAGE DATA EXCHANGE SYSTEM (CHILDES)

The excerpts of child speech we have seen are part of a much larger corpus known as CHILDES, a magnificent resource for serious students of child language. Under the auspices of Brian MacWhinney at Carnegie Mellon University, CHILDES comprises an extensive database of child language transcriptions. Many researchers have donated their original data to this database. The idea is that child language researchers can access and share their data and even, where appropriate, perform analyses on data that were originally gathered by other researchers. Data are available from more than 25 different languages with children of different ages in a wide range of settings. These include data on bilingual acquisition, and on children with language delays or disorders. Also available is a sophisticated software package known as CLAN (Computerized Language Analysis) that allows one to do all manner of automated analyses, including word searches, frequency counts and interactional analyses. In some cases, original audio and video recordings are available, too. On top of this, there is a very useful online discussion forum (known as InfoCHILDES). Access to CHILDES is not automatic, and may well be one step beyond what you need if you're new to the world of child language, but if you have a serious interest, check out the CHILDES website (http://childes.psy.cmu.edu).

BOX 1.4 NOAM CHOMSKY

When:	Born in Philadelphia, USA, in 1928.
Where:	Based since 1955 at the Massachusetts Institute of Technology, Boston, USA.
What:	Linguistics, philosophy of mind and politics.
Famous for:	In the world of child language, Chomsky is best known for the idea that much of what we know about grammar is innate, that is, genetically determined.

(Continued)

Noam Chomsky is perhaps the most influential academic alive today. We know this because huge numbers of people throughout the world have cited, and continue to cite, his work. More than that, the influence of Chomsky's ideas can be traced directly in a vast amount of research, especially in the fields of linguistics, psychology and philosophy. The whole research enterprise now known as cognitive science owes a particular debt to Chomsky's work. In particular, he has changed the way we think about language and the way it is acquired.

Chomsky first made an impact in **linguistics** in the 1950s. Before Chomsky, the study of language was something akin to solving a newspaper crossword puzzle. Language was treated like an object 'out there' (on paper, in recordings), with patterns, regularities and peculiarities to be identified. With the advent of Chomsky, though, linguistics was rapidly turned into a branch of the biological sciences. The focus ever since has been on explaining how language is acquired and represented in the minds of human beings. The quintessence of Chomsky's position with regard to child language is his **nativism**: he believes that much of the child's knowledge of grammar is genetically determined (see Chapter 8).

Chomsky has also had a parallel career as a political maverick, turning out books, essays, speeches and interviews in a sustained campaign against what he maintains is the malign influence of the US Government and its allies. Chomsky paints a deeply sceptical picture of the motives of the United States. He argues that the US has used every means at its disposal to maintain its position as the richest and most powerful country on earth, including subversive means such as assassination, covert support for military coups and terrorist assaults. As the invasion of Iraq in 2003 demonstrates, the US also adopts openly aggressive manoeuvres, in what Chomsky (1985: 47) regards as a self-appointed 'freedom to rob and exploit'. Chomsky has also been concerned to debunk the myths and obfuscations that the US Government has, in his view, generated to justify its actions and keep the general populace in a state of ignorance and confusion. If you need a break from child language (not yet, surely!), you will find a recommendation for further reading on Chomsky's political ideas at the end of this chapter.

The second figure I mentioned, Noam Chomsky, does not do empirical research on child language. But Chomsky's impact on research in the field has been phenomenal (see Box 1.4; see also **innateness of language**). There is one Big Idea for which Chomsky is especially well known, namely, that *language is innate*. This is a fascinating idea, but before we dip a toe into the waters of nature–nurture, let me offer you a flotation device: Chomsky does not, to my knowledge, baldly say that 'language is innate' (though see Smith, 2004: 167). As a typical academic, Chomsky qualifies much of what he says, in ways that will become apparent. So you may be disappointed to find our Big Idea shrinking a little:

the form of the language that is acquired is *largely* determined by internal factors (Chomsky, 1966: 64, my emphasis)

But even after this qualification, I hope you will come to appreciate just how radical and even counter-intuitive Chomsky's position on language acquisition remains. If nothing else, it seems odd to suggest that we are all born with the same knowledge of language when something like 7,000 different languages are currently spoken throughout the world (Gordon, 2005). Did *I* inherit English, while my neighbour inherited Bengali? Patently, no. Chomsky has something quite different in mind. Hold that thought for a moment (actually, hold it until Chapter 8), and let me just slip in a further word of caution: students of child language should take care in the way they represent Chomsky's ideas. It is very easy both to overstate and misinterpret Chomsky's position (see Botha, 1989). I shall try not to fall into this trap myself, but it is always a good idea to check the original sources for yourself (try Chomsky, 1975, for a classic position statement).

BOX 1.5 LANGUAGE DEVELOPMENT OR LANGUAGE ACQUISITION? THE CULTURE OF CHILD LANGUAGE RESEARCH

Is language acquired? Or does it develop? You will have noticed both words in the title of this book and might assume that they are interchangeable. Both words call attention to how children end up knowing their native language (or languages). But, in fact, there *is* a difference, somewhat subtle, but nevertheless useful for the student of child language to be aware of. In brief, nativists tend to avoid the phrase *language development*, preferring the notion of *language acquisition*. I cannot actually find an explicit nativist repudiation of the term *language development* in the literature. But at the same time, it is difficult to find a nativist with a preference for the term. See for example, the indexes in Jackendoff (1993) or Smith (2004). Non-nativists, on the other hand, sometimes show the opposite tendency, avoiding the phrase *language acquisition* (Dąbrowska, 2004, has a telling index in this case, though see Rowland, 2014, for a shift away from this position).

The difference seems to be tangled up with a third concept, that of *learning*. For Chomsky, language is not something that we learn. He argues that 'we misdescribe the process when we call it "learning"' (1980a: 134). Hence, 'we do not really learn language; rather grammar grows in the mind' (ibid.: 134). This idea relates directly to the characterization of language as a mental organ. In the newborn baby, the organs of the body, such as the liver, grow, largely according to a genetic blueprint. As a mental organ, language – for Chomsky – is subject to its own, genetically determined processes of growth. As it happens, the idea that language simply grows is quite old: 'the speech

(Continued)

learning of children is ... a growth of speech capacity via maturation and practice' (von Humboldt, 1836/1988: 37).

Given this distaste for the concept of learning, one begins to see why the term *development* is also avoided by nativists. In essence, the term *development* tends to imply some form of learning (though, strictly speaking, it includes genetic factors also). Thus, the notion of development in psychology is associated with figures like Piaget, who considered the child's experience, and the knowledge that the child constructs from that experience, to be of fundamental importance (see Piattelli-Palmarini, 1980). In the field of second language learning, Larsen-Freeman (2015) has recently called for the repudiation of the term *acquisition*. Second language learners typically arrive at different endpoints in their learning; they do not 'acquire' language *in toto* like some item in a shop.

As a shorthand for spotting an author's theoretical bias, the preference for *language development* versus *language acquisition* might prove useful. My own preference is to trample all over these cultural niceties and use both terms in a directly interchangeable fashion. I will even resort to *language learning* at times.

Chomsky's position on language has polarized opinion within the child language research community. Researchers tend to align themselves very clearly either for or against the idea that language – especially grammar – is innate. It is as well to remember this when you approach the primary literature (see Box 1.5). Although there is some communication across the divide, it can be fractious and unproductive at times. As we shall see, there are occasions when competing and quite different explanations are pretty much equally good at accounting for particular facts of child language as we currently understand them. In other cases, nativists and non-nativists are interested in different phenomena and are therefore unlikely to coincide in debate with one another. The lack of communication is problematic, but should not be overstated. Child language research is a thriving field of enquiry that has blossomed enormously over the past 50 years. In the past 15 years, in particular, a number of alternatives to the nativist credo have been developed that provide genuine and serious challenges to Chomsky's theory. Meanwhile, Chomsky's own ideas have undergone a major process of change and development throughout the 1990s and into the current century. There is, then, a wealth of ideas that promises to drive the field of child language forward.

The lie of the land

As we progress through the rest of the book, the nature–nurture issue will come in and out of focus, depending on the particular topic under discussion. It is by no means the only issue of interest in child language research. But in common with the rest of developmental psychology, the contribution of genetics to behaviour is a prominent theme. Accordingly, Chapter 2 deals with the question of whether language is a uniquely human trait. It does this by asking if animals can acquire language when given the opportunity. Then, in Chapter 3 we will consider if the human ability to acquire language is confined to a specific period of time early on in development, a so-called *critical period*. If there is a universal timetable for the development of language, then genetic factors might well be implicated. The topics of animal learning and critical periods have attracted a good deal of attention, in part because of the fascination people have for stories of animal and human learning in unusual circumstances. It would be fair to say, though, that active research in both these areas is not so intense at present. I have included them here, though, because they provide enduring evidence on the biological basis of language. They also provide good opportunities for considering two other vital issues in research on child language. The first issue is very basic: we must be clear about what language *is*. Chomsky has argued that this question takes priority, because 'there is little point in speculating about the process of acquisition without a much better understanding of what is acquired' (1959: 55). Although fundamental, it will become apparent that questions about what language is and questions about what is acquired are not easily answered. Beyond this issue, we will consider research methods in child language. Our discussion of *The cat in the hat* (above) has touched on the need for ingenuity and rigour in research on child language. This theme is expanded in Chapter 3.

In Chapter 4, we will shift the focus away from the child's genetic endowment towards the child's *environment*. We will examine the linguistic input that the child encounters and consider its role in facilitating language learning. Chapter 5 looks at language learning in the first year of life, culminating at about the age of 12 months in the child's first word. We will see that, even though the child does not produce much recognizable language, the child's knowledge of language expands enormously in the first year. Chapter 6 looks at word learning, in particular, the constraints on word learning that somehow allow the child to overcome the *gavagai* problem. Chapter 7 moves on to morphology and considers how research has informed our understanding of the representation of language in the mind. Chapters 8 and 9 deal with what is, for some, the holy grail of language acquisition: grammar. How does the child acquire something so complex and abstract as grammar? In Chapter 8, the answer we consider comes from the nativist perspective: knowledge of grammar is largely innate. In Chapter 9, we consider what is currently the most prominent non-nativist alternative: usage-based theory. Human beings are intelligent creatures, capable of acquiring all manner of skills and knowledge. Maybe grammar is just another (admittedly complex) system of knowledge that we pick up using our general, all-purpose learning capacities.

IN A NUTSHELL

- Children seem to acquire language quickly and effortlessly. By the time they reach school, they have acquired a rich system of knowledge, including an abstract system of grammar that allows them to combine words in complex, grammatically correct sentences.

- There are several different levels of language, including: phonology (speech sounds); vocabulary; morphology (parts of words); and grammar. They are acquired at the same time, and interact with one another in development.

- Language learning begins in the womb. The foetus can learn to recognize a story from its intonational properties.

- Vocabulary learning seems rapid. By the age of six years, the average child has a vocabulary somewhere between 10,000 and 14,000 words.

- In working out the meaning of a word, the child faces Quine's *gavagai* problem: how to determine what a word refers to, given the infinite possibilities.

- We know that children can analyse the internal structure of words from Berko's *wug* test, in which the child is prompted to supply inflectional morphemes for nonsense words (*'One wug, two ...' / 'wugS'*).

- Children demonstrate some understanding of syntax – the rules governing how words are put together in sentences – as early as the second year of life. For example, children acquiring English realize that changes in word order can fundamentally alter the meaning of a sentence.

- Language development can seem rapid and effortless, especially when compared with certain milestones in other developmental domains (perceptual, cognitive and social). But we should be cautious. Comparisons are difficult to make and it is not even clear how to determine what would count as 'rapid learning'.

FURTHER READING

Aitchison, J. (2010). *Aitchison's linguistics* (7th ed.). London: Hodder Headline.

This book has been around, in one format or another, since 1972 and is written by the pre-eminent writer of student-friendly books on language-related topics. I provide definitions of linguistic concepts (even exercises) throughout the book. But Aitchison's book provides more detail and could therefore prove useful when accessing original research on child language.

Chomsky, N. (2005). *Imperial ambitions: Conversations with Noam Chomsky on the post 9/11 world: Interviews with David Barsamian*. London: Hamish Hamilton.

For all those whose horizons extend beyond child language, this book provides an insight into Chomsky's political views. Chomsky's output in politics is, like his work in linguistics and philosophy, prodigious, making him seem like a latter-day Renaissance man. Put it this way: I doubt Professor Chomsky spends much time on the golf course.

WEBSITES

- **Estimating vocabulary size**: www.testyourvocab.com

  There are several websites which offer a free assessment of your vocabulary size. This one is as good as any other, and includes an interesting description of the rationale used to arrive at the estimate.

- **Child language data**: www.childes.talkbank.org

  The Child Language Data Exchange System (CHILDES) affords access for serious students to many original transcripts, in addition to a range of automated tools for analysing child language data (see Box 1.3).

Still want more? For links to online resources relevant to this chapter and a quiz to test your understanding, visit the companion website at **https://study.sagepub.com/saxton2e**

2

Can Animals Acquire Human Language? Shakespeare's Typewriter

CONTENTS

OVERVIEW

We start this chapter with a basic question: what is language? Taking care to distinguish between three separate concepts – language, talk and communication – we go on to consider some of the key differences between animal communication systems and language. No animal acquires language spontaneously, but can they be taught? We review evidence of attempts to teach a range of animals, including chimpanzees, monkeys, dogs and parrots. In some ways, animals have surprising linguistic gifts. Yet they fall far short of being able to string words together into grammatical sentences. We will see that attempts to teach the grammatical rules of a natural human language are overly ambitious. But the ability to refer to objects with words is now well established for many animals. Recent research also looks at basic psycholinguistic mechanisms, in particular, the processing of speech sounds. This research has shown that cotton-top tamarin monkeys can identify word-like units in a continuous stream of speech, in a way that is similar (though not identical) to the way human infants go about it. It emerges that humans and animals share many basic capacities that can be harnessed in the acquisition of language. At the same time, there remain clear differences between humans and non-humans. Language is a very human phenomenon.

What is language?

The infinite monkey theorem

The legend goes that if you sit a monkey down at a typewriter for an infinite length of time, then eventually, by hitting the keys at random, the monkey will type out the complete works of Shakespeare. This is one version of the infinite monkey theorem. You will not be surprised that the shelf life of this theorem is something less than infinity, once we hold it up to even the most casual scrutiny. First, monkeys are not random letter generators. Second, we are seduced by this problem into thinking about infinity as a vast but finite number. Third, it seduces *me* into showing you a picture of a chimpanzee (not a monkey) sitting at a typewriter (Figure 2.1). Fourth, the monkey would, in all likelihood, be dead long before the first **sentence** had been typed. And fifth, even Shakespeare would have trouble producing the complete works of Shakespeare, given that he couldn't type.

Our sense of the ridiculous is provoked by this scenario. We find it laughable to think that a monkey could generate Shakespeare's plays or even a simple 'Hello, how are you?' Monkeys do not have language. But this theorem suggests that they could acquire language, given sufficient time and an appropriate means of expression. The underlying assumption, therefore, is that humans and monkeys are not qualitatively different when it comes to language. The difference is merely quantitative. From this line of thinking it follows that animals (perhaps the more intelligent ones, at least) could acquire language, if they went about it in the right way. In fact, there have been several attempts to talk to the animals, and to get them to talk back to us.

Figure 2.1 The infinite monkey theorem

Source: Wikipedia: Infinite Monkey Theorem
http://en.wikipedia.org/wiki/Infinite_monkey_theorem

We will examine some of these efforts in this chapter and, in the process, we will discover how this comparative approach can help clarify what, precisely, is unique, and possibly biologically determined, about the human capacity to acquire language.

Language, talk and communication

So … can animals talk? At first glance, this question seems absurd. We do not find sheep debating the pros and cons of a vegetarian diet. Nor do we hear pigeons chatting about life in Trafalgar Square. But this question is deceptively simple. A number of bird species, including mynah birds and parrots, have astonishing abilities to mimic the human voice. Do these birds talk? Evidently *talk* refers to the physical act of producing human speech sounds, but its meaning can be wider, including the communication of ideas via speech. Some parrots can talk in the former sense, but can they hold a conversation? In contrast, many deaf people cannot talk, in the sense of being able to produce speech sounds with great accuracy or fluency, but they *can* hold conversations every bit as sophisticated as those of hearing people, through the medium of sign language. When we consider the biological basis of language, it is this latter, conversational, meaning of talk that holds more interest. Perhaps we should abandon all talk of talk and go straight to the heart of the matter: do parrots (or any other animal) have language?

But before we get to language, we must dispense with *communication*. Many people believe that (at least some) animals have language, because they use the terms *language* and *communication* interchangeably. But they are not the same thing. Many, possibly all, animals communicate, in the sense that they intentionally convey information to each other. To this end, dogs bark, sheep bleat and lions roar. But they do not have language. The upshot is that we must be careful to distinguish the concepts of talk, communication and language. It is the biological basis of language that we are concerned with here.

The design of language

Language has a number of characteristics that sets it apart from animal communication. The American linguist, Charles Hockett, worked on this problem for many years, finally coming up with a list of 16 defining characteristics (Hockett, 1963). As we shall see, most of these so-called design features are shared to some extent with animal communication systems. On this approach, it is the combination of all 16 features that distinguishes human language. We will focus on just four of Hockett's design features here (but see Box 2.1 for the complete list):

- creativity
- semanticity
- arbitrariness
- displacement

Hockett (1963) had two kinds of linguistic creativity in mind. The first refers to the creation of new words and idioms, a process that takes place all the time, and with especial enthusiasm among young people (Cheshire, 1982; see also Discussion point 2.1 below). The second kind of creativity refers to our ability to produce and understand new messages. In recent times, Chomsky (1965), in particular, has emphasized the importance of this latter kind of creativity, reviving a very old observation in linguistics (von Humboldt, 1836/1988): the rules of **grammar** (a limited, or finite, set of rules) allow us to construct an infinite variety of new utterances. New sentences are created all the time.

Two aspects of child speech demonstrate that linguistic creativity is in evidence very early on: (1) novel utterances; and (2) grammatical errors. With regard to novelty, Chomsky (1959: 42) pointed out that 'a child will be able to construct and understand utterances which are quite new, and are, at the same time, acceptable sentences in his language'. The following sentences from Alex, aged four years, are in all likelihood, novel:

> *No, he bit this little tiger from this set.*
> *You stood on my botty.*
> *Yes, he slid down to the bottom with Panda.*
> *Frog fell over and Bee fell over and Soldier fell over.*
> *When I was building the zoo, I jumped down and hurt myself.*

The examples above are grammatical sentences. The ones below (also from Alex) contain errors and, therefore, we can be even more confident that they are novel utterances, because young children are very rarely exposed to ungrammatical speech (Newport, Gleitman & Gleitman, 1977; see also Chapter 4). This means that errors have not been imitated.

> *She's too wide asleep, I think.*
> *I like Shinji because he's the goodest.*

Last day, when you had some toast, how many did you have?
Look, my scratches are going who I got at Colin's house.
I had a happy fry tuckey.

Incidentally, the 'happy fry tuckey' was a Kentucky Fried Chicken Happy Meal. Naturally, Alex was given this by his mother. *I* only ever gave him organic fish and vegetables. Cough. Both novel utterances and errors provide strong evidence that the child is an active producer of their own language, using a system of rules to assemble their own sentences. Throughout our lives, we create entirely new sentences at will, and the people listening to us can, for the most part, understand them. Creativity appears to be one of the few characteristics of language that is unequivocally unique to human language. Animal communication systems simply do not yield creative potential.

BOX 2.1 HOCKETT'S DESIGN FEATURES

Charles Hockett set out 16 different characteristics which together help define human language and crystallize what sets it apart from animal communication systems (Hockett & Altmann, 1968).

1 *Vocal-auditory channel.* The conduit for language is sound (the human voice), transmitted to a hearing mechanism (the ears and auditory channel).
2 *Broadcast transmission and directional reception.* Sound is transmitted (broadcast) in every direction, but the listener perceives it as coming from a particular source.
3 *Rapid fading.* Speech sounds do not last very long; they are transitory.
4 *Interchangeability.* We can switch between transmitting and receiving linguistic signals.
5 *Complete feedback.* Speakers can hear what they are saying: they receive feedback on the signal they are sending out.
6 *Specialization.* The organs used for producing speech (including lips, tongue, larynx and throat) are specially adapted for language; they are not simply used for breathing and eating.
7 *Semanticity.* Linguistic signals (words) can be used to refer to actions, objects and ideas.
8 *Arbitrariness.* There is no intrinsic, necessary relationship between a word and the concept it denotes. There is nothing (in principle) to prevent us from dropping the word *cat* and switching to *zug* to denote the same object.

(Continued)

---

9   *Discreteness*. Language makes use of discrete units, for example, the two speech sounds (phonemes) /p/ and /b/. The point at which the vocal cords begin to vibrate can vary, with more /p/-like sounds shading gradually into more /b/-like sounds. But we *perceive* a sharp cut-off between the two sounds (they are discrete), even though, physically, they figure on a single continuum (see Chapter 6).

10 *Displacement*. We can talk about things that are remote in time or space.

11 *Creativity*. We can extend the repertoire of language by coining new words and expressions. Also, we can produce and understand sentences that have never before been uttered. (Hockett used the term *openness*, but *creativity* is preferred these days).

12 *Cultural tradition*. Language is transmitted from one generation to the next by teaching and learning.

13 *Duality of patterning*. Languages have two levels: meaningful units at one level (words or **morphemes**) are created by combining meaning*less* units at the second level (**phonemes**).

14 *Prevarication*. Human beings can lie. They also write novels and talk about entirely hypothetical entities.

15 *Reflexiveness*. Language can be used to think and talk about language: we have so-called **metalinguistic skills**.

16 *Learnability*. We have the capacity to learn new languages beyond our native tongue.

DISCUSSION POINT 2.1
CREATION OF NEW WORDS

Identify words and phrases that have only recently come into popular usage. They could well be expressions that you use with your friends, but would hesitate to use with your grandparents. You might think of this as slang or casual speech and would struggle to find such words in a dictionary. List five different words of this kind. For each one, consider the following:

* Think of how the word is pronounced (the sounds). Is it a new sequence of sounds? Or is it an old word form that has been given a new meaning (like *cool* to mean 'admirable' rather than 'low temperature'). Or has it been pieced together from existing words and English sound sequences (like *cowabunga*, an expression of exhilaration for 1960s surfers and Teenage Mutant Ninja Turtles)?

- Does the word denote a new concept (have a new meaning)? If so, consider how you would express this new concept if you did not have this new word.
- If the word is, essentially, a synonym for a word that already exists, why do you think it has come into being?

The second of Hockett's design features, semanticity, describes our use of symbols to refer to (or 'mean') something. These symbols are words, ostensibly sequences of speech sounds that can be used to refer to objects, actions or ideas. The word *cat* refers to a furry domestic animal with whiskers and a tendency to sit on just that part of the paper you're trying to read. What is more, the word *cat* can be used to pick out (or 'mean') all exemplars of this kind of animal. *Cat* denotes a category of objects. Do animals have anything that equates to words? One example might be the danger cry of the white-handed gibbon, issued to warn other gibbons about approaching predators, including the clouded leopard (Clarke, Reichard & Zuberbühler, 2006). We might argue that the cry 'means' danger in the way that *cat* 'means' my pet, especially since these gibbons use different calls in different situations. But the gibbon cry might just as easily be a violent emotional response that only incidentally communicates information to other gibbons. Even if the gibbon cry has meaning, it is highly general in its scope, which, if your life is in peril, might not be all that helpful. The type and number of predators, their proximity, the direction they are moving in: none of these are specified by the danger cry. Instead, the gibbon call seems to apply to a total situation. And although other gibbons can obtain information from these calls, it is not clear that there has been any intention, in the human sense, to communicate that information to them (Seyfarth & Cheney, 2003). The (potential) semanticity of animal calls remains a matter for debate. But whichever way one looks at it, human beings far outstrip animals in their deployment of semanticity (Chomsky, 2011). There are many (many) thousands of words in English, compared to the extremely limited repertoires of animal vocal signals. So human beings exploit the benefits of semanticity to a far greater degree than any animal. We shall consider below whether animals can be encouraged to extend their repertoires and behave more like humans with regard to semanticity.

In the meantime, let's consider arbitrariness, another key design feature of language. The central idea here is that word forms – the packages of sound mentioned above – bear no intrinsic relation to their referents (de Saussure, 1916/1974). There is nothing in the nature of a domestic feline animal that forces me to call it *cat*. In Paris, I would use *chat*, while in Tokyo, it would be *neko*. The relation between the referent (the object in the world) and the word form is arbitrary, and the same holds true for the vast majority of words in any language. A tiny handful of exceptions can be found in the form of onomatopoeic words, like *pop*, *crack* and *squash*. Animal cries, on the other hand, are often tied closely in form to the 'meaning' they express. The gibbon danger cry is invested with the heightened emotion of arousal. But if we scour the animal world thoroughly, examples of arbitrary signals can be found. Western gulls, for example, have a wide repertoire of behaviours to denote aggression (Pierotti & Annett, 1994). Most of them, such as striking and grabbing other gulls, or pursuits on the ground with upraised wings, are non-arbitrary. But these gulls also turn away from an opponent and uproot grass with their beaks to display aggression. There is nothing about grass-pulling *per se* that inevitably connects it with aggression. It appears to be an arbitrary signal. The moral: never invite two Western gulls to a garden party. They'll fall out and make a terrible mess of your lawn.

Our final star feature is displacement. This simply refers to our ability to talk about things beyond our immediate situation. Human conversation can be displaced to matters that are remote in both time and space. I can talk about events both past and future, near and far. I am not confined to talking about my immediate context. In contrast, consider once again the gibbon danger cry (poor gibbon, we should get him to a place of safety). The danger signal is only triggered by the sight of an actual predator that is physically present. The gibbon has no signal to inform fellow gibbons that, say, they 'spotted a leopard about half a mile south of here

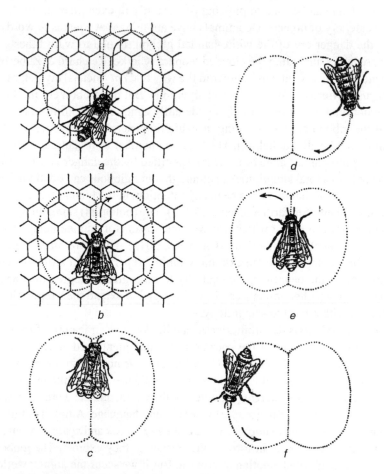

Figure 2.2　The wagging dance of the honey bee

Source: von Frisch, K. (1954). *The dancing bees: An account of the life and senses of the honey bee* (translated by D. Ilse). London: Methuen, Figure 40: The wagging dance, p. 117.

three hours ago'. Nonetheless, danger signals triggered by the sight of a leopard can persist some time after the leopard has disappeared from view. Does that count as displacement? It is debatable. Other animals show more definite signs of displacement in their communication. Most famous in this regard are Karl von Frisch's bees.

Von Frisch (1954) observed that when a bee discovers a good source of nectar, it communicates this information to other bees via a special 'waggle dance' (see Figure 2.2). The dance is performed vertically on a honey comb and comprises a simple figure of eight pattern drawn around a central straight line. During the straight line part of the run, the bee waggles its abdomen before turning left or right. The duration of the waggle phase corresponds to the distance of the food from the hive. Meanwhile, the angle at which the bee departs from the vertical, relative to the sun, during the straight line part of the dance corresponds to the direction of the food source. Amazingly, the bee alters the angle of its dance to accommodate the changing angle of the sun throughout the day. Bees therefore communicate both the direction and distance of remote food sources to other bees, a clear case of displacement. Karl von Frisch won the Nobel Prize for his ingenious work on the bee dance in 1973, and was never short of honey for tea. For our purposes, we can observe that, once again, one of Hockett's design features is not the exclusive preserve of human language. At the same time, it is worth reflecting that displacement is very rare in the animal world. And the kind of displacement we observe in bees, while impressive, is easily outstripped by our own accomplishments. We can talk about *anything* remote from our current location, whereas bees are confined to food sources within flying distance of the hive. They cannot even tell other bees how high a particular food source is. And humans can talk about things remote in time as well as space, and even things that are displaced in the sense of being entirely imaginary. The flexibility and range of the displacement witnessed in human language is massively greater than anything an animal communication system can offer.

DISCUSSION POINT 2.2
DEFINING LANGUAGE

We have considered four of Hockett's design features in some detail. In Box 2.1 you will find the complete set. For each one of the 16 design features, consider the questions below. You might want to split this task among different groups.

- Can you think of any animal communication systems that have a similar feature?
- If the answer is yes, do animals nevertheless differ from humans in the way they exploit this feature?

Returning to our original question – do animals have language? – the answer is clearly 'no'. Animal communication systems share many of their core features with language, but the overlap is highly selective. Bees might show displacement in their communication. But the extent of the displacement they are capable of is strictly limited. Moreover, bees do not use the vocal-auditory channel. They do not demonstrate creativity. Their communication is not arbitrary (there is a direct relation between the angle of the bee dance and the source of nectar). And so on. There are qualitative differences between animal communication and human language. But there are quantitative differences also, often quite dramatic. Humans exploit the potential of the design features to a much greater extent than animals. The 'words' found in gibbon communication could be listed on a single page. Set this against the multiple volumes of the *Oxford English Dictionary*: the contrast in our mutual exploitation of semanticity is readily apparent.

Animals may not have language, but there is a second question we can ask in our exploration of the biology of language: Do animals have the *potential* to acquire language? If so, Hockett's feature of cultural tradition might be the only barrier keeping animals from language. Whatever its biological basis, humans clearly do pass on many aspects of language from one generation to another. These include both the particular **phonemes** of a given language and the vast and arbitrary **lexicon** that must be learned by every child. If language is a cultural artefact, much like fire or clothing, then it might be possible to introduce it to animals. After all, there are several highly impressive cognitive achievements which do not emerge spontaneously in human beings, but which we nevertheless have the capacity to acquire. Consider mathematics or music. Perhaps animals simply need the right opportunities. If an animal could be taught language, then the argument that language is the sole province of human beings would collapse. It would also be much more difficult to argue that language *per se* is coded for in the human (but not any animal) genome. As it happens, a parade of animals, including chimpanzees, gorillas, grey parrots, dogs and dolphins, *have* signed up for Language School. We shall consider how well they got on in the next section.

Teaching words to animals

Talking versus sign language

If you want to teach an animal to talk, it makes sense to try one of our more intelligent neighbours in the animal world. Not only is success more likely, the calibre of conversation should be better than with less bright animals. What would you talk about with a crayfish or a beetle? Accordingly, most efforts to teach language have been directed towards our close evolutionary cousins, the great apes, including chimpanzees, gorillas and orang-utans (see also Herman, Richards & Wolz, 1984, on artificial language learning in dolphins). From the 1930s until the end of the last century, several such attempts were made, beginning with a chimpanzee named Gua who was raised like a human infant by Winthrop and Luella Kellog (1933). The Kellogs wanted Gua to *talk* in both senses described above: to communicate ideas via language, but also to engage in the physical act of producing speech sounds. This latter enterprise, in particular, was doomed to failure. It turns out that the chimpanzee's vocal apparatus – in particular, the proportions of the tongue, the angle of the airway and the relatively high position of the larynx – render human speech sounds all but impossible (Nishimura, 2005). Another chimpanzee, Viki, did produce three words: *mama*, *papa* and *cup*. She pronounced them 'softly, and hoarsely, but quite acceptably' (Hayes & Hayes,

1951: 107). But this meagre outcome was achieved only after three years of intensive training. Astonishingly, an elephant called Koshik has produced human speech recently. Koshik imitated a few words of Korean well enough for native speakers to transcribe accurately (Stoeger, Mietchen, Oh, De Silva, Herbst, Kwon & Fitch, 2012). He did so by placing his trunk inside his mouth to alter the acoustic properties of the vocal tract. As yet, though, there is no indication that Koshik understands what he is saying.

Returning to chimpanzees, research moved on to sign language, which does not depend on the production of speech sounds. Moreover, primates, including chimpanzees, gorillas and orang-utans, have all proved to be manually dextrous enough to communicate through the use of gesture. The first of the signing apes, Washoe, was born some time in 1965 and started learning an adapted version of American Sign Language (ASL) at about 10 months of age. By 36 months, Washoe was credited with knowing 85 separate signs (Gardner & Gardner, 1969). Her vocabulary eventually rose to 132 signs after four years of training (Fouts & Fouts, 2004). Washoe's use of signs was noteworthy in two respects: (1) spontaneity; and (2) generalization. First, Washoe did not always need to be prompted to use signs once they had been learned, but could do so spontaneously. And second, she sometimes generalized their use to a range of objects and events around her. The ability to generalize is an important aspect of reference, allowing us to apply a word to all members of a category. The word *apple* can be applied to all apples – red, green, large, small – not just one particular object in my fruit bowl. This is because the word *apple* is used to refer to a category of objects. We will consider how children tackle generalization of word meanings in Chapter 6. For the moment, we can note that chimpanzees are able to generalize their use of words beyond the immediate context in which they are learned.

Lexigrams

Sign language is not the only medium available for teaching language to apes. This sentence demonstrates the potential to represent linguistic information visually via printed symbols (letters). And while no chimpanzee has been taught to read and write, efforts have been made to use visual symbols (called 'lexigrams') that represent whole words (Savage-Rumbaugh, Murphy, Sevcik, Brakke, Williams & Rumbaugh, 1993). This system has a direct counterpart in Chinese characters: a single symbol can represent an entire word, whereas in English, we construct written words from one or more letters, each representing different **phonemes**. In teaching lexigrams, the chimpanzee is presented with a keyboard containing numerous different symbols constructed from different combinations of shapes and colours. By pressing one of the symbols, a speech synthesizer produces the spoken version of the word. The greatest success with the lexigram keyboard has been achieved with bonobo (or pygmy) chimpanzees, a species that is noted both for high intelligence and prolific sexual activity (de Waal, 1995). Kanzi, a male bonobo born in 1980 was exposed to lexigrams from the age of six months. Four years of effort had previously gone into trying to teach Kanzi's adoptive mother, Matata, how to use the lexigram keyboard, but to no avail. Kanzi, on the other hand, did much better, acquiring signs by observing his mother's training sessions. Kanzi's first 10 words were *orange*, *peanut*, *banana*, *apple*, *bedroom*, *chase*, *Austin*, *sweet potato*, *raisin* and *ball*. Kanzi would get on well with Jamie Oliver.

In the more popular end of the scientific press, Sue Savage-Rumbaugh claims that Kanzi can recognize and use 348 different lexigram symbols (Raffaele, 2006). More astonishing, in the same article it is claimed that Kanzi *understands* more than 3,000 spoken English words. We will consider Kanzi's comprehension of spoken English below, but these figures have not been corroborated and are, in all likelihood, highly inflated. For one thing, this figure seems to be based simply on the number of words that Kanzi was exposed to. That is a far (ape) cry from systematically testing comprehension of each word in isolation. More reliable estimates point to a stark contrast in the size of ape and child vocabularies. While apes seem to peak at a few hundred words, the language learning child soon dwarfs this figure.

The vogue for teaching apes to talk was at its height in the 1970s, and there was a point during that decade when it looked as though language could no longer be seen as the sole preserve of human beings. If apes can acquire words and combine them into novel utterances, one might assume (as the vast majority of their trainers did assume) that they had conquered language. But there are several factors that must temper this enthusiasm. First, the word learning of apes is slow and effortful compared to children. Children can acquire words on a single exposure, a process known as *fast mapping* (Carey, 1978; see also Chapter 6). This contrasts with the efforts of Kanzi and another bonobo, Panbanisha, who required in the region of 32–65 exposures to learn each new word (Lyn & Savage-Rumbaugh, 2000). What is more, the bonobos were tested within one hour of training for signs of comprehension. In consequence, it is not clear how long the bonobos' learning lasted, whereas for the child, of course, words can be lodged in the mind for a lifetime. Word learning in the chimpanzee is clearly a laborious task that they do not take to naturally. The motivation is often driven by reward – food, play, toys – rather than a desire to communicate meanings and hold a conversation either with their trainers or each other. In addition, the categories of words acquired are confined almost exclusively to objects and actions, with none of the wide variety of semantic categories witnessed in human vocabularies (Seidenberg & Petitto, 1979). But even on the most sceptical interpretation, we must still allow that chimpanzees have the capacity to acquire words. The arbitrary nature of words, their semanticity, and their spontaneous, generalized use in displaced communication have all been reliably observed.

Barking up the right tree: Word learning in dogs

Before we move on to consider the holy grail of language learning – grammar – let's consider how dogs and parrots have tried to get in on the word-learning act. Kaminski, Call & Fischer (2004) report that Rico, a border collie dog, acquired the meanings of more than 200 items and can retrieve named objects up to four weeks after the original training session. Moreover, Rico seemed to be using *exclusion learning*, also witnessed in young children (Heibeck & Markman, 1987). Presented with an array of objects, for which the names of all but one are already known, children infer that a novel word must refer to the single nameless object on display. Thus, if a two-year-old is shown an apple, a ball and a whisk and is asked to retrieve the whisk, they can do so, even if, previously, they only knew the labels *ball* and *apple*. Kaminski et al. (2004) claim that Rico can do this too, reporting an accuracy level of 93 per cent on 40 trials. It is unlikely that Rico simply has a novelty preference, because he is also able to retrieve familiar objects as well as new ones. As Bloom (2004: 1605) remarks, 'for psychologists, dogs may be the new chimpanzees'. But Bloom also sounds a note of caution (see also Markman & Abelev, 2004). Rico may be doing nothing more than responding to an entire situation ('fetch X'). There is a difference between a simple association between two items (a word and an object) and the act of reference. This observation was made in the nineteenth century by Taine (1877: 254) who remarked: 'There is nothing more in this than an association for the dog between a sound and some sensation of taste'. In contrast to this kind of associative learning, Bloom (2004) points out that, for the two-year-old child, the word *sock* does not mean 'fetch the sock' or 'go to the sock'. Instead, the child appreciates that the word refers to a category of objects and can be used to talk about different socks, request a sock, or notice the absence of one.

Bloom's concerns have been addressed more recently by Pilley & Reid (2011), who started out by shopping for hundreds of soft toys (yes, hundreds), plus a number of Frisbees and balls thrown in. So to speak. Each object was distinct and was labelled in marker pen with a unique name. Over the course of three years, Chaser was trained for 4–5 hours per day and learned the names for 1,022 of these toys. Remarkably, even several months after training was complete, Chaser was 92 per cent accurate when asked to retrieve a toy from an array of eight objects. There is also evidence that Chaser's understanding of words goes beyond a global response to an entire situation ('fetch the ball'). Chaser could respond appropriately to three different commands (*take*, *paw* and *nose*) when combined with an object name (Pilley, 2013). She seemed to understand the notion of reference, in particular, that words can refer to a given object quite independent of any actions which that object might be associated with. Chaser also seemed to understand that **common nouns** refer to an entire category of objects, even though most of the words she was trained on were treated as **proper nouns**. For example, a single object could be labelled in three different ways: as a toy; a ball; or by its specific name.

Like children (and Rico), Chaser was able to infer the name of a new object by exclusion (cf. Greer & Du, 2015). For example, Chaser was presented with eight objects, all of which were familiar (Sugardaddy, Valentine, Wow, Pregnant, Backpack, Tortoise, Red Riding Hood and ABC – there's a sad story struggling to get out in that list). A novel object was then added to this collection, and Chaser was asked to fetch *Airborne*, a word which was also novel to her. Because she knew all the other object names, she inferred that the new name – Airborne – must refer to the only novel object. This kind of learning is not confined to language. Nor is it confined to human beings. Learning by exclusion in non-linguistic domains has been observed in parrots (Pepperberg, Koepke, Livingston, Girard & Leigh, 2013), macaques, baboons, capuchins and squirrel monkeys (Marsh, Vining, Levendoski, Judge & Call, 2015). Evidently, both children and dogs can recruit a domain-general learning mechanism in the acquisition of new word meanings (more on this in Chapter 10). Even more startling, there are parallels between the way *pigeons* learn to categorize objects and the way children acquire words. Wassermann, Brooks & McMurray (2015) trained pigeons to sort 128 objects into 16 human language categories. Like word-learning children, the pigeons were guided by the perceptual coherence of the different object categories (e.g., shape), and moreover, they generalized their learning to novel objects.

Chaser's lexical prowess puts her fellow collie, Rico, in the shade, but more startling, she outstrips even Kanzi by a wide margin, having learned roughly three times as many words. This is puzzling, if one considers that chimpanzees are renowned for their intelligence (Mandalaywala, Fleener & Maestripieri, 2015) and, what's more, are much closer to humans, phylogenetically, than dogs. But there is a great disparity between chimps and dogs in their willingness to be directed by humans. Domestic dogs can recognize when particular actions are intended as communicative signals, including pointing, the direction of someone's gaze and high-pitched vocalizations (Tomasello & Kaminski, 2009). Of note, human infants also tune in with alacrity to these self-same signals (see Chapter 4). These skills appear to be largely untaught in dogs, since they are witnessed in puppies as young as six weeks old (Kaminski, Shulz & Tomasello, 2012). Dogs have been domesticated for thousands of years. It is possible, therefore, that the long, intertwined history of humans and dogs underpins canine sensitivity to the communicative intentionality of human behaviours (Hare, Rosati, Kaminski, Bräuer, Call & Tomasello, 2010). Unlike chimps, dogs are dependent on humans for food and shelter. It is perhaps not surprising, therefore, that they are so responsive to the communicative signals of human beings. In contrast, chimpanzees are much less inclined to communicate spontaneously with a human, even when supplied with the means to do so. The cognitive skills needed to acquire language are of little use if the *motivation* to learn and use language is missing in the first place. Unlike Chaser, Kanzi was not a willing player of the Language Game.

Alex, the non-parroting parrot

Perhaps even more impressive than Chaser is the case of Alex, an African grey parrot, bought from a pet shop in 1977 when he was about one-year-old. For 30 years, until his death in September 2007, Alex was involved in a programme of research that transformed our view of animal learning (Pepperberg, 2006). While Rico can understand English commands, Alex could both understand and speak for himself, making use of parrots' celebrated vocal mimicry skills. Alex could label 50 different objects, including seven colours and five shapes, as well as being able to discriminate different quantities up to and including six. Remarkably, Alex could answer different questions about the same object (Pepperberg, 2010). Shown a scrap of yellow wool, Alex could answer correctly if the question was either 'What matter?' or 'What colour?' Alex even mastered the number words from one to eight, demonstrating knowledge of cardinality – the fact that each number word denotes a collection of a given size (Pepperberg & Carey, 2012). Alex learned via the so-called Model/Rival technique in which he first observes two humans, one 'training' the other, with success being rewarded by receiving the object that is being named. Alex thus observes and competes with a human being for the objects being labelled. Rewarding Alex with the actual object proved far more successful than providing something extrinsic to the learning situation, like food. This is different from Rico, of course, who must have to watch his weight, given the number of snacks on offer.

We can see, then, that both dog and parrot learned labels for objects in ways that differ quite fundamentally from the way a young child learns words. Pepperberg (2006: 78) asserts that Alex 'demonstrates intriguing communicative parallels with young humans, despite his phylogenetic distance'. In assessing this claim, we should perhaps focus on the judicious use of the word 'parallel'. Alex's use of his 50-word vocabulary bears some resemblance to that of a young child.

But the route he took to get there is very different and his mental representation of words is also very likely quite different from that of a human learner. Shown a wooden block, Alex can correctly answer a range of different questions about it, including: 'What colour?', 'What shape?', 'What matter?' (wooden) and 'What toy?' But each answer has to be trained separately. When different attributes, like colour and shape, are presented together, learning does not take place. When asked 'What colour?', another parrot called Griffin answers with an object name, like 'cup'. In contrast, the young child can integrate the different attributes of an object into a coherent network of interrelated meanings.

Animal grammar

Combining words

As soon as a language learner begins to combine two or more words together into single utterances, it becomes possible to broach the issue of grammar. And it is here, perhaps, that the real battles have been fought in what the Gardners ruefully refer to as the 'chimp-language wars' (Gardner & Gardner, 1991). We can start by confirming that chimpanzees do produce multi-word sequences. Washoe came out with phrases like *gimme tickle* ('come and tickle me'), *open food drink* ('open the fridge') and *sweet go* ('let's go to the raspberry bushes'). Moreover, this language learning feat is not confined to Washoe. Several other primates have been observed producing sign combinations, including other chimpanzees (Terrace, 1979; Asano, Kojima, Matsuzawa, Kubota & Murofushi, 1982), a gorilla (Patterson, 1978; Patterson, Tanner & Mayer, 1988) and an orang-utan (Miles, 1983).

Rivas (2005) analysed a large corpus of signing behaviour from five chimpanzees and reports that 33 per cent of their output comprised two or more signs. The question that then follows concerns rule-governed behaviour. Are words being combined in a systematic way that conforms to the rules of grammar? The easiest way of tackling this question is to look for consistency in the way words are combined. Some combinations look promising in this regard, for example, *eat apple* and *drink coffee*. Children's earliest two-word utterances look very similar: *Mommy letter*; *finger stuck*; and *empty garbage*. In both ape and child, we can see that the basic word order of English has been preserved, even though there are several words (and bits of words) missing. Thus, *eat apple* might be glossed as *I want to eat an apple*, while *finger stuck* might be more fully rendered as *my finger is stuck*. So far so good. But whereas the child maintains the correct word order throughout their language learning, chimpanzees are far less reliable. For example, although Kanzi had a preference for the correct word order, he was nevertheless quite happy to switch words around: *bite tomato* alternating with *tomato bite*. But think of the famous contrast in newspaper headlines: 'Dog bites man' is not news, whereas 'Man bites dog' *is* news. Switching the word order makes a big difference in how the sequence of words is interpreted. Nim, however, switched the order of words around with alacrity: *eat Nim* occurred 302 times, compared with 209 instances of *Nim eat*, seemingly with no regard for the potential impact it might have on the message conveyed. Across a range of chimpanzees, object and action signs tend to occur in initial position, with request markers like *that*, *there*, and *good* occurring in final position.

This makes sense if one considers that the crux of a message, a particular object or action that is being requested, is most salient to the chimpanzee and hence more naturally takes first position in an utterance. Hence, the order of words is dictated by **pragmatic**, rather than syntactic, factors. In other cases, two-word combinations seem to be completely haphazard in a way that child utterances are not: *chase toothbrush, flower peekaboo, sodapop brush, drink gum*. Longer combinations look even less like grammatical sentences:

Multi-sign combinations made by chimpanzees (Rivas, 2005)

> *nut brush toothbrush*
> *cheese drink Tatu*
> *flower gimme flower*
> *banana toothbrush that*
> *flower drink gum toothbrush*
> *drink there brush clothes*

As the signing sequences increase in length, they rely increasingly on repetition:

Four-sign sequences by Nim (Terrace, 1979)

> *eat drink eat drink*
> *drink eat drink eat*
> *Nim eat Nim eat*
> *me Nim eat me*
> *Drink eat me Nim*
> *eat Grape eat Nim*

Anyone would think the poor ape was being deprived of food. Maybe if he learnt to ask nicely, he'd have more success. But it would seem that this feat is beyond both Nim and all other chimpanzees. The longer the sequences, the more repetitive the ape becomes. Hence, no extra meanings are being conveyed in longer utterances, and any semblance of regularity or consistency is diminished. Rivas (2005) reports one sequence of 22 signs from a chimpanzee, and while he does not spell it out, two sequences, each comprising 16 signs *are* detailed:

Sixteen-sign sequences by Washoe and Nim (Rivas, 2005)

Washoe: flower hurry flower hug go flower book flower gimme flower gimme flower hug hurry drink gimme

Nim: give orange me give eat orange me eat orange give me eat orange give me you

What we see, then, is a complete lack of regard for the niceties of grammar (Yang, 2013). And this is the case even when, arguably, the demands placed on chimpanzees are considerably curtailed in comparison with young children. This is because Washoe, Nim, Kanzi and the rest have never been taught **morphology**, the aspect of grammar concerned with the internal structure of words (see Chapter 7). Thus Nim could only ever produce the bald utterance *Nim eat*, not having been exposed to the subtleties of *Nim is eating* or *Nim ate*. In other ways, too, the language that chimpanzees have been exposed to constitutes a stripped down version of a fully fledged natural language. Given that the linguistic demands placed on them have been reduced in this way, one might have expected more from the learning they did undertake. But even with much of the grammatical clutter brushed to one side for them, chimpanzees clearly cannot acquire even basic aspects of grammar, like consistent use of word order.

Comprehension of spoken English by Kanzi

Before we finally give up the ghost, we should take into account the distinction between production and comprehension. So far our emphasis has been on the language that chimpanzees can produce themselves. But we might also consider what they can understand. Perhaps the neuromotor co-ordination required to produce signs or press lexigram symbols obscures the chimpanzee's true level of linguistic competence. It is certainly well known that young children experience a lag between comprehension and production. Two-year-olds generally understand far more words than they can actually utter themselves (Griffiths, 1986; see also Chapter 6). It is conceivable, then, that chimpanzees are in the same boat. Accordingly, Savage-Rumbaugh et al. (1993) tested Kanzi's ability to follow complex instructions, issued in spoken English. Recall that Kanzi's language learning was always, in a sense, bilingual, involving exposure to both lexigrams and spoken English. Typical instructions are shown below:

> *Go to the microwave and get the shoe*
> *Give the monster mask to Kelly*
> *Turn the flashlight on*
> *Give the big tomato to Liz*
> *Take the ice back to the refrigerator*

Savage-Rumbaugh et al. (1993) report an overall success rate of 71 per cent in Kanzi's ability to carry out instructions of this kind. But the criteria for judging success are extremely liberal. More to the point, there is no evidence that Kanzi can understand every word addressed to him. And the basis on which he acts can very often be ascribed to pragmatic factors, rather than his interpretation of grammatical rules to get at meaning. For example, if you hand me a flashlight I will probably turn it on, because that's what one does with flashlights. If I hear *Give the big tomato to Liz*, I would only need to know the words *tomato* and *Liz* to guess that these two 'objects' should be married up. As it happens, Kanzi took two tomatoes of different sizes, and gave them both to Liz. This response was scored as 'Partially Correct', even though the intention of the sentence was to distinguish between large and small exemplars of a category (*tomato*). Using a stricter definition of 'correct', where Kanzi performs the requested action immediately, and where we include only blind trials in which the instructor is out of sight, Kanzi's success rate drops to 59 per cent. And, as noted, this success may be achieved without a knowledge of grammar. Instructions can often be carried out correctly from an understanding of one or two individual word meanings. Overall, then, the work on Kanzi's comprehension does not lend any extra confidence to the idea that apes can acquire grammar.

43

The linguistic limitations of animals

Research on ape language dwindled fast in the 1980s, largely in the wake of the scepticism expressed by Terrace (1979), a 'chimp insider' who set in motion an increasingly acrimonious debate (for example, Wallman, 1992, 1993; Lieberman, 1993). In consequence, it is difficult to find a balanced approach to this topic, so reader beware. Nativists tend to be extremely dismissive of apes' linguistic abilities (for example, Pinker, 1994) while others, especially ape researchers, tend towards excesses in the opposite direction (for example, Savage-Rumbaugh et al., 1993). In fact, both sides of the argument have some merit. Apes – and other animals – have demonstrated abilities that no-one dreamed of a century ago. As we have observed, they are capable of acquiring information about individual words. In so doing, some of Hockett's (1963) defining features of language have been assailed. Čadková (2015) suggests that these abilities evolved in parallel across different species, independently from one another. She further argues that if language cannot be considered the exclusive 'quality' of a single species, then Hockett's design features are undermined and in need of a total rethink: language should no longer be considered the sole preserve of human beings. Hockett overemphasized spoken language (vocal-auditory channel, broadcast transmission, rapid fading, specialization) at the expense of alternative media for language, including sign language and writing (Čadková, 2015). But Hockett's features retain their value for research. It is the combination of all 16 design features which together identify language. Moreover, some of Hockett's features, like duality of patterning, do seem to remain the sole preserve of human language.

When provided with an appropriate medium (e.g., lexigrams), chimpanzee words show semanticity, arbitrariness and, sometimes, displacement. And the essential symbolic function of words appears to be within the grasp of chimpanzees. There has even been at least one case of cultural transmission, where one chimpanzee (Kanzi) has learned words from another chimpanzee (his mother), rather than from a human trainer. At the same time, though, we should be clear that chimpanzee word learning does not have the same flavour as that of a child engaged in the same task. It is slow, effortful, and very limited in scope. And the lexical knowledge that the chimpanzee acquires is far less rich than that attained by the human child. Children acquire information about the grammatical categories of individual words, including information about what *kinds* of words can go together in words and phrases (for example, the **article** *the* is followed by a **noun** in phrases like *the dog*, *the biscuit*, and so on). Beyond word learning, no animal has succeeded in acquiring grammar, not even the star turn, Kanzi. And with respect to the *purpose* of language, it is also apparent that no non-human animal really gets it. No amount of intensive training will ever induce a chimpanzee to express an opinion, ask a question, or phone a friend for a chat. Their use of language is almost tool-like, an instrument used to obtain food or some other desired goal. There is no compunction on the part of a chimpanzee to engage in conversation.

Maybe we have been asking too much of our primate cousins. The Hayes wanted Viki to speak, while the Gardners wanted Washoe to sign like a deaf person. The methods of training chimpanzees did improve with each attempt, most notably with the lexigram keyboard introduced by Savage-Rumbaugh. However, it is one thing to adapt the medium of communication to chimpanzee tastes – it is quite another to consider how suitable the learning task is in the first place. The aim has been to teach language to a primate – words and grammar – the whole kit and caboodle. In this respect, we have certainly expected too much of chimpanzees. Weiss & Newport (2006: 247) point out that 'this paradigm disadvantages primates in that it requires them to acquire a heterospecific (another species') system of communication'. The fact that chimpanzees can acquire any aspects of language at all is therefore surprising and leads us to suspect that some similarities do exist across species in the way that linguistic information is processed. We will pursue this idea further in the next section.

Is speech special?

Categorical perception in infants and primates

As noted, efforts to teach Language (with a capital L) to chimpanzees faded away with the twentieth century, the last major attempt being Savage-Rumbaugh et al. (1993). However, comparative research has been reinvigorated by a change of direction. This new line of enquiry examines the extent to which basic psycholinguistic mechanisms are shared across species, in particular, the rapid, automatic processing of speech sounds. Very early in life, human infants demonstrate an ability to process speech in a very adult-like manner. In particular, infants discriminate between different speech sounds, or **phonemes**, in a categorical manner (Eimas, Siqueland, Jusczyk & Vigorito, 1971; see Box 2.2). For example, the phoneme /p/ can be pronounced in many different ways. But we do not perceive any of these differences. Our perceptual systems place all the different /p/s in a single box (or category) marked /p/. We will examine categorical perception in much more detail in Chapter 5. For the moment, we maintain the focus on our comparison between humans and non-humans.

The discovery of categorical perception in 1971 pointed to a language-specific, uniquely human, inborn ability. However, it was not long before human infants were placed in an unlikely menagerie that included chinchillas, macaques, budgerigars and even Japanese quails. These animals, too, can make categorical phonemic distinctions, a finding which suggests a general property of avian and mammalian auditory systems (Kuhl & Miller, 1975; Kuhl & Padden, 1983; Dooling & Brown, 1990; Kluender, 1991). This finding seems rather odd at first, because only humans have speech. Why would chinchillas need to distinguish /p/ from /b/? Kuhl (2004) suggests that, in evolution, categorical perception for sound came first. As language evolved, it exploited a domain-general auditory capacity that is shared with other animals. The processing of sound for communication might then have become more specialized. Of note, adults use different brain regions for processing speech versus non-speech sounds (Vouloumanos, Kiehl, Werker & Liddle, 2001). But then again, monkeys recruit different brain regions for processing communicative calls versus other kinds of auditory stimulus. Moreover, monkey calls are processed in regions of the left hemisphere that correspond well with brain regions used by humans for speech processing (Poremba, Malloy, Saunders, Carson, Herscovitch & Mishkin, 2004).

BOX 2.2 PHONEMES AND THE NOTATION FOR SPEECH SOUNDS

In order to represent the speech sounds in words (the **phonemes**), there is a special notation system. Phonemes are not the same as letters, but confusingly, there is some overlap in the notation systems. Some phonemic symbols look like ordinary English letters (for example, / p, b, t /), while others require symbols that are not found in the conventional alphabet (for example, θ, ə, æ).

The easiest way to identify a phonological representation is through the use of slash brackets. Thus, the word *cat* can be spelled with the letters c-a-t, or represented phonemically as / k æ t / within slash brackets. Observe the use of /k/ to represent what is often called a 'hard C' in English. The use of /k/ to represent this phoneme allows us to distinguish the hard C in *cat*, /k/, from the 'soft C' in *ceiling*, /s/. And it also allows us to recognize that the words *cat* and *king* start with the same sound, or phoneme, /k/, despite the idiosyncrasies of the English spelling system.

Note also that the vowel in *cat* is represented by the symbol /æ/. Vowel sounds, in particular, tend to have curious symbols, not found in the English alphabet, but this can apply to consonants also. For example, in *king*, the final sound is spelled –NG (yes, it's one sound, not two). The phonemic symbol for this phoneme is /ŋ/.

The full range of possible human speech sounds is encompassed within a single notation system known as the International Phonetic Alphabet (IPA) (see the website listing at the end of Chapter 5). The IPA system allows any word from any language to be transcribed, providing an accurate record of how to pronounce it. A simplified version, listing the phonemes of English, is provided in Appendix 2.

But humans and non-humans are not identical when it comes to speech processing. First, although animals perceive speech categorically, animal phoneme boundaries are different from those perceived by humans in about one third of cases studied so far (Sinnott, 1998). Second, it has been argued that infants have a preference for listening to speech over other sounds. For example, newborn infant brains respond more strongly to samples of Infant Directed Speech than they do to the same samples played backwards (Peña, Maki, Kovačič, Dehaene-Lambertz, Koizumi, Bouquet & Mehler, 2003). Infant preferences have also been examined by manufacturing synthetic sound samples that resemble speech on several dimensions. These include the fundamental frequency (which provides information on **pitch**), duration, pitch contour, amplitude and intensity (Vouloumanos & Werker, 2007). Given a choice between real speech and the non-speech analogue, infants preferred human speech. But despite the strenuous efforts to come up with a speech-like alternative for infants to listen to, Rosen & Iverson (2007) point out that the simulation of voice pitch remains very crude. It is very difficult to establish whether infants prefer speech over other sounds. This follows from the difficulty in constructing a sound stimulus that has the qualities of speech without actually being speech. What we do know is that the preference for speech is not present at birth. Neonates are equally happy listening to either human speech or rhesus monkey vocalizations, though both of these are preferred to synthetic (non-primate) sounds (Vouloumanos, Hauser, Werker & Martin, 2010; Shultz & Vouloumanos, 2010). By three months, any bias for monkey vocalizations has dropped away. Hence, speech may be something that infants focus on very early in life due to a massive amount of exposure.

But there is a third way in which speech can be seen as special. Human infants demonstrate categorical perception effortlessly, whereas it takes many thousands of training trials of supervised learning (operant conditioning) to induce categorical perception in animals. We must also set this great learning effort against the fact that 'humans do not just make one-bit discriminations between pairs of phonemes. Rather, they can process a continuous, information-rich stream of speech' (Pinker & Jackendoff, 2005: 207). It seems that once again we have an example of overlap (not identity) between human and animal cognition: animals can process speech sounds in a way that is analogous to human perception. The contrast lies in the facility with which humans execute the processing and learning of linguistic stimuli. This observation echoes our conclusions (above) about vocabulary learning in chimpanzees. It all comes much more naturally to us. There may not be anything inherently special about speech as an acoustic experience, but there is certainly something special about what we do with speech in the development of a linguistic system. This point has been underscored recently by Marcus, Fernandes & Johnson (2007), who showed that infants learn rules more easily from speech stimuli than from non-speech stimuli (though see Saffran, Pollak, Seibel & Shkolnik, 2007, for contrasting evidence). Overall, the picture is somewhat mixed. There is evidence that speech is processed differently from other acoustic signals from very early on in life. At the same time, there are signs that some animals can also process speech categorically. Some animals also dedicate brain regions to communicative calls corresponding to brain regions that humans use for speech processing. We may not yet be able to declare unequivocally that speech is special to humans but, clearly, what we do with it, in terms of processing and learning, *is* special.

Statistical learning

Recent comparative research has examined our ability to process and remember information from extended sequences of speech. Infants can learn to recognize particular **syllable** patterns that occur repeatedly within a long, uninterrupted sequence of syllables (Saffran, Aslin & Newport, 1996). For example, an infant can learn to recognize the sequence *golabu* within a longer sequence, like the following:

padoti*golabu*padotibidakutupirotupiro*golabu*bidaku

This remarkable ability is often referred to as *statistical learning* and provides one key to explaining how young children begin to isolate individual words from the torrent of speech assailing their ears. How do infants do this? Why is it called *statistical* learning? We shall return to these questions in Chapter 5. For the moment, we want to know if animals also possess the ability to recognize specific, word-like sequences of speech. For those of you who have to go out now, the answer is *yes*. For those of you who can stay a little longer, we must qualify that *yes*: humans and primates are similar, but not identical.

In one respect, cotton-top tamarin monkeys perform like human infants (Hauser, Newport & Aslin, 2001). They can isolate predictable syllable sequences (nonsense words, like *golabu*) from a continuous stream of speech. Two basic processing abilities therefore seem to be shared between humans and monkeys. First, there is the ability to distinguish one syllable from another and treat them as elementary units. Second, we share an ability to keep track of the serial order in which those syllables occur, together with information about which syllable sequences co-occur regularly. However, subsequent research points to subtle differences between human adults and tamarins (Newport, Hauser, Spaepen & Aslin, 2004). Syllables might not, in fact, be the basic unit of analysis. Accordingly, this later study teased apart two factors in the speech stream that could be used as the basis for learning about the serial order of word-like sequences. The first was the syllable (for example, *go, la, bu*) and the second was the phoneme, either **consonants** (for example, /g, l, b/) or **vowels** (for example, (/o, æ, u/). When we listen to a continuous stream of speech, do we pay attention to whole syllables or individual phonetic segments? The answer seems to be that humans prefer phonemes, while tamarins have a penchant for syllables. Both monkeys and adults were exposed to 21 minutes of continuous speech, of the *padotigolabu* kind. Humans did well at identifying words (predictable stretches of speech) when the stimuli contained predictable relations between either consonants or vowels. The tamarins did well when the predictability of the stimuli lay either in the syllable structure or in the vowels. Vowels are sometimes described as the nucleus of the syllable and it might be argued that vowels and/or syllables are relatively large, holistic units of speech. In contrast, humans can cope with the more fine-grained phonetic distinctions to be found between different consonants. The basis for this cross-species difference is not entirely clear yet, but the fact that it exists is important in helping explain the human facility for language.

Back to grammar: Infants versus monkeys

The new approach to comparative learning has recently ventured into the domain of grammar (Saffran, Hauser, Seibel, Kapfhamer, Tsao & Cushman, 2008). Concordant with this new approach, the task presented to learners is highly focused. No attempt was made to teach the whole of Grammar (with a capital G) as in Savage-Rumbaugh et al. (1993). Instead, a language was constructed with very simple grammatical rules. The aim was to see if tamarins can acquire *any* kind of rule characteristic of human language. The focus was on so-called *predictive dependencies*, whereby the presence of one word can be used to predict the presence of another in a phrase. For example, the presence of an article like *the* means we can predict fairly certainly that a noun (*nematode*, perhaps) will follow, either directly (*the nematode*) or very soon (*the white nematode*). Articles do not occur by themselves. Whereas I can predict a noun from the presence of an article, the reverse is not true. Nouns can occur with or without an article (*I like nematodes, My friend named his baby Nematode*, and so on). Saffran et al. (2008) constructed two artificial, miniature languages, one with, and one without, predictive dependencies. Following training, they found that 12-month-old infants could distinguish between grammatical and ungrammatical sentences from the Predictive language, but not from the Non-predictive one. Tamarins, meanwhile, performed in a similar fashion to human infants, but only on simple dependency relationships. When the complexity of test materials was increased, tamarins dropped out of the race, leaving human infants out in the lead. We find another example, therefore, of subtle differences between humans and non-humans that have very large ramifications. Tamarins are capable of learning simple rules, even rules that look language-like (Neiworth, 2013). But the degree of complexity is strictly limited. In this vein, another study has found that rats can learn a simple rule (Murphy, Mondragon & Murphy, 2008). The rule determines the order of two kinds of element (A and B) in three-element sequences. Rats can distinguish AAB from ABA sequences. Zebra finches have also been trained to discriminate patterns of this kind, using elements of songs (Chen, Rossum & ten Cate, 2015). Both rats and finches attend to repeated A or B elements and demonstrate rule-governed behaviour. But the complexity of rules which can be acquired, and the ability to generalize them to novel elements is strictly limited (ten Cate, 2014). Overall, we can see that animals are capable of learning rules, even the kinds of rules that appear in human language. They are strictly limited, however, with regard to the complexity of the rules that can be acquired.

The language faculty: Broad and narrow

In our day trip to the zoo, the overriding interest has been in discovering what, if anything, is special about language. A recent approach to this issue divides the faculty of language into two components: broad and narrow (Hauser, Chomsky & Fitch, 2002). The faculty of language – broad (FLB) embraces the biological capacity that we have, as human beings, to acquire language. FLB is one of the defining characteristics that distinguishes human beings from other animals. At the same time, much of the biological capacity underpinning the broad faculty is assumed to derive from shared origins with animal communication. For example, parts of the human conceptual system, in particular those aspects of cognition that allow causal, spatial and social reasoning, are present in other animals, especially other primates (Buttelman, Carpenter, Call & Tomasello, 2007). The mechanisms of FLB, therefore, are shared with other animals, 'in more or less the same form as they exist in humans, with differences of quantity rather than kind' (Hauser et al., 2002: 1573). Embedded within FLB, as a subset, is the faculty of language – narrow (FLN). FLN comprises just those phenomena that are unique, both to language and to human beings (see Figure 2.3).

What does FLN consist of? The answer is an open question. Some authors, like Pinker & Jackendoff (2005) argue that there are numerous aspects of language that are uniquely human, including: speech perception, speech production, **phonology**, words and **grammar**. They acknowledge that, for several of these phenomena, animals display an ability to learn at least something. But Pinker & Jackendoff emphasize the gulf that generally exists between humans and non-humans. The speed and facility of human learning goes way beyond any animal achievement, and the full complexity of what can be learned also leaves animals way behind in the slow lane. Pinker & Jackendoff (2005) emphasize that many aspects of human conceptual understanding would be impossible without language. These range from seemingly simple concepts like

Table 2.1 Aspects of language witnessed in animal learning

Aspect of language	Animal	Examples and related references
Differentiation of speech versus non-speech sounds	Monkey	Different brain regions used for communicative stimuli versus other auditory stimuli (Poremba et al., 2004)
Categorical perception of speech sounds	Chinchilla, macaque, budgerigar, Japanese quail	Birds distinguish sounds based on the same Voice Onset Time boundaries as humans (Beckers, 2011), including budgerigars (Dooling & Brown, 1990) and Japanese quail (Kluender, 1991). Categorical perception is also seen in chinchillas (Kuhl & Miller, 1975) and macaques (Kuhl & Padden, 1983)
Voice recognition	Cat	Cats recognize the unique auditory qualities of their owners' voices (Saito & Shinozuka, 2013)
Perception: ability to distinguish dialect, gender and age of human speakers	Elephant	African elephants are especially wary when they hear the speech of young Maasai men – a group who pose a distinct threat to them (McComb, Shannon, Sayialel & Moss, 2014)
Talking: production of speech sounds	Grey parrot, mynah, parakeet, budgerigar, cockatoo, starling, elephant	Alex (parrot) produced English words spontaneously to make requests (Pepperberg, 2010). Cf. Klatt & Stefanski (1974), Ohms, Beckers, ten Cate & Suthers (2012), Stoeger et al. (2012)
Words (comprehension)	Grey parrot, dog, chimpanzee, bonobo	Chaser (dog) learned more than 1,000 object names (Pilley & Reid, 2011) Washoe (chimpanzee) acquired ASL signs (Gardner & Gardner, 1969) Kanzi (bonobo) acquired lexigrams (Savage-Rumbaugh et al., 1993) Alex the parrot had a vocabulary in excess of 100 words (Pepperberg, 2010)
Words (production)	Chimpanzee, bonobo, dolphin	Bottlenose dolphins label themselves with a unique signature whistle (King & Janik, 2013). Cf. Savage-Rumbaugh et al. (1993)

Aspect of language	Animal	Examples and related references
Learning words by mutual exclusion	Dog, parrot	Chaser: could use a new word to select a novel object from an array of known objects (Pilley & Reid, 2011). Cf. Pepperberg (2010)
Acquiring object name categories via perceptual categories	Pigeon	Pigeons were guided by object shape in sorting objects into 16 human language categories (Wasserman et al., 2015)
Recognizing words in running speech	Cotton-top tamarins	Tamarins identified predictable syllable sequences in a continuous speech stream (Hauser et al., 2001)
Word combinations (comprehension)	Grey parrot, chimpanzee, bonobo, gorilla, dog, dolphin, any animal trained to follow multi-word commands	Kanzi (bonobo) could follow commands such as 'Go to the microwave and get the shoe' (Savage-Rumbaugh et al., 1993). Cf. Muncer & Ettlinger (1981), Herman, Kuczaj & Holder (1993), Patterson (1978), Pepperberg & Carey (2012), Pilley (2013)
Word combinations (production)	Chimpanzee, bonobo, dog, parrot, mynah	Alex the parrot produced utterances like 'Go back' and 'I want some water' (Pepperberg, 2010). Cf. Gardner & Gardner (1969), Klatt & Stefanski (1974), Pepperberg (2010), Pilley (2013)
Simple rule learning	Cotton-top tamarins, rhesus macaques, rats	Rats learned a rule based on CVCVCV consonant-vowel sequences (de la Mora & Toro, 2013). Cf. Hauser et al. (2001), Wilson et al. (2015)
Hierarchical organization of structures (cf. grammar)	Zebra finch and other song birds, humpback whale	The zebra finch song comprises notes and syllables which combine to form higher-order units (Yu & Margoliash, 1996). Cf. Berwick, Okanoya, Beckers & Bolhuis (2011), Cholewiak, Sousa-Lima & Cerchio (2013)

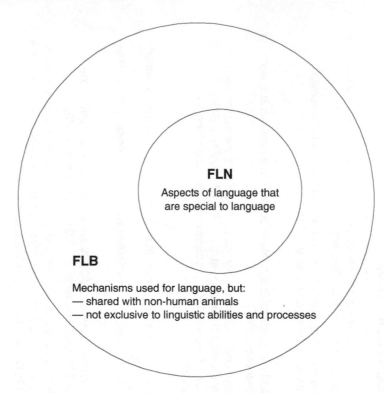

Figure 2.3 The faculty of language: broad (FLB) and narrow (FLN)

a week, to the possibility that numbers could not exist without language. The narrow faculty of language does not look so very narrow on this view. However, other authors have a much more restricted view of FLN. Chomsky has argued that a single, very simple property of language underpins what is both unique to language and uniquely human (Berwick & Chomsky, 2016). This property, known as Merge, allows two linguistic units to combine to form a distinct new unit. When the adjective *crazy* is combined with the noun *Trump*, we get a new unit, the noun phrase *crazy Trump* (we also get a shiver down the spine). This new unit, with its internal structure, allows for the possibility of hierarchical structure in language.

So that's the long and the short of it. Or rather, the broad and the narrow. The distinction between FLB and FLN may have some mileage for conceptualizing the human faculty of language. At present, there are clearly some rather strong disagreements as to which aspects of language should be allocated to each component, broad versus narrow. And therefore, there remain disagreements about what, if anything, is unique to humans about language. That no non-human acquires language spontaneously we can all agree on. There is also broad agreement that some aspects of language can be acquired by animals, but in a different way from human infants. The huge effort chimps expend on acquiring just a few dozen words is one example of this difference. But recent comparative research *has* shown that humans and primates share some basic mechanisms for processing speech, albeit with certain differences. Echoing Darwin, Bekoff (2013) reminds us recently that 'the differences among various animals are differences in degree rather than kind'. We see, then, that the linguistic gulf between humans and other animals is not as wide as might have been expected.

IN A NUTSHELL

- Language, talk and communication are distinct concepts: the central question concerns animals' capacity to acquire language.

- Animal communication systems overlap in various ways with language. But animal communication remains strictly limited in key ways, including its lack of creativity, semanticity, arbitrariness and displacement.

- Numerous attempts have been made to teach language to animals, including chimpanzees, gorillas, orang-utans, dolphins, dogs, parrots and cotton-top tamarin monkeys.

- Chimpanzees, dogs and parrots are capable of acquiring words, at least with regard to the pairing of a word form with a concrete concept. Animal vocabularies do not exceed a few hundred items.

- Animals cannot acquire grammar. Chimpanzees can combine words into multi-word utterances, but there is no sign that they do so in any consistent, rule-governed manner. However, some animals, including rats and zebra finches, can learn simple rules based on the order of elements and can distinguish AAB from ABA sequences.

- Recent research examines the extent to which basic psycholinguistic mechanisms are shared. In particular, research has focused on the ability to process and learn from rapid sequences of speech sounds.

- Cotton-top tamarins can perceive phonemes and identify word-like units in continuous speech. The way they do so may differ somewhat from humans. Some phoneme boundaries differ and, whereas monkeys identify whole syllables as the unit of analysis, humans prefer phonetic segments.

- A recent way of conceptualizing language draws a distinction between broad and narrow components of the language faculty (FLB and FLN). One controversial view claims that FLN comprises a single feature, the grammatical property of Merge (Berwick & Chomsky, 2016). On this hypothesis, all other aspects of language belong in FLB and the mechanisms that support them are shared with animals.

FURTHER READING

Hauser, M., Chomsky, N. & Fitch, T. (2002). The faculty of language: What is it, who has it, and how did it evolve? *Science, 298(5598)*, 1569–1579.

This is the article that started a furore about what is, and is not, special about language. The authors suggest that a single property of grammar (recursion) is unique to humans. Other properties of language are shared, to some extent, with animals.

Pinker, S. & Jackendoff, R. (2005). The faculty of language: What's special about it? *Cognition, 95(2)*, 201–236.

And this is the furore that was started. Pinker & Jackendoff reply to Hauser et al. (2002), arguing that numerous aspects of language are special to humans.

WEBSITES

- **Friends of Washoe**: www.friendsofwashoe.org/

  Google *friends of Washoe*. This site provides interesting background information on Washoe, the first chimpanzee to acquire (aspects of) human sign language.

- **The Alex Foundation**: www.alexfoundation.org

  Dedicated to the most famous talking parrot in the world. Even though he died in September 2007, his legacy lives on in an organization dedicated to the advancement of study on the cognitive and linguistic abilities of parrots.

VIDEO

- A Conversation With Koko The Gorilla – PBS Nature (1999)

  www.youtube.com/watch?v=teB-Icrog6E

- Washoe, Koko, and the social exchange of language.

  www.youtube.com/watch?v=3V_rAY0g9DM

- Kanzi with lexigram

  www.youtube.com/watch?v=wRM7vTrIIis

- Kanzi understands spoken language

  www.youtube.com/watch?v=TaNtf-MviLE

- South Korean elephant can talk

  www.youtube.com/watch?v=vLUz7E5gU2c

Still want more? For links to online resources relevant to this chapter and a quiz to test your understanding, visit the companion website at **https://study.sagepub.com/saxton2e**

3

The Critical Period Hypothesis: Now or Never?

CONTENTS

OVERVIEW

By the end of this chapter you should be able to summarize Eric Lenneberg's hypothesis that there is a critical period for language development. You should be able to evaluate the relative importance of five key features that have been used to define a critical period:

1   period of peak plasticity
2   cut-off point
3   occur early in development
4   brief
5   deprivation has permanent and irreversible effects

You should have a good idea about how to design a scientifically valid test of the critical period hypothesis, and use this knowledge to assess the value of research on language development. In this regard, you should be able to evaluate what different populations of late language learners can tell us about a critical period for language, including feral children, isolated children, second language learners and deaf language learners. This evidence reveals the need to distinguish multiple critical periods for different aspects of language, in particular phonology and syntax. While there is broad (though not universal) support for the critical period hypothesis in first language acquisition, it will become apparent that support is far less clear-cut when we examine the case of second language learning in adults.

What is a critical period?

A musical interlude

At the age of nine I had my first piano lesson. The excitement of this occasion was punctured by my teacher, who announced that I should have started learning four or five years earlier. It was made pretty clear that I now had no chance of becoming the next Horovitz (a famous pianist, not a breakfast cereal). Neither strenuous efforts on my part, nor the ministrations of my piano teacher, could ever compensate for the advantage of starting early. On this view, the same teaching provided to both a four-year-old and a nine-year-old would benefit the younger child more. My piano teacher may have been right, since I've yet to make my debut at Carnegie Hall. Perhaps unconsciously, my teacher was advocating her belief in a *critical period* for music.

Beyond music, the general idea is that a particular kind of experience has a greater effect on development when supplied during a given (critical) period than at other times. If the key experience is not available during the critical period, there is a negative effect on development, more strongly negative than if the experience is missing outside the critical period. Thus, according to the kind of experience, or lack of it, the effects on development can be either positive or negative. Interest in critical periods has been widespread and not confined to music. Over the past 80 years, a whole slew of critical periods has been identified for a wide range of biological, social and behavioural aspects of development. Let's begin by seeing how this idea might apply to language. We shall then take a detour into physiology, to discover how to design a rigorous critical period study. We shall then come back to language development to see if we can match the physiologists for rigour. You will discover that, on the whole, we can't. But you will also see that much has been learnt about the critical period for language acquisition, and, in consequence, something about the biological basis of language.

Lenneberg's critical period hypothesis

The idea that there might be a critical period for language first took flight in the 1960s. Eric Lenneberg (1967) – inspired by the explosion of interest in Chomsky's ideas on language – marshalled a wide range of evidence on language learning and brain development in support of his thesis:

> Between the ages of two and three years language emerges by an interaction of maturation and self-programmed learning. Between the ages of three and the early teens the possibility for primary language acquisition continues to be good ... After puberty, the ability for self-organization and adjustment to the physiological demands of verbal behavior quickly declines. The brain behaves as if it had become set in its ways and primary, basic, skills not acquired by that time usually remain deficient for life. (Lenneberg, 1967: 158)

Lenneberg's hypothesis has been around for a long time but continues to stimulate research. We should note straightaway, though, that, in pretty much every detail, Lenneberg turned out to be wrong (Snow, 1987). For example, language acquisition begins before birth, not at two years (see Chapter 1). And the offset of any critical period – the point at which sensitivity starts to decline – must be more like five years, not the early teens, since most of the basic grammar we acquire is in place by age five (see Chapters 8 and 9).

Disputes about the details of Lenneberg's proposals have not detracted from their core validity. It remains plausible that language development is subject to critical period effects. But we begin our exploration, not with language in humans, but with vision in cats. The scientific rigour afforded by animal research provides a useful benchmark for judging the value of empirical findings in the domain of child language. It also provides an excellent framework for exploring the characteristic features of critical periods in general, before we consider the special case of language.

Designing research on critical periods

Cats' eyes: An example from animal development

We begin by taking a close look at research on the development of vision in kittens. Our interest in this case is twofold. First, the series of experiments in question provides a model of how to go about doing research on critical periods; so good, in fact, that the two authors, David Hubel and Torsten Wiesel, won the Nobel Prize in 1981. A second reason for looking at Hubel & Wiesel's work is that it provides an example of how development can be arrested, or seriously ruptured, when essential experiences are *absent* during a critical period. In this respect, there is a direct parallel with research on language acquisition.

Hubel & Wiesel (1963) monitored the effects of visual deprivation on neural activity in the cat visual cortex. Kittens were deprived of normal visual experience via surgical closure of the right eye. Not to put too fine a point on it, the eyelids were sewn (or sutured) together (see Discussion point 3.1, below). Two factors were systematically varied: (1) the age at which visual deprivation occurred; and (2) the duration of that deprivation. Thus, the age at the time of eye closure ranged from 10 days through to adulthood, while the length of time that the right eye remained closed ranged from three days through to 180 days. Following the period of deprivation, the sutured eye was re-opened and the kitten's responses to visual stimuli were recorded. Measurements were taken from groups of cells in the striate cortex, which is part of the 'grey matter' of the brain's outer surfaces, in this case towards the 'rear', where brain areas controlling vision are located. Groups of cells in this region are organized into so-called *ocular dominance columns*. Most of the cells in a column tend to respond to visual input from one eye or the other. So the aim was to gauge the effects of deprivation on columns that would normally respond to input from the sutured (right) eye. Measures were taken by first anaesthetizing the kittens, a procedure which prevented eye movements and which also allowed recordings of electrical activity to be made from individual cells via tungsten microelectrodes inserted into the cortex.

In a series of studies, Hubel & Wiesel (1963, 1970) found that if the right eye is kept closed for the first 10–12 weeks after birth, it renders the kitten blind in that eye. In effect, inputs to the deprived eye become disconnected from the brain, so visual stimulation produces no effect when the right eye is re-opened. What is more, this effect seems to be permanent. Even very brief periods of deprivation, as little as three days in some cases, can have drastic effects. There is a 'use it or lose it' principle at work here. Susceptibility to deprivation begins in the fourth week after birth, at about the time that kittens begin using their eyes. And the effects of deprivation were found to be strongest six to eight weeks after birth, declining thereafter until about 16 weeks. Tests on older cats, though, revealed that the visual system becomes remarkably robust when faced with deprivation, provided the deprivation starts beyond the critical period. In one case, eyelid closure was maintained in an adult cat for 16 months with no adverse effects when the eye was re-opened. It appears very clearly, therefore, that the same experience has dramatically different effects, depending on when it occurs in life. In the case of cat vision, the critical period is very limited and occurs early on in development.

DISCUSSION POINT 3.1
ETHICS IN SCIENCE

George Bernard Shaw once argued that 'if you cannot attain to knowledge without torturing a dog, you must do without knowledge' (Shaw, 1911: xlvii). To consider this position, the following website may prove useful: www.peta.org. Consider the following:

- Scientific testing with animals has the potential to save millions of lives, as when new drugs and medical procedures are discovered. In such cases, is animal testing justifiable?
- Can animal testing ever be justified in psychology?

How to identify a critical period

At this point, it is useful to consider the methodology of critical period research, since it will better enable us to appreciate the value of research devoted to language. We can again take Hubel & Wiesel (1963) as the benchmark of rigour in the way they designed their experiments. Bruer (2001) provides a useful analysis of their design and points out that there are two sensible approaches:

a   Give the participants the same experience (in both quality and duration), but at different stages in development; or

b   Systematically vary the duration of the target experience, but ensure that the starting point is the same for all participants.

Both of these research designs avoid the confound of a practice effect. To illustrate this point, let's return briefly to my early life at the piano. I started learning the piano at the age of nine. Mozart, meanwhile, was picking out tunes on the harpsichord at the tender age of three. He learned his first piece, a scherzo by Wagenseil, a few days before his fifth birthday. And by the age of 12, Mozart was entertaining the crowned heads of Europe, at which age, I was playing like I'd traded my hands in for flippers. But just a second, maybe this is not a fair comparison. Natural genius aside, Mozart had six more years of practice than me. This means that both kinds of design, above, are violated. With respect to Design (a), Mozart and me differ in terms of both duration and quality of experience (Mozart's father was no musical slouch himself and provided his son with a rich musical experience). With respect to Design (b), of course, Mozart and me started learning at different ages.

Hubel & Wiesel conducted careful experiments that conformed to both kinds of design outlined above. They were also careful about two other factors that should be taken into account in work of this kind. The first consideration is the need to be clear about what the target experience is. In the case of cat vision, it was simply normal exposure to objects and light in the visual field. The second point of concern is the outcome measure. That is, how do we measure the effects of experience on the participants? Again, for Hubel & Wiesel, the answer is very straightforward. How well did the cats see at the end of the deprivation period? The answer could be determined unequivocally, by counting the number of cells in the ocular dominance columns that responded to stimulation. In physiological studies of this kind, both the experience and the outcome measure can be clearly defined. As we shall see below, the same cannot be said for language.

Just before we launch off into linguistic waters, it is worthwhile summarizing the key features of critical periods from classic research like that of Hubel & Wiesel:

1   period of peak plasticity, when the system is especially open to experience
2   cut-off point, beyond which plasticity is greatly reduced – the environment no longer has any effect
3   tend to occur early in development
4   tend to be brief
5   effects of deprivation are permanent and irreversible

It is worth pointing out that none of these five features is entirely sacrosanct. In fact, there are problems with all of them. For example, critical periods are not always brief and are not always characterized by a sharp cut-off point (Bruer, 2001). Instead, there is often a gradual decline in plasticity. As we shall see, this latter point has special relevance for research on language learning. With regard to timing, critical periods do seem to be brief and feature early in development (though 13 years for language could be seen as stretching the point somewhat). The general point is that critical periods are a *developmental* phenomenon. They are associated with genetically determined periods of growth during which the system is especially plastic, in the sense that it is especially receptive to particular environmental inputs. Once development is complete, there is no need for the system to be susceptible to key learning experiences any longer. Hence, one encounters critical periods early in an organism's life.

The effects of deprivation during the critical period are not always absolutely permanent, even in the case of cat vision (Chow & Stewart, 1972; Harweth, Smith, Crawford & van Noorden, 1989). When it comes to language learning, we shall see that our ability to acquire a second language as adults presents a special puzzle. Given that our five defining features are not chiselled in marble for us, some scientists prefer the phrase *sensitive period*, instead of critical period. The term sensitive period carries with it the idea of an extended period during which receptivity to experience peaks and then very gradually declines (for example, Immelmann & Suomi, 1981). Despite this care in defining terms, the phrase critical period tends to be far more popular, especially among language researchers. And the concept of a sensitive period brings its own complications (see Freedman, 1979, as your guide through the minefield). In the domain of language acquisition, the term critical period dominates the literature, so we shall retain it here.

The effects of linguistic deprivation

Now that we know how to design a good test of the critical period hypothesis, what would be the perfect experiment in the domain of language acquisition? If we follow the precepts laid down above, we might vary the age of exposure to language for different children, while keeping the length of exposure constant. This would mean keeping children waiting somewhere, for different lengths of time, until we were ready to start talking to them, or rather, supplying linguistic experience. Alternatively, we could vary the amount of exposure to language, while keeping the age at which we start constant. Of course, no-one in their right mind would attempt a study like this. Sadly, though, the callousness and depravity that one human being can inflict on another has yielded several cases where children appear to have been deliberately denied access to language.

The royal prerogative: Experiments on people

Every so often, history relates how some bored, sadistic monarch decides to experiment on the effects of linguistic deprivation. At least four cases are well known, if not well attested, thanks to Campbell & Grieve (1982):

> Psamtik I, Saitic king of Egypt (7th century BCE)
> Frederick II of Sicily (1192–1250)
> James IV of Scotland (1473–1513)
> Akbar the Great of India (1542–1605)

In each case, one or more children were deliberately deprived of language in order to gauge the effects. Psamtik I thought he would establish beyond doubt what the original language of the world was. He assumed that the first word uttered by a child, if they had never heard any-one speak, would be in this original language. Psamtik naturally placed his money on Ancient Egyptian (though, of course, the language was not so ancient in his day). But he was wrong: the winner was Phrygian, the language of an Indo-European people settled in Anatolia (part of modern Turkey). See Campbell & Grieve (1982) for a fascinating review of the four cases listed above. Cutting to the chase, we can conclude that these Royals were not so hot at science, and also that science reporting left much to be desired in days gone by. For example, the story of Psamtik I is not a contemporary account, being retold a couple of centuries later by Herodotus (485–425 BCE). What is more, some of the details Herodotus includes betray the story as apoc-ryphal, including the use of goats' milk to suckle infants. It turns out that in Egypt at this time, the only use for goats' milk was in the relief of anal dysfunction! All four cases listed above could have been rigorous, albeit deeply unpleasant experiments on linguistic deprivation, but apart from the case of Akbar, we do not know for certain that they even took place.

Feral children

Deliberate experiments aside, numerous cases have been reported of children who have been deprived of normal social contact and exposure to language. Perhaps the earliest report is the legend of Romulus and Remus, twin boys raised by wolves. Many such children have been dis-covered in the wild, having been abandoned by their parents, with animals like wolves, jackals and leopards taking over the parental role. It remains a mystery what brings out the nurturing side of these animals in the face of a perfectly good meal like a human infant. On discovery, these chil-dren are notably reluctant to relinquish either their animal habits or diet. Typically, also, they have an aversion to human company and can endure extremes of temperature. A systematic description is provided by Linnaeus in the tenth edition of his *Systemae Naturae*, published in 1758. Linnaeus classified these children as Homo Ferus, a separate subdivision of Homo Sapiens. Homo Ferus was distinguished by the features of tetrapus, hursutus and mutus, which for those of us with little Latin and less Greek, means that they walked on all fours, were hairy, and were without speech. Of course, it is the lack of speech that interests us, and the fact that all of these children suffered a period of linguistic deprivation in early childhood. See Table 3.1 for a few examples of feral children who have been discovered over the past three centuries.

Do these cases shed any light on the critical period hypothesis? In many cases, no, since they often turn out to be hoaxes. A case in point is the Nullarbor Nymph who was supposedly found hopping about with kangaroos in the Australian outback in 1971. Other cases may be true, but are difficult or impossible to verify, including the Irish sheep-boy of 1672 and the Mauritanian gazelle boy of 1900. There is, though, a small number of well-attested cases. One of these is Victor, the Wild Boy of Aveyron, and in our review of his case we need to consider the following factors: the period of deprivation; his age on discovery; and how well he did subsequently in the task of acquiring language. Victor was discovered in France at the turn of the nineteenth century, at the age of something like 10 or 12. He was eventually taken to Paris under the care of a young doctor called Itard. But despite concerted efforts, attempts to civilize Victor and teach him language were almost entirely unsuccessful. He acquired only two spoken expressions – 'Oh, Dieu!' and 'Lait!' – and while calls for God and milk can be useful, they do not constitute a full-blown command of French.

Itard's first report on Victor was written in 1801 and promised much, but five years later, the tone of his second report was much more pessimistic. Itard concluded, with remarkable prescience, that the 'imitative force … and the apprenticeship of speech, … which is very energetic and active during the first years of … life, wanes rapidly with age' (cited in Lane, 1976: 129). On the face of it, Victor seems to confirm Lenneberg's hypothesis. But precisely how old was Victor when he turned up in Aveyron? Also, how old was he when he was abandoned? Clearly, it is impossible to specify the length of linguistic deprivation, which means that one of the fundamental maxims of critical period research is violated. In addition, we have very little idea whether Victor's other cognitive faculties, like hearing, vision and general intelligence, were normal. Impairments to any of these might account for poor language learning, independent of the effects of a critical period. So although many of the details of Victor's case are well attested, we nevertheless lack vital information when viewing his case as a test of the critical period hypothesis.

Genie

Feral children aside, we might also consider children who have been brought up in isolation. These children have not been abandoned, but have been brought up in circumstances of extreme deprivation, including lack of exposure to language. Given the terrible cruelty involved, it is fortunate that such cases are surpassingly rare. The most detailed account we have is of Genie, a girl who came to light in 1970, aged 13, in Los Angeles. Genie had been raised in circumstances of truly awful deprivation and maltreatment. She spent her days physically restrained, harnessed to a potty seat, unable to move anything but her hands and feet. When not forgotten, Genie would be transferred at nights into an equally restrictive sleeping bag, designed by her father to prevent movement of her limbs. Her days and nights were spent confined in this way in a bare room with almost no tactile or visual stimulation. Genie was rarely spoken to and any attempts on her part to vocalize were met with a beating from her father. She was therefore raised in virtual silence. Interest in Genie was intense.

Table 3.1 Feral children throughout history and reported effects of early deprivation on language learning

Child	Location	Date when discovered	Age at discovery (years)	Language learning	Notes
Wild Peter of Hanover	Germany	1724	13	Peter never learned to talk.	Peter was the first celebrity feral child. He was brought to England as the 'possession' of George I. Daniel Defoe worried about whether Peter had a soul and whether he could think without language.
Kasper Hauser	Germany	1828	17	Kasper could already talk and subsequently learned to read and write also.	Kasper claimed to have been kept in isolation for several years. It was believed that he was heir to the throne of Baden. He was assassinated in 1833.
Amala and Kamala (sisters)	Midnapore, India	1920	1½ and 8	Amala began to babble; Kamala acquired a vocabulary of about 40 words after several years.	Amala lived only one further year after discovery, while Kamala lived to be 18.
Anna	Illinois, USA	1937	5	Some words and a few multi-word utterances.	Anna died four years after discovery.
Majola children	South Africa	2004	14, 18, 22 and 26	None of these children of farm workers could speak when discovered recently.	Brought up in an isolated shack away from society, all four are mentally retarded, as is their mother.

Chomsky's ideas on the biological origins of language were beginning to take hold and Lenneberg's hypothesis was hot off the press (Chomsky, 1965, 1966; Lenneberg, 1967). Genie seemed to present an ideal opportunity to test out the critical period hypothesis. Given that Genie was found at puberty, she should not have been able to catch up with her peers. In the event, a great deal of value and interest was discovered in the study of Genie (see below). At the same time, though, you may not be surprised to learn that, in common with other cases of deprivation, a lack of scientific rigour strictly curtails the scope of any conclusions we can draw about critical periods.

It is usually reported that Genie had absolutely no language when she was found (for example, Hoff, 2001). However, some sources report that Genie did understand a handful of words when discovered (Rymer, 1993). These included *Mother*, *walk*, and *go*, together with colour terms like *red*, *blue* and *green*. Recordings of Genie reveal a very strange, high-pitched fluting quality, far removed from normal speech. Rymer (1993) suggests that she could produce two expressions when first found: *stopit* and *nomore*. Observe that these expressions are written as single words, because there is no evidence that Genie could analyse them into their component parts (see Chapter 9 on holophrases).

Different critical periods for different aspects of language

A concerted effort was made to teach Genie language (Curtiss, 1977). Before we consider how well she did, we must tackle a major problem. So far, we have the prediction that language is subject to critical period effects. But you will recall from Chapters 1 and 2 that *language* is a nebulous term. The researchers working with Genie were well aware of this problem, observing that we lack an 'adequate definition of the innate behavior to be elicited' (Curtiss, Fromkin, Krashen, Rigler & Rigler, 1974: 540). We must therefore be much more precise. Which aspects of language, in particular, are subject to critical period effects? It is entirely possible that multiple features of linguistic development are involved (Long, 2005).

We can begin to tackle this issue by considering each major level of language separately: **phonology**, vocabulary, **morphology** and **syntax**. With regard to phonology (speech sounds), several authors have suggested that the development of a native speaker-like accent is subject to its own critical period effect, quite independent of any other aspect of language (for example, Bongaerts, Planken & Schils, 1995; Spaai, Derksen, Hermes & Kaufholz, 1996; Pallier, Bosch & Sebastián-Gallés, 1997; though see Yeni-Komshian, Flege & Liu, 2000, for a contrary view). Adults learning a foreign language are almost always betrayed by their non-native accent, regardless of how good their grammar and vocabulary might be (see below). In fact, it has been suggested that our ability to acquire a flawless accent in a second language has lapsed by the age of five or thereabouts (Scovel, 1988). Beyond accent, there is now good evidence that numerous aspects of early phonological development are subject to critical period effects (Werker & Hensch, 2015). These include the attunement of the infant to properties of the native language such as rhythm, stress, melody and the particular phonemes and

66

phoneme combinations which are permitted. We can see these effects quite clearly in babies who are born pre-term. These babies start to experience the world in advance of babies born at full-term (40 weeks), including listening to and processing speech sounds. Does this extra experience make any difference to the infant's ability to discriminate between different phonemes (for example, /b/ versus /g/)? The answer seems to be no, at least for infants with a gestational age of less than 30 weeks (Key, Lambert, Aschner & Maitre, 2012). Instead, a certain level of maturation is required before infants can make certain phoneme discriminations. The notion of multiple critical periods is lent weight in a recent study by Huang (2014). She reports separate critical period effects for accent and grammar within a single group of individuals, 118 Mandarin-speaking immigrants to the US.

What about the **lexicon**? If vocabulary learning is taken as the target behaviour, then we might argue that the case of Genie refutes the critical period hypothesis, since she acquired a vocabulary of several hundred words that she could both understand and produce. At the same time, Genie's word-learning pales into insignificance when compared with the prowess of a typical two-year-old, both in terms of vocabulary size and the speed at which it is acquired. The plasticity of Genie's word-learning mechanisms has clearly declined, relative to a typical toddler. There is some independent evidence that word learning in typically developing children is subject to critical period effects (Hernandez & Li, 2007). Recall for words learned early in life tends to be both faster and more accurate (Morrison & Ellis, 2000).

Before we shift the focus to syntax, let's first insert a note on **morphology**, which is concerned with the internal structure of complex words. If need be, shoot back to Chapter 1 for a quick reminder and if that doesn't do the trick, lurch to the end of the book, for more information from the Glossary. Then settle down and consider the following **sentence**: Genie's morphology is very poor.

> *Small two cup*
> *Like chew meat*

These typical utterances are notable for their lack of **inflectional morphemes**: **two cup* instead of *two cups*, **chew meat* instead of *chewing meat*. As we shall see below, other research on critical periods supports the idea that morphology suffers when language learning starts late in life.

Turning to syntax, the two examples above demonstrate that Genie did acquire multi-word speech. In fact, some of Genie's productions are perfectly acceptable. These include *Grandma gave me cereal*, and *I like Dave's car*, as well as phrases like *In the backyard*, *My house*, and *Mark's room*. However, her route to this achievement was not typical. Genie took some time to reach the two-word stage and hung around for quite a while before moving on. A typically developing two-year-old reaches this milestone once they have acquired about 50 words (Bates & Goodman, 1999). Genie, meanwhile, commanded some 200 words before she began to combine them into two-word utterances. Also, the two-word stage lasts just six to eight weeks in a typical toddler. But in Genie, the two-word stage lasted much longer – more than five months – before she developed further.

BOX 3.1   CONTENT VERSUS FUNCTION WORDS

The words in a sentence can be divided into two major categories: content words and function words. Content words carry the burden of meaning in a sentence. Of note is the fact that they can be interpreted in isolation. That is, we can work out their meaning without referring to the other words in the sentence. Nor do we need to take note of who is talking, or anything else about the context, in order to interpret them. Content words typically fall into one of the major sub-classes of **parts of speech**: verbs; nouns; adjectives; and adverbs.

verbs:	run, talk, govern, think
nouns:	car, lion, museum, truth
adjectives:	hot, desperate, green, clever
adverbs:	quickly, happily, deliberately, badly

In contrast, function words are like the icing on the cake. They give us a more precise idea about who is doing what to whom in a sentence. Typical function words include the following:

articles:	a, the, some
prepositions:	in, under, above, for, with
quantifiers:	some, many, all
pronouns:	I, you, he, she, it, we, they
auxiliary verbs:	can, could, may, might, should, will

To fully understand function words, we often need to refer to the context of utterance. When someone says: *I like New York in June*, we cannot determine what *I* refers to unless we know who is talking. When I say *I*, I'm referring to me, but when you say *I*, the word suddenly refers to you. A rough rule of thumb for deciding which words are content words and which are function words is to think of a text message (30 years ago, I would have said a telegram). To avoid repetitive strain injury, when keying text in on a mobile phone, it is commonplace to eliminate all but the most essential words in a message. So instead of texting *My train has been delayed by 30 minutes*, you might send *Train delayed 30 mins*. As you can see, the words that get transmitted tend to be content words, because they carry the essence of our meaning.

The existence of multi-word speech is important, because it means that syntax was a possible acquisition for Genie. The next consideration, therefore, is whether she combined words according to the rules of syntax. To help us decide, here are some more of Genie's multi-word utterances:

Like good Harry at hospital
No more have
Dentist say drink water
Tell door lock
Glass is break
Another house blue car

Unfortunately, this looks like linguistic spaghetti. To illustrate what is wrong, we can focus on two aspects of syntax: function words and word order. Function words are generally small words, like *a*, *the*, *we*, *of*, *some*, that tend not to have much meaning by themselves (see Box 3.1). Evidently, Genie displays poor control over function words, often omitting them:

Cookie sleep car
Bus have big mirror

In both examples, function words have been omitted. *Cookie sleep car*, is probably better rendered as: *Cookie is sleeping in the car* (on the assumption that *Cookie* is someone's name). *Bus have big mirror* would be better as *The bus has a big mirror*. Another aspect of Genie's syntax we can consider is word order. The main components of a prototypical sentence are **subject, object** and **verb** and many languages possess a default way of ordering them. English grammar is very strict about word order, the default being Subject–Verb–Object. Hence, English is known as an SVO language. If you're a bit rusty on subject, verb and object, limber up on them in the Glossary Gymnasium and then try the following Exercise.

EXERCISE 3.1
SUBJECT, VERB AND OBJECT

1   Identify the subject of the sentence in the following examples:

    (a)   Gordon's hair looks like nylon.
    (b)   I couldn't help noticing the baby elephant in your fridge.
    (c)   The man who lives next door to me has a fondness for figs.
    (d)   The end of the world is nigh.
    (e)   Have you ever seen a Buster Keaton movie?

2   Now find the verb:

    (a)   Nigella licked her spoon in a rather suggestive fashion.
    (b)   Now is the winter of our discontent.

(Continued)

(c) Henrietta scoffed a big bag of toffees on the bus.

(d) Fly me to the moon.

(e) Play it again, Sam.

3   Finally, locate the object:

(a) That really takes the biscuit.

(b) Frankly, my dear, I don't give a damn.

(c) I simply adore champagne.

(d) How many cream buns can you eat at one sitting?

(e) I'll make him an offer he can't refuse.

answers at the back of the book

Before that ocean of learning evaporates, let's harness it to evaluate Genie's control of English word order. I have parsed three of Genie's sentences, below, with regard to subject, verb and object. You might want to extend this exercise for yourself with some of Genie's other multi-word productions (my own analyses are in the Answers section).

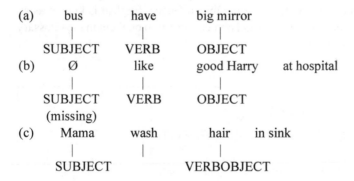

What we see is that Genie's basic word order is generally correct. That is, when she produces at least two of the three main sentential building blocks, they tend to be placed in the right position, relative to one another.

Evidently, Genie's ability to acquire syntax was seriously impaired. But we have also seen that in at least one respect – basic word order – Genie does not do too badly. Some aspects of syntax may thus be immune to critical period effects. Or, alternatively, there may be multiple critical periods that conceivably apply within (as well as across) different levels of language. There are several different components of syntax (the same applies to phonology, vocabulary and morphology). So we may have to ask which particular aspects of syntax, if any, are subject to critical period effects. We might consider knowledge of grammatical categories, like noun and preposition (see Box 1.2). Or knowledge of basic word order. Or knowledge of particular complex constructions, like **relative clauses**. Although several studies examine specific aspects of language (for example,

Johnson & Newport, 1989; Sorace, 1993), none has yet considered syntax at this level of detail. In fact, there is something fairly arbitrary in the selection of those aspects of grammar that have been examined. But unless we specify precisely which aspects of language might be affected by critical period effects, assessing the effects of linguistic deprivation becomes problematic. In effect, we are left without a proper measure of the behaviour we are interested in. As Medawar (1967: 109) observes, 'it is not informative to study variations of behaviour unless we know beforehand the norm from which the variants depart'.

How well does Genie support the critical period hypothesis? From a scientific standpoint, the really interesting aspect of Genie's case is that she was discovered at the age of 13, which matches Lenneberg's cut-off point (the onset of puberty). Language learning should be impossible. In fact, though, we have encountered something of a mixed bag. Genie did learn to produce speech sounds, though with a distinctly odd pronunciation. She did acquire a few hundred words, before reaching a plateau, though her word learning did not mirror the speed and ease enjoyed by a typical child. Genie also acquired some rudimentary aspects of syntax, most notably basic word order. In other respects, though, Genie's syntax was nothing like that of a mature native speaker, even after several years of effort were put into supporting her language development.

As it happens, there is a further complication with Genie's history that makes her case less than ideal as a test of the critical period hypothesis. The brain comes in two halves, or hemispheres (left and right), and in most people, language tends to be processed in the left hemisphere (Broca, 1865; Obler & Gjerlow, 1999). Unusually, it was found that Genie processes language on the *right* side of her brain. The indications are that Genie's left hemisphere was atrophied. It is possible, therefore, that her impaired language learning was due to a general cognitive deficit, and not related to her language faculty *per se*. All in all, the case of Genie does not provide a definitive test of the critical period hypothesis. But the fact that she acquired some aspects of language provides a salutary lesson. There may be multiple critical periods affecting different aspects of language. We must therefore be precise about which particular aspects of language we predict are subject to critical period effects. In this vein, current research points to at least two separate critical periods, for phonology and syntax, respectively.

DISCUSSION POINT 3.2
GENIE AND THE CRITICAL PERIOD HYPOTHESIS

Review the evidence on Genie and consider the following points:

- What aspects of language did Genie acquire?
- What aspects of language did Genie fail to acquire?
- Given that Genie did acquire some aspects of language, what are the implications for Lenneberg's original hypothesis?
- How plausible is the idea that there are multiple critical periods, each one dedicated to a different aspect of language?
- What is the relevance of the critical period hypothesis for the nature–nurture debate?

A happier ending: The case of Isabelle

We can contrast Genie's case with that of Isabelle, a girl who also suffered abnormal depriva-tion in her early years (Brown, 1958). Isabelle was discovered in Ohio in the 1930s at the age of six-and-a-half. An illegitimate child, Isabelle was kept hidden from the world in a darkened room. This cruelty was compounded by the fact that Isabelle was deprived of linguistic input of any kind, because her mother was both deaf and mute. When discovered, the only sounds Isabelle made were a kind of croaking noise, and at first, it was thought that, like her mother, she was deaf. However, Isabelle made remarkable progress. Her language learning was so rapid that she began to put words together in sentences within two months. Within a year, she was beginning to learn how to read. And by the age of eight-and-a-half, Isabelle's language was so sophisticated that she appeared to have fully caught up with her peers. Her IQ also showed rapid improvements. Having initially scored so low that her IQ was almost off the scale, within two years, Isabelle had a normal IQ.

We suggested above that the offset for the critical period may be more like five years than 13. But recall that 'offset' simply means the point at which sensitivity begins to wane. The terminus is a separate concept, denoting the very end of the line for a critical period. Beyond the terminus (still often designated as puberty), first language learning should be impossible. Hence, the case of Isabelle shows that even in the period when sensitivity to language experience is in decline, acquisition is nevertheless still possible. Firsthand details of Isabelle's language are not readily available, and we must rely on Brown's summary from 1958. It would be fascinating, though, to probe the state of Isabelle's language abilities in more detail. With an offset for the critical period at five years, we would predict subtle deficits in Isabelle's language. As with other cases of depri-vation, though, the case of Isabelle is far from ideal as a rigorous test of Lenneberg's hypothesis. As it stands, we can say that what information we have on Isabelle is consistent with the critical period hypothesis.

Conclusions from cases of deprivation

Over the centuries, numerous cases of feral and isolated children have been reported. Many such cases are vague and uninformative, while others turned out to be hoaxes. However, that still leaves several genuine cases. But even these desperately unfortunate children do not provide the basis for good science. There are simply too many unknown factors that cannot be accounted for. These include the precise period of deprivation and the precise kind of deprivation. It is often assumed that these children had no exposure to language at all during their early years, but there is generally no way of being certain. As Lenneberg himself observed: 'The only safe conclusions to be drawn from the multitude of reports is that life in dark closets, wolves' dens, forests, or sadistic parents' backyards is not conducive to good health and normal development' (1967: 142). The very fact that cognitive and emotional development are likely to be abnormal means that poor linguistic development may be due to these factors, rather than due to anything exclusively language-related.

And yet. There remains something tantalizingly plausible about the basic idea that critical periods exist for particular aspects of language. What we need, though, is a more reliable evidence base than abused and neglected children. To this end, psychologists have turned their attention to two other populations of language learners: deaf people and people who learn a second language. As we shall see, in both cases, the start of language learning is often delayed, according to individual circumstances. We can therefore compare the effects of early versus late acquisition. The critical period hypothesis predicts that the later in life language learning begins, the less successful it is likely to be. We can start by looking at the case of second language learning, before concluding with the case of deaf children acquiring their first language. A major advantage of these two populations is that they have not deliberately been denied access to a first language. And other aspects of development tend to be normal, including social, emotional and cognitive development. Effects of late language learning can therefore not so easily be ascribed to non-linguistic abnormalities in development.

Age of acquisition effects in second language learning

Like many people condemned to life in a monolingual culture, my experience of second language learning has been less than triumphant. A life speaking English was interrupted at the age of 12, when lessons in French, German and Latin were introduced at school. There followed four years reminiscent of life at Bletchley Park during World War II. The cryptographers at Bletchley Park were faced with breaking the code of the German Enigma machine, an early example of *Vorsprung durch technik* that could encode a given message in 150 million million million different ways. Feeling like a cryptographer, I was faced with cracking the code of three European languages (one of them dead). Vocabulary was deduced from miscellaneous lists of words, written out with translations. Grammar came via the use of coloured inks to denote different verb endings and case markings. And any attempt to speak these languages was an act of declamation, not communication. After four years, I would have struggled to order a glass of absinthe in Paris. And not just because I was still underage.

Why was I so bad at learning new languages? Was I past it at the age of 12? According to Lenneberg (1967), the answer is *yes*. On this view, attempts to learn a new language post-puberty must proceed without the benefit of the specialized faculty for language acquisition. Therefore, whatever we do learn must be achieved by making use of general cognitive learning mechanisms. This position has intuitive appeal. It chimes with the experience of many adults who migrate from one country to another. For many such people, even decades after settling in a new country, their mastery of the host language remains distinctly non-native. In this section, we will examine age effects in language acquisition in populations that have not been abused or otherwise deprived in terms of emotional, cognitive and educational development. Apart from starting to learn language at different points in life, these people can be considered normal. We are therefore provided with a useful new method of tackling the critical period hypothesis. One quick note. To save excessive wear on my typing fingers, I will alternate at times between L1 for 'first language' and L2 for 'second language'.

Early versus late starters: Effects on language outcomes

The effects of age of acquisition were investigated by Johnson & Newport (1989, 1991). Their first study investigated 46 people with Chinese or Korean as a first language. These people had moved to the United States at different ages, ranging from 3 to 39 years. Thus, the age at which they began to learn English varied widely, extending quite far either side of the critical period boundary. Although age of acquisition varied, the length of exposure to L2 English was controlled for. Participants were allocated to two groups, corresponding to early versus late arrival in the US. For the early arrivals, the average length of stay in the US was 9.8 years, compared with 9.9 years for the late arrivals. This is encouraging, because, as a design feature, this study seems to adhere to one of the research maxims outlined above: *give participants the same length of experience*, but at different stages in development. Our only quibble would be that we are dealing with averages here. Within the sample as a whole, length of exposure ranged quite widely, from 3 to 26 years. However, it is possible, statistically, to separate out the effects of experience from the variable of interest, which is the age at which language learning began.

Johnson & Newport (1989) asked their participants to judge 276 English sentences on 12 different aspects of morphology and syntax. Half of the sentences were perfectly grammatical, while the remainder were tampered with in some way, as below:

> *The farmer bought two pig at the market.*
> *Three bat flew into our attic last night.*

I hope you agree that both of these sentences sound wrong. More to the point, they are wrong for the same reason: the absence of the plural morpheme -*s* (two pigS; three batS). A native speaker should have no trouble rejecting these sentences. As it happens, a control group of 23 native speakers did do extremely well, though, curiously, their performance is not absolutely perfect, as Figure 3.1 reveals. We also see a strong age of acquisition effect for the Korean and Chinese learners. Intuitions about L2 English grammar are native-like only for those people who arrived in the US before the age of seven. Thereafter, there is a marked decline in performance. It is unlikely that late-arrivals are simply guessing about grammaticality, since their performance is well above chance. Instead, they are being inconsistent. They are more prone than native speakers to vacillate between accepting or rejecting test sentences. Looking at Figure 3.1, it looks as though inconsistency increases with age of arrival. But that is not quite right. All of these learners are inconsistent (apart from the native speakers and early arrivals). This leads to problems in interpreting these data. How do we compare Learner A, who scores 30 per cent on a grammar test, with Learner B, who scores 70 per cent? It seems nonsensical to conclude that Learner B knows 40 per cent more grammar than Learner A. Perhaps it is not the ability to acquire grammar that is subject to the critical period phenomenon. Instead, it might be an issue of control. People who start learning early in life seem to have greater control and are more rigorous in applying the rules than late learners. Plausibly, therefore, there is a critical period for the development of our ability to *process* language (cf., Herschensohn, 2007: 226).

For Johnson & Newport, the key finding is the fairly sharp decline in grammatical ability beyond puberty. If a second language is acquired at *any* age in adulthood (20, 40, 70), the outcome, they argue, will be similar, and similarly disappointing. This pattern is, of course, entirely consistent with the critical period hypothesis. During the critical period, learning is possible, but the efficiency of that learning declines as the period of maximum receptivity to the input wanes. Johnson & Newport (1989) controlled for a number of possible confounding factors, including amount of formal instruction, and the attitudes and motivation of participants with regard to learning English. But none of these factors were significant. What we are left with is a clear age of acquisition effect that has been repeated in several other studies (for example, Coppieters, 1987; Schachter, 1990; Johnson & Newport, 1991; Lee, 1992; Sorace, 1993; DeKeyser, 2000).

Age effects may not be due to a critical period

Before we pack our bags and go home, we have to face the fact that considerable controversy persists in the interpretation of findings on second language research (Hyltenstam & Abrahamsson, 2000). There are three main sticking points:

1   There may be no qualitative changes in learning after the cut-off point.
2   Some late learners do seem to achieve native-like competence in a second language.
3   There may be no sharp cut-off point at puberty in L2 ability (despite the picture painted in Figure 3.1).

The first issue concerns the kind of learning that takes place, both during and beyond the critical period. If we compare the L1 toddler and the L2 adult (post-puberty), the language learning processes deployed by each should be different in kind. While the L1 toddler is often characterized as a sponge, naturally soaking up language (Murphy, 2010), the L2 adult is painted more like me at school, engaged in effortful, conscious learning. Hence, some authors argue that the end of the critical period should be marked by *qualitative* differences in the kinds of learning that take place (for example, Hakuta, 2001). The argument goes like this: if the biologically determined learning mechanisms, available during the critical period, are no longer available, then any learning that takes place will depend on alternative learning mechanisms. As a result, the kind of learning that takes place in adulthood will be qualitatively different from that which takes place during childhood. However, available evidence suggests that early and late starters learn in similar ways, and make similar kinds of errors (for example, Bialystok & Hakuta, 1994, 1999; Juffs & Harrington, 1995; Bialystok & Miller, 1999). In other words, the kind of learning that takes place looks remarkably similar either side of the purported critical period barrier. This is an interesting observation, but we need to exercise caution in how we interpret it. The product of learning (language **performance** on grammaticality judgement tasks) does indeed look similar. But we currently have no way of knowing if the *mechanisms* by which that learning came about are the same or different for children and adults. In this vein, it has been argued that adults inevitably learn languages in a different way from children (Newport, Bavelier & Neville, 2001).

My memories of language learning at school illustrate a common story of deliberate, strategic and effortful learning that bears no resemblance to the way a toddler goes about it. It is difficult to argue against this image of the adult language learner. At the same time, it does not mean that less

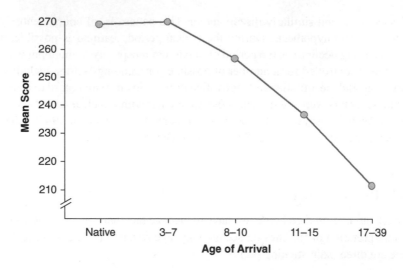

Figure 3.1 Number of correct judgements of English sentences (out of 276 total) according to age of first exposure to English

Source: Johnson, J.S. & Newport, E.L. (1989). Critical period effects in second language learning: The influence of maturational state on the acquisition of English as a second language. *Cognitive Psychology*, 21, 60–99.

conscious processes, possibly more akin to those of a child, are not also working in tandem with more explicit processes. As yet, though, no attempt has been made to distinguish among these possible mechanisms in adults. We should also point out that, scientifically, we are faced with two problems: (1) we may apply different learning mechanisms to language learning in early versus later life; and (2) both the quantity and quality of input for learning may differ in early versus later life. We will examine the input to L1 learning in Chapter 4. But we can note, in passing, that the input and settings in which second languages are learned (both for children and adults) have a profound influence on the learning outcomes (see Murphy, 2010, for a review).

The second argument against critical periods from our list concerns native speaker status. If we accept the critical period phenomenon as real, but also accept that many adults learn second languages to a very high standard, we are left to ask how they do it. It has often been suggested that 'humans bring many high-level cognitive abilities to the task of learning a language, and might be capable of using systems to acquire a second language other than the ones they use for primary language acquisition' (Newport et al., 2001: 496). For example, some authors point to a general analytic verbal ability (think crosswords and Scrabble) as the only significant predictor of second language success beyond puberty (Harley & Hart, 1997). These abilities must be so good that, in a limited number of cases, they lead to native-like levels of performance (for example, Birdsong, 1992; Ioup, Boustagui, El Tigi & Moselle, 1994; White & Genesee, 1996; Bialystok, 1997). We might quibble about how perfect perfection is, because native-like is not the same as native (for example, DeKeyser, 2000), but the main point is that sightings of native-level late second language learners are extremely rare. What we do find, though, are considerable numbers of late learners who do very well indeed in their second language. Whichever way we look at it, therefore, humans must have remarkable general learning abilities to compensate for the loss of any natural, dedicated disposition for language learning. If you examine Johnson & Newport's data again (Figure 3.1), you will see that even the worst adults achieve roughly 75 per cent accuracy on the grammar tests. And although there is individual variation in performance, most people do pretty well. It is worth considering what this means for the portrait painted by Chomsky, where language is described as an object of learning so abstract, complex and difficult that specialized, innate resources are necessary to account for its acquisition.

We come now to our third point, which concerns the definite cut-off point at puberty predicted by Lenneberg (1967). Some authors argue that there is, in fact, no sudden plummet in ability. Instead, they emphasize the more gradual, long slow decline of our cognitive faculties that comes to us all with increasing age. Hearing, vision, general problem-solving skills and memory (both long-term and short-term) get progressively weaker with age (Seifert, Hoffnung & Hoffnung, 2000). It is conceivable, therefore, that receptivity to language remains strong throughout life, but that deterioration in these other, non-linguistic, functions mediates increasingly poor language learning. These effects are in force throughout adult life, which means that late L2 learning, in particular, may be prey to this slide into the Pit of All-Round Poor Learning. What we have, then, are two factors, one or both of which might influence later language learning: (1) a critical period; and (2) a decline in general cognition. If the second factor alone is at work, then the dramatic cut-off point, so vivid in Figure 3.1, should not exist. Put another way, perhaps Johnson & Newport (1989) would not find this definite kink in the graph if they had done a bigger, better, more powerful study.

Hakuta, Bialystok & Wiley (2003) attempted just such a study. They used data on two million speakers of Spanish and over 300,000 Chinese speakers from the 1990 US census. The census provided information on age, education, and age of arrival in the United States. In addition, respondents had also been asked to rate their own English ability. Hence, Hakuta et al. (2003) had the same ingredients in their study as found in Johnson & Newport (1989), only on a massively greater scale. Hakuta et al. found a typical age-related decline in English ability (English being the second language of respondents). But there was no evidence for a significant break or cut-off point, when either 15 or 20 years of age were taken as possible end-points for a critical period. In other words, the statistical model that best described the data showed a *gradual* decline with age. Moreover, it was found that the amount of formal education was important for explaining reported levels of English proficiency. Once in America, the more time spent in school and college, the better one's English becomes. For this reason, Hakuta et al. (2003) argue that, at least for adult L2 learning, there is no critical period, only a general tailing off caused by an age-related decline in general cognition. Hakuta et al.'s results have recently been replicated in an experimental study by Huang (2014). She found that Mandarin-speaking immigrants to the US show a steady decline in grammatical ability in English, depending on their age of arrival in America. Children who were five years old on arrival show near native-like proficiency, while those arriving at the age of 30 years performed much less well. Like Hakuta et al., Huang's study controlled for factors like amount of education and length of residence. Huang (2015) has also reviewed numerous studies on age of acquisition effects and finds no clear advantage for an early start in life when learning a second language.

What are we to make of the clash between Johnson & Newport, on the one hand, and Hakuta et al. and Huang, on the other? First, there are huge differences in sample sizes. The data from Hakuta et al. (2003), with more than two million participants, are bound to be more reliable than the 46 in Johnson & Newport (1989) (see Gravetter & Walnau, 1992, on sample sizes). But the measure of English proficiency adopted in Hakuta et al. (2003) seems extremely weak. Respondents rate themselves (not a good start) and do so on a very simplistic scale. They are asked to say if they speak English 'not at all', 'not well', 'well', 'very well' or 'speak English only'. Hence, there is no adequate definition of the target behaviour (language) that may, or may not, be subject to a critical period effect. In particular, the top of the scale – 'speak English only' – can, ostensibly, encompass a multitude of linguistic virtues and sins. I could speak anything between really bad English all the time (possibly without even knowing it) right through to speaking perfect English all the time, with native-like fluency. Overall, the evidence lined up on each side of this issue suffers from its own weaknesses. As Bialystok & Miller (1999: 127) point out, critical period studies 'use different methodologies, engage different subject groups, administer different types of tasks, and assess different linguistic features. The lack of consensus in outcomes is hardly surprising'.

Abrupt cut-off point or gradual decline? As we have seen, research on adult L2 learning is not yet decisive on this point, possibly because it has been looking in the wrong places. Instead of a dramatic cut-off at 15 or 20 years, as sought by Hakuta et al. (2003), there may instead be an off-set in ability at about five years. The notion of an off-set is different from that of a cut-off point. By off-set is meant the point where the system ceases to be maximally receptive to the effects of the environment. That is, the period of peak plasticity ends. Thereafter, there will be a decline (not a complete cessation) in receptivity to language experience. Some time beyond this off-set, there may be a definite cut-off point for the critical (or sensitive) period. Puberty still seems like the best bet for such a final cut-off point. Subsequent to the critical period cut-off, a more general decline in cognitive functioning begins to reveal itself. Adults who exploit general learning mechanisms to acquire an additional language often do remarkably well, despite the end of the critical period. But they perform increasingly poorly over time, as general cognition deteriorates.

Plastic fantastic: The receptive brain

Evidently, the evidence for a sudden cut-off is not yet clear. But more important, the significance of any definite cut-off is also less than clear. Advocates of the critical period hypothesis now suggest that the existence of a critical (or sensitive) period is not dependent on the existence of this kind of cut-off. Newport et al. (2001) take this tack and cite evidence from animal critical periods – in particular the hearing systems of owls – in support of this view. More important than a sudden cut-off is evidence that the child undergoes a period of peak plasticity. This, at least, is a *sine qua non* ('without which nothing') of critical periods. Of course, plastic in this context does not mean 'Tupperware' or 'polythene'. It means something more like 'mouldable', 'flexible' or 'adaptable'. A plastic learning system (the brain) is one that can be moulded in different ways according to the particular inputs it is exposed to (or deprived of). Hence the familiar idea that the child is especially receptive to language during the projected critical period. We can look for signs of brain plasticity in patients who undergo radical brain surgery, especially in those rare cases where an entire brain hemisphere must be removed (hemispherectomy). We noted above that, in most people, specialization for many language functions resides in the left hemisphere. If this hemisphere is removed in an adult, the effects on language are catastrophic and permanent. But Lenneberg (1967) suggested that language learning *is* possible in cases where the hemispherectomy takes place before the age of two. This follows from an assumption that the brain, as a whole, is still sufficiently plastic for the right hemisphere to take over the language functions normally engaged by the left. In essence, Lenneberg was right. Recovery from severe left hemisphere damage is both possible and strongest for the very youngest children (see Herschensohn, 2007). Plasticity is at a peak in the first few years of life, and then wanes slowly as brain development proceeds into adulthood. In fact, the human brain is not fully mature until 15–20 years of age, 'a long developmental period during which environmental input could shape brain systems' (Neville & Bruer, 2001: 152; cf., Pallier, Dehaene, Poline, Le Bihan, Argenti, Dupoux & Mehler, 2003). Overall, we see that a period of plasticity, with an off-set and subsequent decline, is crucial to the definition of a critical period. And as we have seen, the concept of an off-set is far less drastic than Lenneberg's (1967) original belief in a screeching, dead halt cut-off point.

Deafness and late language learning

Deaf children and adults comprise a further population of language learners that have contributed to the critical period debate. We will have less to say about the research in this area, because it parallels the research on both isolated children and second language learners. The essential ingredients are the same, with the focus on the effects of early versus late language learning. Deaf children provide a testing ground because they often start life in a linguistic vacuum. This is because more than 90 per cent of deaf children are born to hearing parents (Meadow, 1980). Access to language is therefore severely limited. In the past, it often took many months, even years, before children were diagnosed. Happily, serious hearing loss can now be identified in the first week of life (Google: *newborn hearing screening programme* for information on the NHS programme). Not surprisingly, early diagnosis goes hand in hand with enhanced language development (Yoshinaga-Itano, 2003). But even with the best will in the world, hearing parents of deaf children have a steep hill to climb in providing adequate language input. These parents can only start learning sign language once their child has been diagnosed with hearing loss. Effectively, these parents are learning a second language. Imagine if I had been forced to teach my son, Alex, Japanese instead of English when he was born. As it happens, we did cart Alex off to Japan when he was 10 weeks old. But in the following year, the only Japanese he heard were screams of 'kawai!' ('cute') from the locals. It is not surprising, therefore, that Alex did not learn much Japanese. Nor is it surprising that hearing parents of deaf children face a monumental task if they want to gain fluency in what is, in effect, a foreign language for them.

Two more cases of linguistic deprivation: Chelsea and E.M.

It can often be several years before deaf children gain access to native speakers of sign language and begin properly acquiring their first full-fledged language. For some children, access to sign language only begins when they start school at about the age of five. For others, they may have to wait until the age of 11 before going to a specialist secondary school. There are also individuals who reach maturity without having acquired language at all. A case in point is Chelsea, a deaf woman who did not start learning language until her early thirties (Curtiss, 1988). The results were similar to Genie, in the sense that Chelsea managed to acquire items of vocabulary, but stringing them together into grammatical sentences was beyond her. Chelsea produced utterances like *Orange Tim car in*, *The woman is bus the going*, and *Banana the eat*. Despite their ungrammaticality, note that these verbal concoctions are not random. For example, the article *the* is correctly associated with a noun (*woman*, *bus*, *banana*), though, of course, the order is not consistent, even within the same utterance (*the woman* versus *bus the*).

A further example of linguistic, but not social, deprivation is provided by Ramirez, Lieberman & Mayberry (2013). They studied three deaf children who were not exposed to language of any kind until they were about 14 years old. Between one and two years later, after an immersive experience with American Sign Language, it was found that they were acquiring vocabulary in a manner which paralleled that of normally developing toddlers. In particular, they acquired a high proportion of concrete vocabulary items (words for things which can be seen and/or touched), with significantly fewer class items like **prepositions** (for example, in English *by*, *from*, *up*, *on*). It will be interesting to chart how their language continues to develop. A hint is provided by the case study of E.M., a deaf boy studied by Grimshaw, Adelstein, Bryden & MacKinnon (1998). E.M. was raised in a rural area, where he received little formal education before the age of 12, and where he was cut off from the deaf community. At the age of 15, he was fitted with hearing aids that enabled him to hear speech at conversational level, and at this point, he began to learn Spanish. After four years, Grimshaw et al. (1998) tested E.M.'s comprehension on a range of 12 grammatical features. For some of the structures, like the use of pronouns (for example, *he*, *she*, *it*), E.M. performed at chance levels. For other features, E.M.'s performance differed from chance, but was nevertheless not perfect. For example, his understanding of the singular–plural distinction (*cat* versus *cats*) was good, but not perfect, at roughly 85 per cent. What is fascinating about E.M. and many, if not all, of the late language learners reported in the literature, is that they have clearly learned something about grammar. Scoring 85 per cent on a grammar test would attract accolades at school, but in the critical period literature, it is taken as evidence that specialized language learning mechanisms have been switched off. E.M.'s problem is not a lack of grammar, but a lack of *consistency* in applying his knowledge of grammar. His control over the rules does not seem to be as well developed as that of a native speaker, but he does at least have appropriate grammatical features in his repertoire. Of course, this is exactly what we saw with the late second language learners described above. Evidently, linguistic deprivation seems to have had a permanent effect on E.M.'s ability to acquire and/or use the rules of grammar. And it is worth bearing in mind that E.M. did not suffer the physical and psychological abuse that Genie was subject to. His social and cognitive development appear to have been normal, so there must be something about grammar learning *per se* that is affected by late exposure.

Early versus late learning of American Sign Language

Single case studies on deaf children have also been supplemented by more wide-ranging studies that have compared the effects of different starting ages on language learning. Elissa Newport conducted a series of studies that complement her work on second language learning reported above (Newport, 1988, 1990). Three groups of American Sign Language (ASL) learners were identified, so-called native, early, and late. The native learners were exposed to ASL from birth by deaf parents. Early learners began learning ASL between the ages of four and six years, while late learners did not start until the age of 12. On average, the participants in all three groups had been using ASL for 30 years at the time of testing, so the amount of experience with ASL was controlled for. As with second-language learners, Newport found that late language learners in particular did less well, especially on tests of **morphology**. Even early learners showed some deficits compared to the native signers. Newport's findings have been replicated in a number of studies (for example, Mayberry & Eichen, 1991; Emmorey, Bellugi, Friederici & Horn, 1995). It has also been found that late learners process vocabulary in real time less efficiently than native sign language users (Lieberman, Borovsky, Hatrak & Mayberry, 2015).

In addition, it has been shown that native and late deaf signers differ in terms of brain organization. There are several sophisticated techniques for detecting which parts of the brain are especially active during particular activities (see Obler & Gjerlow, 1999, on matters grey). A number of studies support the idea that language is organized differently in the brains of native versus late ASL learners (for example, Wuillemin, Richardson & Lynch, 1994; Neville, Coffey, Lawson, Fischer, Emmorey & Bellugi, 1997; Newman, Bavelier, Corina, Jezzard & Neville, 2002; though see Perani et al., 1998, for an opposing view from the second language literature). The feature of language that distinguishes late from early second language learners appears to be grammar. This finding has emerged by examining brain activity in Broca's area, the region of the left hemisphere that is especially associated with grammar processing (among other functions). In late L2 learners, activity in Broca's area is especially high for L2 compared with L1. Significantly, this is the case regardless of how proficient the learner is in their second language (Wartenburger, Heekeren, Abutalebi, Cappa, Villringer & Perani, 2003). In contrast, people who acquire their second language early in life (early bilinguals) show similar levels of activity in Broca's area for both L1 and L2. Vocabulary is a further domain where differences can be observed in cerebral activity between late and early deaf learners (Ramirez, Leonard, Torres, Hatrak, Halgren & Mayberry, 2014).

Research on brain activity adds to our conviction that, when it comes to the acquisition of both syntax and phonology, age matters. These findings are clear. Their interpretation is much less clear. The problem we face is that an age effect is not necessarily the same thing as a critical period effect. As we discovered, the thrust of Hakuta et al. (2003) is that we experience a long slow decline in the power of our general learning mechanisms that progressively hinders our ability to acquire language. Hence, age effects may not be caused by a language-specific critical period. But age effects are at least compatible with the critical period hypothesis, especially if we relinquish Lenneberg's expectation that there is a clearly demarcated termination point (Newport et al., 2001). We have also shifted the goal posts with regard to the start and end points, for both syntax and phonology. Critical periods for language probably begin before birth. Their off-set, the age at which peak sensitivity ends, seems to be around age five. And thereafter, there is a gradual decline in sensitivity to language. Some authors continue to believe in a complete termination at about puberty, while others adhere to the idea of a continual decline into adulthood and old age.

To conclude, it is difficult to deny the intuitive appeal of the idea that language learning in later life is qualitatively different from the effortless blooming of the toddler's linguistic capacity. The following conclusion seems reasonable, therefore:

> The development of neural architecture dedicated to native language grammar, lexicon and processing is a clearly biological characteristic of typical human growth during the first few years of life that presents the onset and peak of sensitivity of a representative critical period. (Herschensohn, 2007: 226)

However, this chapter has revealed that there is still a great deal we need to confirm, before we can fully accept Lenneberg's original proposal. The perfect critical period experiment is beyond our grasp, while the evidence that is at our disposal is either incomplete or inadequate, or both. What good evidence we do have is at least consistent with the idea that critical periods exist in first language acquisition for both phonology and syntax. Future research on brain functioning and brain development, together with more substantial behavioural data, will surely provide us with more decisive evidence on critical periods for language.

IN A NUTSHELL

- Critical periods in development are biologically determined.

- The effects of the environment on development are especially strong during the critical period and have a much weaker effect once the critical period has ended.

- The critical period is like a 'window of opportunity' for development. If development does not take place during this period, it may not be possible at all thereafter.

- Environmental deprivation has its strongest effects during the critical period. If the organism is deprived of vital input during this period, development may be permanently hindered, even if the input is supplied subsequently.

- In the domain of language, different populations have been studied: feral, abused and neglected children, in addition to deaf people and second language learners.

- Research on language as a critical period phenomenon suffers from a lack of rigour:

  o it is not clear precisely which aspects of language are subject to critical period effects

  o most research does not have sufficiently tight control over the length and quality of environmental experience

  o many of the subject populations studied may have cognitive deficits that affect language learning, quite apart from any critical period effects (for example, Genie).

- It is controversial whether there is a clear cut-off point at puberty in language learning ability. The alternative concept of an off-set may be more valid. An off-set marks the end of a period of peak plasticity, after which receptivity to the environment declines (rather than terminates altogether).

- Evidence for critical period effects in adult second language learning is far from decisive. The influence and gradual decline of general cognitive learning mechanisms greatly complicates empirical enquiry.

- Different aspects of language are probably subject to their own critical period effects, in particular phonology, syntax and language processing.

- On balance, available evidence favours the existence of critical periods in first language development.

FURTHER READING

Curtiss, S., Fromkin, V., Krashen, S., Rigler, D. & Rigler, M. (1974). The linguistic development of Genie. *Language, 50(3)*, 528–554.

A golden oldie, but still worth reading for the detailed examples of Genie's actual speech. You may be surprised at the positive spin put on Genie's grammatical prowess, in light of the discussion in this chapter. A chance to make up your own mind by looking at some of the original data.

Rymer, R. (1993). *Genie: A scientific tragedy*. Harmondsworth: Penguin.

A highly accessible account of Genie: how she came to light and how her story unfolded subsequently. Light on the science of the critical period, but rich in insights about a remarkable person.

Werker, J.F. & Hensch, T.K. (2015). Critical periods in speech perception: New directions. *Annual Review of Psychology, 66*, 173–196.

A thorough review of research on speech perception in particular, with an emphasis on the biological underpinnings of critical periods.

Blom, E. & Paradis, J. (2016). Introduction: Special issue on age effects in child language acquisition. *Journal of Child Language, 43(3)*, 473–478.

These authors introduce a wide range of up-to-date articles on age effects in language acquisition, including the impact of cochlear implants on hearing-impaired children and issues raised in bilingual settings.

WEBSITES AND VIDEO

- **Genie**

  Search on YouTube for *Genie (Secret of the Wild Child)* for an interesting documentary about Genie.

- **Testing on animals in scientific research**: www.peta.org and http://www.ca-biomed.org/csbr/pdf/fs-whynecessary.pdf

  These two sites provide strongly conflicting views on a deeply controversial topic.

Still want more? For links to online resources relevant to this chapter and a quiz to test your understanding, visit the companion website at **https://study.sagepub.com/saxton2e**

4

Input and Interaction: Tutorials for Toddlers

CONTENTS

OVERVIEW

By the end of this chapter you should be able to describe Child Directed Speech (CDS). This is the special register adopted by adults and older children when talking to young children. You will gain some appreciation of specific modifications which are made at the levels of phonology, vocabulary, morphology and syntax. It will become apparent that, in several instances, CDS functions to facilitate language development. You will also gain an understanding of individual differences in CDS. In particular, you will be able to describe how socioeconomic status affects the amount and quality of language children hear, and also, how these differences impact on language development.

This chapter will also introduce you to the difference between input (the language forms children hear) and interaction (the way language is used in conversation). With regard to interaction, you should be able to assess the importance of imitation (both verbal and non-verbal) for language acquisition. You should also be able to describe a special form of verbal imitation, the adult recast, and describe its potential as a form of corrective input for child grammatical errors. You will also gain some understanding of cross-cultural research on the child's linguistic environment and be able to evaluate the claim that at least some aspects of CDS may be an inevitable feature of adult–child conversation.

Talking to young children

To many people, there is nothing special or mysterious about child language development. If you grab a representative of the people – the man on the Clapham Omnibus – and ask him how children learn language, it's an even bet he'll tell you that they learn it from their parents. And who will contradict him? A child born to Tagalog-speaking parents in the Philippines will grow up speaking Tagalog. The child born to Inuktitut-speaking parents in the Arctic region of Canada will learn Inuktitut. My own parents are monolingual English speakers, and here I am, thinking, speaking, reading, and occasionally writing, in English. In one sense, therefore, no-one can argue with the man on the bus. Children learn language from their parents. Unfortunately, though, this formulation does not get us very far.

The real problem is to understand *how* the child learns. We need to find out what learning mechanisms and conceptual knowledge the child applics to the task of language acquisition. In other words, we want to lift the lid on the machinery of language acquisition, all of which resides in the child. The language children hear from parents and others is merely the fuel that allows the machine to run and produce a mature knowledge of language as its end product. Linguistic input is certainly an essential ingredient, which is why we will examine it in this chapter. But we should not forget that, ultimately, we want to establish how the child's language learning capacities engage with and learn from the available linguistic environment. If we torture the fuel metaphor just a little further, one question, of considerable interest, crops up straightaway. Does our language learning machine require low-grade fuel or a high octane deluxe grade? Some machines run very well on low-grade fuel. When it comes to language acquisition, we find that nativists, in particular, adopt this 'low grade' view. In a well-known statement, Chomsky (1965: 31) described the input available to the language learning child as 'fairly degenerate in quality', characterized by 'fragments and deviant expressions of a variety of sorts' (ibid.: 201). However, as soon as researchers began to examine the way parents talk to their children, it became apparent that they adapt their speech in numerous ways at every level of linguistic analysis (Snow, 1972; Phillips, 1973). In other words, parents seem to provide high octane input as the fuel for language acquisition.

The way in which parents speak to their children constitutes a special register or style, which has been given many names over the years (see Box 4.1). We will favour **Child Directed Speech** (CDS), with a brief diversion into Infant Direct Speech (see Saxton, 2008, for a justification). A critical distinction is between *input* and *interaction*. Input constitutes the particular language forms that the child hears, while interaction refers to the way in which those forms are used in adult–child discourse. Imitation, broadly construed, is a critical form of interaction for language development which includes both verbal and non-verbal behaviour. We will discover that CDS facilitates language acquisition. But many researchers downplay the importance of 'high octane' CDS, on the grounds that it is not universally available to all children. We examine the evidence for this assumption in what follows.

BOX 4.1   TERMS OF ENGAGEMENT

The register used by parents and others to talk to young children has been given many names since the late nineteenth century. Here are 15 of the most prominent:

1 baby talk (Lukens, 1894)
2 nursery talk (Jakobson, 1941/1968)
3 motherese (Newport, 1975)
4 caregiver speech (Ochs, 1982)
5 caretaker talk (Schachter, Fosha, Stemp, Brotman & Ganger, 1976)
6 verbal stimuli (Skinner, 1957)
7 exposure language (Gillette, Gleitman, Gleitman & Lederer, 1999)
8 input language (Ninio, 1986)
9 linguistic input (Schlesinger, 1977)
10 primary linguistic data (Chomsky, 1965)
11 Infant Directed Speech (Cooper & Aslin, 1990)
12 Child Directed Speech (Warren-Leubecker & Bohannon, 1984)
13 caregiver talk (Cole & St. Clair Stokes, 1984)
14 verbal environment (Chomsky, 1980a)
15 parentese (Ramírez-Esparza, García-Sierra & Kuhl, 2014)

(Continued)

There are prizes for those who can dig up any more. Not big prizes, mind you – I'm not a banker.

One might ask if it matters which term one chooses. In fact, it does matter. The people doing the talking (e.g., parent or elder sibling) and the person being addressed (e.g., infant or toddler) can have a significant influence on both the quantity and quality of language used. Probably the most useful term is Child Directed Speech, hence its use in this chapter. For a guided tour through the jargon jungle, see Saxton (2008).

Characteristics of Child Directed Speech

Child Directed Speech is a special register, which means that it constitutes a distinct mode of speech. The term *register* is borrowed from sociolinguistics, and overlaps with the concepts of style and dialect (Saxton, 2008). Although it is not well defined, the central idea is neverthe-less fairly straightforward. We talk in different ways to different people in different settings. Consider how you might converse with the Queen at a palace garden party (converse, mind you – not talk). Now compare that with the kind of chat you might have with a close friend. You would, in all likelihood, adopt a separate register for each occasion. We can establish that CDS is a distinct register by comparing it with *Adult* Directed Speech (ADS) (Hills, 2013). This comparison can provide a scientific control. The ideal study would take a group of adults and record each person in conversation with another adult and also, on a separate occasion, in conversation with a young child. This method allows one to identify what is special or distinc-tive about Child Directed Speech. Fortunately, this approach was taken by Snow (1972), who provided the first major study in this field, and therefore the first challenge to Chomsky's belief that the input is 'degenerate'.

Phonology

If you have ever spoken to a baby, you may well have found yourself riding a linguistic roller-coaster. People tend to exaggerate their intonation, producing great swooping curves of sound over an extended pitch range. At the same time, the overall pitch tends to be higher than normal (Garnica, 1977; Stern, Spieker, Barnett & MacKain, 1983; Fernald, Taeschner, Dunn, Papousek, Deboysson-Bardies & Fukui, 1989; Werker & McLeod, 1989). In particular, mothers are espe-cially prone to raise their pitch when the infant shows signs of positive emotional engagement (Smith & Trainor, 2008). Speech also tends to be slower, with syllable-lengthening, longer pauses and fewer dysfluencies (Broen, 1972; Fernald & Simon, 1984; Fernald, 1989; Albin & Echols, 1996). In addition, there is evidence that individual phonemes are pronounced with greater clarity than is the case in Adult Directed Speech. For example, in ADS, the phonemes /t, d, n/ are often not pronounced fully when they are followed by certain phonemes (/b, p, m, g, k/). Instead, they assimilate to these following phonemes. This means that the sounds take on each other's acoustic properties in certain respects. Infants, by contrast, are more likely to hear canonical, fully pronounced versions of the /t, d, n/ phonemes (Dilley, Millett, Devin McAuley & Bergeson, 2014). Parents may well gravitate towards this manner of speech because infants prefer to listen to it. In fact, some infants have a stronger preference for listening to ADS than others. And those infants who pay particular attention at 12 months have acquired relatively large vocabularies by the age of 18 months (Vouloumanos & Curtin, 2014). From the adult's point of view, ADS provides the best method to grab the infant's attention and, in the process, convey a mood of positive affect (Fernald, 1989). On occasion, this exaggerated intonation is lampooned as a minority pursuit, indulged in only by the privileged Western mothers mentioned above. But this kind of speech has also been observed in languages as diverse as German, Hebrew, Italian, Japanese, Luo (an East African language), and Spanish (see Soderstrom, 2007, for a summary). The phonological adaptations sketched out here figure most prominently during the child's first year. For this reason, some authors refer to Infant Directed Speech (IDS) as a special register, distinct from the Child Directed Speech addressed to older children (Golinkoff, Can, Soderstrom & Hirsh-Pasek, 2015).

Vocabulary

Adult–child conversation with a toddler tends to be about the here-and-now, rather than topics distant in time or space. This means that the words chosen by the adult are likely to be more easily comprehended by the child. In this vein, there is a marked emphasis on concrete, rather than abstract, concepts. *Cup*, *juice* and *tree* are far more likely in speech addressed to two-year-olds than *purity*, *truth* or *beauty*. Moreover, adults tend to place object words at the end of **sentences** and pronounce them relatively loudly, thus giving them special prominence (Messer, 1981). Five topics in particular seem to dominate the conversation: members of the family; animals; parts of the body; food; and clothing (Ferguson, 1977; Ferguson & Debose, 1977). These topics are dictated by the interests of the child, which indicates that, if you want to maintain a toddler's attention, you have to talk about what interests *them*. It is no use launching into a discussion about falling share prices, fiscal prudence and quantitative easing. You will be met with a blank stare. Actually, if you tried that with *me*, you'd be met with a blank stare. As with phonological adaptations, parental lexical choices respond to the needs and interests of the child.

Morphology and syntax

With regard to **morphology**, the frequency with which children are exposed to particular morphemes is reflected in their own speech (Warlaumont & Jarmulowicz, 2012). Some languages, like Russian, have a dauntingly complex system of word endings. But Russian mothers tend to subvert these complexities and, instead, rely heavily on diminutive forms. Equivalents in English might be diminutive forms like *horsie*, *doggie* and *duckie*. Russian mothers alternate between diminutive and morphologically simplified forms within the same stretch of conversation (Kempe, Brooks, Mironova, Pershukova & Fedorova, 2007). In so doing, these mothers may provide an accessible demonstration of the morphological variety typical of Russian, without overwhelming the child with the massive variety witnessed in ADS.

Turning to syntax, sentences in CDS are remarkable for being well-formed grammatically. Although children hear a considerable number of incomplete sentences, these nevertheless comprise legitimate syntactic phrases, for example, **noun phrases** like: *more grape juice*; *a cup*; or *another blue one* (Brown, 1973). One survey by Newport et al. (1977) found just one genuine adult error in a corpus of 1,500 utterances. CDS sentences are not only grammatical, but also relatively short (Barnes, Gutfreund, Satterly & Wells, 1983). In jargonese, we could say that the **MLU** of CDS is lower than in ADS. **Mean Length of Utterance** (MLU) provides a rough and ready measure of syntactic complexity, whereby shorter sentences tend to be simpler. The impression of simplicity is confirmed by the relative scarcity of certain complex structures. Thus, Sachs, Brown & Salerno (1976) report few **subordinate clauses**, **relative clauses**, **sentential complements** and **negations** in CDS.

The **subject** of CDS sentences also has a strong tendency to be an **agent**. We encountered the category of subject in Chapter 3. Agent, or 'doer' of an action is one semantic role that the subject can take on. In fact, we might argue that 'agent-as-subject' is prototypical: *Venus* in *Venus knocked on our door*, or *Paula* in *Paula taught me British Sign Language*. Critically, subjects are not always agents: *The oysters were washed down with champagne* or *The meeting came to order at 10 o'clock*. Neither *the oysters* nor *the meeting* are acting as the agent of any action, yet they each function as the subject. Coming back to CDS, consider the advantage to the child if the majority of subjects they hear *are* agents. Eve's mother produced the following examples, when Eve was 1;7:

Agent as subject of the sentence:

> *you're* dancing
> *Eve* can get the banjo
> *you* broke it
> shall *we* change your diaper?
> *you* make a train

Initially, the child's experience is confined mostly to just one kind of subject and, moreover, it is the prototypical (agent) subject. By confining sentence subjects to agents, the adult makes the relationship between meaning and grammar especially clear for the young child (Rondal & Cession, 1990). The one-to-one mapping between agents and subjects in CDS may well provide the child with an entry point for discovering the grammatical category of subject, a process known as *semantic bootstrapping* (Pinker, 1984). The complexities involved in a range of different subject types are thus introduced later. In fact, it takes several years before children make the connections between different kinds of sentential subject and treat them as a single grammatical category. Four-year-olds have trouble in this regard, and it is not until the age of nine that children demonstrate full control over the subject category (Braine, Brooks, Cowan, Samuels & Tamis-LeMonda, 1993). It is fascinating to discover, therefore, that the child's introduction to the subject category, via CDS, is simplified.

A dynamic register

The register used with children is dynamic. Rather than being a fixed mode of address, adult speech changes continually in concert with the child's developing language. Perhaps the clearest sign of these changes is the shift from infant-directed to child-directed speech. The different names – IDS and CDS – indicate that the changes in adult speech are substantial. But there is no step change from one mode to the other. On a day-to-day basis, the changes are subtle and difficult to detect, but they continue all the way through childhood until a point is reached where the speech addressed to one's offspring can genuinely count as an instance of Adult Directed Speech. Some of the changes over time have been monitored (e.g., Buchan & Jones, 2014), though it must be said that there is far more to learn about the dynamic nature of CDS. One change we do know about concerns tone of voice. From birth to three months, infants respond well to a comforting tone of voice, but subsequently, from three to six months, they come to prefer a more approving tone of voice. Finally, there are signs that, by nine months, infants respond more readily to a directive tone of voice (Kitamura & Lam, 2009). Adults are able to satisfy these changes in infant preferences because they are sensitive to the infant's emotional needs on a moment-to-moment basis (Smith & Trainor, 2008). Snow (1995) refers to these changes over time as a process of 'finetuning' to reflect the continual sensitivity of caregivers to the child's communicative needs. In fact, the notion of finetuning may overstate the case, with some authors arguing that the 'input is only grossly, not finely, tuned' (Hoff, 2004: 924). But the fact that the adult input is tailored in any way at all to the infant's language level deserves our attention.

EXERCISE 4.1
ADULT DIRECTED SPEECH

Make a short audio recording of a conversation between yourself and a friend. Tell your friend that you are doing this, to guarantee both eternal harmony and a proper regard for the ethics of research (see www.beta.bps.org.uk for more information on the ethics of psychology research). Nowadays, you won't need a big reel-to-reel tape recorder; many mobile phones have an audio recording capacity that should suit our rough-and-ready purposes. Try not to be self-conscious and talk about something that you really want to talk about.

Once you have made your recording, transcribe part of your conversation word (and even part-word) for word. Listen with great attention to precisely what was said. We are interested in your speech **performance**, so do not edit out the unintended glitches. You will probably need to listen to each utterance several times before you can get an accurate record. Now consider the following:

(Continued)

- If you were a toddler, what aspects of your conversation would be difficult to follow? Consider phonology, vocabulary and syntax. Consider also any errors, hesitations, repetitions and interruptions to the flow.
- How adequate is your language as a model for learning by a toddler?
- Would it be possible to modify the content of your conversation in any way to improve its 'language teaching' potential? If so, what would you change?

Individual differences and their effects

So far, we have sketched a picture of Child Directed Speech that marks it out quite clearly as a special register, quite different in its characteristics from Adult Directed Speech. In terms of average tendencies, this picture is accurate. But we should also be aware that individual children have different experiences of language. There is considerable variation in both the amount and quality of CDS provided. In this regard, two points are often raised: (1) CDS may be a minority phenomenon, not universally available; and (2) parents who do supply CDS nevertheless differ, in terms of both quantity and quality, in how they talk to children. The assumption that CDS is not available to all children is widely retailed in the child language literature. But as we shall see, below, this assumption is very poorly supported, empirically. Far more convincing is the evidence on the second point – individual differences among parents – and this provides the focus in this section.

Hart & Risley (1995) provide the most substantial demonstration that children differ in the sheer amount of language they hear. They grouped parents into three bands according to socioeconomic status (SES), a variable that generally takes into account level of education, income and job prestige. High-SES parents were professionals, Mid-SES parents were working class, while Low-SES parents were generally on public assistance, a form of social welfare provided in the US.

As Table 4.1 reveals, there are substantial differences in the amount of language different children hear. In fact, both the quantity and *quality* of the input varied among groups. High-SES children are exposed not only to more words, but to a greater variety of words also. This group also receive fewer prohibitions and directives: utterances designed to control child behaviour in some way. High levels of parental prohibition are associated with relatively poor language growth on a range of measures, including MLU, diversity and complexity of vocabulary, and use of different language functions (Taylor, Donovan, Miles & Leavitt, 2009). Furthermore, High-SES parents use longer, syntactically more complex utterances with their children. Generally speaking, more talkative parents tends to use a richer vocabulary and express more complex ideas, regardless of SES (Rowe, 2012). And this input has a beneficial impact on the child's own acquisition of complex grammar (Vasilyeva, Waterfall & Huttenlocher, 2008). High-SES children produce complex structures themselves at an earlier stage than Low-SES children (22 months) and this advantage persists over the next 18 months

Table 4.1 Estimated number of words heard per week by children according to socioeconomic status (after Hart & Risley, 1995)

SES status of parents	Number of words heard per week
High	215,000
Mid	125,000
Low	62,000

or more (see also Hoff, 2006, who reviews the impact of a wide range of social factors on language development). Finally, High-SES parents in China, as measured by parental education level, have children with more advanced vocabulary development (Zhang, Jin, Shen, Zhang & Hoff, 2008).

There are signs that a simple equation – High-SES = 'high talking' – may not hold, not even within the United States. Low-SES Spanish-speaking mothers in San Francisco produce 17.5 utterances per minute, on average, when talking with their 18-month-old children (Hurtado, Marchman & Fernald, 2008). This figure compares with an average of 14.6 per minute for another US sample, this time comprising both Mid- and High-SES speakers of English (Hoff & Naigles, 2002). Low-SES mothers are more talkative than High-SES mothers on this comparison. Apart from SES, these groups also differ in terms of the native language spoken and membership of different sub-cultures. These latter factors probably exert separate influences on the amount of parental speech. It is also worth emphasizing that there can be considerable variation in talkativeness *within* SES bands (Hurtado et al., 2008). The children of talkative mothers heard seven times as many words, and three times as many *different* words, as children of less talkative mothers. In fact, individual parental loquaciousness predicts the child's language development better than the SES group they belong to (Weisleder, Otero, Marchman & Fernald, 2015). Regardless of SES, lexical frequency and lexical diversity co-occur (Song, Spier & Tamis-LeMonda, 2014). And both of these factors have an impact on the child's vocabulary development, with children of talkative mothers developing larger vocabularies (Hart & Risley, 1995; Hoff & Naigles, 2002; Hurtado et al., 2008; Fernald & Weisleder, 2015). In a similar vein, children whose parents engage in more episodes of joint attention and shared book reading develop larger vocabularies by the age of six years (Farrant & Zubrick, 2013).

Hurtado et al. (2008) report a further consequence of being talkative with one's child. They found that the children of talkative mothers were more efficient at processing speech. Pictures of two familiar objects were presented side by side, and one of them was named. Children of talkative mothers looked more quickly to the named target. Lexical knowledge and processing efficiency work together in a synergistic fashion. As vocabulary grows, so too do the processing skills needed to make fine discriminations among words on the basis of their phonological, morphological and semantic characteristics. It makes sense, therefore, that children with large vocabularies are better able to learn words on a single exposure (Gershkoff-Stowe & Hahn, 2007; see also Chapter 6 for more on so-called *fast mapping*).

Overall, we have observed a tendency for High-SES parents to be relatively talkative. It turns out that they also use more *gestures*, with a concomitant beneficial impact on later child vocabulary learning (Schmidt, 1996; Rowe & Goldin-Meadow, 2009a, 2009b; Hall, Rumney, Holler & Kidd, 2013; Stanfield, Williamson & Özçalişkan, 2014). But why should wealthy, well-educated people chatter and gesticulate so much? The answer is not yet clear, though Rowe (2008) does report that *attitudes* towards child-rearing practices differ according to SES status. High-SES parents hold beliefs that reflect the information on offer from textbooks, experts and paediatricians. Of course, now that you've read this chapter you too can feel perfectly justified, when you next meet a toddler, in jabbering on at ten to the dozen while waving your arms about like a windmill.

Child Directed Speech: Summary

If one was asked to design a language course for infants, one might very well come up with something resembling Child Directed Speech. The numerous modifications on display are, without fail, geared towards simplifying and clarifying the object of learning. As a language course, CDS benefits from confining the syllabus to topics that interest the learner. We might also point to the dynamic nature of CDS, because, like any well-designed course, it presents the child with a graded series of lessons. Or, more subtly, the child elicits from parents the input that meets their language learning needs. This view is expressed by Bohannon & Warren-Leubecker (1985: 194), who observe that, 'since the complexity of speech addressed to children is largely determined by cues from the children themselves ..., one might think of language acquisition in this view as a self-paced lesson'. One thing is certain. The input to the child is not, as assumed by Chomsky (1965), degenerate. At the same time, there is variation in the amount and quality of CDS available, with concomitant effects on the rate of language development. Evidently, Child Directed Speech has a facilitative influence on child language development. But facilitative is not the same as necessary. Many researchers assume that CDS cannot be necessary for language development, because they believe that CDS is not supplied to all children everywhere. We shall consider the validity of this assumption. First, though, we turn our attention to the neglected topic of interaction. CDS does not simply comprise a special set of language forms. Language is presented to the child via particular kinds of interaction, including imitation. We begin, though, by considering what happens when the child has linguistic input, but no interaction, at their disposal.

DISCUSSION POINT 4.1
THE INPUT IN LANGUAGE LEARNING

Consider your own experience of learning a second language.

- What age did you start learning?
- What kind of input and/or teaching did you receive?

- What are the similarities in the input available to both second language learners and toddlers acquiring their first language?
- What are the differences?

Hop back to Chapter 3 to help with the following two questions:

- To what extent can differences in the input explain differences in the outcome of learning, when comparing native first language learning with adult second language learning?
- Did the age at which you started learning have an effect on the outcome?

Lack of interaction: Can children learn language from television?

We can demonstrate the difference between input and interaction by switching on the TV. All of a sudden, the child is exposed to linguistic input, but without the benefit of a conversational partner to interact with. We can therefore investigate language acquisition in the absence of interaction. On the whole, the results are disappointing. It has been found that before the age of two years, children are not capable of learning new words from television (Kuhl, Tsao & Liu, 2003; Mumme & Fernald, 2003; Anderson & Pempek, 2005; Krcmar, Grela & Lin, 2007). And if we compare the power of TV with live interaction, then live interaction is clearly superior. In this vein, Patterson (2002) showed that children aged 21–27 months learned new words from a shared book reading activity, but none at all from TV viewing. Moreover, television has no impact on second language development in young children (Snow, Arlman-Rupp, Hassing, Jobse, Joosten & Vorster, 1976). The limitations of television are especially clear in the case of Jim, a hearing child born to deaf parents (Sachs, Bard & Johnson, 1981). Jim's only exposure to English was via television, which he spent a lot of time watching. By the age of 3;9, Jim's language was not merely delayed, it was distinctly odd:

> This is how plane
> I want that make
> House chimney my house my chimney

Rather like the case of Genie discussed in Chapter 3, Jim was able to learn some words, but very little about how to put words together to form grammatical sentences.

Beyond the age of two years, it *is* possible to learn some vocabulary from TV viewing (Rice & Woodsmall, 1988; Barr & Wyss, 2008). But it depends what you watch. Programmes that are not designed expressly for toddlers have no discernible effect (Rice, Huston, Truglio & Wright, 1990). Even some programmes that *are* designed for young children do not have much impact.

For example, regular viewing of *Teletubbies* from the age of six months is associated with relatively low vocabulary scores at three years of age (Linebarger & Walker, 2005). If you're a *Teletubbies* fan, then you will not be surprised by this. You will probably also have a small vocabulary. *Teletubbies* does not contain very much language and the characters are prone to talk in a rather bizarre, fake kind of 'baby talk'. In contrast, other programmes, including *Dora the Explorer*, *Blue's Clues* and *Dragon Tales*, did have a beneficial effect on vocabulary and expressive language scores (Linebarger & Walker, 2005; cf., Uchikoshi, 2005). In one study, children aged 2;6 learned new words from video only when there was some form of reciprocal social interaction with an adult, either on or off screen (O'Doherty, Troseth, Shimpi, Goldberg, Akhtar & Saylor, 2011). Given an optimal programme style, it is perhaps not surprising that three-year-olds can learn some vocabulary from television. By this age, language acquisition has long since taken off in an exponential fashion, with rapid growth in both vocabulary and syntax (Bates, Dale & Thal, 1995). The child is therefore increasingly well equipped, both cognitively and linguistically, to infer word meanings for themselves, even in the absence of interactive support.

Television is not the only source of non-interactive input that might influence the child. Overheard conversations, radio and song lyrics all expose the child to linguistic information. There is some indication that children as young as 18 months can learn new words that they have overheard being used by adults (Akhtar, 2005; Floor & Akhtar, 2006; Gampe, Liebal & Tomasello, 2012). But as with television, the language acquired is confined to a limited range of vocabulary items, at an age when vocabulary learning has already taken off. Somewhat older children (mean age 27 months) can learn rudimentary aspects of word meaning in the absence of social and observational cues (Arunachalam, 2013). However, the amount of speech overheard by the child does not predict vocabulary size, whereas the amount of speech targeted specifically at them does (Shneidman, Arroyo, Levine & Goldin-Meadow, 2013; Weisleder & Fernald, 2013). Of course, many children grow up in a world where the TV is switched on for hours at a time as a backdrop to daily life, thus exposing them to a large amount of overheard language. However, constant background TV interferes with adult–child interaction, with a negative effect on subsequent vocabulary growth (Masur, Flynn & Olson, 2016).

Chomsky (1959: 42) suggested that 'a child may pick up a large part of his vocabulary and "feel" for sentence structure from television'. But most of Chomsky's early assertions about language acquisition are the result of armchair speculation, not empirical enquiry. And most of them, like this one, are wrong. In the nativist approach, the role of the linguistic environment is reduced to a matter of simple and limited exposure to key linguistic forms. The assumption is that limited exposure of this kind will suffice to trigger language acquisition (Lightfoot, 1989, see also Chapter 8). In principle, therefore, the nativist might be content to leave the child, unaccompanied, in front of the TV screen. But as any guilty parent knows, if the child must watch TV, it is better that someone watch with them (Naigles & Mayeux, 2000; Masur & Flynn, 2008). In essence, parents should consider TV viewing in the same way as shared book reading – as an opportunity to interact with the child and provide the framework for extending the child's current state of linguistic knowledge (Vygotsky, 1934/1962; Cameron-Faulkner & Noble, 2013). Left alone, with no more than exposure to linguistic forms, the child cannot acquire syntax. Interaction is essential.

Imitation

We started out this chapter on the Clapham Omnibus, where we heard the common sense view that children learn language from their parents. Even if we accept this view, we still need to know *how* children learn from parental input. To the man on the bus, and many like him, the answer is, once again, entirely obvious: children learn language by imitating their parents. Surprisingly, though, researchers have largely ignored imitation as a serious factor in child language acquisition. Relatively little research effort has been devoted to the issue. Moreover, imitation rarely figures in theoretical debates and does not even feature as an index topic in several recent books in the field (e.g., Cattell, 2000; Karmiloff & Karmiloff-Smith, 2001; Clark, 2003; Hoff & Shatz, 2007). It was not always thus. Imitation of language is mentioned several times by Tiedemann (1787) (see Appendix 1). Tiedemann observed a child of six months and noted that 'his mother said to him the syllable "Ma"; he gazed attentively at her mouth, and attempted to imitate the syllable' (see Murchison & Langer, 1927: 218). Incidentally, infants who are good at observing the mother's mouth (and following her gaze) acquire vocabulary with particular alacrity (Tenenbaum, Sobel, Sheinkopf, Malle & Morgan, 2015).

In this section, we shall demonstrate that imitation, as a special form of interaction between parent and child, is fundamentally important in the study of language acquisition. But before we get started, a note on terminology: I will mostly use the term *imitation* in this section, but when you access the child language literature directly, you will find that *repetition* is often preferred (e.g., Gathercole, 2006; Clark & Bernicot, 2008). The points to be made are not substantively affected in the alternation between these two terms. Repetition can be seen as a particular kind of imitation, one that is often associated with language.

Linguistic creativity: Children make their own sentences

As mentioned, imitation is often downplayed in theories of language acquisition because the child possesses *linguistic creativity*. As speakers of a language, we create genuinely novel sentences all the time, putting words together in sequences that have not been uttered before and which may never occur again. We can do this because grammar allows for infinity in the number of different sentences we can put together, even though the system of grammatical rules is itself finite (von Humboldt, 1836/1988; Chomsky, 1965). Two consequences follow from this observation that have a direct bearing on imitation: (1) it is logically impossible to imitate an infinite number of sentences; and (2) we could not rely on imitation as the source for producing our own sentences. Think how odd it would be to sit around waiting for someone to say a sentence, so that you, as a learner, got an opportunity to use it for yourself, through imitation. You might literally have to wait forever for the right sentence to come along. Not much fun if the sentence is: *Can you tell me where the toilet is, please?* Even if the child were adept at imitating each and every sentence they heard, it would not provide the information needed, in and of itself, to construct new sentences for themselves. In other words, the child cannot imitate grammar (the rules), only the output from those rules (sentences). We will expand on this point in Chapter 8. For now, we can confirm that imitation of sentences does not provide a feasible route into the acquisition of syntax.

Skinner and Chomsky on imitation

It is often wrongly assumed that Chomsky (1959) dismissed imitation as part of his campaign against the behaviourist approach to language acquisition. Chomsky (1959) provides a book review of *Verbal Behavior* (1957), written by B.F. Skinner, the doyen of twentieth-century behaviourism. Ironically, this book review has been far more widely read than the actual book, in which Skinner argued that child efforts to speak are rewarded by parents. Skinner based his position on a form of learning studied extensively by behaviourists, termed *operant conditioning*. Each time the child produces an utterance that comes close to sounding like an acceptable word or sentence, the parent offers a 'reward' in the form of praise or encouragement. On successive occasions, closer approximations to the adult model receive yet further parental rewards. Thus, operant conditioning relies on the learner producing a linguistic behaviour that is progressively shaped through rewards, until the desired behaviour is achieved. Punishments can also be used to 'dissuade' the learner, when behaviours veer away from the desired learning outcome. Operant conditioning is very different from imitation. In fact, Skinner had very little to say on the subject of imitation, other than to reject the idea that humans have an instinct to imitate. Instead, he preferred the phrase *echoic behaviour*, whereby a 'response generates a sound-pattern similar to that of the stimulus. For example, upon hearing the sound Beaver, the speaker says Beaver' (Skinner, 1957: 55). Skinner does not call this behaviour imitation, on the grounds that there is 'no similarity between a pattern of sounds and the muscular responses which produce a similar pattern' (ibid.: 59). This is an astute point, although it does no violence to standard definitions of imitation. For most people, Skinner's 'beaver' example *is* a case of imitation.

The champion of imitation in the Skinner–Chomsky exchange was Chomsky (1959: 42), who insisted that 'children acquire a good deal of their verbal and nonverbal behavior by casual observation and imitation of adults and other children'. Elsewhere, Chomsky talks about children's 'strong tendency to imitate' (ibid.: 43) and castigates Skinner for rejecting the 'innate faculty or tendency to imitate' (ibid.: ff51). Unfortunately, this clear position has been completely reversed in the re-telling. Some recent authors now suggest that it was Chomsky (not Skinner) who rejected imitation as a significant factor (for example, Cattell, 2000; DeHart, Sroufe & Cooper, 2000; Stilwell-Peccei, 2006). In this vein, Owens (2008: 33) asserts that 'an overall imitative language acquisition strategy would be of little value, according to Chomsky (1957), because adult speech provides a very poor model'. This not only misrepresents Chomsky on imitation, it gets the date wrong (there is nothing at all on imitation in Chomsky, 1957). Alarm bells should ring for students at this point: read the original sources for yourself, if you possibly can. None of this would matter, perhaps, if our initial critique of imitation, *vis-à-vis* linguistic creativity, was the last word on the subject. Arguably, though, there is more to say and far more to learn about the function of imitation in language acquisition.

Imitation as a mechanism in cognitive development

The definition of imitation is less straightforward than it might seem. A simple definition might be: *the reproduction of another person's behaviour*. In the context of language, this could mean that, if you first say something, I would repeat it back verbatim. But no matter how good a mimic I am, I will not be able to reproduce precisely your accent, your voice quality, the emotions conveyed in your tone of voice, the speed and rhythms of production, nor the fine-grained acoustic detail in the way each word and phrase is articulated. If you nevertheless recognize that I am imitating you successfully, then that recognition must derive from some abstraction of properties common to your model and my response. Furthermore, this abstraction requires the integration of information from different sensory modalities. As Skinner (1957) observed, the act of producing a burst of speech sound is very different from the act of listening to it, prior to attempting one's own production. Cross-modal co-ordination is therefore required to bridge the gulf between perception and performance (Meltzoff, 2002).

The act of imitation is complex. But these complexities are overcome, to some extent, because the ability to imitate may well be inborn. Infants can imitate adult tongue protrusion within minutes of birth (Meltzoff & Moore, 1983). Within the first week, they can even imitate an adult who raises either one or two fingers (Nagy, Pal, & Orvos, 2014). This ability is all the more remarkable because the newborn infant has not yet seen their own face (Meltzoff & Moore, 1997). In other ways, too, infants have been described as 'prolific imitators' (Marshall & Meltzoff, 2014). The genetic basis of imitation has been challenged recently (Cook, Bird, Catmur, Press & Heyes, 2014). But none deny that the primate brain possesses a dedicated functional capacity for imitation, operating via so-called *mirror neurons*. Research on monkeys shows that these special neurons (in the premotor cortex) discharge both when an action is observed and also when it is performed (Gallese, Fadiga, Fogassi & Rizzolatti, 1996). In monkeys, the sight of another monkey grasping, placing or manipulating an object will cause mirror neurons to fire. Mirror neuron activity is associated with the monkey's own motor response, which often constitutes an imitation. Mirror neurons therefore form a link between an observer and an actor. Mirror neurons have also been discovered in the human brain. At one point, it was believed that mirror neurons could be detected in Broca's area (Rizzolatti & Arbib, 1998), an area in the left hemisphere long known for its importance in the motor planning of speech and probably also in the processing of syntax (Obler & Gjerlow, 1999). However, more recent studies locate the human mirror neuron system more accurately in a region known as *premotor BA6* (a catchy name, I think you'll agree) (Cerri et al., 2015). Whatever the precise location of mirror neurons, their existence points to the intrinsic importance of imitation in human behaviour.

Imitation: Who, when and how?

In the study of imitation, three factors demand attention: (1) the actors: who is imitating whom? (2) the time lag: how long is the delay between model and imitation? and (3) precision: how closely does the imitation match the model? With regard to the actors, imitation can work both ways. The child can imitate the adult, but equally well, the adult can (and does) imitate the child (Olson & Masur, 2012). We will consider one form of adult imitative behaviour in our discussion of corrective input, below. The second factor to consider concerns the time lag between presentation of a model and its subsequent imitation. Imitation can be either immediate or deferred (Stern, 1924). It is easy to establish that an imitation has occurred when it is immediate. But imitation may also be deferred until quite some time after presentation of the model (Meltzoff, 1988). In this case, researchers need to be more resourceful in confirming that a given behaviour does indeed constitute imitation. Perhaps for this reason, child language research on deferred imitation is limited. But there is some evidence that children can imitate utterances first presented several hours or even days earlier (Clark, 1977; Moerk & Moerk, 1979; Snow, 1981). Logically, of course, every time a child uses a new word for the first time, in the immediate absence of a parental model, we witness a case of deferred imitation. The child must have heard each word spoken by a parent at some point previously. Imitation must therefore play an important role in lexical development.

A third factor that has proven important is the fidelity of the imitation to the original model. As noted above, it is pretty much impossible to imitate someone else's verbal behaviour precisely. Nevertheless, most researchers would describe an imitation as 'exact' if the same words are reproduced in the same order. It turns out that this kind of verbatim repetition is rare, accounting for no more than 10 per cent of the child's imitative behaviour (Snow, 1981). It is far more common for the child to incorporate just part of an adult utterance into their own response, which may also embody further additions, reductions or modifications. Strictly speaking, therefore, the child imitates selectively, as shown in the following examples from Nathaniel aged 2;3–2;7 (Snow, 1981):

Mother: *A Dutch house.*
Nathaniel: *Nathaniel Dutch house.*

Mother: *What's this?*
Nathaniel: *What's this a boat.*

Mother: *The pigs are taking a bath.*
Nathaniel: *Taking a bath and make juice.*

Mother: *You like jingle bells.*
Nathaniel: *Like other jingle bells.*

Imitations of various kinds are frequent in adult–child conversation. Clark and Bernicot (2008) analysed nine hours of data from 41 French children and report that both children and adults are very repetitive, with adults having a slight edge on their children (Table 4.2).

Adults also repeat *themselves* a great deal, tending to rely on a restricted repertoire of verbal routines of the form: *Look at NP*, *Here's NP* and *Let's play with NP* (where NP stands for **noun phrase** like *the dog* or *Auntie Mary*). These routines are used to introduce new information, with the noun in the noun phrase often being produced with exaggerated intonation and heavy stress (Broen, 1972). New information appears sentence-finally 75 per cent of the time in CDS, as against 53 per cent for ADS (Fernald & Mazzie, 1991). This is significant, because new information is more exposed in sentence-final position (Slobin, 1973), and young children respond more accurately to new information presented in this way (Shady & Gerken, 1999).

Table 4.2 Rates of repetition by mother and child reported by Clark & Bernicot (2008)

	Repetition rate (per minute)	
Mean age	Mother imitates child	Child imitates mother
2;3	1.21	0.51
3;6	1.45	0.43

Individual differences in imitation

Research is beginning to show that our ability to imitate varies and, moreover, that imitation ability has an impact on language development. This topic has been investigated as part of the Twins Early Development Study in the UK (McEwen, Happé, Bolton, Rijsdijk, Ronald, Dworzynski & Plomin, 2007). McEwen et al. (2007) examined more than 5,000 twins for their ability to imitate non-verbal behaviours like gestures and facial movements. They found that good non-verbal imitators had higher vocabulary scores. This finding is intriguing because the link is between *non*-verbal imitation and language development. McEwen et al. (2007) also used their twin sample to examine the genetic basis of imitation. By comparing identical twins with non-identical twins, they could estimate the **heritability** of imitative capacity (Plomin, 1990). They found that 30 per cent of the variance in imitative skill could be attributed to genetic factors. This is a fairly modest figure and means that environmental factors play an important role in distinguishing between good and poor imitators. It remains for future research to determine more precisely how the child's upbringing affects their capacity to imitate. Perhaps some parents encourage this kind of behaviour through their own example, by providing high levels of imitations themselves.

Individual differences also exist in *verbal* imitative ability (Bloom, Hood & Lightbown, 1974). An important measure of these differences is the *nonword repetition task* (Gathercole, 2006). Children are presented verbally with a series of nonsense words, like *prindle, frescovent* and *stopograttic*, and are asked to repeat each one back to the experimenter. The ability to imitate (or, as the authors prefer, repeat) these words is highly correlated with children's vocabulary level at four, five and six years (Gathercole, Willis, Emslie & Baddeley, 1992; Hoff, Core & Bridges, 2008). Good nonword repetition skills are also found in children who produce relatively long, syntactically complex utterances (Adams & Gathercole, 2000). At the other end of the spectrum, children with serious language impairments do very poorly at repeating back to another person polysyllabic nonwords (Bishop, Adams & Norbury, 2006). The nonword repetition task is generally discussed within the context of individual differences in working memory capacity (Archibald & Gathercole, 2007). But performance on this task also relies on the child's imitative capacity. It is possible, then, that imitative skill is partly constrained by working memory capacity.

Masur & Olson (2008) provide another example of how individual differences in imitative ability have an impact on child language development. These authors examined imitation of both verbal and non-verbal behaviours, by mothers and children. In a longitudinal design, children were tested at four different points between the ages of 10 and 21 months. Mothers imitate their infants' behaviours and infants demonstrate an increasing responsiveness to, and awareness of, being imitated. In response to being imitated by an adult, the child may repeat the imitation back, in return. Thirteen-month-olds who engaged more in this chain of imitation were more lexically advanced at 21 months. And generally speaking, infants who were most responsive to maternal imitations at 10 months were also those children with more advanced vocabularies at 17 and 21 months (see also Olson & Masur, 2015). In a similar vein, verb learning was enhanced in children aged 30 and 36 months when they actively imitated the action associated with a verb, rather than just passively observed it being performed (Gampe, Brauer & Daum, 2016).

Another source of individual differences in imitation is the *motivation* of the child to engage with other people. Imitation is a fundamentally social behaviour, one that assumes a strong impulse to interact with other people. But this impulse is weaker among certain individuals, including those with autism. Of interest, children with autism do not perform well on non-verbal imitation tasks (Vivanti, Nadig, Ozonoff & Rogers, 2008). In fact, these children *can* copy another person's behaviour, but their motivation to do so seems to be depressed by a relative lack of interest in the goals and intentions of other people. Even within this population, though, there is considerable variation in the rate at which children imitate other people. Significantly, among children with autism, the ability to imitate simple sounds at the age of three years predicts general spoken language ability at the age of five years (Thurm, Lord, Lee & Newschaffer, 2007). Good imitators turn out to be good talkers.

Generally speaking, we see that individual differences in imitative behaviour, both verbal and non-verbal, have an impact on language development. But despite individual differences, we have also seen that imitation is a fundamental human capacity. It has a partly genetic basis and exploits a dedicated neurological resource in mirror neurons. With regard to language acquisition, we have argued that it deserves our close attention, as a critical form of interaction between adult and child. In the next section, we will focus on imitation of the child by the adult and consider how it might influence language acquisition. In particular, we consider its potential as a form of correction for child grammatical errors.

Corrective input

We begin this section by describing a special form of adult imitation, the recast. In what follows, we zoom in on one particular kind of adult recast that might function as a form of corrective input for child grammatical errors. More broadly, we consider the significance of findings on corrective input for theories of child language acquisition.

Recasts: Adult repetition of the child

Adult imitation of child speech is often embellished in one way or another. In fact, repetitions with minor variations to the original utterance are the hallmark of adult–child discourse. This kind of adult imitation is often referred to as a *recast*, and was first studied by Roger Brown and his students (Brown & Bellugi, 1964; Cazden, 1965). The following examples are from Brown (1973):

Eve:	*Eve get big stool.*
Mother:	*No, that's the little stool.*
Eve:	*Milk in there.*
Mother:	*There is milk in there.*
Eve:	*Turn after Sarah.*
Mother:	*You have a turn after Sarah.*

Recasts fall out naturally from conversation with a two-year-old. It is unlikely that adults consciously recast child speech, but they do it a lot (see below). The prime function of recasts is to maintain the flow of conversation with a partner who is cognitively and linguistically immature. This is achieved, in part, by reproducing some or all of the child's own words and structures. In so doing, the adult increases the chance of being understood by the child. And, of course, the conversation topic is of interest and relevance to the child, since it follows the child's lead. In essence, the adult adopts the linguistic framework supplied by the child, so any additions or changes they introduce will place the minimum burden on the child's processing and memory resources. In consequence, it is likely that any new or unfamiliar language will be more readily assimilated by the child. In this vein, studies with adults have shown that grammatical forms that have just been used by another speaker are more easily accessed and produced (for example, Kaschak, Loney & Borreggine, 2006). The value of recasts has been established in numerous studies that demonstrate their association with language growth, in both typically and atypically developing children (for example, Seitz & Stewart, 1975; Nelson, Denninger, Bonvillian, Kaplan & Baker, 1984; Hoff-Ginsberg, 1985; Forrest & Elbert 2001; Eadie, Fey, Douglas & Parsons, 2002; Swensen, Naigles & Fein, 2007). Recasts are one sign that adults are being responsive in conversation with children, and parental responsiveness in general is closely linked with language development (Tamis-LeMonda, Kuchirko & Song, 2014).

The 'no negative evidence' assumption

All language learners make errors. In fact, errors are the hallmark of language development. They demonstrate that a recognized, mature end-state has not yet been reached. From about the age of 15 months, when the child begins to put two or more words together in multi-word utterances, very little of the child's output looks adult-like in its grammatical form:

Eve aged 1;6 (Brown, 1973):

> more cookie
> Mommy read
> Fraser water?
> that radio (following the mother's question: *What is that?*)
> dollie celery

All typical children produce errors. But eventually, and just as surely, children retreat from error as they acquire an adult-like, mature knowledge of grammar. The problem, then, is to explain how errors are expunged. The most obvious answer, explored below, is that parents correct their children's errors. But many child language researchers reject this suggestion. Nativists, in particular, have argued that the child receives no help from the linguistic environment in eradicating errors (for example, Weissenborn, Goodluck & Roeper, 1992). In nativist terms, the child receives 'no **negative evidence**', that is, no information about what is, and is not, grammatical. Adherence to this assumption has a radical effect on one's view of the task that faces the language-learning child. If there is no guidance in the input on grammaticality, how does the child acquire this knowledge? The nativist answer is that this knowledge must be innate and will, at some point in development, come to the child's rescue (see Chapter 8). Many non-nativists have also expressed support for the 'no negative evidence' assumption (Ambridge, Pine, Rowland & Young, 2008). These researchers rely on the child's general learning mechanisms to explain how children retreat from error (see Chapter 9). In this section, though, we will argue that the 'no negative evidence' assumption is unfounded. There is evidence that parents *do* correct their children's grammatical errors.

We begin our review of the evidence by returning to the adult recast. Brown & Hanlon (1970: 197) were the first to recognize the corrective potential of adult recasts with their observation that 'repeats of ill-formed utterances usually contained corrections and so could be instructive.'

Eve aged 1;6 (Brown, 1973)

Eve: *Want lunch.*

Mother: *Oh you want lunch then.*

Eve: *Mommy gone.*

Mother: *Mommy's gone.*

Eve: *Fraser coffee.*

Mother: *Fraser's coffee.*

Brown & Hanlon's suggestion concerning the corrective potential of recasts has been ignored for many years. Instead, the focus has been on a different kind of adult response, also investigated by Brown & Hanlon (1970), which they call a Disapproval. Behaviourist in inspiration, it was thought that Disapprovals might function as a form of corrective input. The idea was that parents might explicitly signal their displeasure with ungrammatical child sentences with injunctions like *no, that's wrong*, or *don't say that*. But it turned out that Disapprovals were not contingent on child grammatical errors. Instead, Disapprovals were contingent on the *meaning* of child speech (*No, that's a purple sweater, not a blue one*). The influence of Brown & Hanlon's study has been extensive. Researchers continue to cite the evidence on Disapprovals as evidence that parents do not correct child errors (Tomasello, 2003). But there is more than one way to provide corrective input. Disapprovals are just one possibility, a rather implausible one at that. Far more promising are the special recasts – 'repetitions with corrections' – that Brown & Hanlon (1970) observed, but unfortunately neglected. Attempts to revive interest, beginning with Hirsh-Pasek, Treiman & Schneiderman (1984), have not been universally welcomed (Tomasello, 2009). But we shall give them more leeway than is typical in what follows.

Contrastive discourse

Look again at the three exchanges between Eve and her mother, above. In each case, Eve's utterance is ungrammatical. And in each case, Eve's mother provides grammatical versions of the erroneous elements in Eve's speech. As you can see, the adult response, in each case, is a particular kind of recast. Recall that recasts preserve some of the child's original words, but changes are also introduced. The adult 'expands, deletes, permutes, or otherwise changes the … [child utterance] while maintaining significant overlap in meaning' (Bohannon, Padgett, Nelson & Mark, 1996: 551). Hence, recasts can take many forms. When it comes to corrective input, though, we are interested only in those recasts where the change constitutes the provision of a correct form directly following a child error. It is possible that this kind of recast counts as a form of negative evidence for the child. Negative evidence is a topic that I have investigated myself. The following examples come from a diary study I conducted with my son Alex, when he was four-years-old (Saxton, 1995):

| Alex: | I had all my breakfast and I **drinked** up all the milk |
| Matthew: | You **drank** the whole bowl? |

| Alex: | Listen to me! I was **talked** first |
| Matthew: | You weren't **talking** first! |

| Alex: | I'm **easy to eat** you up. |
| Matthew: | You can **eat** me up **easily**? |

| Alex: | All **by her own**. All **by her own**. All **by her own**. |
| Matthew: | All **by herself**? |

Incidentally, **bold** has been used to highlight errors and correct alternatives. It does not indicate stress, which may well lie elsewhere. To explain how the child might identify the corrective potential in these responses, I formulated the so-called *direct contrast hypothesis* (Saxton, 1997). The prediction is that the correct adult form is especially conspicuous when it directly follows a child error. In the first example above, Alex uses *drinked*, but I counter this directly with the correct version, *drank*. The contrast between the two forms is therefore especially noticeable. It is predicted that the child will recognize their own selection (in this case, *drinked*) as erroneous, and furthermore, will recognize that the adult alternative (*drank*) constitutes the appropriate form.

It has been discovered that contrastive discourse of this kind is very common. In one study, as many as 65 per cent of all child errors met with this kind of correction (Chouinard & Clark, 2003). A large number of other studies also report high levels of contrastive discourse (for example, Hirsh-Pasek et al., 1984; Demetras, Post & Snow, 1986; Penner, 1987; Bohannon & Stanowicz, 1988; Morgan & Travis, 1989; Moerk, 1991; Farrar, 1992; Furrow, Baillie, McLaren & Moore, 1993; Post, 1994; Morgan, Bonamo & Travis, 1995; Strapp, 1999; Strapp & Federico, 2000; Saxton, Backley & Gallaway, 2005). This high prevalence is perhaps not surprising. Young children produce numerous errors, whereas adults do not. The chances are therefore high that errors and their correct counterparts will often be found sitting side-by-side in adult–child conversation.

It is one thing to show that negative evidence is supplied to the child. We also need to determine whether it works. That is, do children pick up on the corrective information on offer, and use it to modify their own developing grammars? If corrective recasts really do function as a form of negative evidence, the child should respond to them by adopting the correct forms offered by the adult. There is evidence that children can, in fact, do this. Some more examples from Alex:

Alex (aged 4;1–4;9)

Alex:	*It's even **gooder** than anything.*
	*It's **gooder**, isn't it?*
Matthew:	*Yes, it is **better**.*
Alex:	***Better**, yeah.*

Matthew:	*What did he do?*
Alex:	*He wiped **him**.*
Matthew:	*He wiped **himself**.*
Alex:	*Yes, he wiped **himself**.*

Alex:	*He's got **little nice** feet.*
Matthew:	*Oh, he has got **nice little** feet.*
Alex:	*Yes, he's got **nice little** toes.*

Alex:	*It's **bored** of being on the bike.*
Matthew:	*It's not **boring**.*
Alex:	*Yes, it's **boring** on the bike.*

Alex:	*That's what happens to Tarzan Dog. He **gets falled over** by Tarzan Man.*
Matthew:	*I **make him fall over**, do I?*
Alex:	*What?*
Matthew:	*I **make him fall over**, do I?*
Alex:	*Yes, you **make Tarzan Dog fall over** with your sword.*

If you have ambitions to be a child language researcher, then it helps to breed your own source of data. Thanks, Alex. We can see in these examples that Alex is sensitive to the linguistic form (not just the meaning) of my utterance. He is capable, on some occasions at least, of switching, from his own erroneous uses to the ones offered by me, in the form of a direct contrast. Experiments and studies using naturalistic conversational data confirm that children are responsive to this kind of correction (Saxton, 1997; Saxton, Kulcsar, Marshall & Rupra, 1998; Saxton, 2000; Strapp, Bleakney, Helmick & Tonkovich, 2008; Laakso & Soininen, 2010; Holtheuer & Rendle-Short, 2013; see also Box 4.2). It has also been shown that the child's immediate responsiveness to negative evidence is not ephemeral: the beneficial effects on the child's grammar can be observed, in some cases, several weeks later (Saxton et al., 1998). In other cases, effects are apparent for some structures, but not for others (Saxton, Houston-Price & Dawson, 2005). Teasing apart the effects of one kind of adult response from all other sources of input influence is no easy matter, empirically. What evidence we have, though, is broadly supportive of the idea that negative evidence can facilitate the acquisition of more adult-like states of grammatical knowledge.

BOX 4.2   NOVEL WORDS (SAXTON, 1997)

The beauty of novel words is that one knows exactly how many times children have heard them and in what context. The novel words in the study described here are **irregular past tense verbs** (Saxton, 1997). Children are first taught the present tense of verbs like *streep* and *pell*. It is important to give children lots of practice at recognizing the new words and getting their tongues round them in different forms (*pell, pells, pelling*). A schedule of multiple training sessions – little and often – works well. The characters shown here were modelled on glove puppets that the children used to act out the verbs.

   The next stage was to elicit a past tense form from the child. This was done by showing a video featuring the familiar puppet characters. A dragon is shown asleep under a tree, snoring loudly. To stop him snoring, one of the characters suggests they sneak up on the dragon and wake him by performing one of the actions. The poor dragon wakes up, roaring loudly, at which point the video is paused and the child is asked: *What happened?* One has thus created a past tense context. The child has never heard the past tense form of these verbs, so they have no choice but to treat the verbs as regular: *He pelled his nose.* But little do they know: these are irregular verbs. We have not only induced a past tense form, but an error also.

(Continued)

sty / stought

prodding action performed with a plastic concertina that makes a honking noise (cf., *buy / bought*)

streep / strept

ejection of a ping pong ball from a cone-shaped launcher towards a target (cf., *creep / crept*)

pell / pold

a beanbag on the end of a string is swung like a bolas at the target (cf., *sell / sold*)

pro / prew

twisting motion applied with a cross-ended stick (cf., *throw/ threw*)

jing / jang

a beanbag is catapulted from a spoon at a target (cf., *sing / sang*)

neak / noke

repeated clapping motion in which target is trapped between the palms (cf., *speak / spoke*)

(Continued)

This means that the child can be corrected:

Child: He *pelled* his nose.

Adult: Oh yes, he *pold* his nose.

Alternatively, the correct irregular past tense form can be modelled as soon as the video is paused, before the child has had a chance to make an error: *Oh look! He pold his nose.* In both cases, the adult models the correct past tense form. The difference is simply that in one condition only, the correct model is supplied in a contrastive way, directly following a child error. If direct contrasts do indeed function as a form of correction for the child, then they should be more likely to reject their own, erroneous version in favour of the correct adult version. And this is precisely what was found.

Note that each novel word sounds like a genuine word (they are phonologically plausible). And the meaning of each verb is also novel. This prevents any form of competition with meanings that already exist in the child's repertoire. Novel words have a long history in child language research (Berko, 1958). As noted, control over the input is their chief virtue. A major limitation is that it is usually only possible to expose children just a handful of times to novel words. Practical considerations prevent children being exposed hundreds (or even thousands) of times, as with many real words. Nevertheless, novel words continue to be a valuable tool in the armoury of child language researchers.

Negative feedback

Another form of corrective input can also be identified, which I term *negative feedback* (to distinguish it from *negative evidence*).

Alex (aged 4;1–4;9)

Alex: *Knights have **horse**, they do.*
Matthew: *They what?*

Alex: *He **slided** down the door.*
Matthew: *He what?*

Alex: *Ouch! It **hurted**.*
Matthew: *Eh?*

Negative feedback is provided when adults seek to clarify what the child has said, following a grammatical error. My responses here can be classified in each case as an error-contingent clarification question (CQ). CQs feature as a significant part of conversation, accounting for something like 5 per cent of all turns in adult–adult discourse (Purver, Ginzburg & Healey, 2001). We constantly need to check on each other's meaning, but my suggestion is that, incidentally, they may help the child check on the syntactic form of their speech. That is, error-contingent clarification questions may function as a form of negative feedback. Children as young as 12 months old respond appropriately to clarification questions, by returning to their original utterance and either repeating or repairing it in some way (Golinkoff, 1986). There is some evidence also that children correct themselves, following the intervention of an error-contingent CQ. They switch from erroneous to correct forms for a wide range of grammatical errors, when supplied with negative feedback (Saxton, 2000; Saxton et al., 2005). If we think about how negative feedback works, then it is quickly apparent that it provides a weaker form of corrective information than negative evidence. This is because the adult provides no correct alternative to the child error. The *prompt hypothesis* predicts that negative feedback provides a cue for the child that, essentially, jogs their memory about language forms they have already learned. Overall, we see that parents provide at least two kinds of corrective signal, both negative evidence and negative feedback.

Corrective input: Summary

The problem of explaining how children overcome their language errors must be addressed in all approaches to language acquisition. Corrective input provides the most straightforward solution to this problem. And the evidence is now quite compelling that parents not only correct grammatical errors, but that children respond accordingly. We know this from a recent meta-analysis conducted by researchers with an interest in therapeutic interventions for children with language delays (Cleave, Becker, Curran, Van Horne & Fey, 2015). In essence, meta-analyses provide a statistical method for throwing the data of numerous studies into a big metaphorical pot to determine, overall, the fundamental trends in the findings. This kind of analysis is especially useful for investigating controversial topics, where conflicting evidence arises over the years. Cleave et al. (2015) deduce that error-contingent recasts are indeed a valuable source of learning for the child. Even so, many researchers continue to adhere to the 'no negative evidence' assumption. For example, a devout non-nativist, Tomasello (2009: 82) remarks that 'adults do not explicitly correct child utterances with any frequency'. But the basis for this assertion is limited to the behaviourist-inspired notion of Disapproval reported by Brown & Hanlon 40 years ago. When I published the first edition of this book, Tomasello was one of many non-nativists who espoused the view that negative evidence is either not available to the child or of little practical use. Since then, though, the ground has begun to shift. For example, Ambridge (2013: 510) explicitly accepts that negative evidence 'likely plays an important role in children's learning'. Ironically, one researcher who has long supported the idea of parental corrections is Chomsky:

> certain signals [child sentences] might be accepted as properly formed sentences, while others are classed as nonsentences, as a result of correction of the learner's attempts on the part of the linguistic community. (Chomsky, 1965: 31)

As with imitation, it is widely – but wrongly – assumed that Chomsky rejected the notion of corrective feedback (e.g., Brooks & Kempe, 2012). But before we get too enthusiastic, it is unlikely that corrective input is either necessary or sufficient to guarantee the successful acquisition of grammar. Other mechanisms are undoubtedly at work. The 'no negative evidence' assumption has created an abiding puzzle, and hence, an abiding prompt to theorizing. It has encouraged the exploration of multiple solutions to the same learning problem, some or all of which may be available to the child (cf., Golinkoff & Hirsh-Pasek, 2008). We shall consider some of these proposals in Chapters 7, 8 and 9. The more suggestions we have to consider, the more likely it is that we shall discover how the child succeeds in acquiring an adult sense of grammaticality.

Universality of CDS

While linguistic input is clearly necessary for language learning, it is less obvious whether Child Directed Speech is necessary. It is conceivable that the many fine adjustments and simplifications typical of CDS are simply icing on the cake: a welcome addition, that may *facilitate* language development, but which are not in any way necessary. To test this idea, all we need to do is find a single child who has been deprived of this special input, but who has nevertheless acquired language normally. In fact, it is widely assumed that many children *are* so deprived. Pinker (1994: 40) asserts that 'in many communities of the world, parents do not indulge their children in Motherese'. He further adds that 'the belief that Motherese is essential to language development is part of the same mentality that sends yuppies to "learning centers" to buy little mittens with bull's-eyes to help their babies find their hands sooner' (ibid.: 40). In fact, Pinker is setting up a straw man here, since no-one, to my knowledge, has argued that CDS is *necessary*, rather than simply facilitative. More to the point, when we look at the empirical evidence, Pinker's assertion is not supported. What evidence we possess indicates that children around the world *are* exposed to at least some of the characteristic features of Child Directed Speech.

A limited number of studies are continually cited in defence of the idea that CDS is not universally available (see Saxton, 2009). We will focus on the best known example, the African-American community of Trackton in South Carolina studied by Heath (1983). The Trackton adults studied by Heath were dumbfounded by the idea that parents should modify their speech when talking to infants:

> Now just how crazy is dat? White folks uh hear dey kids say sump'n, dey say it back to 'em, dey aks 'em 'gain 'n' 'gain 'bout things, like they 'posed to be born knowin'. You think I kin tell Teegie all he gotta know? Ain't no use me tellin' him: learn dis, learn dat. What's dis? What's dat? He just gotta learn, gotta know. (Heath, 1983: 84)

Heath (ibid.: 7) is the first to acknowledge that she is not a psychologist. And this is important because what we have here is an informant who is not the main caregiver of the child and who is reporting on her *beliefs* about child rearing. What her actual practices are remain unclear. In fact, there is a marked contrast between what people *say* they do in talking to children and what they *actually* do. Haggan (2002) conducted interviews with 82 Kuwaiti adults and discovered that 18 of them were adamant that they made no concessions when talking to children. Some even suggested that the use of 'special ways' to communicate would be detrimental to language development (ibid.: 22). Haggan then observed each of these 'CDS sceptics' interacting with a child aged 2–3 years. She found that every single one of these sceptics modified their speech in ways entirely typical of Child Directed Speech. These include the use of short, semantically simple sentences, concrete referents based on the child's own interests and extensive repetitions. Had Haggan stopped her study at the interview stage, she would have been left with a fundamentally mistaken view of how Kuwaiti adults interact with their young children. In a similar vein, Birjandi & Nasrolahi (2012) report that, in the Iranian city of Babol, parents generally deny correcting their children's errors. Nevertheless, a majority of parents do, in fact, supply negative evidence.

As it happens, there is a strong indication that the parents in Trackton do use elements of CDS in their talk with young children. For example, 'when adults do not understand what point the young child is trying to make, they often repeat the last portion – or what is usually the predicate verb phrase – of the child's statement' (Heath, 1983: 93). This kind of interaction sounds remarkably like the recasts described above. More research of a less anthropological flavour, with a stronger psychological bite, would be welcome here. But it is apparent that key pieces of evidence from Heath's study have been overlooked. Instead, much attention has been paid to Heath's observation that 'during the first six months or so, and sometimes throughout the entire first year, babies are not addressed directly by adults' (ibid.: 77). This is a dramatic assertion. Why would parents not talk to their babies? It is suggested that 'for an adult to choose a preverbal infant over an adult as a conversational partner would be considered an affront and a strange behavior as well' (ibid.: 86; cf., Pye, 1986). Again, though, what we need is some hard evidence on what Trackton parents actually do, both in private and in public. What we do know for certain is that parents and others must, and indeed do, start talking to the child at some point. We also know that parents are not the only source of CDS. Children as young as 4;0 modify their speech when talking to toddlers (Shatz & Gelman, 1973; Weppelman, Bostow, Schiffer, Elbert-Perez & Newman, 2003). In Trackton, there is evidence that older children may supply specially modified input for their younger siblings and peers (Heath, 1983: 93).

Every possible feature of CDS does not appear in the speech of every parent throughout the world (Pye, 1986; Lieven, 1994). More likely, there is a 'smorgasbord effect'. The speech of parents in different cultures will express different combinations of CDS features, 'selected' from the full menu. Cross-cultural research does reveal the widespread occurrence of one important CDS feature: the practice of repeating child speech back to them in one form or another. Repetitions, elicited repetitions and recasts have been recorded in the adult input in a wide range of languages. Thus, Mead (1930: 35) remarks of the Manus people of New Guinea that the adult's 'random affection for repetitiousness makes an excellent atmosphere in which the child acquires facility in speech'. In a Danish context, Jespersen (1922: 142) made a similar observation: 'understanding of language is made easier by the habit that mothers and nurses have of repeating the same phrases with slight alterations'. In addition to Manus and Danish, speakers of many other languages provide recasts for their children, including French (Chouinard & Clark, 2003), K'iche'

113

Maya from Guatemala (Pye, 1986), Hebrew (Berman, 1985), Mandarin (Erbaugh, 1992), Persian (Birjandi & Nasrolahi, 2012), Japanese (Clancy, 1985), Korean (Clancy, 1989), Samoan (Ochs, 1982), and Warlpiri from Australia (Bavin, 1992). And, of course, we can also add Trackton in South Carolina to this list.

Generally speaking, the idea that CDS is confined to well-educated, white, middle-class mothers is without foundation. There has not been a great deal of research, and much of it is, in any case, anthropological in nature. It was not designed for the study of language acquisition. Moreover, this research has often been communicated to the child language research community in a partial, inaccurate manner. For example, the recasts found in the speech of Trackton parents are routinely overlooked. At the same time, errors have crept in that betray a lack of direct engagement with the literature. For example, 'Trackton' sometimes appears as 'Tracton' (Hamilton, 1999: 430), while the informant quoted above has been wrongly described as 'Aunt Mae' (Pinker, 1994: 40). She is, in fact, 'Annie Mae'. Moreover, she is not the child's aunt, but his grandmother. Repeat warning: read the original sources for yourself. All in all, the assumption that CDS is absent in some cultures lacks support. In fact, the available evidence points in the opposite direction with at least some standard features of CDS being reported in all cases so far. Undoubtedly, though, we require better evidence on this issue. Future research should tell us much more about the linguistic environments of children throughout the world.

Input and interaction in language acquisition

The child's linguistic environment was a major focus of interest during the 1970s, but since then, interest has declined. We can identify at least three reasons for this decline. First, many of the basic facts about Child Directed Speech were established during this period. And although subsequent studies have refined these findings, they have not substantially altered our view about the nature of CDS. Second, the significance of a special register, directed at young children, was undermined by the assumption that CDS is largely confined to a privileged minority of Western mothers. This assumption still prevails, but we have challenged it here, in our review of cross-cultural research. Third, the locus of interest, in both nativist and non-nativist theories, has shifted firmly to the child. The central aim is to describe and explain the learning mechanisms and knowledge that the child brings to the task of language acquisition. This shift towards the child, away from the environment, is entirely justified. We want to discover how the child acquires language, after all. But the environment still deserves our attention.

As we shall discover in Chapter 9, present theorizing reduces the role of the input to a matter of frequency. The number of times that a child hears a particular linguistic form is held to be the critical environmental factor that contributes to language development. Of course, frequency *is* important (Cameron-Faulkner, 2012; Ambridge, Kidd, Rowland & Theakston, 2015). Children's experience of language differs quite widely with regard to input frequency, with a direct impact on language development. But frequency is not the only factor of interest. Interaction is also critically important, both verbal and non-verbal. In this regard, imitation – as a form of interaction – stands out as a fundamental human behaviour that is implicated in

114

language development. The study of corrective input can be seen as one branch of the broader topic of imitation studies. Language is acquired in the context of interaction with other people and input alone – simple exposure to linguistic forms – will not suffice.

Even if we accept that both input and interaction are essential ingredients for language development, that does not commit us to the need for a special register. In principal, we could speak to a baby or toddler in precisely the same way that we speak to an adult. The assumption that CDS is not universally available leads directly to this conclusion. And yet, my guess is that very few researchers, if any, would advocate withholding CDS and replacing it with Adult Directed Speech. In any event, our review of cross-cultural research revealed that assumptions about the 'non-universality' of CDS are unfounded. At the same time, much more cross-cultural research is needed, designed by psychologists with a direct interest in the environment of the language learning child. Personal guess Number 2 is that parents throughout the world will adopt at least some of the characteristic features of CDS at least some of the time. This belief is based on the assertion that Child Directed Speech is actually inevitable (Saxton, 2009).

Arguably, the only way to engage a young child in conversation is to follow their lead and this includes the choice of conversation topic. Try talking to a two-year-old about your council's recycling policy and see how far you get. Now try talking about the book that the child is holding in their hands. Notice the difference? The young child is constrained, both linguistically and cognitively, and these constraints compel adults (and older children) to adapt to these limitations. Otherwise, communication will not succeed. An adult who fails to engage the child will only succeed if their next attempt dovetails more closely with the child's limited capacity and particular motivation to communicate. It is not surprising, therefore, that parents around the world spend so much time recasting child speech, effectively acting like a mirror, reflecting back the child's own speech with a range of modifications. By following the child's lead in this way, the adult can more easily maintain a conversation that is geared to the level and interests of the child. Observe that the motivation of the adult, conscious or otherwise, is to *communicate* with the child, not teach language. It just so happens that a special form of facilitative input and interaction – Child Directed Speech – falls out naturally from communication with a young child. It is in this sense that CDS might be inevitable. Given that both input and interaction are necessary for language development, it remains possible that at least some aspects of the special register, Child Directed Speech, are essential to guarantee successful language acquisition.

IN A NUTSHELL

- Adults and older children use a special register, known as Child Directed Speech (CDS), when talking to young children. They simplify and clarify their speech in numerous ways, at every level of language, including phonology, vocabulary, morphology and syntax.

- CDS is a dynamic register, with adult speech being tuned, to some extent, to the language level of the child as it changes over time.

- The amount of linguistic input available to children varies quite widely. Children of 'high-talking' parents tend to be relatively advanced in terms of vocabulary and grammar development.

- The child's linguistic environment comprises both input (language forms) and interaction (the way those forms are used in conversation).

- Children cannot acquire language from watching TV, a situation in which they are exposed to input in the absence of interaction. Interaction is therefore essential for language acquisition.

- Imitation, both verbal and non-verbal, is a fundamental aspect of human interaction. Infants who are especially responsive to imitation develop relatively advanced vocabularies.

- Parents frequently imitate their children, repeating back child utterances with modifications (recasts).

- Some adult recasts can function as a form of corrective input for grammatical errors (negative evidence). They present a direct contrast between a child error and a grammatical alternative offered by the adult.

- It is widely assumed that CDS is not universally available, but cross-cultural research does not support that assumption.

- Child Directed Speech may be an inevitable consequence of adapting to the communicative needs of a conversational partner who is both cognitively and linguistically immature.

FURTHER READING

Hoff, E. (2006). How social contexts support and shape language development. *Developmental Review, 26(1)*, 55–88.

This article provides a thorough review of the social factors that affect the amount and quality of talk to young children. It goes beyond the factor of socioeconomic status considered here to include numerous other factors, including ethnicity, multilingualism, and childcare experience.

Matthews, D. (Ed.) (2014). *Pragmatic development in first language acquisition.* Amsterdam: John Benjamins.

Although topics in interaction are touched on in this chapter, we do not explore in any depth how the child comes to use language as a tool for communication. This recent collection does an excellent job of filling the gap.

WEBSITES

- **Effects of TV viewing on child development**:

  Google: *How TV affects your child – KidsHealth* for the following site: http://kidshealth.org/en/parents/tv-affects-child.html. If you still need convincing about the Evils of Television, this site takes you one step beyond language acquisition to summarize the effects of TV viewing on other aspects of child development. A note of warning: this site is not intended for a scientific audience, so be prepared to follow up any points of interest by checking with the original research literature.

Still want more? For links to online resources relevant to this chapter and a quiz to test your understanding, visit the companion website at **https://study.sagepub.com/saxton2e**

5

Language in the First Year: Breaking the Sound Barrier

CONTENTS

OVERVIEW

In this chapter we consider how the child gets started on the task of language acquisition. We focus on infant speech perception in the first year of life and show how the child breaks the sound barrier to discriminate individual speech sounds and words. By the end of the chapter, you will know more about:

- categorical perception: the child's innate mechanisms for distinguishing one phoneme from another.
- specialization towards the native language: how infants tune in to the particular phonological properties of the input language, and why they lose the power to tune in to foreign languages.
- word segmentation: how the child uses the statistical properties of the input and information on prosody to work out where one word stops and the next one begins.
- early grammar: how the infant learns something about grammatical organization in the first year of life before they have uttered their first word.

Hunt the phoneme

In the beginning

As we saw in Chapter 1, language learning begins before the baby is even born. Newborn infants can recognize a story (*The cat in the hat*) that they first heard while still in the womb (DeCasper & Spence, 1986). They do this by hearing and remembering information about the prosodic (musical) qualities of the story. In this chapter, we will pick up the baton from the moment of birth and follow the infant through to their first birthday. For most babies, it takes a whole year of life before they produce their first word. But infants are not idle during this period. They are avid listeners. We will see that infants possess remarkably powerful mechanisms for processing speech. This is just as well, given that the infant is faced with the daunting task of tuning in to the specific properties of their native language (or languages). The 'tuning in' process includes the need to discriminate individual speech sounds (**phonemes**) and information about how phonemes combine with one another into words. As we shall see, the perceptual abilities of the child are used to identify individual sounds, individual words and even some information about the grammatical organization of language. By 12 months, therefore, the typical child is well equipped for the rapid progress in lexical and grammatical development that follows.

Drops of sound in a river of speech

London is one of the most linguistically diverse cities in the world, with more than 300 different languages being spoken by children in schools (Baker & Eversley, 2000). Living in London, I constantly find myself eavesdropping on languages I do not even recognize. It can be quite bamboozling.

Where are the silences between words?

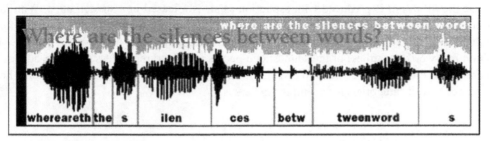

Figure 5.1 A speech waveform of the sentence 'Where are the silences between words?' (from Saffran, 2003: 111)

Where does one word stop and the next one begin? What are the individual sounds that make up each word? Perhaps if I wasn't just idly eavesdropping this would not seem so daunting. After all, within each word, one sound follows another, and, by the same token, one word follows another. It looks as though all I need do is identify the separate elements, like beads on a string. This is quite a nice image, but unfortunately, it is not quite right. Let's throw the necklace out and try a different image. The words we hear in everyday conversation flow together in a fast-moving river of sound. In a river, I cannot tell you where one drop of water ends and the next one begins. In a similar way, within each word, it is generally impossible to tell where one phoneme stops and the next one begins. And the same is true for the boundaries between words. A spectrographic analysis of fluent speech shows that individual phonemes overlap in their physical properties, even at the boundaries of words (Ladefoged, 2006). The infant language learner is thus faced with two **segmentation problems**. In the river of speech, where are the phonemes and where are the words? We will examine each of these problems in more detail, and then consider how the child tackles them (see Figure 5.1).

Let's first think about the task of individuating the phonemes within a word. The languages of the world contain something like 600 consonants and 200 vowels (Ladefoged, 2004). However, each language uses only a fraction of this total number. For example, English has about 45 different phonemes, while Igbo (a West African language) uses more like 35. Meanwhile, Japanese and Warlpiri (an Australian Aboriginal language) make use of roughly 25 each. The infant must therefore hone in on a particular small subset of phonetic units from the full range of possible speech sounds. Let's take a single example, the phoneme /p/. It turns out that there are many different kinds of /p/. The physical properties of the /p/ phoneme vary depending on the age, gender, dialect and emotional state of the speaker. Less obviously, /p/ is altered by the sounds it co-occurs with. Thus, the /p/ sounds in *lap*, *lip*, *lop* and *loop* all differ from one another. This variation is caused by *coarticulation*, the effects of the physical properties of neighbouring sounds (Ladefoged, 2006). In this case, the vowel in each word affects the way the lips, tongue and other articulators position themselves in readiness to pronounce the following /p/ sound. Variation in the /p/ sound is also introduced according to its position within a **syllable**. In *lap*, /p/ is syllable-final, while in *pal*, it is syllable-initial. You can see for yourself how different these two sounds are if you tear off a small strip of paper (not from this page!) and hold it up close to your lips.

121

When you say *lap*, not much happens, but with *pal*, you should blow the paper over. This is because the /p/ in *pal* is produced with aspiration as air is released in a sudden burst. With *lap*, this does not happen, because the syllable-final /p/ is not fully released. We can see, therefore, that there are many kinds of /p/ sounds. But to the untrained ear, a /p/ is a /p/ is a /p/, whatever its position in a word, regardless of the sounds it co-occurs with, and regardless of who produces it. Generally, therefore, adults do not perceive the differences within the /p/ category. They only hear differences across categories, for example, /p/ versus /b/.

Categorical perception

We need to consider how the infant comes to recognize all the different /p/ sounds as a single phoneme, and, further, how /p/ is distinguished from every other phoneme. One answer to this question was provided by Peter Eimas and his colleagues, more than 40 years ago (Eimas et al., 1971). In an ingenious experiment, Eimas et al. (1971) demonstrated that infants perceive speech sounds categorically, in much the same way that adults do. Their study focused on the contrast between /p/ and /b/, two sounds that are almost identical in the way they are produced, apart from the feature of voicing.

We can demonstrate the concept of voicing most easily by taking a sideways step away from /p/ and /b/ to consider another contrasting pair that allow a more leisurely inspection: /s/ versus /z/. To detect the contrast between **voiced and voiceless sounds**, place your fingers on your Adam's apple (therein lie the vocal cords). Take a deep breath and produce a continuous /s/ sound. Without stopping, switch to a /z/ sound. You should notice that, with the shift to /z/, your Adam's apple starts vibrating – an indication of voicing. Next, try alternating between long /s/ and /z/ sounds. You will feel the voicing switch on and off. Now look behind you. If you see someone looking at you strangely, it's time to stop this exercise and leave the room (take the book with you).

If we now turn our attention back to /p/ versus /b/, there is one further detail we need in order to appreciate the study by Eimas et al. (1971). Our perception of voicing is not simply a matter of whether the vocal cords are vibrating or not. It is also a matter of timing. We can see this if we place /p/ and /b/ in syllables: /ba/ and /pa/. When we produce /ba/, the lips are closed initially, before bursting open. In most English speakers, voicing begins just a fraction of a second after the lips have opened. In /pa/, meanwhile, voicing is also switched on when the vowel is produced (all vowels are voiced), but compared to /ba/, the start of voicing is delayed some time after the lips have opened. There is, then, a difference in *voice onset time* (VOT). We perceive a /b/ if voicing starts within 25 msec from when the lips open. And we perceive a /p/ if the VOT is greater than 25 msec. This fine difference in timing is critical for allowing us to differentiate /b/ from /p/, which in turn allows us to distinguish different words in otherwise identical pairs, like *pack-back*, *pull-bull* and *pin-bin*.

Eimas et al. (1971) tested infant sensitivity to voicing by synthesizing a range of syllables that differed incrementally in VOT. Infants were tested on pairs of syllables to see if they could discriminate between them, for example *ba-3* and *pa-1*, in Figure 5.2 below. These two syllables differ in VOT by 20 msec and, to adult ears, cross the boundary between /b/ and /p/. The stimulus pair *pa-1* versus *pa-2*, meanwhile, also differ by 20 msec in VOT, but this time they both lie within the same phoneme category and would sound identical to an adult.

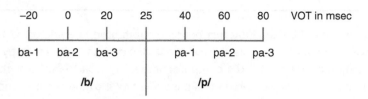

Figure 5.2 Stimuli used by Eimas et al. (1971) to test infant sensitivity to voice onset time (a negative VOT indicates the start of voicing before the release of the lips)

Eimas et al. (1971) used a *high-amplitude sucking* (HAS) procedure to habituate infants (see Box 5.1). The infant is played one syllable, say *ba-3*, repeatedly. In this version of the habituation method, the infant has control over how often they hear the syllable. The faster the infant sucks on a specially rigged dummy, the more often *ba-3* is heard. At first, sucking rate is high, reflecting the high level of infant interest, but eventually the allure of *ba-3* fades and the sucking rate drops off. When habituation is achieved, a new syllable with a different voice onset time is introduced, say, *pa-1*. If the infant can detect a difference between *ba-3* and *pa-1*, then the sucking rate should revive to reflect renewed interest. And this is what Eimas et al. (1971) found: infants hear the difference between /p/ and /b/. Critically, they also discovered that infants were far less sensitive to the contrast *within* a phonemic category. For example, infants who were habituated to *ba-3* showed no revival in sucking rate when *ba-2* was introduced. The two /b/ sounds were not distinguished. As noted above, *ba-2* and *pa-1* both differ from *ba-3* by 20 msec. But only *pa-1* crosses the adult phoneme boundary. Like adults, when VOT is greater than 25 msec, one-month-old infants hear /pa/, when it is lower than 25 msec, they hear /ba/.

BOX 5.1   HABITUATION METHOD

The habituation method provides psychologists with a window on the mental life of infants. Patently, we cannot ask an infant about what they perceive or know and we cannot subject them to experiments where they have to say or do anything in response to instructions. What we *can* do is bore them. In the habituation method, a stimulus is presented to the infant repeatedly. When interest in this first stimulus wanes, a new stimulus is introduced. The question then is, can the infant detect the change of stimulus?

Infant attention can be measured in several different ways by exploiting responses that are already in their behavioural repertoire. These include looking time, head turning, heart rate and the rate of sucking on a dummy. Looking time, in particular, has long been a popular measure of infant interest (e.g., Fantz, 1961).

(Continued)

How can we tell when an infant has become habituated to a stimulus? Csibra (2008) provides a typical example of how this is decided. In Csibra's study, the infant's attention is first drawn to a computer screen by a cartoon. Next, the habituation stimulus is presented (in this case a video showing a box in motion), and the computer begins timing infant looking. When the infant looks away, an experimenter presses a key and the time of that first look is recorded by the computer. Infants who play along with this procedure will then alternate between looking back at the screen for a while and then looking away again. On each occasion, looking time can be measured (each 'look' is termed a *trial*). The average looking time for the first three trials (T1) is calculated, this being the point when infant interest is at its peak. As interest declines, the infant spends less and less time looking at the habituation stimulus. When the average looking time for three subsequent, consecutive trials falls below 50 per cent of T1, then the infant is said to be habituated. At this point, a test stimulus is introduced that differs from the habituated stimulus. Is the infant aware of the switch in stimuli? If looking time shoots up significantly, then the infant is said to have dishabituated. The experimenter thus infers that the infant can distinguish the habituated stimulus from the test stimulus.

If old habits die hard, then new ones die with ease. For this reason, the habituation paradigm has proved to be enormously productive in developmental research, having being used in hundreds of studies. Recently, though, questions have been raised about what prompts infants to dishabituate. One important factor that is often overlooked is that infants vary in terms of the number of trials it takes before they are habituated. For example, in Csibra (2008), infants needed between 6 and 13 trials to reach habituation. This is important because 'fast' and 'slow' habituators differ in their behaviour. For example, in Baillargeon (1987), for infants aged 3–4 months, fast habituators showed 'surprise' at physically impossible events, but slow habituators did not. Evidently, the basis for infant responding is not straightforward (Schoner & Thelen, 2006). Differences in susceptibility to habituation are compounded with the effects of variation in stimulus display and experimental procedure. The power of habituation as an experimental paradigm must therefore be tempered with caution: we still need to explain *why* infants dishabituate on a given occasion.

Since that early study, several other phonemic contrasts have been tested and in almost every case, infant perception seems to match adult perception in being categorical (Werker & Lalonde, 1988; Jusczyk, 1997). A sample of the contrasts that have been tested is listed in Figure 5.3 below.

Phonemic contrast	Study
p — b	Eimas et al. (1971)
b — d	Eimas (1974)
b — w	Hillenbrand, Minifie & Edwards (1979)
b — m	Eimas & Miller (1980a)
r — l	Eimas (1975)
w — j	Jusczyk, Copan & Thompson (1978)
m — n	Eimas & Miller (1980b)
f — θ	Levitt, Jusczyk, Murray & Carden (1988)
v — ð	Levitt et al. (1988)

Figure 5.3   Studies demonstrating categorical perception in infants

For unfamiliar phoneme symbols, see the Pronunciation Guide at the end of the book.

EXERCISE 5.1
PHONOLOGICAL CONTRASTS

You can discover the phonemes in a language by thinking about how different sounds contrast to produce a difference in meaning. For example, the two sequences, *cat – pat* are identical apart from the initial sounds, /k/ and /p/. The contrast between /k/ and /p/ is sufficient to change the meaning, so they are said to constitute a minimal pair. Find the minimal pairs in the following set of words. Then consult the chart of English phonemes at the back of the book and 'translate' the English letters into phonemes (for example, the letter *c* in *cat* is written phonemically as /k/). Remember to concentrate on how the words sound, not on how they are spelled.

dog	catch	funny	ceiling	male
lake	cheese	ship	bog	chip
whale	laze	sham	peas	shack
been	feeling	cap	honey	dean

Another remarkable finding from this research is that very young infants are sensitive to contrasts that do not feature in their own native language. For example, the contrast between /ba/ and /pa/ is not exploited in Kikuyu, a language spoken in Kenya. Nevertheless, one-month-old Kikuyu infants can detect the voicing contrast between these two sounds (Streeter, 1976). In a similar way, English–Canadian infants can distinguish contrasts found in Polish, French and Czech (Trehub, 1976) as well as in Hindi and Nthlakapmx, a North American language

(Werker & Tees, 1984). And yes, that is how you spell it. Just don't ask me how to pronounce it (you'll find out why my Nthlakapmx pronunciation is so poor below). Overall, the large body of research on infant speech perception yields two main conclusions: (1) infant phoneme perception is categorical from the earliest time of testing, suggesting that it is an inborn capacity; and (2) infants can discriminate contrasts that appear in any of the world's languages. For this reason, Kuhl (2004: 833) suggests that infants are born 'citizens of the world', able to acquire the phonemic contrasts of any language. Hence, the task of cutting up the sea of sound into separate phoneme droplets is less bewildering than it seems at first, because, to a large extent, our inborn perceptual mechanisms are geared to do the job for us. The many different kinds of /p/ are grouped, in perception, into a single category from the very start of life.

Specialization towards the native language

Why I don't speak Nthlakapmx

We do not remain citizens of the world for very long. Between the ages of 6–12 months there is a gradual specialization for the native language driven by two complementary processes: both enhancement and decline in perceptual sensitivity. On the one hand, infants tune in to their native language with increasing precision and several months of exposure enhances sensitivity to the particular features of the ambient language. On the other hand, there is a decline in ability to detect contrasts in non-native languages. An early demonstration of this decline is provided by Werker & Tees (1984), who tested infants from an English-speaking background on contrasts found in three languages: (1) English; (2) Hindi; and (3) Nthlakapmx, as shown below. (Incidentally, you may sometimes see Nthlakapmx referred to as the more pronounceable Salish, but this latter is actually a group of North American Languages, of which Nthlakapmx is just one.) (See Table 5.1.)

Werker & Tees (1984) found that at 6–8 months, Canadian–English infants could discriminate all three contrasts. From 8–10 months, though, discrimination of non-native contrasts deteriorated sharply. By 12 months, hardly any infants could distinguish the Hindi or Nthlakapmx contrasts. And this, of course, is why my own Nthlakapmx pronunciation is so dismal. A parallel case is provided in Japanese, in which /ɹ/ and /l/ are not contrastive. This means, that to Japanese speakers, *right* and *light* sound like the same word. Japanese infants seem to lose their ability to detect the /l/ – /ɹ/ contrast by the age of 10–12 months (Tsushima, Takizawa, Sasaki, Nishi, Kohno, Menyuk & Best, 1994; Kuhl, Stevens, Hayashi, Deguchi, Kiritani & Iverson, 2006). Recent evidence from neuroscience confirms these behavioural data. Infant brain responses can be obtained in a non-invasive manner through the use of event related potentials (ERP) (see Figure 10.2). In this technique, electrodes placed on the scalp record electrical activity in the brain. ERP data show changes in activity over time (they do not provide data on *where* activity is located in the brain). It has been found that ERP responses to non-native contrasts are present at 7 months, but have disappeared by 11 months (Rivera-Gaxiola, Silva-Pereyra & Kuhl, 2005). In general, much research now demonstrates that infant sensitivity to non-native contrasts declines from about the age of six months onwards (for example, Werker & Lalonde, 1988; Best & McRoberts, 1989, 2003).

Table 5.1 Phonemic contrasts tested by Werker & Tees (1984)

Language	Contrast	Notes
English	/b/ – /d/	
Hindi	/ʈ/ – /t/	The long tail on the t denotes a retroflex sound, produced with the tip of the tongue curled up
Nthlakapmx	/k'i/ – /q'i/	The inverted comma indicates an ejective sound, produced by air bursting through the vocal cords
		/q/ is produced with the back of the tongue touching the uvula, that little flap you can see hanging down from the back of your mouth when you say *ahhh*

Loss or decline?

Reading the literature, one can sometimes get the impression that infant sensitivity to non-native contrasts ceases altogether by the end of the first year. For example, Maye, Werker & Gerken (2002: B102) assert that 'in many cases … infants *stop* discriminating previously discriminable contrasts'. More likely, though, we are talking about a decline, not a loss. First, a small minority of 12-month-olds still perform well with non-native contrasts (Werker & Tees, 1984). And some of those who show the more usual decline still perform above chance (McMurray & Aslin, 2005; Kuhl et al., 2006). We can also mention here children who move from their birth culture at an early age to be adopted in a different country with a different language – in one study, children from India aged 6–60 months (Singh, Liederman, Mierzejewski & Barnes, 2011). Initial testing suggested that these infants had lost their ability to distinguish contrasts from the birth language. However, after training, performance improved significantly; a group of control children, meanwhile, were immune to the training intervention. In effect, native contrasts can be resuscitated, even if contact with the birth language has been lost. Adults, too, can be trained to perceive neglected contrasts. For example, Japanese adults can recover the ability to distinguish /l/ and /ɹ/ (Flege, Takagi & Mann, 1995, 1996). And, depending on the task they are asked to perform, adults can override categorical perception (Schouten, Gerrits & van Hessen, 2003). Finally, in at least one case, infant ability neither declines nor disappears, but is maintained over the first year. English-learning infants can still distinguish between two click sounds in Zulu, a South African language (Best, McRoberts & Sithole, 1988; Best, McRoberts, Lafleur & Silverisenstadt, 1995). If you've ever heard click sounds in languages, you will realize how distinctive they are and it is perhaps this lack of similarity to other language sounds that helps explain continued facility in discriminating among them.

Enhancement of native contrasts

Infant perception of unfamiliar, non-native languages may decline, but this is compensated by an increase in facility with the native language over the first year. Perception of native language is actively enhanced. For example, Mandarin-learning infants get better at discriminating a contrast in their language between so-called **affricate** and **fricative** sounds (Tsao, Liu & Kuhl, 2006). (In English, the sound made by CH in *chip* is an affricate, while SH in *ship* is a fricative). Enhancement of native contrasts is also necessary, as another look at the /p – b/ contrast will reveal. Some languages do not simply divide the phoneme pie into two neat slices, cutting along the /p – b/ border provided by our auditory systems. Thai, for example, divides up the pie into three phoneme categories: /p/, /b/ and an aspirated /p/. We have already seen that some /p/ sounds are aspirated, while others are not. Native English speakers do not notice the difference, because aspiration is not critical for distinguishing one word from another. But in Thai, aspiration *is* contrastive. We can see how this works in Thai, by representing aspiration with an /h/ (see Table 5.2).

Table 5.2 The use of aspiration to make a phonemic contrast in Thai

Thai word	English translation
/pit/	car
/pʰit/	dog
/bit/	flower

The moral here is, if you're visiting Thai friends and you want to borrow their car, be careful what you ask for. You could end up driving off in their dog. A further lesson is that the boundaries provided by our auditory system are not set in stone. The infant must create categories that correspond precisely with those in the native language (Maye, Weiss & Aslin, 2008).

Language-specific differences can be illustrated in a different way, with our favourite /p/ – /b/ contrast. Once again, voice onset time is the critical factor. We noted above that the /p/ – /b/ VOT boundary is 25 msec for some varieties of English, but this is subverted in other cases, as shown in Table 5.3. It is through subtle acoustic distinctions of this kind that we identify dialectal differences and speakers with foreign accents. In effect, our innate auditory mechanisms do the really hard job of hacking through the /b/ – /p/ phonetic spectrum for us, dividing it into two manageable parts that correspond roughly to what must be acquired. Then, through experience, this initial boundary is finessed until it corresponds more closely with the precise phonemic contrasts in the language being acquired. Even then, there is work to do. Sounds differ in their salience for the child both with respect to their voicing status and their position within a word. Word-final voiced stops like /b, g/ are acquired with relative ease, while their voiceless counterparts, /p, k/, are not acquired, either word-initially or word-finally, until the age of 20 months (Archer, Zamunerb, Engel, Fais & Curtin, 2016).

We need to consider why the infant's perceptual abilities change over time. Unfortunately, explanations are fairly thin on the ground. One possibility is offered by Kuhl (2004) with

Table 5.3 Cross-linguistic differences in voice onset time (VOT) for the /p – b/ contrast

Language	VOT lag between /b/ and /p/ (msec)
European French	0
Canadian French	7
Canadian English	25
Danish	40

Sources: Caramazza & Yeni-Komshian, 1974; Christensen, 1984

her native language neural commitment (NLNC) hypothesis. She suggests that 'language learning produces dedicated neural networks that code the patterns of native-language speech' (ibid.: 838). Once this neural commitment has been made, the potential of the brain to learn language is directed towards the regularities of the native language and, consequently, also interferes with the processing of non-native sound patterns. Certainly, by the time we are adults, larger regions of the brain are activated in response to the native language than to non-native input (Zhang, Kuhl, Imada, Kotani & Tohkura, 2005). But we need equivalent evidence from infants to provide strong confirmation of Kuhl's hypothesis. Rivera-Gaxiola et al. (2005) do show that infant ERP responses are stronger in some infants for native versus non-native contrasts. The strength of ERP response provides a measure of neural commitment, but, as mentioned, ERP data do not provide information on precisely where something is happening in the brain. So there is support for the idea that some neural resources somewhere are committed to the native language, and also that some neural resources somewhere are much less committed to non-native contrasts. But are they one and the same neural resources? The obvious reading of the NLNC hypothesis is that neural resources are used for the native language *at the expense of* the non-native language. But some kind of imaging data would be required to establish if this happens, since imaging data can tell us *where* neural activity is located. We can see that the NLNC hypothesis is somewhat vague about precisely what 'neural commitment' means. It may simply be another way of saying that learning takes place.

In a similar way, Werker & Yeung (2005) talk about *functional reorganization* of perceptual capacities as a result of increasingly selective attention to the properties of the native language. The notion of functional reorganization is reasonable enough as a label we can attach to describe what happens in very broad terms. But it does not provide a satisfying explanation, nor does it generate precise hypotheses that we might test about infant speech perception. Broadly speaking, we can see that increasing commitment to the native language is linked to decreasing ability with non-native speech perception. These two developments are not independent. The fact that infants become more attuned to the subtleties of their native language is not surprising. The native language is pretty much all they hear, after all. But why do we lose our capacity with non-native contrasts? The answer to this question is much more open.

Individual differences in infant speech perception

Intriguingly, evidence is beginning to emerge that infants differ in their perceptual abilities. By seven months, there is a negative correlation between performance on native versus non-native contrasts. This means that infants who do well on native contrasts simultaneously do less well on non-native contrasts. It seems, then, that some children tune in to their native language with relative ease, while at the same time being less fazed by non-native distractions. Of great interest, research is beginning to show that these 'easy tuners' have an advantage when it comes to later language learning (Tsao, Liu & Kuhl, 2004; Newman, Ratner, Jusczyk, Jusczyk & Dow, 2006; Kuhl, Conboy, Coffey-Corina, Padden, Rivera-Gaxiola & Nelson, 2008). Better native phonetic perception is associated with accelerated growth on both vocabulary and grammar more than two years later, at the age of 30 months (Kuhl, Conboy, Padden, Nelson & Pruitt, 2005). It seems somewhat ironic that those children who remain open to non-native contrasts are at a disadvantage for learning their own language. But this 'openness' might better be seen as a deficit that prevents maximal attunement to the ambient language. One further source of individual variation has been identified which stems, not from the infant, but from the linguistic environment. It has been found that infants tune in to their native language more quickly (at six months) if their mothers are especially responsive during interactions (Elsabbagh, Hohenberger, Campos, Van Herwegen, Serres, De Schonen, Aschersleben, & Karmiloff-Smith, 2013). In particular, these mothers produced higher levels of mutual gaze, turn-taking and mutual affect and altered their behaviour in direct response to the infants' behaviour. It would seem that the infant is encouraged by this kind of high quality input to tune in more quickly to their native language.

Summary: Breaking the speech sound barrier

So far, we have seen that the daunting task of identifying individual phonemes is made manageable by an innate capacity to perceive speech sounds categorically. We saw that any given phoneme has many different physical realizations: changes in gender, age and mood of speaker are compounded by changes according to where a phoneme occurs in a syllable and also by the sounds it is surrounded by. But we are born able to ignore these differences and perceive different phonetic realizations of a sound as a single phoneme. We also saw that over the first year of life, two related processes take place. On the one hand, the child tunes into the native language, becoming increasingly adept at identifying the precise phoneme categories of the language being learned. On the other hand, an initial ability to identify phoneme contrasts from any of the world's languages fades away from about the sixth month onwards. In the next section, we will see that the infant is not content to identify the *sounds* of the ambient language. In this regard, Jusczyk comments that:

it seems pretty clear that the basic speech perception capacities that infants possess should prove useful in learning how the sound structure of the native language is organized. What is less obvious is that these same perceptual capacities could play a role in acquiring information about other levels of language structure. (Jusczyk, 1997: 137)

We will turn our attention now to these other levels of language structure and see, first, how infants come to identify individual words in the stream of speech and, second, how they can even identify information about grammar. All before their first birthday, when they break another sound barrier by *producing* a word of their own.

Word segmentation

As you read this **sentence**, the white spaces at the beginning and end of each word perform a great service: they segment the words for you. To see what a great help this is, try reading the following (taken from Kuhl, 2004):

> *theredonateakettleoftenchips*

This exercise is not that easy, even though you have two massive advantages over the infant: (1) you know what a word is already; and (2) you know many thousands of specific words that you can look out for. Even so, this particular example is rather tricky, because it can be **parsed** (cut up) in two different (admittedly rather nonsensical) ways:

> *the red on a tea kettle often chips*
> *there, Don ate a kettle of ten chips*

The spaces between printed words make life easy for the reader. But listeners to spoken language have no such advantage, as we noted earlier, because there are no clear gaps demarcating the end of one word and the start of another. The sounds run into each other. We might also note that the *segmentation problem* is compounded by the fact that human speech is very fast. An average speaker produces something like 200 syllables per minute (Aitchison, 1998). Even allowing for the fact that adults speak relatively slowly to young children (Broen, 1972), the child must therefore process speech at a phenomenal rate.

Despite the complexity of this task, there is evidence that infants can segment words from fluent speech by the age of seven months (Jusczyk & Aslin, 1995). How do they do this? Researchers have examined two broad categories of cue in the speech signal that might help the infant:

- *transitional probabilities*: statistical information on the probability that one syllable will follow another
- *prosodic cues*: information from the 'music' of speech

131

In the following sections, we will look at each one of these potential cues to word boundaries. Before we do so, though, have a go at segmentation yourself with the following exercise.

EXERCISE 5.2
WHERE ARE THE WORDS?

At the start of this chapter, I mentioned the bamboozling experience of eavesdropping idly on a foreign language speaker. But what if we listen carefully? Some research shows that adults can, in fact, detect words in an unfamiliar language (Saffran, Newport & Aslin, 1996), although the first language seems to interfere (Finn & Kam, 2008). Try this out for yourself. If you have a bilingual speaker in your group, record them speaking for no more than two minutes, uninterrupted, about their friends, hobbies, or anything that takes their fancy. Listen very carefully to the recording. Try to write down any words you hear. Afterwards, ask your bilingual informant to check how well you did. You can get some sense of the task facing the infant from this exercise, but don't forget that you started out with one major advantage: you know what a word is, so you know what you're looking for.

The baby statistician

We will first introduce the notion of uncertainty in the input. There is a lot of information in the input that could guide infants in the task of segmentation. But none of this information is 100 per cent reliable (Jusczyk, 1997). This lack of certainty introduces the idea that language learning may involve probabilistic inferences on the part of the child. Box 5.2 discusses probability theory and hints at the massive impact it is beginning to have on theories of child language development. For one thing, probabilistic inference presents a theory of learning that stands in direct conflict with the nativist idea of inborn knowledge. In fact, the statistical properties of language were dismissed by Chomsky (1957) and have taken almost half a century to emerge once more as an important influence on the child. Chomsky (1957: 15) based his argument on a now famous example:

Colourless green ideas sleep furiously

Before Chomsky constructed this sentence, the probability that these particular words had ever been placed in this particular order was (let's lay odds) zero. And yet the sentence is perfectly grammatical, even if it is somewhat difficult to make sense of. This suggests that our analysis of the sentence cannot depend on the probabilities with which words group together (Seidenberg, MacDonald & Saffran, 2002: 553). The low chance of this sentence occurring does not impede our recognition of a grammatical sentence.

BOX 5.2   WHAT ARE THE CHANCES? THE RISE OF PROBABILITY THEORY

The fundamental assumption in probability theory is that learning is an uncertain process. In cognitive science, generally, the brain is viewed as an information processor. Learning takes place when we infer something new, on the basis of what we already know. Given information (something we already know) might come to us from the senses or be drawn from memory. In both cases, we can use this 'old' information to infer something new. We can make either *deductive* or *inductive* inferences.

In a deductive inference, the outcome is certain and incontestably true (because the premises are true).

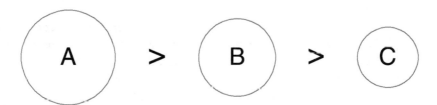

Premises: A is bigger than B
                       B is bigger than C
Deductive inference: A is bigger than C

In fact, we make relatively few deductive inferences in everyday life. Far more common are inductive inferences, in which we go beyond the premises to arrive at a conclusion that is not absolutely certain:

Premise: All the tigers I have ever seen (or heard about) have orange fur and dark stripes.

Inductive inference: The next tiger I see will have orange fur and dark stripes.

The probability that my inference will match reality is high in this case, but it is not 100 per cent. The next tiger I come across might have *white* fur and dark stripes. Although rare, white tigers do exist. So my inductive inference could be proven wrong.

Probability theory provides a method for capturing uncertain inference. It is based on the idea that events have a given probability, or chance, of happening. For example, there is a 50 per cent chance of a tossed coin landing heads up (usually written as a probability of 0.5). Numerous domains of learning and knowledge can be modelled by

(Continued)

the laws of probability, including vision, motor control, causal learning, language at every level (phonological, lexical, morphological, syntactic), in addition to both speech perception and speech production. In the field of language acquisition, probability theory provides a serious (albeit recent) alternative to Chomskyan theory. For Chomsky, a system of rules specifies all and only the 'legal' sentences in a language. These rules are held to determine what is learned about language and how that knowledge is represented in the mind. Chomsky's black-and-white approach to grammaticality stands in sharp contrast with probability theory. Grammaticality can be viewed as a shaded concept, a matter of degree rather than absolute right or wrong. Two people may differ on whether they accept a particular form as grammatical (for example, *shined* as the past tense of *shine*: *Tom shined his torch in my face*). The amount of experience different people have with particular language forms may affect the chances of them being accepted as grammatical.

The rise of probability theory follows in the wake of huge advances in computational technology. Speech recognition, automatic text analysis and machine translation have been made possible through the development of powerful computational systems. Quite simply, probability theory has been harnessed in this research because it works in refining machine capabilities. Almost incidentally, the fallout for cognitive science has been profound. Psychologists interested in how the mind works now have a powerful set of computational and theoretical tools for modelling its functional capacity (Chater & Manning, 2006; Chater, Tenenbaum & Yuille, 2006).

In fact, it has emerged that there are several probabilistic (or statistical) properties of language that the child might make use of in the segmentation of words. For example, in harmonic languages like Turkish and Hungarian, the vowels within a word tend to be either all front vowels or all back vowels. This means that the narrowest point in the airway, where the tongue almost blocks off the air flow, is either at the front of the mouth or the back. Statistically, two vowels of the same kind (front or back) will more likely occur within a word, rather than across a word boundary (Ketrez, 2014). There is a probabilistic cue, therefore, to identify where one word stops and the next one begins. But can the child actually use cues of this kind to segment words? Let's take another example, offered by Saffran, Newport & Aslin (1996): the simple phrase *pretty baby*. What are the chances of one syllable following another? Taking samples of Infant Directed Speech, we can calculate that, within the word *pretty*, the chance of *pre-* being followed by *-tty* is very high, something like 80 per cent. This is why it is difficult to think of another syllable that can follow *pre-* (pronounced as PRI-). Try it for yourself. If we now consider the probability of *-tty* being followed by *ba-*, as it does in *pretty baby*, the chance is much lower, something like 0.03 per cent. This is because there are many other possible syllables that can follow *-tty*: *pretty hat*, *pretty flower*, *pretty perambulator*, and so on. The odds that one particular syllable will be followed by another are often referred to as *transitional probabilities*. In our example, we can see that within the word *pretty*, the transitional probability from one syllable to the next is high, but across words (from *-tty* to *ba-*), the transitional probability is low. In essence, syllable sequences that go together frequently have a relatively high chance of being words. Can the infant compute transitional probabilities? If so, they might use low transitional probabilities as a good (if not perfect) cue for identifying the boundary between one word and the next.

Saffran, Newport & Aslin (1996) tested this possibility by teaching eight-month-old infants a miniature artificial language. They generated four three-syllable words, using a speech synthesizer. In one condition these words were:

> *tupiro*
> *golabu*
> *bidaku*
> *padoti*

These words have been carefully designed so that transitional probabilities within words are 1.0 (that is 100 per cent or totally predictable), while between words, transitional probabilities were only 0.33. Thus, within words of this language, *pi* is always followed by *ro* (in the word *tupiro*), that's to say, a transitional probability of 1.0. Across words, *ro* can be followed by *go, bi* or *pa* (the first part of the other words in the language). Since these three words follow *ro* an equal number of times, the transitional probability is 0.33 (a one in three chance). The words in this language were produced in a monotone female voice with no pauses between words and no other cues to word boundaries like stress or prosody (see below). Try saying the following eight words at a normal speed in a flat voice with no hesitations or pauses:

> *padotigolabupadotibidakutupirotupirogolabubidaku*

There isn't much to learn from this little exercise, though we do gain some idea of what life is like as a speech synthesizer. And it passes the time. Infants listened to an unbroken string of these four novel words, played in random order for two minutes, at the rate of 270 syllables per minute. Following this familiarization phase, infants were exposed to four words repeated continuously, two from the original set (*tupiro* and *golabu*), and also two new words, composed from the same original set of syllables, but in a scrambled order (*dapiku* and *tilado*). It was found that infants listened significantly longer to the new words. There is evidence, then, that 'infants succeeded in learning particular groupings of three-syllable strings – those strings containing higher transitional probabilities surrounded by lower transitional probabilities' (Saffran, Aslin & Newport, 1996: 1928). They succeeded in finding words after only two minutes of listening.

One hiccup is that infants in these experiments come to rely on the fact that all the words they hear have the same number of syllables. In Saffran, Aslin & Newport (1996) all of the words have three syllables and, as we have seen, learning runs smoothly. But if infants are trained on trisyllabic words, but then switch to hear words of just two syllables (or vice versa), they are thrown (Lew-Williams & Saffran, 2012). Word segmentation by the infant is much less impressive. In real life, of course, children are exposed to Syllable Salad, where the words vary much more haphazardly in terms of syllable number. There is a disjunction, then, between the laboratory and the real-life conditions faced by the child. We pursue the issue of **ecological validity** further in the next section. In the meantime, we can consider the relationship between segmentation ability and later word learning. It has been found that infants vary in how well they do on Saffran, Newport & Aslin's task. Moreover, those infants who are proficient at segmentation when they are 7.5 months old turn out to have larger productive vocabularies at 24 months (Singh, Reznick & Xuehua, 2012; Newman, Rowe & Ratner, 2015).

The power of the infant to exploit statistical properties in the input is beginning to transform our view of child language learning (Romberg & Saffran, 2010). Research is by no means confined to the problem of *word* segmentation. The research on categorical perception has also been interpreted in this way, since the child is mapping the probabilities that different phonetic units belong within the same phonemic category, on the basis of experience (Werker & Yeung, 2005). And we will see in Chapter 6 that statistical learning is beginning to be applied in the domain of word learning. Another example is provided in the domain of grammatical rule learning (Marcus, Vijayan, Rao & Vishton, 1999). Using similar methods to Saffran, Newport & Aslin (1996), Marcus et al. created two artificial languages, each one with a very simple rule for putting three syllables together in a particular order:

> ABA   *ga ti ga*
> ABB   *ga ti ti*

Infants were familiarized with one of these two grammars and then, in the test phase, they were exposed to three-syllable sequences containing entirely new syllables. Thus, the infant who has been familiarized on the ABA sequence with *ga ti ga*, would then hear novel syllable strings which were either consistent with the ABA pattern (*wo fe wo*) or inconsistent (*wo fe fe*). The idea is to see if the child can detect the *pattern* they have been trained on (ABA versus ABB). This is why new syllables were used in the test phase (*wo* and *fe*, rather than *ga* and *ti*). Marcus et al. (1999) found that seven-month-old infants had a novelty preference for the inconsistent sequences: they preferred to listen to *wo fe fe* (ABB) if they had been trained on *ga ti ga* (ABA) (see also Gervain & Werker, 2013). These researchers argue that infants have learned rules, not just particular strings of syllables, because the test stimuli were entirely new. However, there is some doubt about whether a grammatical rule (however simple) has been learned (Seidenberg et al., 2002). There are *statistical* regularities in the stimuli used by Marcus that are similar to the kind found in Saffran, Newport & Aslin's (1996) word segmentation study. And the ability to generalize beyond the input to new stimuli is possible both with statistical learning and rule learning.

Studies on statistical learning demonstrate that infants possess very powerful mechanisms for processing and analysing rapid auditory information. Subsequent studies suggest that this ability is not confined to speech, but applies equally well to rapid sequences of auditory tones and even to visual stimuli (Saffran, Johnson, Aslin & Newport, 1999; Fiser & Aslin, 2001). This brings us back, momentarily, to the debate on whether or not 'speech is special'. Cross-domain segmentation abilities suggest that speech does not occupy a privileged position in human cognition. And work on cotton-top tamarins (a kind of monkey) supports this position, since they too can learn from the statistical regularities in speech (Saffran et al., 2008). The ability to perform these kinds of analyses both across species and across different kinds of stimuli suggests a domain-general learning capacity for language (Saffran & Thiessen, 2007).

Learning in the real world

Before we move on from our baby statistician, it is worth pointing out that, in Saffran et al.'s (1996) study, the transitional probabilities within words were fixed in advance at 1.0. But the vast majority of real words in real languages do not enjoy this perfect predictability. Take, for example, the syllable *per-* in words like *perceive, perhaps, personality, persuade*, and so on. The syllables after *per-* are all different, so the chance of correctly predicting what follows plummets accordingly. When transitional probabilities are high, infants can not only segment speech, they can also begin to learn about the meanings of the words identified. In contrast, word learning is relatively poor when the infant has to cope with low transitional probabilities (Hay, Pelucchi, Graf Estes & Saffran, 2011). One other point to note is that, in real life, infants are not exposed to the same four words repeated over and over again. It is impressive that learning can take place after just two minutes of this kind of exposure. But the intensity of the experience lowers its **ecological validity**. One recent study tackled this problem by using words that the child had already learned in isolation (Depaolis, Vihman & Keren-Portnoy, 2014). It was found that infants only became adept at segmenting these words from fluent speech at the age of 12 months. It would seem, then, that the real world places greater demands on the infant's ability to process and remember words than the laboratory.

Ecological validity was improved in a study that looked at the influence of Infant Directed Speech on word segmentation. But instead of using synthesized stimuli, real speakers were recorded producing either Infant Directed Speech (IDS) or Adult Directed Speech (ADS) (Thiessen, Hill & Saffran, 2005). You will recall from Chapter 4 that IDS has a very distinctive quality, especially notable for its high pitch and exaggerated, swooping pitch contours. Thiessen et al. (2005) found that infants could find the word boundaries when listening to Infant Directed Speech, but not from *Adult* Directed Speech. This finding has been replicated more recently (Floccia, Keren-Portnoy, Depaolis, Duffy, Delle Luche, Durrant, White, Goslin & Vihman, 2016). Out of 13 studies, word segmentation was witnessed in just one study, and this was distinguished by the use of an exaggerated form of Infant Directed Speech. These findings might be explained by reference to the power of IDS to grab the infant's attention. Infants may learn more when IDS is used because they are focusing especially closely on the experimental stimuli. Not surprisingly, there is evidence that enhanced attention improves learning and memory (e.g., Rensink, O'Regan & Clark, 2000). Another study can be mentioned which is also grounded more firmly in the real world (Lew-Williams, Pelucchi & Saffran, 2011). Eight-month-old children learning English listened to Italian words, either in running speech or in isolation. These infants segmented the speech and identified Italian word boundaries more effectively when they heard the words in both contexts, as in normal Child Directed Speech. Exposure to fluent speech alone was not sufficient to help these children identify its statistical properties. Learning was therefore most effective when the situation more closely reflected real life. In a similar vein, it has been found that infants are not fazed by a switch from one speaker to another when segmenting words from running speech (Graf Estes, 2012). They can therefore go beyond the artificial, synthesized speech of the laboratory and generalize their learning in ecologically valid settings. Transitional probabilities are clearly a powerful cue that help the infant find word boundaries. But there are other sources of information in the input that the infant might exploit. We next turn our attention to prosodic factors in the input, to consider if they, too, are helpful.

Prosodic cues to speech segmentation

In running speech, some syllables seem to stand out, because they are produced with more energy. In the linguistic parlance, they are *stressed*. The perception of stress is caused by three factors: amplitude (louder syllables are perceived as stressed); duration (longer syllables sound stressed); and an increase in pitch. Of these three cues, an increase in pitch provides the strongest cue that a given syllable is stressed (Fry, 1955). Changes in pitch contribute to the prosody (or 'music') of speech. In normal running speech, the pitch changes continuously, rising and falling, to create a kind of melody. In the process, they contribute to our impression that some syllables are stronger than others. In continuous speech, a pattern of alternating strong and weak syllables can be discerned, as in the following lines from poems (strong syllables have been highlighted).

> And **did** those **feet** in **an**cient **time** … (Blake)
> **Stop** all the **clocks**, **cut** off the **tele**phone … (Auden)
> I **sing** the **bo**dy e**lec**tric … (Whitman)
> **Do** not go **gen**tle into **that** good **night** … (Thomas)

The words in a given language have a characteristic stress pattern. English words tend to have a strong–weak pattern (known as *trochaic*), while other languages, like Polish, prefer an *iambic*, weak–strong pattern. But all languages have exceptions to their general patterns. For example, in English, about 90 per cent of all multisyllabic words do begin with a strong syllable:

water	**bi**cycle	**en**velope
taxi	**pine**apple	**gar**den

Nevertheless, a significant minority of words buck this trend, as in the following:

indi**ges**tion	gui**tar**	re**li**gion
com**pare**	re**solve**	ex**plore**

The prosodic qualities of language are therefore predictable, but not perfectly predictable. They are predictable in a *probabilistic* fashion. There is a parallel, then, with the transitional probabilities of syllables discussed above. The question then becomes: Are infants sensitive to the prosodic qualities of their native language? The short answer is *yes*. We saw in Chapter 1 that the foetus can recognize a piece of poetry from its prosodic properties. Beyond *The Cat in the Hat* studies, we also know that, prior to birth, the foetus has a preference for listening to their own mother's voice (Kisilevsky, Hains, Lee, Xie, Huang, Ye, Zhang & Wang, 2003). This means that the foetus can learn and recognize (at least some of) the unique qualities in a particular speaker's voice. And shortly after birth, newborns can distinguish their native language from a foreign language (Moon, Cooper & Fifer, 1993; Nazzi, Bertoncini & Mehler, 1998). By five months, they can even distinguish one dialect of English from another (Nazzi, Jusczyk & Johnson, 2000). In each case, the infant makes use of prosodic qualities to distinguish one form of speech from another.

But what about the task of segmenting words from the speech stream? Word stress provides a useful cue to the boundaries of words. In English, it would be a good (if not perfect) strategy to assume that each stressed syllable marks the beginning of a word. Between six and nine months, infants do show sensitivity to the stress pattern of their native language (Jusczyk, Houston & Newsome, 1999). In fact, the stress pattern of the language biases the infant in its segmentation behaviour. They can segment words like *king*dom and *ham*let, that begin with a stressed syllable, but not words like *beret* and *device* (Jusczyk, 2002). (If you're wondering about *beret*, this was an American experiment and they follow the French pronunciation (*beret*) – personally, I emphasize the first syllable.) These studies show that infants who hear a phrase like '*guitar is*' assume that *taris* is a word: they assume that the stressed syllable –*tar* marks the start of a word. The infant is thus guided by the predominant trochaic stress pattern of English. Other studies have also demonstrated infant ability to exploit stress cues. For example, Saffran & Thiessen (2003) show that infants can segment words from an iambic language, even when only 80 per cent of the words presented followed the iambic stress pattern. Generally speaking, it is a good strategy to cut up the speech stream according to the position of stressed syllables. The chunks of phonetic information this process yields very often correspond to words and may help focus attention on other cues that can help refine the segmentation process.

One extra segmentation cue is the edge of an utterance. Utterances have a characteristic intonation contour, something like a musical envelope that contains the phonetic information. In particular, there is a coherent pitch contour laid over the whole utterance, an overall pattern of rising and falling. And utterance boundaries generally occur at the point where we take a breath, so pauses are more likely. Not surprisingly, therefore, words placed at the beginning or end of an utterance are more salient (stand out more) than words buried somewhere in the middle (Fougeron & Keating, 1997). Given that Infant Directed Speech is replete with short utterances, infants are exposed to especially high numbers of utterance edges. It turns out that utterance edges are especially good places to find words: eight-month-olds do better at segmenting words from both the beginning and end of utterances than they do from the centre (Seidl & Johnson, 2006).

Most of the word segmentation research discussed here deals with words that begin with a **consonant**. Other research has shown that infants find vowel-initial words especially difficult to segment (Nazzi, Dilley, Jusczyk, Shattuck-Hufnagel & Jusczyk, 2005). In English, they also find **verbs** difficult compared to **nouns**, even when these start with a consonant (Nazzi et al., 2005). One reason for this may be that verbs tend to occur in the centre of utterances, while nouns often begin and end utterances (for example, *Mary had a little lamb*: *Mary* and *lamb* are nouns, while the verb *had* is tucked away in the middle). It is important to remember, therefore, that word segmentation is not a monolithic process. Certain kinds of words are easier to locate in the speech stream than others. A 7.5-month-old can detect, with relative ease, nouns at the edge of an utterance that begin with a consonant (Jusczyk & Aslin, 1995). But it may not be until 16.5 months that verbs beginning with a **vowel** are segmented successfully (Nazzi et al., 2005). Unless, that is, the vowel-initial word (e.g., *eye*, *apple*) is placed at the edge of an utterance. In that case, infants look more precocious, since 11-month-olds can manage the task (Seidl & Johnson, 2008). Overall, we can see that several factors enter into the task of word segmentation, including transitional probabilities, phonological structure, prosodic structure, word class (noun or verb) and utterance position (edge or centre).

Relative cue strength

Do segmentation cues vary in strength? Johnson & Jusczyk (2001) addressed this question by pitting prosodic cues against statistical ones in an artificial language taught to eight-month-olds. Syllables that ended words by statistical rules were given word-initial stress cues (they were high-pitched, louder and longer). If the infant did statistics, they would have found word endings. If they were more musical (tuned into prosody) they would find word beginnings. At eight months, it turns out that prosody wins. However, Thiessen & Saffran (2003) replicated this study, using infants aged seven and nine months. They found that, whereas nine-month-olds preferred stress cues, seven-month-olds did better with statistical cues. There is, then, a developmental progression. Happily, of course, these cues do not conflict with one another in real languages. Evidence from adult artificial language learning confirms this view, since the addition of prosodic cues enhances the learning adults can do from transitional probabilities alone (Saffran, Newport & Aslin, 1996). This confirms what any psychology student already knows: statistics and stress go together.

Another test of relative cue strength is provided by Thiessen & Saffran (2004). You will recall that our perception of stress is caused by increases in three factors: pitch; duration; and loudness. Usually, these three factors co-occur, but Thiessen & Saffran teased them apart and taught infants a language where the only cue to stress was a change in loudness (or amplitude). In fact, the change is even more subtle than that, since only the amplitude of sounds with a relatively high pitch were altered (changes to the so-called *spectral tilt*). For adults, spectral tilt is the weakest index of stress, but nine-month-olds performed well at segmenting the speech stream with only these subtle changes in loudness to help them.

By 12 months, however, infants perform much more like adults, and changes in spectral tilt are much less powerful as a cue to word boundaries. We have another demonstration, therefore, that word boundary cues do differ in strength, but importantly, their strength for the infant varies across the course of development. And the changes take place rapidly. From 9 to 12 months, infant perception shifts so that the speech signal is processed in an integrated, adult-like fashion, being less susceptible to subtle changes in just one factor.

We have seen that the infant's segmentation abilities are impressive, but it is worth asking what kind of words the infant fishes out of the speech stream. Are they just strings of sound with no meaning? If so, the infant would have discovered words in only the baldest sense. In fact, though, research is beginning to show that information on transitional probabilities can enhance the naming of words. In one study, 17-month-olds took part in a statistical word segmentation task of the kind pioneered by Saffran (Estes, Evans, Alibali & Saffran, 2007). In a subsequent task, these words were used to name objects. Exposure to the words in the statistical learning task enhanced performance in the object labelling task that followed. Hence, the statistical task provides the child with information on what constitutes a 'good word' in the language being learned. And this information makes it easier to map from sound to meaning in the labelling task.

DISCUSSION POINT 5.1
INFANTS AND OTHER ANIMALS

In Chapter 2 we reviewed evidence on animal abilities to perceive and process human speech. Refer back to this evidence (especially the section, Is speech special?). Then compare infant and animal learning:

- What are the similarities between animal perception and Infant perception? Consider in particular the perception of phonemes and the statistical learning of word-like units.
- In what ways do infants and non-humans differ? Consider not only the outcomes of learning, but also the way in which learning takes place.
- If tamarin monkeys can process speech in a similar way to human infants, what do you think prevents them from going on to acquire the full complexities of language?

Grammar from the babble

By this stage, we might ask if there are any limits to the child's remarkable segmentation abilities. Phonemes and words come tumbling out of the river of sound with apparent ease. But grammar might be more elusive. We reviewed claims by Marcus et al. (1999; 2007) that infants can use input regularities to learn rules. The rules were very simple, namely, that a sentence must comprise just two kinds of element in simple strings of three (ABB or ABA). You will recall that the jury is still out on whether infants are learning grammatical rules or simply learning statistical regularities. But there is stronger support for a less ambitious claim about grammar learning: infants can use prosodic information to mark off one **clause** from another (Hirsh-Pasek, Kemler Nelson, Jusczyk, Cassidy, Druss & Kennedy, 1987). You can think of a clause as a 'mini-sentence', with each sentence comprising one or more clauses (see the Glossary for a slightly more refined description). Of course, infant ability to demarcate clauses depends on being able to detect clause boundaries. But there are no perfectly predictable prosodic markers of this kind. Instead, there are at least three different cues, all of which are associated with the edges of clauses. Clause boundaries in English are often (if not always) marked by pauses, syllable lengthening and a change in pitch (Price, Ostendorf, Shattuck-Hufnagel & Fong, 1991). Of interest, there is a parallel here between speech and music. These same three cues often mark the end of musical phrases also (Jusczyk, 1997).

Hirsh-Pasek et al. (1987) tested infant sensitivity to clause boundaries. They prepared two sets of stimuli from a single sample of Infant Directed Speech (IDS). In one version, pauses were inserted at clause boundaries, happily coinciding with the other two cues: pitch change and a drawn out final syllable. This coincident version was pitted against a non-coincident version, in which the pauses were inserted between words *within* the clause. It was found that infants as young as seven months preferred to listen to the coincident versions, that is, natural sounding clauses. No such preference was found in a subsequent study that used Adult Directed Speech (Kemler Nelson, Hirsh-Pasek, Jusczyk & Cassidy, 1989). By seven months, therefore, infants are tuned in to the unique, exaggerated prosody of IDS. And they use this special input to help locate groups of words (clauses) critical in the acquisition of grammar. American nine-month-olds still prefer coincident speech samples when exposed to an unfamiliar dialect from Britain (Polka, Jusczyk & Ravchev, 1995). And younger American infants (4.5 months) prefer coincident versions not only in English, but in Polish also (Jusczyk, 1989). However, the penchant for Polish clauses has gone by the age of six months, a finding that is in accord with the research described above showing a loss of non-native sensitivity in the latter half of the first year.

If your ultimate goal is to learn a system of grammatical rules, it is a good start to be able to fish out a chunk of language from the input that corresponds to a chunk of grammar. But the chunk of grammar that we have considered (the clause) is quite a mouthful. Clauses can be any length and vary considerably in their syntactic complexity. Clearly, there is much analysis to do within the unit of the clause. The ability, discussed above, to isolate individual words must be very helpful in this respect. And, one might also predict, a sensitivity to word order would also be very useful. The rules of grammar determine the order in which words are placed in a sentence. Compare the grammatical *When I am an old woman, I shall wear purple* (from the poem by Jenny Joseph), with the ungrammatical *I I purple when woman shall am an wear old*. Word order matters, especially in languages like English. Remarkably, infants are sensitive to changes of word order, provided that the changes take place within the prosodic envelope provided by a clause (Mandel, Kemler Nelson & Jusczyk, 1996; Soderstrom, Blossom, Foygel & Morgan, 2008). Compare the following sentences, bearing in mind that the words *would* and *wood* are pronounced identically, and are therefore indistinguishable to an infant.

(a) Cats would jump benches.   →   Cats jump wood benches.
(b) Cats would. Jump benches.   →   Cats jump. Wood benches.

The examples in (a) comprise single, whole clauses, pronounced naturally as a single prosodic unit. Observe how *would/wood* and *jump* have been switched around to the right of the arrow. The examples in (b), meanwhile, have been constructed from two fragments, with each fragment sounding natural by itself. Placed together, though, the two fragments do not sound like a single unit of speech. Try them for yourself, paying attention to rises and falls in pitch. Mandel et al. (1996) found that two-month-old infants could detect the change in word order, but only when presented within the single prosodic unit, as in (a). The change in word order in (b) takes place across a prosodic boundary, and was not detected by two-month-olds. It seems that their analyses take place within the prosodic unit. And as we saw above, the prosodic unit very often corresponds to the grammatical unit of the clause.

Phonemes, words and grammar: Summary

We have seen that the infant does a remarkable job in perceiving words, and even clauses, in the first year of life. And of course, they achieve this at the same time that they are hunting down the phonemes of the native language. In essence, the infant transforms the flood of sound – with its lack of obvious beginnings and endings – into sequences of language units. Phonemes, words and phrases all exist as distinct units of linguistic analysis, so we can reinvoke the image, cast aside at the start, of beads on a string. The infant has to identify the separate beads and begin to learn how they are strung together. We have reviewed evidence that the infant is well equipped for this herculean task. The (probably innate) ability to perceive phonetic units categorically provides a massive kick-start to the process of phoneme acquisition. And infants are also well equipped to detect regularities in the music of speech – its prosody – that correspond, to a significant degree, with linguistic units, in particular words and clauses. Infants also possess a very impressive ability to process strings of syllables. They can identify, learn and recall the order in which syllables occur in sequences they hear. And they can compute regularities in syllable order across many different strings of syllables. In consequence, the boundary between one word and the next can be predicted, in a probabilistic manner, by working out the likelihood that one syllable follows another. If the chance of this transition is very low, it is likely that one has reached a cut-off point between one word and the next. In the next chapter, we will examine the child's progress in word learning from the second year of life onwards. It is one thing to identify that a certain string of syllables constitutes a distinct unit. It is another thing to know that this unit is a *word* with a meaning and a particular place in the grammar of the language.

IN A NUTSHELL

- Speech cannot be divided easily into separate units of sound or words. Phonemes overlap and merge into one another in a continuous fashion. And there are often no obvious breaks between one word and the next.

- Each language makes use of a small subset of the 800 or so phonetic units that are found in the world's languages.

- The great task for the infant is to penetrate this babble and identify phonemes, words and even units of grammar in the ambient language.

- Infants perceive sounds categorically: physically different kinds of /p/ are perceived as a single sound.

- Commitment to the sounds of the native language increases during the first year, while the ability to detect non-native contrasts declines.

- Infants of seven months can observe, learn and remember statistical regularities in sequences of syllables. They are sensitive to the chances that one syllable will follow another (transitional probabilities). In consequence, infants can make a good 'guess' about where one word stops and the next one begins in running speech.

- Infants can also use prosodic information (especially word stress) to identify where one word stops and the next one begins. Like statistical learning, prosodic information is probabilistic: a stressed syllable in English has a good, but not perfect, chance of signifying the start of a word.

- Infants use multiple cues to identify word boundaries in a probabilistic fashion. None of these cues is reliable by itself. But working in concert, the information in the input is enhanced.

- Infants can even use prosodic information to identify large chunks of grammar (the clause) and are sensitive to changes in word order taking place within a prosodic unit.

FURTHER READING

Jusczyk, P.W. (1997). *The discovery of spoken language*. Cambridge, MA: MIT Press.

This book is not bang up to date, but it still provides a very clear survey of research on early infant perception, with a wealth of material that I could not include here.

Vihman, M.M. (2014). *Phonological development: The first two years* (2nd ed.). Malden, MA: Wiley-Blackwell.

The present chapter has been concerned with infant speech perception, rather than production. This reference fills the gap with a clear review of how children learn to get their tongues round the sounds of their native language.

WEBSITES

- **International Phonetic Association (IPA)**: www.internationalphonetic
association.org/

  The chart at the end of the book shows you the phonemes used in English, but the IPA pages host much more information about phonetics, including a link to the International Phonetic Alphabet that shows you all the symbols used to represent the sounds of the world's languages. There is also information on the special fonts needed to produce the weird squiggles and curlicues for yourself. Google: *International Phonetic Association.*

- **Jenny Saffran**: www.waisman.wisc.edu/pi-Saffran-Jenny.htm

  Google: *Jenny Saffran* to find her academic homepage with a link to useful publications, including Saffran et al. (1996), the study that got the child language world excited about statistics (strange, but true).

- **Patricia Kuhl: TED Talk**: www.ted.com/talks/patricia_kuhl_the_linguistic_genius_of_babies

  Google: *Patricia Kuhl – The linguistic genius of babies,* for a TED talk on the infant's remarkable language segmentation skills and how they change over the first year of life. Observe how Kuhl describes the loss of non-native discriminations in terms of a critical period in development.

Still want more? For links to online resources relevant to this chapter and a quiz to test your understanding, visit the companion website at **https://study.sagepub.com/saxton2e**

6

The Developing Lexicon: What's in a Name?

CONTENTS

OVERVIEW

By the end of this chapter, you should be familiar with the kinds of words that children first learn. We will also consider a common kind of error – overextension – in which words are used with too wide a scope. We will consider three possible causes of overextensions:

- a category error (misclassification of an object)
- a pragmatic error (expediency determines the word chosen)
- a memory failure (the wrong word is retrieved)

We will also investigate the so-called *vocabulary spurt* and consider explanations for the speed with which children learn new words. We then consider solutions to the *gavagai* problem, introduced in Chapter 1: How do children work out what words refer to? Three approaches are considered:

- conceptual biases
- associative learning
- probabilistic learning

Conceptual biases, including the *whole-object bias* and the *shape bias*, determine how the child perceives and interprets objects and actions. The child is thus equipped with expectations that help them interpret what words refer to. Meanwhile, associative learning, long studied in psychology, may explain how biases are acquired in the first place. And finally, we will examine the recent use of probability theory to model word learning in the child. On this approach, the probability of the child converging on the correct meaning of a word increases when the child is equipped with both prior knowledge about the world and increasing experience of the objects in it.

Approaches to word learning

If there is one linguistic concept that almost everyone recognizes, it is the *word*. Words are everywhere. If I don't know the meaning of a word, I can ask someone or reach for a dictionary. If I feel like relaxing I might play Scrabble online (oh dear, the number of hours gone forever). Others do crosswords. Children play *I Spy*. People have an awareness of what a word is, in and of itself. And arguably, *word* is pretty much the only linguistic category that enjoys widespread recognition and **metalinguistic** understanding. Our sense of ease with the concept of word might cause us to take words for granted. In a similar way, learning new words might not seem like such a big deal. Even a word like *axolotl* does not take much effort to learn. Until recently, I had never encountered this word, less yet the species of Mexican salamander it denotes. But my friend Diana is now unaccountably smitten by these strange creatures. In consequence, I have learned the word *axolotl*, and much else besides, concerning Diana's new hobby (no, she doesn't get out much). I was shown the actual creature (an object in the world) and developed an impression (or concept) of the slithery beast (no, not Diana) and, to help matters, was supplied with the word form *axolotl* to name my new concept. Some kind of connections must presumably be made between the object in the world, the concept it inspires, and the word form that labels the concept. In this chapter, we will consider the nature of these connections and the kinds of learning that might be involved to make them. But first, let's sketch out some of the major achievements in early word learning.

First words

Comprehension versus production

Most children produce their first word at around the time of their first birthday, as you will recall from Chapter 1. But the comprehension of words may emerge sooner, as early as seven months in some cases (Harris, Yeeles, Chasin & Oakley, 1995). This disjunction between comprehension and production is a prevalent theme in child language. Children know more than they can say. This is not surprising when you consider that to utter a word, the child must retrieve it from memory, and then formulate and execute a suitable motor-articulatory programme to pronounce it. During speech production, the activation of **voicing** and the movements of the articulators, including lips, tongue and velum (soft palate) are very finely co-ordinated in their movements and timing. It is not easy getting your tongue round words. The most obvious case of the comprehension production disjunction was provided in the last chapter. It takes a year to produce the first word, while speech perception is remarkably sophisticated during this period. As we can see in Figure 6.1, the number of words that children understand grows quickly, reaching about 150 words by 16 months. But only a fraction of that total is *produced* at the same age, something in the region of 30 words. The lag in production is still in evidence at two years, and can even be witnessed in adults (Gershkoff-Stowe & Hahn, 2013).

What do one-year-olds talk about?

The thing about toddlers is that they don't have a terribly wide range of interests. In conversation, the same topics crop up over and over again, irrespective of who their parents are and regardless of where or how they've been brought up.

Given the list of interests in Table 6.1, it is not surprising to find that parental speech to young children is dominated by similar topics (Ferguson, 1977). As we noted in Chapter 4, the parent tends to follow the child's lead as a way of initiating and maintaining the conversation. Another observation that brings no surprises is that early words are easy to pronounce. A number of factors make life easy for the child. For example, *pill* is easier than *spill*, because the latter starts with a consonant cluster, that is, two consonants, /sp/, rather than one, /p/. What's more, *spill* begins with a so-called **fricative**, /s/, a category of sound which is more difficult to produce than others (Stoel-Gammon & Sosa, 2007). Beyond individual sounds, words with one or two syllables, like

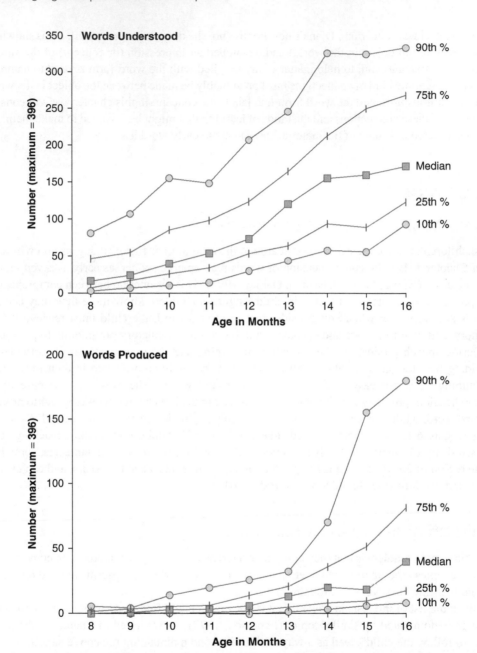

Figure 6.1 Median number of words produced and understood by children aged 8 to 16 months

Source: Adapted from Fenson, L., Dale, P.S., Reznick, J.S., Bates, E., Thal, D.J. & Pethick, S.J. (1994). Variability in early communicative development. *Monographs of the Society for Research in Child Development, 59/5*, Figure 1, p. 35 and Figure 2, p. 38.

Table 6.1 Words in the vocabularies of children younger than 18 months (after Clark, 1979, and Pan, 2005)

Topic	Examples
Food and drink	*bread, cookie, drink, juice, milk*
Family	*mama, dada, baby*
Animals	*dog, kitty, duck, cow, horse, bunny*
Parts of the body	*nose, mouth, foot, ear, hair, hand*
Clothing	*hat, shoe, coat, nappy*
Vehicles	*car, truck, bike, boat, train*
Games and routines	*bye-bye, night-night, upsidaisy, peekaboo, hi, shhh*
Toys	*ball, book, doll, teddy, bubbles*
Familiar objects	*chair, cup, spoon, bottle, key, clock, flower, door*
Actions	*eat, go, up, down, sit, off, back*
Descriptives	*hot, cold, allgone, dirty*
Sound effects	*yum-yum, ouch, moo, woof*

hat or *water,* are easier than polysyllabic horrors like *tyrannosaurus.* Observe that *tyrannosaurus* might well be on the lexical wish list of your average two-year-old. But they are likely to avoid difficult words like this, or at best mangle them, by dropping one or more syllables, and by reducing consonant clusters to something more manageable. For example, *bread* becomes *bed*, *blue* becomes *boo,* and *school* becomes *cool* (Menn & Stoel-Gammon, 2005). Meanwhile, *spaghetti* reduces to *ghetti, banana* to *nana,* and *crocodile* to *crodile* (Stoel-Gammon & Sosa, 2007). We see here a good example of how different levels of language interact in development. The child's lexical production is directly affected by their phonological skills. The number of words produced is limited, while those that *do* appear are often subject to reductions of various kinds.

Overextension

Learning the word *coat* to refer to the garment worn when you go out is useful. But much more useful is an understanding that the word *coat* can be *extended* beyond that particular item of clothing to include your parents' coats, the coats of people you see in the street, coats worn by TV characters, and so on. The extension of meaning to include members of an entire category is an essential part of word learning. In the early stages, though, a limited grasp of word meaning can lead to category errors. In particular, children **overextend** word meanings: they use words beyond their conventional range of meaning. For example, Hildegard, aged 1;0 used the word *Papa* to refer not only to her father, but to her grandfather and even her mother (Leopold, 1939). By 1;2, she was calling any man she met *papa* (history does not record how many paternity suits ensued). Between the ages of 1;6 and 2;6, overextensions are very common, accounting for as many as 40 per cent of child word uses (Rescorla, 1980).

Child overextensions (Leopold, 1939; 1949; Clark, 1973):

(a) *ticktock*
square-faced watch, clock, all clocks and watches, gas meter, fire hose on spool, bath scale with round dial, round eraser

(b) *fly* (insect)
fly, specks of dirt, dust, all small insects, child's own toes, crumbs of bread, toad

(c) *ass*
toy goat on wheels with rough hide, sister, wagon, all things that move, all things with a rough surface

(d) *baby*
self, other children, pictures of children, any child

(e) *sch!*
music, cars and trains, pictures of cars, a toy wheelbarrow, old-fashioned carriages, a riding motion

(f) *choo-choo*
trains, Bradyscope (an early piece of psychological apparatus), planes, wheelbarrow, street-car, trunk

Children overextend word meanings in both production and comprehension. It is not so easy to observe overextension in comprehension, but McDonough (2002) shows how it can be done. She presented children (mean age 1;11) with pictures of three objects, for example, two birds and a hat. McDonough first asked children to place a sticker on a bird and, when successful, they were then asked to place a second sticker on another bird. Observe that the child is not expected to say anything during this experiment; only comprehension is being tested. The test items were sometimes from different domains (e.g., animals and clothing, as in our example) or from the same domain (e.g., all animals: two birds and a pig). Overextension errors were especially high (29 per cent) when the items came from the same domain. This means that, having correctly identified a bird, from a choice of two birds and a pig, the child will, on occasion, place a sticker on the pig when asked to find another bird. Hence, overextension is more likely when objects share certain properties like animacy or shape. McDonough (2002) also reports that overextensions are more frequent for unfamiliar items. Again, this makes sense. The less familiar a given word is, the less likely that the proper scope of its extension will be known. Hence, more errors will be made. But what is the basis of these errors? Three accounts have been offered, which we turn to below: (1) category error; (2) pragmatic error; and (3) retrieval error.

Categorically wrong

A category error occurs when the child's emerging categories diverge from adult norms. For example, the child who mislabels a hippo as *cow* may have mistakenly placed hippos and cows together in the same category (Mervis, 1987). Why would the child do this? In this case, one might conjecture that similarity in shape is driving the child's desire to form a unified herd of hippos and cows. We will look at the influence of shape in more detail below. But shape is not the only basis for overextension errors. If you look again at the examples above, you will see that size, sound, characteristic motion, taste and texture have all been observed as the basis for overextensions. So although hippos might fall (rather heavily) into the *cow* category, shape similarity is not the only possible explanation for the child's error. Cows and hippos also share the same taxonomic category – they are both mammals (see Box 6.1). Perhaps *cow* means *mammal* to this child, in which case, it is quite legitimate to include hippos, too. As Clark (2003) points out, shape similarity and taxonomic level are often confounded, making it difficult to determine the basis for the child's overextension. In both cases, though, we can say that the child's overextension is caused by an immature semantic system leading to one or other kind of category error (Naigles & Gelman, 1995; Gelman, Croft, Fu, Clausner & Gottfried, 1998).

BOX 6.1 PROTOTYPE THEORY AND CATEGORY MEMBERSHIP

Prototype theory is based on the idea that category membership is graded. Concepts may be more or less representative of a particular category (Rosch, 1973). Consider, for example, an ostrich, a penguin and a robin, all members of the bird category. Most people will agree that the robin represents the most birdlike bird among these three (Kintsch, 1981). In other words, robins are prototypical birds, possessing all of the necessary, defining features that define the concept of *bird* (e.g., has feathers, has wings, can fly). Different birds can therefore be more or less typical members of the *bird* category. Ostrich and penguin are less typical, in part because neither of them fly.

Experiments have shown that prototypes possess psychological reality. For example, reaction times are quicker and people are more accurate when asked if a robin is a bird, compared with an ostrich (Kintsch, 1981; Rogers & Patterson, 2007). Also, typical category members, like *robin*, come to mind first when people are asked to list all the birds they can think of (Mervis, Catlin & Rosch, 1976).

Concepts often figure in hierarchical relationships with one another. At the basic level, we find concepts that are most readily learned and retrieved from memory, concepts like *bird*. There is some evidence that children acquire basic-level concepts first (Spaepen & Spelke, 2007; though see Widen & Russell, 2008). Superordinate to *bird* is the category of *animal*. Superordinate categories tend to be abstract and difficult to visualize (what does *animal* look like?). At the subordinate level we find more specific instances of *bird*, like our friends the robin, the ostrich and the penguin.

Problems have been raised with prototype theory, based, for example, on the inherent vagueness of language terms (Hampton, 2007; see also Eysenck & Keane, 2005). Overall, though, prototype theory has stood the test of time remarkably well and remains useful in helping to explain the conceptual development of children.

153

Lexical plugs: Pragmatic errors

A second cause of overextensions is the existence of a lexical gap – a concept, but no word to name it. One way to plug this gap is by resorting to a plausible word that has already been acquired. Take the child who possesses the word *dog*, but not the word *horse*. What does she do when presented for the first time with a horse? One solution is to reach for *dog* and use that – a pragmatic solution in which 'it is almost as if the child were reasoning: "I know about dogs, that thing is not a dog, I don't know what to call it, but it is like a dog!"' (Bloom, 1973: 79). In this way, all four-legged creatures can end up being labelled *dogs* for a time. Pragmatic errors reveal that the boundaries of lexical categories can be rather fluid. Gaps can also be filled by the invention of a new word altogether, something that young children do on occasion. Examples include the use of *pourer* for *cup*, *bee-house* instead of *beehive* and *plant-man* for *gardener* (Clark, 1993; Becker, 1994). The origins of these words are readily apparent in the child's existing vocabulary and demonstrate the child's willingness and ability to be creative with the linguistic resources at their disposal.

Losing it: Retrieval failures

The third possible cause of overextensions is a simple failure to retrieve the correct word from memory. The word that *is* selected usually bears some resemblance to the target word. The resemblance is usually based on a confluence of perceptual and taxonomic similarities (like our cow/hippo example, above), but can sometimes be based on perceptual similarity alone, as in *ball* for *apple*. More rarely, the child might select a word that sounds like the target, for example, *moon* instead of *spoon* (Gershkoff-Stowe, 2002). In each case, the child knows the target word, but simply slips up in production, producing a related alternative. Chomsky (1965) would describe this phenomenon in terms of the difference between **competence** and **performance**. The child's performance (the word that is produced) does not reflect the knowledge they possess. And children do sometimes produce errors, even when they have demonstrated their comprehension of an object name (Huttenlocher, 1974). In particular, children approaching their second birthday start making errors when naming objects, despite previous correct performance (Dapretto & Bjork, 2000). This deterioration in performance coincides with the early stages of rapid vocabulary growth and indicates that performance factors (unreliable retrieval from memory) can mask the child's true level of understanding. Failures in memory retrieval have been implicated in other kinds of language error, most notable morphological errors (see Chapter 7).

Lexical processing

We have seen that there are three plausible causes for children's overextension errors: (1) an immature category; (2) a lexical gap (pragmatic); and (3) a faulty retrieval from memory. These explanations are not mutually exclusive; they might all have some validity. Gershkoff-Stowe, Connell & Smith (2006) bring all three together under the broad umbrella of lexical processing.

Research with adults suggests that when we name an object, there are three levels of processing, namely, object, concept and word (Johnson, Paivio & Clark, 1996; see also Figure 6.2 below). Naming starts at the object level, in the act of perceiving a particular object. This perception then activates our concept (or memory) of what we have seen. Catching sight of a chair will thus activate the concept of *chair* in the mind. At the same time, several related concepts will also be activated (for example, sofa, table, stool, bookshelf). Each activated concept, in turn, causes the activation of the word that labels the concept. Several words are thus activated in parallel. The word which receives the highest level of activation is the one that wins out and is actually produced. Factors affecting level of activation include perceptual similarity, practice and context (Brown & Watson, 1987; Martin, Weisberg & Saffran, 1989; Gershkoff-Stowe, 2001). First, activation is stronger the more closely the object resembles an existing concept (e.g., the sight of a robin will activate the concept *bird* more strongly than the sight of a penguin). Practice also increases activation, as seen when high frequency words are recalled relatively quickly. And finally, activation is increased if a concept, or a related one, has been activated recently. This recency effect is an example of priming and has been the subject of scores of studies in cognitive psychology (Anderson, 1983).

So how does this model of lexical retrieval help account for our three different kinds of overextension? First, category errors arise when a novel object – for which the child has no name – activates an existing, similar concept (and its associated name). In (a) above, we know that Hildegard possesses the concept *wristwatch* and a name for it, *ticktock*. Imagine that she then sees a gas meter for the first time. The perceptual similarity (a dial with moving hands behind a glass face) might prompt the activation of the *wristwatch* concept and hence the associated name, *ticktock*. To be a genuine category error we would have to be confident that Hildegard truly considered the gas meter to be an instantiation of her concept *wristwatch*. This is perfectly possible, but it would be very difficult to establish empirically. How could we be sure that Hildegard was not making the second kind of error, based on pragmatic necessity? In that case, the word *ticktock* would have been activated by the sight of the gas meter (by perceptual similarity) and would have been used by Hildegard as a handy means of talking about the gas meter in the absence of a suitable name. Hildegard would be perfectly aware that gas meters and wristwatches are different things, but would be plugging a lexical gap by labelling the gas meter *ticktock*.

The third type of overextension is caused by a retrieval error. Gershkoff-Stowe et al. (2006) demonstrate that recently activated concepts can lead to overextensions, because, on occasion, their continued high activation level leads them to be selected, in place of the correct, similar concept. Gershkoff-Stowe (2001) suggests that young children are especially vulnerable to this kind of error in the early stages of word learning. The child's lack of experience, compared to an adult, means they have had less chance to form strong links from object to concept, and from concept to word. In consequence, competition from a recently activated concept is more likely to interfere in the word retrieval process, leading to an incorrect selection. Overall, the lexical retrieval model helps explain three seemingly disparate causes for overextension errors. At the same time, it is apparent that actually teasing apart which particular cause is responsible for which particular error brings on an empirical migraine.

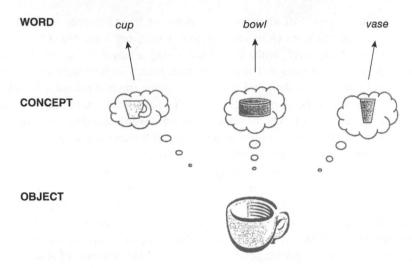

Figure 6.2 Levels of processing in object naming

Source: From Gershkoff-Stowe, L., Connell, B. & Smith, L. (2006). Priming overgeneralizations in two- and four-year-old children. *Journal of Child Language*, *33/3*, 461–486, Figure 1, p. 464: Levels of processing and lexical competition involved in naming a perceived object.

Up, up and away: The vocabulary spurt

One of the most repeated facts about word learning is that children start out slowly, but then, suddenly, go into orbit with a step change in their rate of learning (Goldfield & Reznick, 1992). Following production of the first word at about the age of 12 months, further words are added rather slowly. By about 18 months of age, the child has clawed their way to a productive vocabulary of about 50 words. But from this point onwards, there is a sudden acceleration in the rate of learning. One of the first studies to identify a vocabulary spurt was Dromi (1987). Figure 6.3 shows data from Dromi's daughter, Keren, who was followed longitudinally between the ages of 10 and 17 months. Ages are shown in months, with days in parentheses (for example, 13(11) = 13 months and 11 days).

As you can see, Keren's spurt takes place at about the age of 15 months. Others have suggested 18 months (for example, Bloom, 1973) or even 21 months as the age at which the naming explosion takes place (Plunkett & Wood, 2004). Recent evidence points to a shift in brain activation patterns between the ages of 20 and 24 months which are associated with a sudden growth in vocabulary (Borgström, Torkildsen & Lindgren, 2015). Perhaps the critical factor for the start of the spurt is not age, but the size of the child's productive vocabulary. But even then, the issue is not that straightforward. Many studies suggest 50 words as the critical mass required to trigger a spurt, but others argue that 100 words is more appropriate (Bates, Marchman, Thal, Fenson, Dale, Reznick, Reilly & Hartung, 1994). Clearly, there are disagreements about when the spurt begins. But the idea that a spurt does take place enjoys wide acceptance (Kauschke & Hofmeister, 2002; though see below).

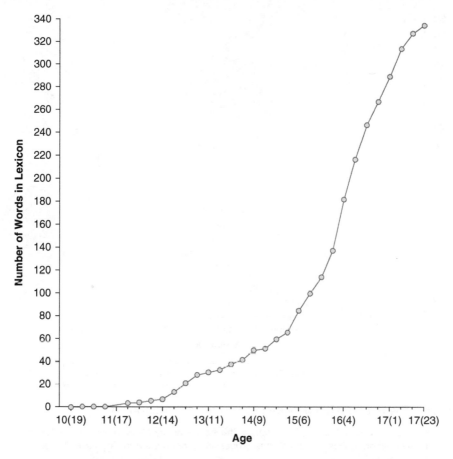

Figure 6.3 The vocabulary spurt in a child at the one-word stage

Source: From Dromi, E. (1987). *Early lexical development*. Cambridge: Cambridge University Press. Figure 1, p. 111: Keren's cumulative lexicon at the one-word stage.

Why so fast?

Diesendruck (2007) suggests that prodigious word learning is related to a generally impressive capacity for learning. Other authors, too, ascribe the child's lexical prowess to general cognitive abilities (Bloom, 2000; Poulin-Dubois & Graham, 2007). These include an extensive knowledge about the properties of objects and the relations they can enter into with one another. Children are also equipped with sophisticated social–cognitive skills that allow them to interpret what adults are referring to. These latter skills include *theory of mind*, that is, the ability to attribute mental states (including beliefs, desires and intentions) to oneself and others (Premack & Woodruff, 1978). The child's increasing memory capacity and general learning abilities probably do contribute

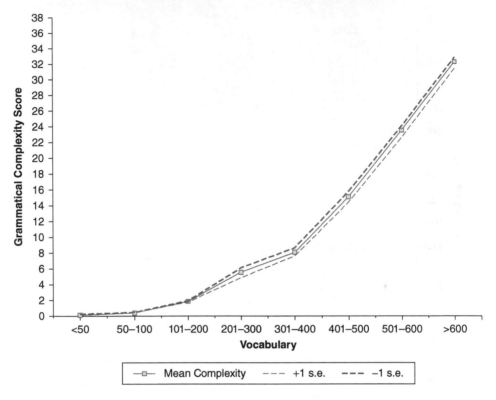

Figure 6.4 The relationship between grammar and vocabulary

Source: From Bates, E. & Goodman, J.C. (1997). On the inseparability of grammar and the lexicon: Evidence from acquisition, aphasia and real-time processing. *Language and Cognitive Processes, 12(5–6)*, 507–584, p. 517, Figure 2.

to an explanation of rapid word learning. But that is not the same as a spurt. Perhaps a further candidate, the onset of combinatorial speech, holds the key. Bates & Goodman (1997) observe a close interrelationship between words and grammar and certainly, the point at which word learning takes off in earnest (roughly 18 months) is also the point at which the child begins to put words together in multi-word sequences. As Figure 6.4 shows, there is a very strong relationship between the size of the child's vocabulary and the grammatical complexity of their utterances. Moreover, this relationship is non-linear. This means that growth (in both vocabulary and grammar) is not steady, but increases rapidly after a phase where growth has been more sedate. This tight relationship between vocabulary and grammar persists until the child is at least 30 months old (Fenson et al., 1994). In a similar vein, early vocabulary learning also predicts the child's facility with literacy at the age of ten years (Song, Su, Kang, Liu, Zhang, McBride-Chang, Tardif, Li, Liang, Zhang & Shu, 2015).

Spurt? What spurt?

The sudden acceleration in rate of word learning has variously been described as a burst, a spurt or an explosion. All very exciting, but not necessarily true. Bloom (2004) suggests that the vocabulary spurt is actually a myth. First, no-one seems to agree on what counts as a spurt.

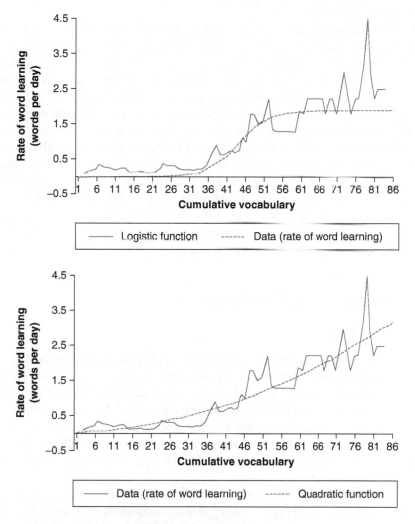

Figure 6.5 Different ways of modelling vocabulary growth

Source: Ganger, J. & Brent, M.R. (2004). Reexamining the vocabulary spurt. *Developmental Psychology*, *40/4*, 621–632. Figure 1: A spurtlike function (logistic) superimposed on slightly modified data from Child 041B (p. 623), and Figure 2: A nonspurtlike curve (quadratic) superimposed on the same data shown in Figure 1 (p. 623).

We have already seen that disagreement exists about both the age and vocabulary size marking the onset of the spurt. There is no consensus, either, on what *rate* of learning might identify a spurt. On one view, the spurt has started when the child has accrued ten or more new object names in a single three-week period (Gopnik & Meltzoff, 1986). Mervis & Bertrand (1995), meanwhile, look for ten or more words in a *two*-week period, at least half of which are object names. But perhaps this is nit-picking. Most authors do use roughly similar criteria, however arbitrarily chosen they might seem.

Perhaps more seriously, there is evidence that the vocabulary spurt is a minority taste. Ganger & Brent (2004) examined the growth curves for 38 children, looking for a kink, or inflection point, in the graph that would indicate a dramatic shift in rate of learning. As shown in Figure 6.5, different kinds of growth curve can be fitted to the same set of data. Statistical methods can help choose which curve function models the data most closely. Ganger & Brent were looking for a logistic function, essentially a growth curve with a kink in it that would denote a spurt. But this kind of curve was rarely the best model of the data, being most suitable for only five out of the 38 children they examined. Unless all children show a spurt, its significance in theories of language development remains unclear. If we accept the existence of a spurt, then we must thereby accept a discontinuity in development – a qualitative shift from one stage to another. But shifts of this kind are difficult to explain and, wherever possible, are avoided in theorizing, if only for the sake of parsimony (Pinker, 1984). Nevertheless, the fact that some children undergo a spurt requires explanation. Perhaps individual differences, in the constitution of either the child or the input (or both), hold the key.

The rate of word learning

Ten words a day?

Spurt or no spurt, the rate at which the child learns words appears prodigious. The child shifts from knowing just a handful of words at 18 months to several thousand by five years. But how fast is that? A figure that is often bandied about is a rate of 10 words per day. But this figure, which finds its origins in Carey (1978), overstates the case. And it also masks considerable variation over time. Children do not actually hit their peak until they are about 10 years old. The estimates shown in Table 6.2 assume an average vocabulary size of 60,000 words by the time of (American) High School graduation (Anglin, 1993). Word learning begins quite slowly but then picks up speed throughout the school years.

The figures in Table 6.2 represent our current best estimates of vocabulary growth, but, as we pointed out in Chapter 1, estimating vocabulary size is a notoriously difficult venture. In addition, quoting average figures can be deceptive, because it breeds the idea that the child is moving along at a constant rate. In fact, it is very difficult to determine, in absolute terms, whether word learning is fast or slow (see Chapter 8 where this issue is considered in relation to grammar). What we *can* say is that, within each age band, there will be times of accelerated growth, balanced by times when things ease off (Bloom, 2004).

Table 6.2 Average number of words learned per day (based on Anglin, 1993)

Age range (years)	Words per day
1;0 – 1;4	0.3
1;4 – 1;11	0.8
1;11 – 2;6	1.6
2;6 – 6;0	3.6
6;0 – 8;0	6.6
8;0 – 10;0	12.1
10;0 – 17;0	7.8

Fast mapping

We have established that children are capable of learning words quickly. But how do they manage it? One answer is that children often need very little experience to learn and retain (at least *something* about) individual words. In fact, a single exposure to a new word can be sufficient to lodge it in the child's head. The first study to show this *fast mapping* effect was conducted by Carey & Bartlett (1978). They taught three- and four-year-old children a new colour term, *chromium*, which they used for a shade of olive green. (Yes, chromium is a shiny metal, but these children were not to know that.) Given a choice of two trays – one blue, one chromium – children were asked to 'Bring me the chromium tray, not the blue one, the chromium one'. If you had never before heard the word *chromium*, what would *you* do? These children fetched the olive-green coloured tray and, moreover, they retained some understanding of *chromium* as a colour name even after six weeks (Carey, 1978). Fast mapping ability improves during development, with four-year-olds out-performing their 18-month-old peers (Schmidt, Oliveira, Santos Lotério & Gomes, 2016). But retention from fast mapping is not always good (Horst & Samuelson, 2008). While children can learn something from very limited experience, the benefits of practice, through repeated exposure, should not be underestimated. Practice with one set of words can even lead children to cope better in learning an entirely different set of words (Gershkoff-Stowe & Hahn, 2007).

Slow mapping: The gradual accretion of meaning

At the start of this chapter, I noted that *axolotl* is a new word for me. Maybe for you, too. If so, you may at least recall that axolotls are a kind of salamander from Mexico. This means that without ever meeting a real-life axolotl, you can begin to use the word successfully. But there is more to know about the meaning of *axolotl*. They can regenerate entire limbs, should they happen to lose one. They remain in the larval stage of development throughout their lives, failing to undergo metamorphosis. And so on. The concept of *axolotl* is not an all-or-nothing affair. As adults, then, we often have only partial knowledge of a word's meaning. Malapropisms provide another example of partial lexical knowledge:

> *He is the very pine-apple of politeness.* (Mrs Malaprop, from Sheridan's play *The Rivals*)
> *We heard the ocean is infatuated with sharks.* (Stan Laurel)
> *Republicans understand the importance of bondage between a mother and child.* (Dan Quayle)

For children, too, it can take some time to acquire the full meaning of a word, especially abstract terms like *truth* or *purity*, or complex verbs like *pour* and *fill* (Gropen, Pinker, Hollander & Goldberg, 1991). Try 'pouring the glass with milk' or 'filling milk into the glass', if you think the meanings of *pour* and *fill* are straightforward. Not surprisingly, therefore, children do not learn all there is to know about a word straightaway. Notice how, in this case at least, we have turned the comprehension–production disjunction on its head. *Full* comprehension of a word often lags behind the ability to produce it. Generally speaking, we can see that an adult-like ability to understand and use words may take several years to achieve.

EXERCISE 6.1

Give yourself three days to learn 30 new words, but do it in a language that is completely foreign to you. You should be able to find reference materials in your University library for Mandarin or Swedish or whatever language takes your fancy. Compile a list containing concrete objects and actions, that is, things you can see or touch, like *cup*, t*able*, *eat*, *jump*. Avoid abstract words like *constitution*, *beauty*, *decide*. On Day 1 make a set of drawings depicting each word. Then start practising. On Day 3, test yourself by naming each picture. Then consider the following points:

- How well did you do? 100 per cent correct?
- How many times did you have to repeat the words to make them stick (if they did stick, that is)?
- What kind of exposure did you have to each word?
- Would a different method of learning have been more effective?
- How does the way you learned these words differ from the way a two-year-old would have learned them? See also the Website recommendations at end of this chapter.

Biases

The return of the *gavagai* problem

Remember what *gavagai* means? If your fast mapping is not so fast any more, slip back to Chapter 1, or see if the following brief reminder works. Let's take a two-year-old and show her a corkscrew. For the sake of both the argument and her liver, let's assume that corkscrews are a novel item for this child. What does the word *corkscrew* refer to? Following Quine (1960), we cannot assume a priori that the word denotes the whole object. In principle, there is nothing to stop the child assuming that the word refers to the handle of the corkscrew alone, or the corkscrew plus the bottle it is opening, or the corkscrew as it appears at 7am on Sunday morning (quite evil). And so on. This infinity of referents is logically possible. Patently, though, children are not misled in this way. They do not lurch all over the place, mislabelling concepts and acquiring bizarre word meanings. But what stops the child from doing this? The answer that has dominated research on word learning for the past 20 years or so is the notion of a *learning bias*. If children are biased to pay attention to certain aspects of a scene, they are more likely to make the same connections between the world and its words as adults do. We can begin to explore the topic of word-learning biases through a more general bias: the dominance of nouns over other kinds of word in the child's early vocabulary.

A noun bias in the child and in research

Nouns, in the form of object names, have a special place in the child's early vocabulary. In every language studied so far, object names occur with an unusually high frequency when compared with the vocabularies of older children and adults. This pattern holds for Dutch, English, French, Hebrew, Italian, Korean and Spanish (Bornstein, Cote, Maital, Painter, Park, Pascual, Venuti & Vyt, 2004). It also holds for less well studied languages like Tzeltal (a Mayan language spoken in Mexico), Kaluli (spoken in Western Samoa) and Navajo (a native American language) (Gentner & Boroditsky, 2001). There may be some exceptions, though. Children learning Chinese, Korean or Japanese may learn verbs earlier than nouns, or possibly at the same time, with no privileged place for nouns (Tardif, 1996; Choi, 1998). But the picture is far from clear. Other studies report the opposite, more conventional pattern of noun dominance, even if verbs are learned earlier than in English (for example, Au, Dapretto & Song, 1994; Rescorla, Lee, Oh & Kim, 2013; Hao, Liu, Shu, Xing, Jiang & Li, 2015). The confused picture may stem from the methods used in these studies. For example, the method of data collection influences the kind of language produced by the child. Both Chinese- and English-speaking children produce more nouns when reading books with their parents than when playing with toys (Tardif, Gelman & Xu, 1999). In addition, many studies rely on parental checklists. In this approach, parents are given a list of words and asked to check those which, in their opinion, their child is already producing. But as noted above, child usage does not always give the best indicator of child comprehension. Experimental approaches provide much clearer

163

support for the dominance of nouns over verbs. In a novel word learning study, three-year-olds learning English, Japanese and Chinese all succeeded in acquiring new nouns but not new verbs (Imai, Li, Haryu, Okada, Hirsh-Pasek, Golinkoff & Shigematsu, 2008).

Nouns are easy

The research on nouns versus verbs leads us to ask two questions. First, why are nouns so easy? And second, why are verbs so difficult? If we look at nouns first, it is important to note that we are not talking about just any kind of noun. The nouns children first acquire are typically object names that refer to physically manifest things I can see and touch, like jelly or mud. But many nouns are abstract, like *happiness*, *purity* or *antidisestablishmentarianism* (second appearance for this word – look it up: it's the longest conventional word in English). Other nouns *are* concrete, but refer to things or events that are difficult to observe directly, or point out in a simple way, for example, *symbiosis* or *sunshine* or *fission*. It is only certain kinds of noun – object names – that children learn with particular ease. Having said that, not *all* nouns in the child's early vocabulary are object names: some of the nouns in the child's first 50 words refer to parts, actions, locations and substances (Bloom, Tinker & Margulis, 1993). Object names might be easy, but other kinds of noun are not impossible.

We have now narrowed our question about the noun bias down to the following: what is it about object names that children find relatively easy? The answer lies in the nature of objects and how we perceive them. It seems that we are born viewing the world in terms of whole objects (Spelke, 1994). We expect objects to adhere to certain principles, namely: cohesion, continuity, solidity and contact. Cohesion refers to the fact that objects comprise a connected and bounded region of matter. Continuity decrees that objects follow a continuous path through space. Only in *Doctor Who*, and the like, do objects disappear in one place and pop up in another. Solidity, meanwhile, suggests we have a (reasonable) belief that one object cannot pass through another (again, *Doctor Who* fans notwithstanding). And finally, the principle of contact determines that inanimate objects move only when they are touched by another object or person. There is good evidence from developmental psychology that we are born with these expectations and that we view the world as a place comprising separate, whole objects (Spelke & Kinzler, 2007).

Some authors talk in terms of a universal whole-object bias (for example, Imai et al., 2008) that compels the child to assume that words refer to whole objects. Indeed, if a 12-month-old hears a new word, their initial assumption is that it refers to an object category (Waxman & Markow, 1995). So powerful is this bias, the perception of angles in geometric figures can be skewed (Gibson, Congdon & Levine, 2015). Erroneously, four-year-olds are swayed by perception of an object – specifically, the length of the lines in a figure – when making judgements about the size of its angles. There is evidence, also, that the whole object bias is more powerful than other word-learning biases. Three-year-olds retain object words learned from fast mapping after one week, but failed to recall words describing shape, texture or colour (Holland, Simpson & Riggs, 2015). Observe how the whole-object bias greatly reduces the complexity of Quine's *gavagai* problem. It would simply never occur to a child that a word might refer to just part of an object or include entities beyond an object's boundaries.

The whole-object bias is part of human cognition generally (Patterson, Bly, Porcelli & Rypma, 2007). It is not part of language and does not compel us to use language to name objects. Many animals, including rats and monkeys, have been shown to possess a whole-object bias (Winters, Saksida & Bussey, 2008). But humans are unique in exploiting their whole-object bias in the naming of objects. What prompts us to do this? The answer may lie in the property of *shared intentionality*. Humans, unlike chimpanzees, seem compelled to share their attention and interest in what they are doing, including picking out objects of interest to talk about (Tomasello & Carpenter, 2007; see also Chapter 9). Shared intentionality, combined with the whole-object bias, may therefore explain the dominance of object names in early child vocabularies. Object names not only make possible the learning of other kinds of noun, they provide a framework for learning verbs. For example, if one knows the object names *ball* and *girl*, it will be easier to grasp the meaning of the verb *kick* when viewing a scene described by *The girl kicked the ball*.

Verbs are hard

Now let's tackle the second question: why are verbs so difficult? As with object names, the answer seems to lie partly in the way we perceive and think about the world. Actions are inherently more difficult than objects to pick out as discrete entities from the environment (Gentner, 1982, 2006). With objects, the cohesion principle ensures that the boundaries of an object are easy to detect. In contrast, deciding where an action begins and ends is not always straightforward. Also, many actions change as they unfold over time (think of dancing or swimming). There is some evidence that children perform better when the visual salience of an action is improved (Abbot-Smith, Imai, Durrant & Nurmsoo, 2017). Generally speaking, though, children seem to have more difficulty encoding (and later recalling) actions than they do objects (Imai, Haryu & Okada, 2005). Verbs are also difficult for distributional reasons. This point relates to our discussion in Chapter 5, where we discovered the statistical exploits of the preverbal infant. It turns out that nouns are more predictable than verbs with regard to the linguistic contexts in which they occur. For example, the probability of *the* being followed by a noun is 0.19 (almost 1 in 5). Verbs are significantly less predictable. But in one experiment, the predictability of verbs was increased by increasing the number of times infants heard them with the morpheme *–ing* (*jumping, diving, running*) (Willits, Seidenberg & Saffran, 2015). Given this leg-up, infants as young as 7.5 months found verbs less taxing to identify. The distributional properties of nouns and verbs therefore contribute to the relative ease with which they are learned.

Children also have difficulty in extending verb meanings to new instances. For example, I may first encounter the verb *jump* in the **sentence** *Simon is jumping on the bed*. Generalizing beyond this context, I might change the **agent** (*Martine is jumping on the bed*). I might also change the **object**, the thing being jumped on (*Simon is jumping on the sofa*). In one study, children were provided with unusual (novel) objects that were paired with novel actions. For example, a rugby ball-shaped object with fins was paired with the action of lightly tossing and catching it with both hands (Imai et al., 2005). It was found that three-year-olds can generalize verb use to a new agent (as with the switch from Simon to Martine), but only when the original object was used (the bed). Of course, actions can often be applied to more than one object. The action of cutting can be

165

applied to a potato, a cabbage or my finger. But object and action seem to be fused together conceptually for three-year-olds. When the action was applied to a different object (as in the sofa), children failed to generalize their knowledge of the new verb. By five years, in contrast, children could cope with changes in either actor or object.

Why are verb meanings less easily extended than noun meanings? The answer to this question is not so clear. The child may sometimes need to witness specific actor–object combinations several times before they can be encoded and identified as nameable actions. That is, the child needs more experience with verbs than with nouns. And the reason for this may lie in the relative difficulty we have in perceiving actions as discrete events in the world. This problem arises for the simplest kind of verbs – concrete actions depicting events that we can readily perceive and participate in. Once the hurdle of concrete actions has been crossed, the child still faces other kinds of verbs, a situation paralleling the case for nouns discussed above. For example, some verbs have concrete referents, but are not so easily observed, like *putrefy* or *indulge*. Yet others are abstract, like *sanctify* or *excel*. The naming of concrete objects is therefore only the first, most tractable, step in learning the full range of word types that must be acquired.

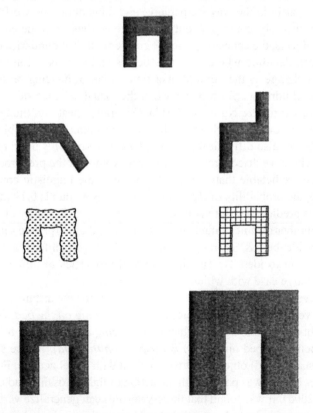

Figure 6.6 Stimuli used in a study demonstrating the shape bias in early word learning (from Landau, Smith & Jones, 1988)

The shape bias

As we have seen, the whole-object bias provides a good launching pad in the task of object naming. But it will only get the child so far. Object names must also be extended appropriately to new examples from the same category. We have already hinted that the child might make use of an object's shape in this respect. In addition to the whole-object bias, then, a shape bias has also been proposed. An early demonstration of the shape bias is provided by Landau, Smith & Jones (1988). In their experiment, they created a real object from wood and named it a *dax* (as shown at the top of Figure 6.6). Children were told 'this is a dax' and then asked about each of the remaining objects in Figure 6.6 with the question, 'Is this a dax?' For children aged two and three years, a new object was accepted as a dax if it had the same shape as the original dax. Other factors, meanwhile, were overridden, including size, colour, pattern, material and texture. The shape bias is a developmental phenomenon, with children becoming progressively more adept at using shape to guide word learning between the ages of 12 and 24 months (Hupp, 2015). In some cases, as in Spanish-speaking children, the shape bias develops more slowly, if at all (Hahn & Cantrell, 2012). But generally speaking, the shape bias is a pervasive factor in early word learning (Samuelson, Horst, Schutte & Dobbertin, 2008).

The rise and fall of word learning biases

Associative learning: The origin of biases?

The shape bias has come to dominate research on children's early extension of word meaning. But other biases have also been documented in the literature. The most prominent of these are summarized in Table 6.3. There is a general consensus that these special biases exist and greatly facilitate children's learning of new categories and words. But two important questions remain unanswered. First, where do these biases come from? And second, where do they go? You will not be surprised that the first question – the question of origin – reduces quickly to our old friend nature–nurture. It is possible that children are born with particular ways of perceiving and conceptualizing the world. These cognitive dispositions are then later harnessed in the acquisition of word meaning. A strong candidate in this regard is the whole-object bias, which many researchers consider to be a biologically determined system quite independent of language (Spelke & Kinzler, 2007). Other researchers sometimes point to the universality of word learning biases, but do not equate that universality with a genetic origin (for example, Imai & Haryu, 2004). This caution applies even though the focus is on the child's conceptual, rather than linguistic, knowledge. On the whole, word learning researchers have been more hesitant when it comes to grasping the nativist nettle than in other areas of child language, like grammar or morphology (see Chapters 7 and 8).

The alternative to nativist accounts rests on the child's ability to learn. And in research on the shape bias, we find the most fully developed account of how the child might *acquire* conceptual knowledge of shape through perceiving and interacting with objects in the world (Smith, 2001; Colunga & Smith, 2008). This approach is known as the Attentional Learning Account (ALA)

Table 6.3 Word learning biases

Bias	Description	Evidence	Key studies
Whole object	New words name whole objects, not parts or properties.	12-month-old infants are shown a complex object that could be construed as two separate objects. A novel word is associated with the whole object, not the parts, as measured by infant looking times.	Hollich & Golinkoff (2007)
Shape	Objects that have the same shape will have the same name.	A novel object is labelled a *dax*. New objects are also labelled dax if they have the same shape as the first, regardless of size, texture or colour.	Landau et al. (1988)
Mutual exclusivity	Words are mutually exclusive: each object will have one and only one label.	The child is shown two objects, one of which has a familiar label and one of which does not. Given a new label, children assume that it applies to the unfamiliar object.	Markman & Wachtel (1988)
Taxonomic bias	Children classify objects according to taxonomic categories (e.g., animal) rather than themes (e.g., animal plus its food plus its habitat, and so on).	A picture of a dog is labelled as a *dax*. When asked to choose another dax from pictures of a dog, a cat and a bone, they choose the cat.	Markman & Hutchinson (1984)
Basic level	Categories are easier to conceptualize and remember at the basic-level (e.g., *cat*, rather than *Tiddles* or *mammal*).	A significant proportion of children's early vocabulary comprises basic-level terms.	Mervis (1987)

and relies on the well-established phenomenon of *associative learning*. Associative learning takes place when two perceptual cues co-occur in a predictable way. The presence of one cue can be taken as a reliable (if not perfect) indication that the second cue will also be present. Once an association has been formed, then the presence of one cue will automatically direct the learner's attention to the second cue. Attention thus becomes selective. In the word learning context, attention becomes selectively focused on object shape as a reliable cue to an object's category, as indicated by its name. In this regard, it is telling that more than 90 per cent of the **count nouns** first acquired by children are most easily categorized according to their shape (Smith, 2000). Shape is therefore a reliable cue to the name that an object will be labelled with in episodes where parents say things like 'This is a _____'. In this way, the linguistic cue becomes associated with the perceptual cue of shape. The shape bias ends up being specific to the domain of language, but it 'emerges from very general learning processes, processes that in and of themselves have no domain-specific content' (Smith, 1999: 182).

The importance of associative learning for word learning is not contested. But not all researchers agree that the ALA can explain the origins of conceptual knowledge about shape (or indeed, other aspects of conceptual knowledge). A major sticking point has been the age at which the child demonstrates their knowledge of shape in categorization tasks. In early versions of the ALA, it was assumed that the child required considerable experience of object–word pairings for the shape bias to emerge. It was suggested that this point might not be reached until about age 2;6 when the child's vocabulary is something like 50–100 words. However, recent studies have shown that conceptual categories are in evidence much earlier — as young as 12 months – and, moreover, they are not necessarily bound to the act of naming (Samuelson & Smith, 2005; Booth & Waxman, 2008; Hupp, 2008). For example, Waxman & Markow (1995) showed that 12-month-old children can form different animal categories (e.g., duck, lion, bear, dog), much earlier than suggested by the ALA account. Moreover, it is not clear that these younger children are using shape as the basis for categorization. Other factors, like the particular form and position of head, eyes and legs may explain children's success (Gershkoff-Stowe & Smith, 2004). It does seem that children have already developed certain key aspects of conceptual knowledge before they begin the task of word learning. The further development of conceptual knowledge then becomes intertwined with further advances in vocabulary acquisition. The way in which associative learning interacts with conceptual knowledge has not yet been determined (Elman, 2008). We must watch this space (with attention to its shape) for further clarification.

Where do biases go?

Perhaps more mysterious than the issue of where biases come from is the question of where they go, or rather, the question of how children override their biases as learning progresses. Biases are helpful in the early stages of word learning, but they must be overcome at some point. A quick look at the lexicon beyond the realm of concrete count nouns reveals why this must be so. Take, for example, the whole-object bias. Many words do not refer to whole-objects at all, but, instead, are used to refer to parts of objects (like the leg of a chair) or properties (like the colour of the chair). And many (many) other words have nothing to do with objects at all, for example, those words used for actions, events and relations. Another bias, mutual exclusivity, is overridden very early on (Markman, 1990). This bias decrees that there should be one, and only one, label for each object (see Table 6.3). But at the age of two years, my son Alex called our pet both by its name (*Michelangelo*) as well as by the basic-level term, *cat*. (Incidentally, Michelangelo was named after a ninja turtle, not a Renaissance artist.) Mutual exclusivity can be overridden, but, to complicate matters, it does not entirely disappear (Jaswal, 2010). Children can be seen adhering to mutual exclusivity years later, at the age of six (Davidson & Tell, 2005). The example of different names for our pet could also be seen as a case of overriding the basic-level assumption (see Box 6.1). While *cat* is the basic-level term, the child also acquires both superordinate (*animal*) and subordinate terms (*Michelangelo*). As learning progresses, many other terms could be recruited for our cat, including *feline*, *pet*, *mammal* and *moggy*. In a similar vein, the child can go beyond the taxonomic bias by the age of four years (Srinivasan & Snedeker, 2014).

Even the mighty shape bias disappears when children are presented with complex-shaped objects or when they are not forced to choose – as in many experiments – one object from an array of objects (Cimpian & Markman, 2005). Another way to overcome the shape bias is to provide a strong hint of animacy by adding eyes to the test object and by manipulating the texture (e.g., making it furry or feathered) (Jones, Smith & Landau, 1991). In other words, children's attention *can* be drawn beyond the perceptual attributes of shape during the process of categorization and naming. As children get older, they become increasingly adept in this regard. For example, children aged three and four years can focus on an artefact's function – what it is used for – something that is not always obvious from appearance alone (Kemler Nelson, Frankenfield, Morris & Blair, 2000). Children can also attend to other conceptual distinctions, including real versus toy animals (Carey, 1985), rigid objects versus non-solid substances (Soja, Carey & Spelke, 1991), and animate versus inanimate (Jones et al., 1991). As children's conceptual knowledge about objects increases, it can be deployed with increasing sophistication in the acquisition of new words.

Biases do have an important part to play in vocabulary acquisition and the fact that they can, indeed must, be overridden is important also. We might think of these biases as a series of springboards that help get the child started, both in the early stages of word learning, but also later on, when particular words are new to the child. They help narrow down the range of possible hypotheses about what words mean. In this way, they go a long way to solving Quine's *gavagai* problem. What we do not yet know is where these biases come from. As noted, most researchers commit happily to the idea that the whole-object bias is innate, but there is much more evasion for other biases (e.g., Imai & Haryu, 2004). If the question of origins has not yet been answered satisfactorily, even less is known about the disappearance of word learning biases. Numerous studies demonstrate that the child can be flexible in what they attend to when categorizing and naming. But as yet, it is not clear how or why word learning biases operate at some times, but not at others. What we are left with at present is simply the fact that these biases exist, that they have a universal currency in children learning very different languages, and that they are used to guide the expansion of children's vocabularies.

Some lexical gaps

The origin and demise of word learning biases are but two mysteries that remain unresolved in research on word learning. Before we move on, it is worth pointing out some other rather large gaps in our knowledge about word learning. As we have seen, a large amount of research effort has been devoted to just one very specific kind of word, namely, concrete count nouns (like *chair*, *dog*, *tree*). In recent years, the palette of enquiry has been expanded somewhat to encompass verbs (e.g., Hirsh-Pasek & Golinkoff, 2006; Golinkoff & Hirsh-Pasek, 2008) and **adjectives** (Ninio, 2004; Mintz, 2005; Booth & Waxman, 2009; Hall, Williams & Bélanger, 2015), but we still know relatively little about other types of word, including **articles** (*a*, *the*, *some*), **prepositions** (*by*, *through*, *from*) and **pronouns** (*he*, *she*, *they*) among others. Evidently, there is still a lot to learn about how children acquire their knowledge of words.

Computational modelling based on probability theory

Innate biases and associative learning have recently joined forces under the flag of probability theory. To remind yourself about the basic precepts of this approach, slide back to Box 5.2. The aim is to devise a computer program that can model child word learning. To do this successfully, modellers aim to simulate the conditions of learning in the following ways: (1) equip the model at the outset with the same knowledge that the child brings to word learning; (2) provide the model with input that equates to that experienced by the child; and (3) show that the outcome of learning is the same as the child's. With regard to (1), the learner's initial beliefs are sometimes known as the learner's *hypothesis space*. The hypotheses that a learner can entertain about word meaning are constrained within this space by the knowledge and learning mechanisms that are brought to the acquisition process. With regard to (2), the input can be simulated in various ways, but emphasis is often placed on frequency (see Chapter 9). Ideally, the frequency of exposure to the words being learned should equate to that experienced by the child. The context in which words are presented should also be similar. Finally, the success of a simulation can be judged quite straightforwardly by comparing how well the model does with how well the child does. The model should achieve a similar degree of success to the child, not only in terms of accuracy, but also in terms of errors. We want our model to behave like the child, so similar kinds of errors should occur (for example, overextensions) at similar frequencies.

To date, Xu & Tenenbaum (2007) provide the most serious attempt to model word learning computationally. Their approach is based on Bayes' theorem, named after an eighteenth-century mathematician, Thomas Bayes (1702–1761). Bayes' theorem provides a formula for calculating the probability that a belief is true. In this case, we are concerned with learners' beliefs (or hypotheses) about word meanings. Support for a given hypothesis accumulates with experience, to the point where the chance that it is correct becomes very high. Nevertheless, the learner must always make some leap of faith beyond the evidence (an inductive inference). We can see this more clearly if we resurrect Quine's *gavagai* problem. First, let's take the issue of prior knowledge (or beliefs). We have seen that there are good grounds for equipping the learner with a whole-object bias at the outset of learning. In so doing, we greatly narrow down the hypothesis space (the kinds of hypotheses that will be entertained). The learner is much more likely to predict that *gavagai* means *rabbit* (the whole object) rather than *the rabbit's left ear* or *the rabbit plus the ground it is touching*. Even so, the learner cannot be absolutely certain that *gavagai* means *rabbit*. But the chances of being correct have increased. In addition to prior knowledge, we can think about the effects of the input. As experience is accumulated, the learner will probably encounter *gavagai* in different times and places. But the pairing of the word *gavagai* with the actual rabbit will remain constant. In consequence, increasing experience will strengthen the association between *gavagai* and the rabbit. Taken together, we can see how prior knowledge and experience constrain probabilistic reasoning, in the process of honing in on the meaning of *gavagai*.

Xu & Tenenbaum's model was presented with the task of learning 24 object names. Pairs of objects drawn from this set were rated by 22 adults according to their similarity with one another (on a scale from 1 to 9). These ratings were then used to inform the hypothesis space of the model. The objects were organized into a hierarchy of clusters, based on how closely the objects were judged to resemble one another. Similarity judgements can be based on shape, size, colour, texture, animacy, and many other properties (both perceptual and non-perceptual). Some or all of these relevant distinguishing properties might enter into a given judgement, plus information gleaned from prior experience with the objects. The model's hypothesis space, therefore, is very rich in terms of the prior knowledge it brings to the learning task, going well beyond the whole-object bias. One limitation is thus that a whole raft of word learning biases are conflated together. As noted, the prior knowledge of the model was based on adult ratings of the objects. But the basis for those ratings was not established. Future work might tease apart the differential effects of different kinds of prior knowledge. Even if we cannot be certain which aspects of prior knowledge were critical, the model was nevertheless very successful at categorizing the objects in the same way as three- and four-year-old children.

Another successful feature of the model is that it took into account the fact that our experience with different words will vary greatly. Hence, the model used probabilistic inference to arrive at different degrees of knowledge about a word's meaning, based on the particular level of input experienced. In consequence, the model ended up with a more extensive knowledge of some words than others. This attempt to capture different degrees of knowledge about particular words is especially valuable, since it chimes well with the observation, made above, that understanding of word meaning accumulates gradually. Xu & Tenenbaum (2007: 270) conclude that 'only a combination of sophisticated mental representations and sophisticated statistical inference machinery will be able to explain how adults and children can learn so many words, so fast and so accurately'. But where do the 'sophisticated mental representations' (the learner's prior knowledge) come from? Are they innate? Or are they learned, as a prelude to word learning proper? Modelling approaches do not yet provide an answer. But given the way that probabilistic machine learning closely models young children's behaviour, we must take seriously the idea that word learning is, in part at least, a statistical process, based on the laws of probability.

IN A NUTSHELL

- Comprehension of words precedes the child's ability to produce them: children know more than they can say.

- Overextension of a word's meaning is a common error in the early stages of vocabulary learning.

- Three possible causes of overextensions are: (1) a category error (the child misclassifies objects); (2) a pragmatic error (plugging a lexical gap); and (3) a memory retrieval error (the wrong word is selected).

- Some, but possibly not all, children undergo a vocabulary spurt – a sudden acceleration in the rate of word learning, at about 18 months.

- Whether or not there is a spurt, lexical acquisition appears to be fast, peaking during the late primary school years.

- Knowledge of individual word meanings is acquired gradually.

- Conceptual biases, including the whole-object bias and the shape bias, provide solutions to Quine's *gavagai* problem. They explain how children are constrained in the meanings they ascribe to words.

- Concrete count nouns dominate children's early vocabularies. Other kinds of noun, and verbs, are more challenging.

- Conceptual biases may be innate, though few researchers adopt an avowedly nativist stance.

- Associative learning has been used to explain the origins of word learning biases, but biases appear much earlier than this account might predict.

- Children must override conceptual biases in order to expand their vocabularies.

- We still require satisfactory explanations both for the origin of biases and for how they are overcome in development.

- Probability theory provides a method of modelling child word learning computationally. It combines a rich prior knowledge, based on conceptual biases, with statistical learning.

FURTHER READING

Hall, D.G. & Waxman, S.R. (Eds.) (2004). *Weaving a lexicon.* Cambridge, MA: MIT Press.

This book presents a wide-ranging collection of papers from specialists in lexical acquisition. It covers the period of early word learning and claims also to look at later acquisition. Be warned, though: 'later' means 'post-first year, but still pre-school' in a language acquisition context. Nevertheless, this is a weighty tome that covers all the major bases of research in the field.

Hirsh-Pasek, K. & Golinkoff, R.M. (Eds.) (2006). *Action meets word: How children learn verbs*. Oxford: Oxford University Press.

Another sizeable collection of papers, this book considers verb learning and, in the process, makes a concerted effort to break away from the massive research focus on early concrete nouns. These papers set the research ball rolling in a new and potentially exciting direction, by addressing a question we touched on here: why are verbs relatively difficult to acquire?

WEBSITES

- **Online Scrabble**: www.isc.ro

  Play to your heart's content when you should be writing an essay and learn two things about language acquisition: (1) we continue to acquire new words throughout the lifespan; and (2) we can learn and use words without any idea what they mean or even what grammatical category they belong to. Try *vly*, *euoi* and *zati* for size – all English words.

- **Tips on vocabulary learning**: www.sheppardsoftware.com/ vocabulary_tips.htm

  A commercial site, but here they offer you ten free tips on how to improve your vocabulary. Does the young child use any of these methods? Do you? What are the differences between child and adult word learning?

- **Wordbank**: http://wordbank.stanford.edu

  An open database on children's vocabulary growth which contains data on more than 60,000 children across 21 languages. You can explore a wealth of data profiles and analyses or even use free software to do your own investigations (see also Frank, Braginsky, Yurovsky & Marchman, 2016).

Still want more? For links to online resources relevant to this chapter and a quiz to test your understanding, visit the companion website at **https://study.sagepub.com/saxton2e**

7

The Acquisition of Morphology: Linguistic Lego

CONTENTS

OVERVIEW

Morphology is concerned with the internal structure of words, with *morpheme* being defined as the smallest unit of meaning in a language. By the end of this chapter, you should be able to describe three different ways of constructing complex words from morphemes:

- inflection (*jump* + *-ed* → *jumped*)
- derivation (*inspect* + *-ion* → *inspection*)
- compounding (*lady* + *bird* → *ladybird*)

We shall examine how the child acquires these three processes. It will become apparent that a great deal of attention has focused on just one aspect of inflectional morphology: the English past tense. Researchers have investigated the way we learn and represent regular past tense forms (*moved, pushed*) versus irregular forms (*fallen, held*). You should develop an understanding of the regular–irregular distinction, in relation to two competing accounts of how we represent past tense morphology:

- single-route
- dual-route

The first approach, advocated by computer modellers in the connectionist tradition, argues that all past tense forms are learned in the same way. The second argues that two systems are required: grammar (for regular forms) and the lexicon (for irregular forms). You should come to appreciate arguments on both sides of this debate and gain some insight into why it remains unresolved after 30 years of enquiry.

We will also look at the acquisition of both derivation and compounding. You should become familiar with the way children acquire complex compounds like *bus drivers* and *dog catchers*, which combine all three morphological processes. We will examine the nativist suggestion that children may be born knowing how to assemble words of this kind. We will conclude by looking at the development of morphology in the school years. The acquisition of explicit knowledge about morphology facilitates acquisition in other domains, including vocabulary, reading and spelling.

Inflection

Begin this chapter with a deep breath. Hold it for a few seconds and then release. Repeat this cycle until you achieve a state of complete tranquillity. Then get ready to analyse the internal structure of words in terms of inflectional, derivational and compound **morphology**. Deep breathing may or may not help, but we do need to learn something about morphology in order to appreciate the task which faces the language-learning child. The complexities of complex words can overwhelm, especially if we look beyond English. In Finnish, for example, it has been estimated that the morphological system yields more than 2,000 possible word forms for nouns (Karlsson & Koskenniemi, 1985). Despite this huge complexity, every typically developing child born to Finnish-speaking parents acquires Finnish morphology. If *they* can do it, so can you. Or rather, you can discover, without *too* much pain, the essentials of morphology. Let's start with a definition. Morphemes can be defined as the smallest unit of meaning in a language. These units can be smaller than a word, which means that every word comprises one or more morphemes. The study of morphology is therefore concerned with the internal structure of words. Inflection, derivation and compounding provide three different ways of constructing complex words, each of which pose different challenges for the language-learning child. We will start with inflection, where our first observation is that this aspect of morphology has devoured the lion's share of research effort. In fact, just one aspect of inflection in a single language – the English past tense – has been (almost) all-consuming. But we shall try to throw the net wider, once we have worked out what all the fuss is about with inflection.

Inflection is a process that changes the grammatical function of a **lexeme** through the expression of properties such as number, gender, **case** and tense. We can take inflection for number as an example. In English, there is no inflection to mark a singular noun (*one beetle, one atom*). But we do add -*s* to mark plurality (*two beetles, twelve atoms*). Inflection does not create a new lexeme, that is, a new word with a distinct meaning. Instead, inflection yields a range of different **word forms** that fulfil particular grammatical functions. As we can see, one such function is the expression of plurality. English is rather feeble when it comes to inflection, having only eight different inflectional forms (see **inflectional morpheme** in the Glossary). Other languages, including Finnish and Russian, have vastly more complex systems of inflection. One complication in English (and other languages) is that inflectional paradigms can have exceptions, which leads to a traditional distinction between regular and irregular forms. The regular inflection for plural is -*s* (*trees, planes, ideas*). But there are exceptions. I can roast *two geese*, not **gooses*, for *three women*, not **womans* (I hope they're hungry). *Goose* and *woman* are irregular nouns. Similarly, the past tense in English has a regular pattern, which (roughly speaking) involves adding -*ed*. I can say that yesterday, I *washed, shaved* and *talked*. But again, there are irregular exceptions. These include *ate* instead of **eated, drove* instead of **drived*, and *bought*, not **buyed*. Pinker and Prince (1988) suggest there are 181 irregular verbs in English, but the list is not immutable. New irregular forms do emerge from time to time. For example, it is common (in the UK) to hear *text* as the past tense form for *text* (e.g., *He text me last night*), rather than the regular form *texted*. The verb *text* is similar, therefore to verbs like *cut* and *shut*, which also show no change from present to past forms. Pinker (1999: 15) suggests that, 'whereas regulars are orderly and predictable, irregulars are chaotic and idiosyncratic'. Thus, the past tense of *sing* is *sang*, but for *bring*, we say *brought* (not **brang*). The past tense of *drink* is *drank*, but for *think* it is *thought* (not **thank*). Viewed in this way, it is difficult to discern any pattern among different irregular forms. But there *is* some order in the chaos Pinker perceives, as we shall see, and this has a direct bearing on how the child might acquire categories like the past tense.

A moment ago we were rather rough in our handling of the regular inflection, -*ed*. Let's smooth things out now, to help with the discussion that follows. If we focus on the way -*ed* is pronounced, it becomes apparent that it varies. Consider *phoned*, where -*ed* is pronounced /d/. The final phoneme of the root form, *phone*, is /n/ (think sounds, not spelling). /n/ is a **voiced** sound and so is /d/. Next up is *danced*, which ends in /t/, a **voiceless** sound. The final phoneme of the root form, *dance*, is /s/, which is also voiceless. Hence, *-ed* can be pronounced as either /d/ or /t/. The choice is determined by the voicing of the final sound in the stem: the inflection takes on the same voicing state as the root. In grown up linguistic talk, which you can drop into your next conversation with Chomsky, we say that the past tense inflection is *phonologically conditioned*. One further wrinkle. Some regular verbs insert a vowel before /d/ (e.g., *wanted*, *batted*, *patted* and *carted*). Again, this is phonologically conditioned: observe that the root form ends in /t/ in each case.

The acquisition of inflection

Whole word learning

In principle, a child could get by in life without any knowledge of morphology, nor any of the skills required to dissect words into their constituent morphemes. All we would need is a powerful long-term memory storage system, something which humans do, in fact, possess. Using a sufficiently extensive memory, we could learn every word form as it stands, with no reference to or acknowledgement of any internal morphological structure. On this model of learning, the child would treat words like *parrots*, *believing* and *wanted* as indivisible wholes. The child would never need to analyse words into their constituent parts (e.g., *parrot + -s*). But none of the analyses in Table 7.1 would be done at any point in the course of acquisition.

Table 7.1   Analysis of words into constituent morphemes

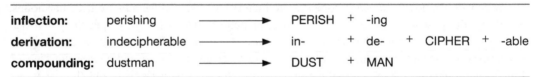

inflection:	perishing	⟶	PERISH	+	-ing				
derivation:	indecipherable	⟶	in-	+	de-	+	CIPHER	+	-able
compounding:	dustman	⟶	DUST	+	MAN				

There is, in fact, some evidence that children do start out as 'whole word' learners, with no regard for the internal structure of words. For example, children acquiring Hungarian produce correctly inflected words, even during the one-word stage (MacWhinney, 1985). However, it is unlikely that the child has assembled these words from separate morphemes, or has any knowledge that these words can be broken down to yield distinct units of meaning. This is because, initially, there are no signs of child productivity. Children do not produce inflected words of their own, but confine their output to words they have been exposed to in parental input. This phenomenon has been observed in languages with rich inflectional systems, including Hungarian and Turkish (MacWhinney, 1985; Aksu-Koç & Slobin, 1985; Aksu-Koç, 1997). In the absence of productivity, these early words are best regarded as unanalysed wholes, even if

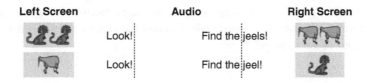

Figure 7.1 Testing the comprehension of the plural marker -s (after Jolly & Plunkett, 2008)

they *seem* morphologically complex from an adult perspective. It takes some time for children to work out the meanings of inflections. This becomes apparent if we give children a choice of two pictures to look at, one depicting a single novel object, the other depicting two novel objects (see Figure 7.1).

If the child hears *Look at the jeels!*, they should look at the two-object picture, if, that is, they understand the meaning of the plural inflection -s. By the same token, children should focus on the single-object picture if they hear *Look at the jeel!* However, Jolly & Plunkett (2008) found that 24-month-olds are insensitive to the plural marker. It is not until 30 months that children's viewing is guided by the presence or absence of the plural marker. The task in this experiment taps into children's *comprehension* of language. But we know that they correctly *produce* plural markers of their own well before 30 months. In a similar fashion, Dispaldro & Benelli (2012) report that Italian children only begin to understand that singular forms refer to one object at about age four, while they are at least six years old before they comprehend that plural forms refer to 'more than one'. There is increasing evidence, therefore, that correct production of morphologically complex words does not necessarily mean that the child grasps either the form or meaning of a word's internal structure.

In fact, we know that, eventually, the child does begin to analyse the internal structure of words. A simple demonstration of this fact was provided in Chapter 1 with Berko's (1958) *wug* test. You may recall that four-year-olds can pluralize a nonsense word like *wug* – to produce *wugs* – even though we can be sure they have never heard the plural form. The child is therefore being productive in applying the plural inflectional morpheme -s to the noun *wug*. A number of factors seem to nudge the child into realizing the ways in which language encodes the distinction between single versus multiple entities (Lanter & Basche, 2014). One such factor is the complexity of singular–plural morphology in a given language. Russian, with its complex morphology, presents the child with multiple cues for learning the singular–plural distinction, whereas Japanese and English are much simpler. Accordingly, Russian children show signs of understanding the singular–plural distinction earlier than their Japanese and English contemporaries (Sarnecka, Kamenskaya, Yamana & Yudovina, 2004). Parallel findings have been reported for the acquisition of plural morphology within a single language, the dialectal variants of Spanish found in Chile and Mexico (Miller & Schmitt, 2012). The richness of the input has a direct influence on learning. Chilean children hear fewer full-form plural endings and, consequently, take longer to acquire the plural marker than their Mexican counterparts. This finding is confirmed in a large study across six different languages: Croatian, Dutch, French, German, Greek and Russian (Xanthos, Laaha, Gillis et al., 2011).

179

The complexities of the particular language being learned are reflected directly in the morphological richness of the input available to children, which in turn has a direct impact on the speed at which morphological features are acquired.

The past tense debate: Rules or connections?

Back in the 1980s, when telephones were stupid (or at least, not yet smartphones), we did at least have some form of computers, however large and unwieldy. Thanks to computational power, a debate was launched by Rumelhart & McClelland, in 1986, which has rumbled on for many years. The questions thrown up by these researchers strike at the core of how fundamental aspects of language are acquired and then represented in the human mind. The frenzy of controversy is largely in abatement these days, but not because the issues have been resolved, nor because the questions raised have become any less interesting. Rather, as is tantalisingly often the case, in both child language and psychology more widely, we lack the wherewithal to resolve the matter one way or the other. In addition, we shall see that concessions have been made, perforce, on both sides of the debate. The result has been a blurring of theoretical boundaries which makes adjudicating between the two sides more difficult. The two competing approaches are known as: (1) single-route; and (2) dual-route theories. Connectionist theorists provide the best-known single-route accounts, while so-called Words and Rules theory is the most prominent dual-route model. A good deal of the battle has been fought on the terrain of cognitive psychology, with the focus on how inflections are represented in the adult mind, rather than acquired by the child. But we shall try to keep the spotlight trained on the issue of *acquisition*.

A dual-route account: Words and Rules theory

As the name suggests, Words and Rules (WR) theory claims that language offers two ways of representing grammatical categories like past tense: **regular past tense forms** are generated by a rule, while **irregular forms** are stored in the lexicon. The mental lexicon is conceived as part of declarative memory, our long-term repository of facts. The 'facts' that are stored about each word include information about meaning, pronunciation and grammatical category (e.g., verb). Together, this information comprises the *lexical entry* for a word. Regular forms are produced by a mental production line that puts words together at the time of speaking. The regular rule can apply to any word with the symbol V (verb) as part of its lexical entry. For example, the word *talk* is a candidate for undergoing the regular rule, because it will be marked as V in its lexical entry. The past tense rule is enacted by retrieving the base form, *talk* (from lexical memory), together with the past tense morpheme *-ed*. An operation that merges the two elements is also required to allow $V + -ed$ to be concatenated into a single word online. This unification rule, $V + -ed$, is a grammatical process that pays no heed to any non-grammatical aspects of the base form (semantic or phonological). The grammatical rule 'add *-ed*' thus applies to any regular verb with equal facility. The second system produces irregular past tense forms. They are simply acquired and stored as whole forms in the mental lexicon. They are also retrieved from memory, as and when required, like any other word. In consequence, an irregular form like *bought* is treated as an unanalysed whole, even though we could argue that it bears some kind of inflection for past tense – a vowel change plus word-final /t/ in this case. In summary, WR theory depends on two systems – lexicon and grammar – for producing past tense (and other) inflected forms.

Over the past 30 years or so, a wealth of evidence has been brought to bear in favour of Words and Rules theory (e.g., Jaeger, Lockwood, Kemmerer, Van Valin, Murphy & Khalak, 1996; Clahsen, Hadler & Weyerts, 2004; Ullman, Pancheva, Love, Yee, Swinney & Hickok 2005; Shankweiler, Palumbo, Fulbright, Mencl, Van Dyke, Kollia, et al., 2010; Magen, 2014; Smith-Lock, 2015). In its first blush of youth, Words and Rules theory provided a very straight-forward account of inflection. But life (and child language) is rarely that simple. Take, for example, the 'blind' nature of the regular rule, 'add -*ed*'. The rule is blind in the sense that it should apply to any word marked V (verb), with no regard for any other factors like meaning or sound. But this is not the case. It has been discovered that the rule applies in a graded way, being influenced by the phonological properties of particular verbs (Albright & Hayes, 2003). The phonology of most verbs does not allow us to predict whether they will be regular or irregular. But verbs that end with an unvoiced **fricative** /s, f, ʃ, ʧ/ as in *place, laugh, wish* and *itch* are different. They are always regular. This is probably why novel verbs ending with an unvoiced fricative are more likely to be treated as regular than other verbs (Albright & Hayes, 2003). This finding suggests that the regular past tense rule is not blind to phonological factors in the way that Words and Rules theory assumes (see also Harris & Humphreys, 2015). In consequence, the bedrock of Words and Rules, which is the operation of rules over linguistic symbols, is called into question. Albright & Hayes (2003) demonstrated that regular verbs are not all equal. Another source of inequality is in the *frequency* of regular verbs. Many regulars occur only rarely in conversation, but there are some high frequency regular verbs (for example, *looked, robbed, dropped*) (Clahsen et al., 2004). Reaction time data from children aged eight to 12 years suggest that high frequency regulars often behave like irregular forms, being produced as pre-packaged whole forms, rather than being put together online (Dye, Walenski, Prado, Mostofsky & Ullman, 2013). Hence, Words and Rules theory has been amended: regular forms are not inevitably produced online by a grammatical process.

The acquisition of words and rules

Let's now consider the *acquisition* of words and rules. We can quickly dispatch the 'words' part of this double act to models of lexical acquisition (see Chapter 6). The way in which irregular plurals and past tense forms are learned is not assumed to differ from the way in which any other word is acquired. Having said that, the meanings 'more than one' for plurals and 'before now' for past tense have to be acquired as part of the lexical entries for irregulars. With respect to the rules part of WR theory, it is clear that particular rules must be learned from experience. They could not possibly be innate, because languages vary in how they mark tense: 'add -*ed*' is fine for English, but it does not work for Japanese. Some languages, including Chinese, do not even mark tense on verbs.

181

We know that children begin to segment words into roots and affixes some time in their second year (Slobin, 1978). What we do *not* yet know is how they do it. Pinker (1999: 193) suggests that it may not be such a difficult task: 'by subtracting *walk* from *walked*, *push* from *pushed*, and so on, the child can isolate *-ed*'. But if it is so straightforward, why do children not perform this analysis much earlier in development? After all, they solve the seemingly harder task of segmenting phonemes and words from continuous speech in the first year of life (Chapter 5). But whereas words are isolated before the child's first birthday, inflections are not produced until the child is about two years old, and are not fully comprehended until about the age of three. One more paradox for the pot, it would seem. What we do know is that there is a close relationship between the frequency of inflections in Child Directed Speech and the order they are acquired. The more frequent a given suffix in CDS, the sooner it is acquired (Warlaumont & Jarmulowicz, 2012).

DISCUSSION POINT 7.1
THE SEGMENTATION PROBLEM IN MORPHOLOGY

As we have seen, little attention has been paid to the issue of how children identify bound morphemes as units of language in their own right within words. Go back to Chapter 5 and review the evidence on the segmentation of words from continuous speech by infants. Compare the evidence on segmentation for both words and morphemes, respectively. The following recent article will be helpful:

Marchetto, E. & Bonatti, L.L. (2015). Finding words and word structure in artificial speech: The development of infants' sensitivity to morphosyntactic regularities. *Journal of Child Language, 42(4)*, 873–902.

- Seven-month-old infants can distinguish word-like units, but what do they actually know about such words?
- At seven months, what else is there to learn about words? A stopover in Chapter 6 might help with this question.
- Why do you think there seems to be a disjunction between the age at which the child segments words versus bound morphemes? Consider the kinds of knowledge on display and the difference between comprehension and production when you discuss this issue. Consider also the different kinds of data that are brought to bear on this issue in the different domains of morphology and word learning.

The blocking hypothesis

One of the hallmarks of child language, observed with delight by hordes of parents, is the **over-regularization error** (OR). Even into the school years, children misapply a regular inflection to

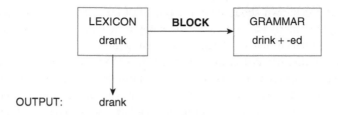

Figure 7.2   The mechanism for blocking overregularized forms

irregular forms. For example, at one point or another, many children add the regular *-ed'* to the irregular verb *break*. The result is *breaked*, instead of *broke*. 'How cute!' you doubtless cry. And now you can also cry: 'That's an overregularization!' (not so cute). WR theory needs to account for the emergence of overregularization errors and also for their eventual disappearance. It does this by proposing a blocking mechanism that connects lexicon and grammar. On this account, when an irregular form like *drank* is retrieved from memory, an inhibitory signal is sent from the lexicon to the grammar, thereby suppressing the regular process (*drink + -ed*) (see Figure 7.2).

On this view, both lexicon and grammar are activated in parallel every time we produce a past tense form. In the case of an irregular verb like *drink*, the activation of *drank* simultaneously blocks the production of *drinked* (Marcus, Pinker, Ullman, Hollander, Rosen & Xu, 1992). It is assumed that blocking is an innate mechanism, 'built in to the circuitry that drives language acquisition' (Pinker, 1999: 197). We should be clear, though, that there is no evidence to support this claim. Blocking prevents the occurrence of past tense and plural errors. Which is all very well, apart from one small matter. As noted above, errors do occur (see below).

Alex (aged 4;1–4;9)

> Daniel's **broked** my mast
>
> And he **sticked** his tongue out at Snow White.
>
> In the old days, they **eated** bad things.
>
> Well, Tippy **bited** me.
>
> I **drawed** a picture of a pirate today.
>
> He **shooted** the fish.
>
> I wish you **buyed** some for me.

If blocking exists, there must be some spanner in the works, preventing its smooth operation. Marcus et al. (1992) suggest that blocking is vulnerable in young children, because their memory retrieval system is immature and sometimes lets them down. If the child fails to retrieve *drove*, the regular rule proceeds unhindered, to give *drived*. Errors like *drived* are therefore caused by lapses in memory retrieval. This explanation seems to solve the problem of past tense errors, but it does so by sweeping the detritus of child language under the carpet of cognitive psychology.

However, very little is known about the development of lexical retrieval. Generally speaking, in fact, the blocking hypothesis has attracted remarkably little empirical attention.

One source of evidence that *has* been considered centres on the frequency of overregularization errors. Originally, Marcus et al. (1992) suggested that overregularization rates are low (4.2 per cent), because the regular process is overwhelmingly blocked by the presence of irregular forms in the child's repertoire. But Maslen, Theakston, Lieven & Tomasello (2004) report OR rates as high as 43 per cent in one case. It turns out that OR rates can be very high for brief periods of development, especially for high frequency verbs (Maratsos, 2000). In fact, even adherents of Words and Rules theory now acknowledge that past tense errors are common (for example, Pinker & Ullman, 2002: 456). A further problem is that overregularization errors seem to start at different points in development for different inflections. Thus plural ORs (*foots*, *mouses*) appear in child speech three months before their past tense counterparts (Maslen et al., 2004). This finding is problematic for the blocking hypothesis. Once the process of inflection is available to children, it should apply to nouns and verbs equally well (Marcus, 1995). One more point of discomfort for the blocking account is the occurrence of blended past tense forms. These are forms like *droved*, where the irregular form (*drove*) has been retrieved, but where the suffixation of the regular *-ed* ending seems to have taken place, too. Such forms are embarrassing to the blocking hypothesis because they suggest that retrieval of the irregular form has failed to block the default regular process. In summary, what little evidence we currently have does not favour the blocking hypothesis. The concept of blocking (or inhibition) is very well established in cognitive psychology (e.g., Sumner & Samuel, 2007). But within Words and Rules theory, blocking stands on shaky ground. An alternative account is required for the emergence, and eventual disappearance, of overregularization errors.

Words and Rules: The story so far

Let's have a quick recap on where we've got to with the dual-route model, before we look at the alternative, single-route approach. We have seen that WR theory provides a very simple model of the English past tense (and the plural), based on the distinction between regular and irregular forms. Regular past tense forms are assembled online by a grammatical process, while irregulars are retrieved as whole forms from the lexicon. Meanwhile, overregularization errors are prevented by a blocking mechanism, inhibiting the regular process when an irregular verb is activated. Occasional child errors are then attributed to an immature memory retrieval system. We have already seen that the simplicity of this model is belied by the complexities of language. Three problems have arisen so far. First, the past tense rule ('add *-ed*') should apply equally well to any regular verb, but it does not. Second, high frequency regular verbs seem to behave like irregular verbs, stored as whole forms in the lexicon. And third, the blocking hypothesis is not well supported. As we proceed into connectionist waters, one further fundamental challenge for WR theory will emerge: the validity of the basic distinction between regular versus irregular. Seemingly so clear-cut in English, this distinction begins to look illusory when other languages (like Polish) enter the fray. But place that thought on hold for the time being, while we head down a single route to the past tense.

Connectionism and a single-route account

Connectionist models are computer simulations that aim to emulate the language learning behaviours of the child. The more closely the computer model echoes child language data, the more plausible it becomes that the *way* in which the computer learns reflects the way in which the child learns. The startling discovery by connectionist modellers was that a single route for learning the past tense may suffice. The single system is a pattern associator, which detects and exploits the numerous regularities and quasi-regularities that exist across the board among both regular and irregular verbs. The fallout from the single-route model has been dramatic. It calls into question the distinction between regular and irregular in inflectional morphology. It further suggests that morphemes are not explicitly represented as discrete entities. And the need for linguistic symbols like V, together with the rules for combining symbols, are dispensed with. These are all foundational assumptions of modern (and ancient) linguistic theory, so it is no wonder that the advent of connectionism, about 30 years ago, was heralded as the dawn of a new age in linguistics and cognitive science.

Irregular past tense forms are neither chaotic nor idiosyncratic, in the way characterized by Pinker (1999). Arguably, only two verbs in English are genuinely irregular, the so-called suppletive forms *be* (past tense *was* or *were*) and *go* (past tense *went*). For the remaining irregulars we can detect nine different clusters of verbs, each with its own pattern for the formation of past tense forms (McClelland & Patterson, 2002). For example, 28 verbs which end in /d/ or /t/ have identical forms in both present and past tense, including *cut*, *hit* and *bid*. Another group, also ending in either /d/ or /t/ simply change the vowel in the past tense, for example *hide/hid*, *slide/slid* and *fight/fought*. Yet another group replaces word-final /d/ with /t/ to produce the past tense form: *send/sent*, *bend/bent* and *build/built*. By this point, your cunning eye will have detected a pattern, based on the popularity of /d/ and /t/ for past tense endings. Fully, 59 per cent of the 181 irregular verbs listed by Pinker & Prince (1988) take word-final /d/ or /t/. And you will recall that these two phonemes constitute the realizations of the regular past tense morpheme *-ed*. Connectionist models exploit the systematic patterns that exist among sub-groups of irregulars, including the frequent appearance of /d/ and /t/. They treat the learning problem for these patterns as identical to the problem of finding the pattern in regular verbs. Hence, all verbs are learned by the same model in the same way at the same time, by establishing the various patterns of association that exist across present and past tense forms in different sub-groups of verbs.

In the connectionist approach, learning is achieved by a network of units that correspond, metaphorically, to neurons in the brain. Each unit is connected to many other units, in a way that mirrors the synaptic connections between neurons. The level of activation for a given unit is computed from the activation levels of all the units feeding into it. If the overall activation level is sufficiently high, the unit will be switched on, causing it to send a signal via all of its connections to the output layer. If, on the other hand, the activation level of a unit does not exceed a critical threshold, it remains switched off.

The sample network in Figure 7.3 looks complicated enough with its numerous connections. But the real thing is even more bamboozling. In Rumelhart & McClelland (1986), the input and output layers each contain 460 separate units, each of which is switched either on or off for a given learning trial. The task of the network is to match the root form of a verb with the correct past tense form. It does this by gradually forming patterns of association between the features of words. The association is not between the whole words, *drive* and *drove*, but between parts of words: *dr-* and *dr-*, *dri-* and *dro-*, *-ive* and *-ove*, and so on. At the same time, other associations are inhibited, for example, between *-rive* and *-rived*, to discourage *drived* as the output for *drive*. The focus on features allows the network to detect the patterns that exist among different families of verbs. For example, most of the units that are turned on when *shrink* is entered will also be activated when *stink* is entered. The output from the network gradually converges on the correct form.

In Rumelhart & McClelland's (1986) original model, 420 verbs were each entered into the model 200 times, yielding a total of 84,000 trials. The end result of all this activity was very impressive. The model converted most of the input verbs into their correct past tense counterparts, both regular (*seem/seemed*, *melt/melted*) and irregular (*make/made*, *sing/sang*). The next challenge was to see if the model could generalize beyond the verbs it had been trained on and generate appropriate past tense forms for 86 unfamiliar verbs. The model managed to add *-ed* to three quarters of the new regular verbs. It did so by analogy with the verbs in its training set. The model also generated some overregularization errors, similar to those made by children, like

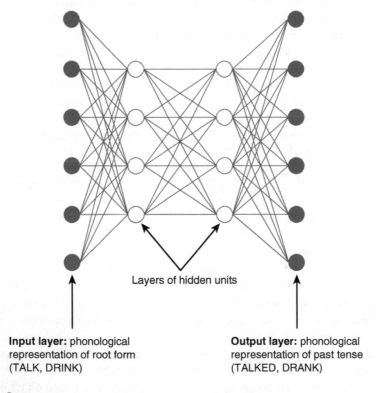

Layers of hidden units

Input layer: phonological representation of root form (TALK, DRINK)

Output layer: phonological representation of past tense (TALKED, DRANK)

Figure 7.3   Connectionist model of past tense inflection

gived and *digged*. Intriguingly, these errors emerged after an initial period when the correct irregular form was produced, somewhat like children (though see below). The model also did well in recognizing clusters of irregular verbs. It could therefore cope with a new verb like *cling/clung* by analogy with *ring/rung* and *sing/sung*. The model also produced blended forms, like *gaved* and *stepted*, which we have seen are a feature of child language, but which are not easily accommodated by Words and Rules theory. Overall, then, the achievements of connectionist models provide a serious challenge to the idea that we need two systems for producing past tense forms. Maybe just one system – a simple pattern associator – is all that is required.

Problems with connectionist models

All is not entirely rosy in the connectionist garden. Early models suffered from a number of deficiencies (see Pinker & Prince, 1988, for a full account). One problem was the presence of a 'teacher' in the model, essentially a way to compare its output against the target and adjust learning where the two did not match. This 'teacher' can be seen as a form of corrective input, a concept which, you will recall, is anathema to many theorists, both nativist and non-nativist (but see Chapter 4 for an alternative view). Another problem was with **homophones** like *brake* and *break*. Connectionist models that input only information about phonology will treat these two verbs as identical, because they sound the same. Yet one is regular, while the other is irregular (*brake/braked* versus *break/broke*). A third problem is with novel and very low frequency regular verbs. Connectionist models have difficulty in generalizing to novel words that differ from those in their training set. They either produce odd blends (like *trilb/ treelilt*) or no output at all. The failure of connectionist models in this regard may be inherent in their design (Marcus, 2001). Children and adults, in contrast, can cope with the extremes of novelty and inflect whatever verb comes their way. Even odd concoctions that violate the phonological constraints of English, like *ploamph*, can be accommodated by people (*ploamphed*), but not by connectionist models.

A fourth problem for connectionism, which we can mention briefly, is the modelling of *U-shaped development*, a phrase that captures the dip in performance we mentioned earlier: errors with irregulars creep in after a period of correct performance, before being phased out again. The U-shape appears if we make a graph with percentage correct use on the vertical axis, and time on the horizontal axis. Unhappily, Rumelhart & McClelland based their model on inaccurate descriptions of this U-shape. They assumed a simple developmental sequence for irregulars: *correct → error → correct*. But correct uses never disappear. In fact, even when overregularization errors emerge, they remain in the minority, with correct forms predominating. Hence, the kind of U-shaped behaviour generated by Rumelhart & McClelland's model is not the kind actually exhibited by children. We have made brief mention of just four problems with early connectionist models: the presence of a teacher; homophones; low frequency and/or unusual verbs; and the course of U-shaped development. Most of these problems have, to some extent, been addressed in subsequent versions of connectionist models. But no model has accommodated all of these problems in a single, supersize solution to all connectionist headaches. Instead, individual models have chipped away at individual problems.

Crosslinguistic evidence

Despite the massive amount of research on inflection, the scope of that research is surprisingly narrow. The English past tense has devoured the lion's share of attention, with a few scraps thrown to English plurals. But we should recall that inflection in English is a paltry affair. Inflection in other languages, like Finnish, Hungarian and Russian, is vastly more complex, but relatively little is yet known about the acquisition of these inflection systems in their own right. Even where crosslinguistic research has been undertaken, much of it is designed to contribute to the debate inspired by the English past tense. Notable exceptions include research on the acquisition of plurals in German (Szagun, 2001) and Arabic (Albirini, 2015). These languages each have complex systems for pluralisation and, not surprisingly, children are well into their school years before adult-like control is achieved. For example, in Jordanian Arabic, children start out with a single default (or regular) plural form – so-called 'feminine sound' plurals – but, later on, they come to utilise two default forms, as witnessed in the adult language (Albirini, 2015). The notion of two regular plural forms is, of course, alien to English. What's more, the plot thickens. Jordanian Arabic actually presents children with four separate plural forms which are not mastered until about the age of eight years. Critically, the acquisition of these forms is not driven solely by considerations of default forms. In the early years, frequency and productivity of plural forms have a strong influence on acquisition, with predictability emerging as a further influence in the later years. Frequency also figures large in a recent study of Finnish past tense acquisition (Kirjavainen, Nikolaev & Kidd, 2012). Recall that, according to Words and Rules theory, the regular past tense rule ('add -*ed*') applies to any and all regular verbs with equal facility. There should be no differences among verbs. But Kirjavainen et al. (2012) show that both frequency and phonological factors affect children's production of past tense forms. They conclude that the single associative mechanism envisaged by connectionists can account for the data. If we look beyond English, therefore, regularity may not be the main factor driving acquisition of inflected forms. Even more startling, crosslinguistic research now indicates that the distinction between regular and irregular, seemingly so clear in English, is all but illusory in other languages. Dąbrowska (2005) offers the genitive and dative systems in Polish as a case in point (see **case**). There is no default regular marker in Polish and most forms have irregular versions. In addition, both semantic and phonological properties influence how nouns are inflected, contra Words and Rules theory (Ramscar, Dye & Hübner, 2013). And regularity is a poor predictor of productivity in Polish adults, again contra Words and Rules theory. These findings suggest that the regular–irregular distinction may be an artefact, something we impose on the data of English, without it possessing any genuine psychological significance. But there is a fly in this ointment. While Polish tells us to forget about the regular–irregular distinction, up pops Hungarian. Like Polish, Hungarian has its complications when viewed through the simplistic lens of English. For example, it is an agglutinative language, which means that words can contain several morphemes, essentially combined in (sometimes quite long) chains to express features such as number, tense and gender. A recent reaction time study on both noun and verb morphology in Hungarian found evidence in *favour* of the regular–irregular distinction (Nemeth, Janacsek,

Turi, Lukacs, Peckham, Szanka, Gazso, Lovassy & Ullman, 2015). On the whole, though, it is perhaps quite telling that the weight of crosslinguistic evidence tends to favour the single route approach (in this vein, see also Nicoladis & Paradis, 2012).

Summary: One route or two?

The debate between single-route versus dual-route theories has generated a huge amount of research. A wide range of methodologies has been applied, including computer modelling and reaction time studies. More recently, evidence has been forthcoming from neuroscience, throwing data on brain responses into the pot. But not even this multiple-method approach has been able to provide definitive evidence in favour of one theory over the other. In this vein, a number of recent studies have recruited evidence on brain responses to support Words and Rules theory (e.g., Bakker, MacGregor, Pulvermüller & Shtyrov, 2013; Regel, Opitz, Müller & Friederici, 2015). But similar methods also yield evidence for a single route, by demonstrating that morphologically complex words are retrieved as whole words, rather than being the product of online rules (Hanna & Pulvermüller, 2014; see also Danko, Boytsova, Solovjeva, Chernigovskaya & Medvedev, 2014). And so the controversy rumbles on, with no killer blow (or even peaceful resolution) in sight. A major difficulty is that most of the findings can be accounted for by both single-route and dual-route theories, while evidence in favour of one theory over the other tends to be fairly weak (for recent examples, see Ambridge, 2010; Magen, 2014). To accommodate contrary findings, substantial modification of the original theories has proven necessary. For example, we noted that Words and Rules theory now accepts the need for a pattern associator in lexical memory. This acknowledges the way irregular verbs are organized in distinct sub-groups. They are not just a list of unconnected exceptions to the regular pattern. WR theory also accepts that high frequency regulars may be stored in memory, not assembled online. What remains, though, is the insistence that we have two systems for producing inflected forms. Inflection is conceived as a mental process, available to us for producing complex words. This idea is not accepted by many connectionists. But it is less controversial than the notion that inflection is a default process that applies unfailingly to regular forms. This is because the notion of regular versus irregular is very hard to maintain when we look beyond the confines of English. Pattern associators, too, have their problems. In particular, they are nowhere near as proficient as the young child in generalizing acquired patterns to new forms, especially if those forms are rare or unusual in some way. The debate, therefore, continues. To date, there is no incontrovertible proof that linguistic symbols and rules are redundant concepts in psychology. But connectionism has demonstrated that a world without symbols and rules is at least conceivable. As Seidenberg (1992: 93) puts it, 'any system can be described by a set of rules if the rules do not have to apply to all cases'. In the absence of agreement, we will let Groucho Marx have the final word:

> Pardon me. I was using the subjunctive instead of the past tense. We're way past tents. We're living in bungalows now.
>
> (*Animal Crackers*, 1930)

We *are* way past the past tense now and heading for the bungalow where compounding and derivation live.

Compounding and derivation

Beyond inflection, you will recall that language offers two further ways of constructing complex words: compounding and derivation. In both cases, the outcome is a new lexeme, with its own meaning. Derived words are formed by the addition of an inflection to a word, as in *confusion* (*confuse* + *-ion*), while compounds are made by joining two words together, as in *apple juice*. We shall consider the mechanics of each process first and then consider how the child tackles the acquisition of these morphological processes.

Derivation

Derivation creates new **lexemes**, through the addition of morphemes to a base form (see Box 7.1). This process can be fairly straightforward, as in the derivation of the noun *driver*, from the verb *drive* plus *-er*. But it can also be more complex, with more than one bound morpheme involved in the creation of a word. The word *unbelievable*, for example, can be analysed as *un-* + *believe* + *-able*. Anglin (1993) identifies in excess of 100 different derivational **affixes** in English. Try your hand with a few of them in the Exercise below.

EXERCISE 7.1
DERIVED FORMS

What is the root in each of the following derived forms? What grammatical category does the root belong to? What category does the derived form belong to? Look up noun, verb and adjective in the Glossary if you need a kick start.

obesity	selection	realize	playful
unholy	swimmer	successful	speciality
repellent	curable	reorganize	membership
Londoner	blacken	clearance	accidental

BOX 7.1   DERIVATIONAL MORPHOLOGY

Derivational morphology creates new **lexemes**, words with different meanings from the roots they are derived from. A derived word may therefore have its own separate dictionary entry. Sometimes the grammatical category also changes. For example, the

---

adjective *desirable* is derived from the verb *desire*, as shown in the table below. The table also shows how, in English, derivational morphemes can be **prefixes** or **suffixes**, attaching to the left or right of a word, respectively.

Root form			Derived form	
		Verb	Noun	Adjective
Verb	→	**re**paint	driver	desir**able**
		undo	flatter**y**	resent**ful**
Noun	→	demon**ize**	child**hood**	self**ish**
		vaccin**ate**	lion**ess**	whole**some**
Adjective	→	weak**en**	craz**iness**	**un**happy
		pur**ify**	desper**ation**	yellow**ish**

Most derivational processes are productive, that is, they can apply to a range of different words. For example, the suffix *-able* (meaning 'able to be') can be added to pretty much any verb in English: *doable, driveable, changeable.* Admittedly, some such forms sound a bit odd (*smellable, feelable, takeable*), but *-able* still stands as a highly productive morpheme, used in the creation of new words. Another highly productive morpheme in English is *-er*, used to denote 'someone who performs an action', as in *lover, walker* and *baker.* Other morphemes are less productive, being restricted to a narrower range of root forms. For example, the suffix *-ity* can only be added to a fairly limited range of adjectives to produce nominal forms (*curiosity, sincerity, sanity,* but not **warmity, *sadity, *bitterity*). As we shall see, variations in productivity have an impact on the child's acquisition of morphology.

Compounding

Like derivation, compounding also results in a new lexeme, but this time, it is formed by bringing two or more lexemes together, most commonly some combination of nouns and adjectives in English. For example, *wind* and *mill* (two nouns) can be compounded to produce the noun, *windmill.* Notice how the meaning of the compound is not necessarily just the sum of its parts. It typically takes on a meaning of its own. Another point to note is that compounds can be written as a single word (*runway*), with a hyphen (*part-time*) or as two separate words (*table tennis*). Nowadays, we even have the spectre of capital letters word-internally (*PowerPoint, SlideShare*). The choice of one written form over another does not seem to be systematic and does not affect the linguistic status of compounds.

The internal structure of compounds can be analysed into a **head** and a **modifier**. In English, the head appears on the right. Broadly speaking, the head determines the meaning of the compound and also dictates which grammatical category it belongs to. For example, in *watertight*, the head element is an adjective, *tight*, so the compound is also an adjective. In *daredevil*, the head element, *devil*, is a noun, and the compound is a noun. The head element is also the part of the compound that can be modified by inflection. For example, the plural of *landlord* is *landlords*. The plural marker *-s* is added to the head, *lord*, not to the modifier, *land* (**landslord*). How do we know that *two landlords* is correct while **two landslord* is wrong? More to the point, how does the child acquire this knowledge? We shall return to this question below. Our final observation is that inflection, derivation and compounding do not exist in isolation from one another. We have just seen that compounds can be inflected (*landlords*). But they can also include derived forms, yielding so-called synthetic compounds. For example, *train driver* contains the derived form *driver* (*drive + -er*), while *washing machine* contains *washing* (*wash + -ing*). We thus reach the pinnacle of morphological complexity, where inflection, derivation and compounding are combined. We shall consider how the child copes with this morphological mayhem below (see Table 7.2).

Table 7.2 All three morphological processes combined

shooting stars	derivation	*shoot + -ing*
	compounding	*shooting + star*
	inflection	*shooting star + -s*
bus conductors	derivation	*conduct + -or*
	compounding	*bus + conductor*
	inflection	*bus conductor + -s*
given names	derivation	*give + -en*
	compounding	*given + name*
	inflection	*given name + -s*

EXERCISE 7.2
MORPHOLOGICAL PROCESSES

In the following compounds, identify which morphological processes have been applied: inflection, derivation and/or compounding. Be careful. Sometimes more than one morphological process is involved in the creation of a word form. Sometimes, none at all (a root form by itself).

airheads	sampling	insider	elephant
disgraceful	pleased	coffee table	recycles
hat maker	indefatigable	reasserted	sweetcorn
monster	washing machine	dressmakers	unhappily

We will cover both kinds of process in this section, if only because research studies have often brought them together. You might wonder why inflection has been left out of this party, and you would be right to wonder. In fact, studies are beginning to suggest that different morphological processes may be quite intimately related. In this vein, Rabin & Deacon (2008) asked children aged 7 to 10 to complete word fragments like *ne _ _*. Possible answers include *nest, next, neat* and *need*. Before doing this task, children were primed in different ways, by giving them a list of words to read. In amongst this list, some children saw the inflected word *needs*, others saw the derived word *needy*, while others saw a control word *needle*. The initial sound sequence of *needle* (*need*) is shared by *needs* and *needy*, but it has a different root from *need*. It was found that *needs* and *needy*, but not *needle*, were effective prompts. Moreover, children were equally likely to complete *ne _ _* as *need* when primed with inflected and derived forms (*needs* or *needy*). In consequence, Rabin & Deacon (2008) argue that inflected and derived forms may be mentally represented by children in a similar way, according to morphological principles.

Derivation: The influence of productivity

Derivation creates new words through the addition of affixes to a stem. Affixes vary in terms of their productivity, which is a measure of how many different words they can attach to. Try Exercise 7.3 below to get a feeling for the way in which productivity varies across different affixes.

EXERCISE 7.3
PRODUCTIVITY OF DERIVATIONAL SUFFIXES

Try deriving new words by adding the following suffixes to nouns, verbs and adjectives chosen at random. Identify the category (noun, verb, adjective) of both the original word (the root) and the derived form. You will find that you cannot just add any affix to any word. There are constraints. Also, some affixes apply to a wider range of words than others. That is, they are more or less productive. Which affix do you think is the most productive in the following list?

pre-	de-	-ity
in-	-cy	-less
under-	-able	-er

Children acquire the most productive suffixes first. For example, there are three different suffixes in English that are used to mark an agent, the doer of an action: *-ian*; *-er*; and *-ist*. Picture a small band of *musicians* with *trumpeter*, *drummer*, *pianist* and *violinist*. If you're feeling strong, repeat Exercise 7.3 and think of more examples for each suffix (*physician*, *golfer*, *chemist* …). You will probably discover that *-er* is far more productive than the other two, and this is because

-*ist* and -*ian* are largely confined to words with Greek and Latin roots. Not surprisingly, children can use -*er* to mark novel agents from the age of two or three, whereas creative uses of -*ist* and -*ian* lag behind by a year or two (Clark & Hecht, 1982). Examples of productivity with -*er* are provided by Clark (2003) in a child aged 2;2 to 2;9:

> *Come here, brusher.*
>
> *Herb a bad guy, because I a gunner.*
>
> *I'm a big reacher.*
>
> *I'm going to shut that door hard because I'm a shutter.*
>
> *I have a sip. I am a sipper.*

In fact, -*er* is one of the earliest suffixes witnessed, together with the diminutive suffix -*ie*, as in *doggie* and *horsie*. The influence of affix productivity has also been observed in other languages. For example, children learning Hebrew acquire the most productive suffixes early and use them more readily in their own complex word production (Berman, 1987).

Productivity can also be gauged across different morphological processes. At the start of this chapter we observed that languages exploit inflection, derivation and compounding to different degrees. That is, each process is more or less productive, and these differences are reflected in the rate of acquisition by the child. In French and Hebrew, for example, derivation is much more productive than compounding. Accordingly, children acquire derived forms before compounds in these two languages. In German, meanwhile, the reverse is true. Children acquire compounds, which are especially productive in German, before derived forms (Clark, 1993). Now that compounds have cropped up again, let's explore further.

Early compounds

Compounds are in evidence very early on in children's speech output. In one recent study of Finnish, Estonian and Sami (the latter being native to northern Europe), children as young as 1;10 showed evidence of compounds (Argus, Laalo & Johansen Ijäs, 2014). Initially, however, children do not treat compounds as complex words (Berman, 1987). Instead, they seem to follow the 'whole-word' pattern of learning which we encountered above with inflected words. The internal structure of a compound like *football* is not analysed into its component parts (*foot + ball*), even if the child has acquired each component as an individual word in its own right. Instead, *football* is understood as an indivisible linguistic unit, in much the same way as other polysyllabic words, like *ballet* or *tennis*. The treatment of compounds as whole words, or *holophrases*, can persist into the school years for particular compounds. For example, Berko (1958) found that 98 per cent of four- to seven-year-olds were not aware that *birthday* referred to a particular day. Nevertheless, from three years on, children begin to recognize the distinct components in some compounds. In one test of this development, Nicoladis (2003) asked children to pick out the correct referent for novel compounds from a choice of four pictures, as in Figure 7.4.

Figure 7.4 Comprehension of a novel compound ('sun bag') by three- and four-year-olds (Nicoladis, 2003)

Three-year-olds are more prone than four-year-olds to select a single object from this array, rather than two interacting objects. It takes time, therefore, to realize that interacting objects are most readily labelled by a compound noun. Errors in the analysis of compounds can still be discerned in primary school-aged children, as the following definitions reveal (Berko, 1958: 170):

Breakfast is called breakfast because you have to eat it fast when you rush to school.

Friday is a day when you have fried fish.

An *airplane* is called an airplane because it is a plain thing that goes in the air.

Although the child may sometimes miss the mark in their analyses, the critical point to note is that they can perform such analyses at all. In fact, from the age of two, English-speaking children begin to construct compounds for themselves, as in *house-smoke*, for smoke from a chimney, and *cup-egg*, for a boiled egg (Clark, 1981).

Do you remember that compounds comprise a head and a modifier? Of course you do. In English, the order of these elements is modifier + head. The head element determines the essential meaning of the compound. In *blackboard* the head is *board*, modified by *black*. Children's knowledge of the modifier + head order was tested by asking them to interpret novel compounds

195

(Clark, Gelman & Lane, 1985). As you may imagine, a pencil-tree will look very different from a tree-pencil, but even children as young as 2;4 succeed on this task 49 per cent of the time, rising to 96 per cent by the age of 4;0. In Hebrew, the order is reversed, but Berman & Clark (1989) demonstrated that children begin to discern the correct order from 2;5. The four-year-old whose comprehension of compounds is almost perfect, may nevertheless *produce* ordering errors. For example, when asked 'What could you call someone who pulls wagons', observed responses included *A pull-wagon* and *A puller-wagon* (Clark, Hecht & Mulford, 1986). But the head element, *pull(er)* should appear to the right (*wagon puller*). Hence, comprehension of the correct ordering for head and modifier precedes the child's production ability.

Relating the parts to the whole in compounds

In compounds, the relationship between head and modifier can take on many different forms. The so-called *thematic relation* between head and modifier determines how a given compound must be interpreted. Krott, Gagné & Nicoladis (2009) provide the following examples:

chocolate muffin	a muffin that HAS chocolate in it
cardboard box	a box that is MADE OF cardboard
mountain bird	a bird that is LOCATED on mountains
mountain magazine	a magazine ABOUT mountains

If the meaning of a compound is unfamiliar, then the appropriate thematic relation between the component parts must be inferred. In some cases, there are morphological markers available to help out. For example, in *bus driver*, the *-er* suffix can be used to deduce the relationship between *bus* and *driver*: *-er* is agentive, so *driver* is a 'person who drives'. It then follows that *bus* is what the driver drives, yielding the thematic relation OF ('a driver OF buses'). In other cases, the use of a new compound in context will help the child interpret its meaning and the relations between the components. A third way to solve this problem is to rely on prior learning to work out the meaning of new compounds. They could do so by drawing an analogy between the new compound and ones they already know. If *chocolate muffin* is new, then the child might rely on knowledge of other chocolaty compounds to deduce its meaning. In this vein, Krott & Nicoladis (2005) report that four- and five-year-olds do indeed infer the thematic relations of new compounds by analogy with familiar compounds.

Learning by analogy is a useful strategy, but it will not always work by itself. The problem is that some compounds have a number of competing interpretations, as we have seen with *mountain bird* versus *mountain magazine*. When there is competition of this kind, Krott et al. (2009) suggest that the child will prefer the most frequently encountered interpretation for any new compound. For example, for *mountain*, the most frequent thematic relation is LOCATED (*mountain bird, mountain goat, mountain lion*, and so on). And it turns out that, by the age of four years, children choose the most frequent thematic relation for novel compounds about 40 per cent of the time (Krott et al., 2009). If this figure does not impress you, remember that children manage this with no contextual or linguistic support. Their responses in this study are based solely on the ability to recognize analogies between new compounds and previously learned ones.

Complex compounds: Three processes combined

Near the start of this chapter we ascended to the summit of Morphology Mountain without oxygen, and planted a flag in words that combine all three morphological processes. Words that incorporate inflection, derivation *and* compounding include *train drivers*, *flower sellers* and *alto saxophonists* (see also Table 7.1). In this section, we shall see that three-year-old children cope well with this complexity, since they demonstrate surprisingly adult-like intuitions about complex compounds. Young children do so well, in fact, that some authors assume that the rules underlying the construction of such compounds must be innate (Gordon, 1985). So what *are* these rules? Kiparsky (1983) provides the most popular analysis, known as level ordering, which predicts that production of complex compounds passes through three hierarchically sequenced levels (see Table 7.3).

Table 7.3 Level ordering (Kiparsky, 1983)

Level 1	retrieval of base forms	head, man, men, hunt
Level 2	derivation and compounding	head hunter, man hunter, men hunter
Level 3	regular plural inflection, -s	head hunters, man hunters, men hunters

Looking at the compounds that emerge from this sequence, you might possibly wince at *men hunters*, with its irregular plural modifier, *men*. *Men hunters* might give you pause for thought (see below), but that's nothing compared to *heads hunter*. That one really jars. According to Kiparsky, such forms are prevented because the plural inflection *-s* can only be added *after* compounding has taken place, not before. This is why regular plural forms, like *heads*, cannot occur within compounds. If you agree with Kiparsky, and give the green light to *men hunter*, then we need to explain why *irregular* plurals *can* occur within compounds. According to level ordering, the reason is that irregular plurals like *men* are retrieved like any other word from the lexicon at Level 1. Compounding then takes place at Level 2 (*men + hunter*). If we wanted to, we could then even inflect the whole compound at Level 3 to yield *men hunters* (with the same meaning as *man hunters*: 'several people who hunt men').

Gordon (1985: 79) laid his hands on a Cookie Monster puppet and tested the level ordering hypothesis with children aged 3;2 to 5;10. The following introduction was made:

Do you know who this is? … It's the Cookie Monster. Do you know what he likes to eat? (Answer: Cookies). Yes – and do you know what else he likes to eat? – He likes to eat all sorts of things …

After a period of training, children were asked to name other objects that Cookie Monster might eat. These included a rat, a collection of four rats, a mouse and four mice. Gordon does not say if these were real rats and mice. The child was then asked, for example, 'What do you call someone who eats rats?' *Rat* and *mouse* have similar meanings, but you will have picked up that *rat* is regular, while *mouse* is irregular. Therefore, level ordering predicts the following possible responses:

197

rat eater	YES
rats eater	NO
mouse eater	YES
mice eater	YES

When faced with a rat or a mouse, most people scream. But these children blithely produced compounds like *rat eater* and *mouse eater* on 98 per cent of occasions. When asked simply to name a group of mice, some of the younger children overregularized and said *mouses*. But these same children reduced *mouses* to the singular form when the compound was elicited, giving *mouse eater*. Children who used the correct irregular *mice*, also used it in the compound, *mice eater*, 90 per cent of the time. Only *rats eater* was conspicuous by its absence. It seems, therefore, that Kiparsky's level ordering model correctly predicts child speech. Irregular plurals can appear within compounds, regular plurals cannot. Gordon (1985) asserts that knowledge of level ordering is innate. He suggests that children could not have learned these constraints because they are not exposed to relevant information in the input which could assist learning. Thus, children avoid compounds that are prohibited by level ordering (*rats eater*), while producing compounds that *are* permitted (*mice eater*), despite having heard neither of them. If three-year-olds possess this knowledge in the absence of help from the input, it is assumed that the knowledge is innate. This line of reasoning is often used to support nativist claims and we will examine it in more detail in the next chapter. For the moment, it is worth pointing out that Gordon (1985) did not actually examine the input to children. He relied instead on an early database of adult written English (Kučera & Francis, 1967). Laying that aside, though, other problems have arisen with the level ordering account.

In the first place, there are exceptions. In English, it *is* possible to have a regular plural in modifier position: *drinks cabinet, weapons inspector, Parks Commission, awards ceremony, sports announcer*. It is also possible in other languages, including French, where there is a head + modifier order in compounds. The word for *nutcracker* in French – *casse-noisettes* – glosses as 'break hazelnuts' with a regular plural modifier, *noisettes*. If level ordering exists, neither French nor English should allow regular plurals in compounds. A second problem is that studies since Gordon (1985) have found that children do produce regular plurals inside compounds sometimes. In this respect, Nicoladis (2003) discovered an interesting crosslinguistic difference between monolingual English-speaking children and bilingual children acquiring French and English. The bilingual children produced English *rats-eater* compounds on 15 per cent of occasions, compared with just 2 per cent for mono-lingual English speakers. French is more lenient than English in allowing such compounds, which helps explain this pattern of findings. In contrast, level ordering hits the buffers as an explanation. If level ordering is an innate constraint on children, it should apply to speakers of all languages equally. It turns out that children in the early stages of learning about compounds are very likely to produce regular plural compounds. Nicoladis & Murphy (2004) report that 50 per cent of children who make other kinds of compound error (for example, *ringer-bell* instead of *bell-ringer*) also produce *rats-eater* errors. In contrast, those children who are error-free on the *bell-ringer* front cannot be induced to produce *rats-eater*. There is a developmental progression, therefore, in which children *learn* to avoid regular plurals in compounds.

Perhaps the most interesting finding from Gordon (1985), which still requires explanation, is the propensity of children to say *mice eater*. The viability of level ordering depends crucially on the acceptability of irregular plurals in non-head position. However, I suggested, above, that you might balk at *mice eater*. If so, you are joined by the adults studied by Haskell, MacDonald & Seidenberg (2003). They found a hierarchy of acceptability for different modifiers:

regular singular   >   irregular plural   >   regular plural
rat eater   *mice eater*   *rats eater*

Haskell et al. (2003) argue that phonological and semantic factors influence the acceptability of different compounds (though see Berent & Pinker, 2008, for a counterblast). In any event, according to level ordering, we should be equally happy with both *rat eater* and *mice eater*. But this is not the case. Not only do adults avoid producing compounds like *mice eater* (Murphy, 2000), they are not that keen when they hear them either (Haskell et al., 2003). So why do *children* produce compounds like *mice eater*? Buck-Gengler, Menn & Healy (2004) focus on the preference even young children have for singular forms within compounds. Gordon (1985) showed that, even when the child has just named a group of *rats* in the plural, their subsequent compound will be *rat eater*, with a singular *rat* modifier. Access to the singular form (*rat*) is straightforward, even when the plural form (*rats*) has been produced. But access to the singular form may be less straightforward for irregulars. Having named a group of *mice*, it is more likely that a subsequent compound will be *mice eater*, because the singular form (*mouse*) is relatively difficult to access when first primed with *mice*. Haskell et al. (2003) report reaction time data from adults in support of this idea. What we need now, therefore, are some equivalent data from young children. In any event, we have seen that children's understanding of how compounds are assembled and interpreted develops gradually over the pre-school years. In the next section, we will see how morphological knowledge continues to grow past the age of five and influence development in other domains of language and learning.

Morphology in the school years

Morphological awareness

Once children have acquired some knowledge of morphology, they will find themselves in possession of a very useful tool for learning in other domains, including the lexicon, literacy and spelling. But children differ in their level of morphological prowess and the rate at which they learn. And these individual differences have a lasting impact on later linguistic development. This was demonstrated in a study of Finnish inflection, which, you will remember, allows for more than 2,000 possible nominal forms. Lyytinen & Lyytinen (2004) showed that children with a more advanced knowledge of inflection at two years have a higher vocabulary level at five years. You can also see the impact of complex morphology in any Helsinki supermarket. The aisles are littered with screaming toddlers who've just been told they have to learn Finnish morphology. Individual differences can also be seen in children acquiring Cantonese, Mandarin and Korean (McBride-Chang, Tardif, Cho, Shu, Fletcher, Stokes, Wong & Leung, 2008). In these languages, compounding is enormously productive as a way of creating new words. In Mandarin, for example, *baseball* ('bang-qiu') emerged from the fusion of the words for *stick* ('bang') and *ball* ('qiu'). And there are thousands more where that came from. In fact, McBride-Chang et al. (2008) argue that compounding is so prevalent in these languages that this aspect of morphological knowledge is essential for the comprehension and production of even minimally complex words. This study demonstrated that knowledge of morphology and lexical knowledge are intimately linked. Four- and five-year-olds with a large vocabulary do well on tests of morphological awareness when tested one year later. Causation runs in the opposite direction also. A high level of morphological awareness at four years predicts a more extensive vocabulary by age five. Hence, these two abilities feed off each other to encourage mutual growth. The critical factor seems to be **metalinguistic awareness**, specifically, *morphological* awareness. McBride-Chang et al. tested children's awareness of and ability to manipulate morphological structures. They did not simply measure how accurate children were in their use of morphemes. Metalinguistic skills clearly provide a significant boost to the child's learning in both lexical and morphological domains.

Connections with vocabulary, reading and spelling

Metalinguistic skills are sometimes exploited explicitly in classroom settings. The child's ability to reflect consciously on language structure provides teachers with an opportunity to intervene systematically and supply useful information. Nippold (2016) provides examples from American textbooks which show how morphology is sometimes incorporated into the school curriculum. For example, one student workbook provides a table of derivational suffixes, with definitions and examples of the following kind:

> **-able** 'capable of being, worthy of,' as in *lovable*
> **-er** 'one who performs an action,' as in *baker*
> **-ful** 'full of, characterized by,' as in *painful*

Another text described by Nippold (2016) provides step-by-step instructions on how to determine the meaning of an unfamiliar compound word, starting out with the injunction to segment the word into its constituent roots (for example, *rowboat* = row/boat, *snowstorm* = snow/storm). There is, then, a clear expectation that explicit instruction will enhance both literacy and word learning. As we have seen, evidence from child language research is beginning to confirm the validity of these assumptions.

One recent study has demonstrated that morphological awareness can be enhanced through direct intervention in the classroom. Ravid & Geiger (2009) implemented a three-month programme with children aged 9–10 years in Israeli schools, with the aim of increasing awareness of Hebrew morphology. This study is distinguished by the decision to incorporate linguistic humour into the teaching materials. For example, a particular noun pattern was introduced, CaCéCet, which is used in Hebrew to designate different diseases (where C stands for consonant). Children were encouraged to play around with this format and come up with novel diseases of their own, one such being *dabéret*, which glosses as 'talkativeness'. You may not split your sides at this sample of merry-making, but I guess you had to be there. To nine-year-old speakers of Hebrew, this is hilarious. More to the point, it is instructive. Post-intervention, child scores on tests of inflection and derivation, and on their awareness of these categories, had increased significantly. Morphological intervention has recently proven effective with children learning Arabic, also in Israeli schools (Taha & Saiegh-Haddad, 2016).

Morphological awareness in teachers

In contrast to explicit teaching, there are settings where morphology is largely absent from teachers' training and understanding. One study in the UK found that, in a sample of 51 London teachers, not one used the word *morpheme*, either in the classroom or in interviews about their practice (Hurry, Nunes, Bryant, Pretzlik, Parker, Curno & Midgley, 2005). Many of these teachers did have some explicit awareness of words like *prefix* and *suffix*, but the fundamental importance of morphemes, including their crucial role in generating complex words, was neither remarked upon nor observed in classroom practice. Curiously, this lack of awareness existed, despite explicit reference to morphology in the UK National Curriculum. The story has a happy ending, though. Hurry et al. (2005) incorporated an intervention programme for these teachers into their study, which proved to be very successful. In particular, increased morphological awareness in teachers was associated with subsequent gains in the spelling prowess of the children they taught (aged 7–11 years).

The impact of morphological knowledge on spelling is not confined to English. Similar effects have been witnessed for Hebrew (Levin, Ravid & Rapaport, 2001; Gillis & Ravid, 2006). Moreover, there is evidence that children as young as five years recruit their knowledge of inflection and derivation in the service of spelling (see Pacton & Deacon, 2008). At the same time, children with depressed morphological skills, including those with dyslexia, experience problems in reading and spelling (Siegel, 2008). In a similar vein, Freyd & Baron (1982) report quite dramatic differences in levels of morphological awareness among different groups of children. They showed that advanced 10-year-olds were significantly better at defining complex derived words than average 13-year-olds. Tellingly, the younger, precocious children actively analysed derived words into their constituent morphemes. Many of the older children, meanwhile, showed no evidence of using morphological knowledge to help them define words like *numberless, endurance, invaluable* and *solidify*. These older children did improve after a classroom intervention, though. It is possible, therefore, that for some children, morphological awareness develops spontaneously, while for others, explicit teaching may be required. Overall, we see that significant individual differences exist in levels of morphological awareness among children. And these differences have a direct impact, not only on the ability to analyse words, but also on the development of related skills, including reading and spelling.

IN A NUTSHELL

- Children acquire three different processes for producing and understanding complex words: inflection; derivation; and compounding.

- In the early stages, children are 'whole-word' learners. They produce morphologically complex words without any appreciation of their internal structure.

201

- English past tense inflection has dominated research over the past 30 years, with debate centred on the regular–irregular distinction:

  o The single-route model argues that both regular and irregular past tense forms can be learned by a single process, using a pattern associator that learns all new forms by analogy with known verbs. Models that achieve this kind of learning nevertheless have problems learning the past tense of new or unusual verbs that differ from anything they have been trained on previously.

  o The dual-route model argues that regular forms are assembled online through a grammatical process ('add -ed'), while irregular forms are stored as whole-word forms in the lexicon. But the regular–irregular distinction may be illusory. It may look defensible for English, but far less so for other languages, like Polish.

- Derivational morphemes differ in their degree of productivity, with more productive forms being acquired early.

- The interpretation of new compounds is facilitated in three ways: (1) use of contextual information; (2) use of linguistic context; and (3) drawing analogies between new compounds and previously learned ones.

- For complex compounds, level ordering theory predicts that compounds must be assembled before inflection takes place (*rat* + *eater* → *rat eater*; then *rat eater* + *-s* → *rat eaters*). Inflection should not be possible before compounding (*rat* + *s* → *rats*; then *rats* + *eater* →*rats eater*).

  o Even three-year-old children avoid *rats eater* compounds.

  o The argument that level-ordering is innate has been challenged. Recent evidence suggests that children gradually learn the constraints governing the formation of complex words.

- Children can develop an explicit awareness of morphology in the school years, sometimes through explicit teaching.

- Knowledge of morphology can help children develop in other domains, including vocabulary, reading and spelling.

FURTHER READING

Pinker, S. (1999). *Words and rules: The ingredients of language*. New York: Perennial.

One thing you are guaranteed in a book by Steven Pinker is a tidal wave of fascinating detail. No argument is left to its own devices. All are supported by evidence.

At the same time you will have no trouble picking out the broad themes in Pinker's defence of Words and Rules theory.

Seidenberg, M.S. (1992). Connectionism without tears. In S. Davis (Ed.), *Connectionism: Theory and practice* (pp. 84–122). New York: Oxford University Press.

I found this chapter too late, so my own tears flowed freely. A bit like when I first saw *Bambi*. Save money on Kleenex and read this chapter. It may be getting on in years, but it still provides a good starting point for the connectionist take on language learning.

WEBSITES

- **Jean Berko Gleason's academic homepage**: www.bu.edu/psych/faculty/gleason/

  A pioneer in the field of child language research, Jean Berko Gleason's *wugs* and *nizzes* remain relevant more than half a century after their first appearance. There is a link on this site to Berko (1958), the original article in *Word*, which is still well worth reading. You can also access the original pictures of her novel creatures. Don't expect great art, but do expect great ingenuity and a lasting influence.

Still want more? For links to online resources relevant to this chapter and a quiz to test your understanding, visit the companion website at **https://study.sagepub.com/saxton2e**

8

Linguistic Nativism: To the Grammar Born

CONTENTS

OVERVIEW

By the end of this chapter you should be familiar with the concept of Universal Grammar (UG) and the main arguments in favour of the idea that it is innate. You should be able to describe the problem of linguistic diversity: if we are born with the same knowledge of grammar, why do the grammars of the world's languages seem so different? You should be able to describe two approaches to this problem:

- core UG versus peripheral, language-specific aspects of grammar
- parameters: UG does allow for some variation among languages

You should also develop an awareness that arguments in favour of UG rest largely on the assumption that the child's linguistic environment is impoverished: the information it supplies is too meagre to explain the rich knowledge of grammar that every typical child attains. In this regard, you should be able to describe one of Chomsky's best-known examples of a property of grammar (structure dependence) that we all seem to acquire despite limited experience. You should also be able to summarize other arguments in favour of linguistic nativism: language acquisition seems quick and effortless, even though children are not explicitly taught anything about language, and even though it is assumed they receive no help in the form of corrections for grammatical errors. Finally, you should gain some idea about how well supported, empirically, Chomsky's theory of Universal Grammar is.

Universal Grammar

In this chapter, we will focus on the 'nature side' of the nature–nurture argument (see Box 8.1). In particular, we will examine the theory that knowledge of grammar is genetically determined. If your eyebrows shoot up at this idea, you are not alone. Many people find this notion deeply implausible. Nevertheless, the concept of innate grammar has proven remarkably tenacious over the past half century, due in large part to the efforts of Noam Chomsky (see Box 1.4). He argues that children are born with a *Universal Grammar*, or UG. The idea is that 'certain aspects of our knowledge and understanding are innate, part of our biological endowment, genetically determined, on a par with the elements of our common nature that causes us to grow arms and legs rather than wings' (Chomsky, 1988: 4). On this view, language is an organ of the body, albeit a mental organ, and like other organs it grows according to a genetic blueprint. Notice, therefore, that *innate* does not necessarily mean 'present at birth'. Babies are not born talking. But nor are they born with adult arms and legs. The development of arms and legs and (for Chomsky) language, depends on maturation: growth that unfolds over time according to a biological timetable. On this view, we are all born with the same potential for language (Universal Grammar), which then develops into knowledge of particular languages (Swahili, Greek, Gujarati, and so on) according to our individual experience. UG thus corresponds to the initial state of the language faculty at birth. Language acquisition is the process whereby 'a person proceeds from a genetically determined initial state S_0 through a sequence of states S_1, S_2, ..., finally reaching a 'steady state' S_s which then seems to change only marginally (say, by the addition of new vocabulary)' (Chomsky, 1980b: 37). The steady state (S_s) corresponds to knowledge of a recognizable language like Polish or Vietnamese. Chomsky summarizes the difference between UG and the particular languages we end up acquiring in the following way:

> The grammar of a particular language is an account of the state of the language faculty after it has been presented with the data of experience; universal grammar is an account of the initial state of the language faculty before any experience. (Chomsky, 1988: 61)

BOX 8.1 THE ORIGINS OF 'NATURE–NURTURE'

'Nature–nurture' is an elegant phrase that has entered the language. It encapsulates an important issue in the life sciences and provides an easy reference point for anyone with an interest in the origins of human behaviour. To students of psychology, it might sometimes seem that this phrase is quite modern, coinciding with the massive increase in research on genetics over the past 50 years or so. But in fact, the phrase is very old. Francis Galton, the nineteenth century eugenicist, is often credited as the first to popularize this phrase (Fancher, 1979). Others (including Conley, 1984) point out that Shakespeare juxtaposes nature and nurture in about 1610 in his play *The Tempest*. In Act IV, Scene I of this play, the central character, Prospero, fulminates against Caliban:

> A devil, a born devil, on whose nature
> Nurture can never stick.

But it turns out that Shakespeare was not the originator of this famous phrase. In 1582, about 30 years before *The Tempest*, an Elizabethan head teacher called Richard Mulcaster argued that 'Nature makes the boy toward; nurture sees him forward'. As Teigen (1984: 363) observes, Mulcaster stressed the 'harmony and mutual dependence' of nature and nurture. These two concepts were not, originally, set up in opposition to one another in the manner so prevalent these days.

How plausible is the notion of a *universal* grammar? If we sign up for this idea, we must tackle three complementary questions:

1   How does UG theory cope with linguistic diversity – the fact that the grammars of the world's languages seem to differ greatly?
2   Why suppose that UG is present at birth?
3   Precisely which aspects of grammar are universal?

In the following sections, we will consider each of these questions in turn. Before we do, though, it is worth pointing out that the concept of **innate** is not straightforward (Maratsos, 1999; Scholz & Pullum, 2006). Mameli & Bateson (2006) offer 26 different definitions of 'innate', none of which is entirely satisfactory. They identify the following definition as the one adhered to by Chomsky:

> A trait is innate if and only if its development doesn't involve the extraction of information from the environment. (Mameli & Bateson, 2006: 159)

On this approach, the proof that language is innate comes from a demonstration that the child's linguistic environment is not responsible for language acquisition. If the information required for learning does not come from the environment, then it must derive from the genome. Of note, Chomsky's argument does not rely on any simple equation of 'innate' with the concept of 'genetic determination'. Rather, 'innate' is equated with a lack of environmental influence. One problem with this definition is that it does not cover all traits that one finds in nature. Mameli & Bateson (2006) point out that scars or calluses are not readily considered innate, but neither do they stem from the extraction of information from the environment. With regard to language, this definition faces a further profound empirical problem. Currently, we have no principled way of distinguishing experience that provides information for learning from experience that merely provides developmental support (Lehrman, 1970).

We will explore Chomsky's ideas about lack of information in the environment below. In the meantime, Jackendoff (1997: 6) encapsulates the nativist position for us: 'the human genome specifies the growth of the brain in such a way that UG is an emergent functional property of the neural wiring'. On this view, therefore, the form that language takes is inevitable, because it is predetermined in the human genome. In his later writings, though, Jackendoff (2002: 71–72) blurs the edges of Chomsky's position, by dropping the equation of UG with innate knowledge:

> Universal Grammar is not the grammar of any single language: it is the prespecification in the brain that permits the learning of language to take place. So the grammar acquiring capacity is what Chomsky claims is innate.

There is a fundamental difference between innate knowledge and an innate grammar acquiring capacity. Inheriting knowledge of the category of noun is not the same as being born with the capacity to acquire this knowledge. It is worth repeating Chomsky's own words on this issue:

> certain aspects of our knowledge and understanding are innate, part of our biological endowment, genetically determined. (Chomsky, 1988: 4)

If we compare these two definitions, we see that Jackendoff presents us with a far less radical version of the nativist position (cf., Pearl, 2014). It is patently obvious that we are endowed with the mental machinery that permits the acquisition of grammar. Where researchers still disagree is on the issue of how specialized that mental machinery is. Nativists argue that the grammar acquiring capacity is dedicated exclusively to language. Non-nativists, on the other hand, consider grammar to be simply one of many mental achievements acquired by general-purpose cognitive learning mechanisms. We will examine the non-nativist approach to grammar in the next chapter. In the meantime, we can note that Chomsky promulgates a somewhat startling belief: some of our *knowledge* of grammar is innate. And lest we think that Chomsky is out on a limb here, swaying in the breeze all by himself, rest assured that he is not alone:

> The interesting claim that nativism makes is that there are innate ideas, not simply that there are innate learning mechanisms. (Valian, 2014: 90)

DISCUSSION POINT 8.1
NATURE–NURTURE BEYOND LANGUAGE

The nature–nurture question extends far beyond the confines of child language. Think, for example, of the controversy that rages over race and IQ. Herrnstein & Murray (1994), in particular, are famous (infamous, even) for suggesting that African Americans not only do less well on IQ tests than white Americans, but that *genetic* factors play a significant role in explaining the observed differences (see Mackintosh, 1998, for a survey of this issue that is both balanced and thorough).

- List different domains of human behaviour. Start your list with language and IQ, but add as many others as you can: different facets of personality, perhaps, musical ability, and ...?
- Review your list and consider your intuitions about the extent to which genetic factors are responsible both for similarities and differences among people.
- Do you have different intuitions about the role of genes for different domains of behaviour? If so, why?
- In what ways might the nature–nurture issue, as it applies to language, be more than just a scientific issue? What political and social implications might there be?

The problem of linguistic diversity

How can we all be born with the same knowledge of grammar, when people around the world grow up speaking such a massive array of different languages? One recent estimate puts the figure at 6,912 separate languages (Gordon, 2005). To the casual observer, the grammatical systems of the world's languages seem quite different from one another. For example, Japanese treat adjectives as though they were verbs. In Russian, verbs of motion are marked to show whether you go on foot or by transport; they also indicate whether you are going one-way or making a round trip. Yucatec Maya, meanwhile, a central American language spoken in Belize and Guatemala, places the **verb** at the beginning of the **sentence**, usually followed by the **object**, then **subject**.

Yucatec Maya, then, is a VOS language, while English is SVO (*My friend dances like a lunatic* could be glossed something like: *dances – like a lunatic – my friend* in Yucatec Maya). A quick world tour would reveal many grammatical idiosyncrasies that seem exotic from the standpoint of English and which differentiate one language from another. But why do languages differ in these ways? Linguists have grappled with this question for centuries. One explanation, offered by von Humboldt, suggested that geopolitical factors underlay linguistic diversity: 'the structure of languages differs among mankind, because and insofar as the mental individuality of nations is itself different' (1836/1988: 47). Social and political factors have also been emphasized by anthropologists who paint a picture of each human language as a repository of linguistic and cultural uniqueness. UG theorists adopt a radically different perspective, offering three different observations on the issue of linguistic diversity:

1   Fundamentally, human languages share many grammatical properties that may not always be obvious at first glance.
2   There are some differences between the grammars of different languages, but these are not part of UG, and are therefore peripheral.
3   UG offers a menu of options for certain properties of grammar (parameters of variation). Different languages have 'chosen' different options, but they all fall within UG.

To take the first point, there are many ways in which languages resemble one another. To take a simple example, all languages seem to have grammatical categories like **noun** and **verb**. Other categories are also widespread, including, **preposition**, **determiner** and syntactic features like gender, tense and number. Valian (2014) argues that it is not necessary for every language to express every feature of UG – the absence of tense in Chinese provides a case in point. Of course, this creates a headache. How do we establish that a given near-universal feature is actually part of UG? And if it is part of UG, why is it not expressed in every human language? Absolute universals are rare (Evans & Levinson, 2009), but the hunt for them is a longstanding project within linguistics (for example, Greenberg, 1966). In Chomsky's approach, when a universal property of language is discovered, it becomes a likely candidate for inclusion as part of UG. It should also be borne in mind that properties of UG may not be obvious from the surface properties of different languages. We may need to dig beneath the surface to demonstrate the fundamental similarities that unite different languages. We will look in more detail below at one aspect of UG, known as structure dependence. In the meantime, let's consider the second point from our list above.

Core versus periphery

For Chomsky, Universal Grammar comprises a set of core linguistic properties, common to all human languages. But this leaves a considerable number of other, peripheral properties of grammar that are not part of UG. These latter aspects of grammar can be unique to particular languages (or groups of languages). For example, languages often have idiomatic expressions whose meaning is quite different from their literal interpretation: *Tim's got ants in his pants* or *Naomi only made it by the skin of her teeth*. The periphery also contains examples that violate the principles of UG.

For instance, the English sentence *The more the merrier* should not be grammatical because it lacks a verb (Cook, 1988). Similarly, a sentence like *Myself, I wouldn't go there* should not be possible (Salkie, 1990). According to UG, reflexive elements like *myself* should refer back to a person or thing that has already been introduced, as in *Patricia made the cheese soufflé herself*. In this example, the antecedent of *herself* is *Patricia*. But in *Myself, I wouldn't go there, myself* does not have an antecedent. This latter example (and others like it) should set alarm bells ringing. If Universal Grammar constrains the form of human languages, how can we violate its principles with such alacrity? Moreover, the core–periphery distinction begins to look like a convenient way of disposing of awkward examples that do not fit the theory. Quirky aspects of grammar that are not easily explained can be assigned to the periphery.

The concept of peripheral grammar goes some way to explaining the diversity we see, both within and across different languages. It is worth pointing out that anything on the periphery presents a learning problem. No helping hand is available from Universal Grammar, which suggests that the child must be equipped with general learning mechanisms that are not dedicated specially to language, but which *are* capable of acquiring at least some aspects of grammar. How these general learning mechanisms might operate is an issue that has never been broached by UG theorists. The existence of a periphery, though, demonstrates that Universal Grammar cannot account for the acquisition of all aspects of grammar in human languages.

Parameters of variation

Some of the variety between languages is encompassed within UG via the notion of *parameters* of variation (Chomsky, 1981). The idea is that UG presents a limited range of options or parameters. On this view, the '"menu choices" languages opt for can vary, but what's on the menu does not' (Berwick & Chomsky, 2016: 55). Each individual language (like English or Japanese) has 'chosen' one of the parameter settings available. An example will help illustrate this idea (see also Box 1.2 on Syntactic Categories). In English, **verb phrases** can be formed by a verb followed by a noun phrase:

Verb Phrase	$\rightarrow$	Verb	+	Noun Phrase
		eat	+	a biscuit
		take	+	your time
		open	+	the door

The **head** of the verb phrase (VP) in these examples is the verb (*eat, take, open*) and in each case it is followed by a **complement** noun phrase. Our simple rule captures this regularity of English: VP → V + NP. But this rule misses out on the chance to capture a much broader generalization. The interesting property of grammar here is the order of heads and complements within phrases. In our Verb Phrase, the order is 'head followed by complement'. And it turns out that, in English, this head + complement ordering applies to every kind of phrase (including Noun Phrase, Adjective Phrase and Prepositional Phrase). In other languages, like Japanese, the order is reversed: complement + head. The so-called Head Parameter can then be invoked to capture this property of human languages. Universal Grammar presents two choices: head-first or head-last. For the language-learning child, life is made much simpler than having to learn the rules for each kind of noun phrase, each kind of verb phrase, and so on, separately. Instead, the child simply needs to discover the order of heads and complements in the language they are exposed to. Once the Head Parameter is set, the child will know the order of constituents in every kind of grammatical phrase. Thus, parameters can be seen as a kind of switch that needs to be set one way or the other. In this way, parameters 'reduce the difficulty of the learning problem' for the child (Gibson & Wexler, 1994: 407).

Setting parameters: Triggers

We must next explain how parameters are set, that is, we must explain how the child comes to know which kind of language they are learning (e.g., head-first or head-last). The answer provided by UG theory is through the action of a *trigger*. 'Parameters are alleged to be unacquired. What is acquired is a particular setting of a parameter by the process of being triggered by an environmental stimulus' (Scholz & Pullum, 2006: 63). The trigger is generally taken to be exposure to a relevant phrase in the language being learned (see the section on imitating grammar, below). The child exposed to Japanese will hear phrases where the head comes last, while the child learning English will hear head-first phrases. In principle, exposure to a single relevant example could trigger the setting of the parameter, bringing with it a wide range of syntactic knowledge. At this point, though, we run into a problem. The notion of 'simple exposure' as a trigger for this kind of learning is deceptive. In order for the head parameter to be triggered, the child would need to have learnt a substantial amount about language. They have to recognize grammatical phrases for what they are, which, in turn, requires the child to understand in advance the notions of head and complement. Once these concepts are in place, then exposure to a phrase (the trigger) will allow the child to recognize the order of these critical elements (head first or last) and hence set the parameter accordingly. But how does the child come to know what heads and complements are in the first place? UG theory currently offers no answer to this question, which is unfortunate, because it goes to the heart of the problem facing the language-learning child. Universal Grammar may furnish the child with knowledge about grammar, but somehow the child has to recognize the expression of that knowledge in the language they experience. This conundrum has been described recently as the *linking problem* (Ambridge, Pine & Lieven, 2014) and strikes at the heart of the nativist enterprise. Providing the child with innate knowledge of grammar seems to cut through the learning problem thrown up by a supposedly impoverished input. But it throws up the equally vexing problem of how that innate knowledge makes contact with the linguistic input children hear. On this view, Universal Grammar does not simplify the learning problem facing the child.

The concept of trigger being considered here assumes that some information in the environment, the trigger, is directly relevant to what is acquired (in this case, an actual example of head–complement ordering). But the term trigger has been used with different meanings over the years (Stich, 1975). An alternative view is to look at triggers as a kind of catalyst, a concept borrowed from chemistry to denote something that causes a chemical reaction, but which is itself unaffected by it. Either way, though, the child is faced with the prior problem of identifying both heads and complements for what they are. As Smith (2004: 80) admits, this leads to a 'vacuous claim – the child only needs to learn what it needs to learn'. The unanswered question remains: how does the child link their innate knowledge to the input they hear?

The concept of parameters seems to present an elegant solution to the problem of linguistic diversity. A wide range of seemingly disparate facts about different languages can be captured by a single parameter with a very limited range of settings (usually just two). At the same time, it is interesting to note that after almost 30 years of effort, disappointingly few parameters have actually been established within linguistic theory. Fewer still have been investigated empirically using data from child language development (though see Hyams, 1992; Snyder, 2007). Critically, there is currently no convincing explanation for how the child might set parameters.

Arguments for linguistic nativism

Some initial observations

We can start with the observation that, to some eyes, language development looks very fast. As noted in Chapter 1, every typically developing infant undergoes a dramatic transformation. Capable of little more than belching and wailing at birth, it is not so long before the child can hold their own in conversation, expressing their opinions, desires and interests. It has been suggested that children 'display virtual adult competence by age 3 or 4' (McGilvray, 2006: 107). By 'competence', McGilvray has in mind the mental representation of a mature system of adult grammar. While many would regard McGilvray's assertion as extreme, most would nevertheless agree that children do seem to soak up language like a sponge. Moreover, nativists emphasize that children achieve the feat of language acquisition with very little help from parents and others. Contrary to the picture of the input presented in Chapter 4, it is argued that the input for language learning is seriously underdetermined. This means that the input lacks critical information needed to permit successful language acquisition.

To summarize, then, nativists present us with a paradox. On the one hand, grammar is portrayed as a highly abstract, complex system of knowledge. On the other hand, the input is too poor in quality to explain how language could be learned. Despite this contradiction, children nevertheless seem to acquire language, both rapidly and with ease. We are thus skewered by a simple point of logic: 'if the child's linguistic experience does not provide the basis for establishing a particular aspect of linguistic knowledge, there must be another source for that knowledge' (Lightfoot, 2005: 50). As we have seen, that alternative source of knowledge is held to be Universal Grammar. Of course, this argument is only as sound as the assumptions on which it rests:

1   limited exposure to linguistic input
2   no teaching: children acquire language with no help from parents or others
3   speed: children acquire language quickly
4   ease: language is acquired with little ostensible effort
5   poverty of stimulus: the quality of information available in the input is too meagre to account for the rich system of language that children acquire.

We shall consider each one of these assumptions in more detail.

Limited exposure to linguistic input

The first assumption is encapsulated by Chomsky (1975: 4) with his suggestion that 'a normal child acquires … [language] knowledge on relatively slight exposure'. The amount of input available appears very limited if we compare it to the full range of sentences the child might possibly be exposed to. In fact, there is literally no end to the number of different possible sentences we might produce or hear. The rules of grammar provide a toolkit for producing an infinite number of sentences. It is always possible to produce a novel sentence, one that has never before been uttered, by simply adding another phrase. For example, *The cat in the hat* can become *The cat in the hat on the moon*, which can, in turn, become *The cat in the hat on the moon ate a sandwich*, and so on. This property of language was encapsulated by the German philosopher, Wilhem von Humboldt (1836/1988: 91), who observed that language can 'make infinite employment of finite means'. We see, then, that the language-learning child is exposed to a fraction only of the possible sentences. Moreover, each child is exposed to a unique, and therefore idiosyncratic, sample. To compensate for the child's lack of input, Universal Grammar is invoked by nativist theorists.

Before we subscribe to Chomsky's position we should consider how appropriate it is to present the child's learning task in this way. The child is not attempting the impossible, by trying to acquire every sentence of the language. Instead, the goal is to acquire the system of rules that will allow any sentence to be interpreted. And as von Humboldt points out, the system of rules is finite. The child therefore uses a finite sample of sentences to acquire a finite system of rules. Put in these terms, the task facing the child seems more tractable. Moreover, one might argue that children are exposed to a very large amount of language. On a standard estimate, children are exposed to language for about 10 hours per day (Clark, 2003; Tomasello & Stahl, 2004) which must amount to millions of words within the first five years (I say 'must' because no-one has actually counted). As we saw in Chapter 4, the amount of input varies according to the child's individual circumstances. And the differences do impact on the pace of language development. But even in cases of relative deprivation, the number of sentences heard in the early years must still run into the millions. Viewed in this way, the child's input sample does not seem all that 'slight'.

No direct instruction

The second assumption underpinning UG concerns the role of instruction. Chomsky argues that no-one teaches pre-school children how to talk. Parents and teachers often object at this point, being very clear in their own minds that they do teach their children language. For older children, there is some justification for this view. At school, children *are* explicitly taught hundreds, if not thousands, of new words. Indeed, intervention programmes have been devised to increase children's vocabularies, on the basis that explicit instruction is both possible and beneficial (for example, Nash & Snowling, 2006). But grammar, not vocabulary, is the focus here. And more to the point, most researchers do not focus on school-aged children. As noted above, by the age of four or five the child's knowledge of grammar rivals that of any adult.

214

So any explicit teaching at school could only tinker round the edges of an already mature system. In any event, direct instruction is probably impossible. How would we give a grammar lesson to a one-year-old? At this age, the child does not possess the language to understand explicit instruction *in* language *about* language. That is, Eve lacks the requisite **metalinguistic abilities**. Typical estimates suggest that the ability to think about and analyse language structure (for example, work out the number of syllables in a word) does not emerge in any serious way until about the fourth or fifth year (Bowey, 2005; though see Clark, 2003). But the child seems to get by just fine without sophisticated metalinguistic skill or direct instruction, as we can see from Eve's linguistic prowess.

But Chomsky may be leading us down a blind alley. His assumption is that direct instruction would be the best source of input for a language learner. But thousands of adult second language learners, struggling in evening classes, can attest that overt teaching about grammar does not bring them to the point of fluency, however hard they try. We have even less reason to suppose that direct instruction would be the best resource for the toddler. If the metaphor of teaching is at all helpful, then we might cast Child Directed Speech as a better form of instruction. As we saw in Chapter 4, parents modify and simplify their speech in myriad ways to support the acquisition needs of the child (Clark, 2003). CDS is closely geared to the language-learning needs of a cognitively and linguistically naive learner, in a way that explicit teaching could never be.

Ease and speed of language acquisition

We can take the next two assumptions together, namely, that language is acquired with ease and at high speed. Moreover, the facility with language learning is witnessed in all typically developing children, irrespective of their general intelligence or memory capacity. Von Humboldt (1836/1988: 58) made this observation in the nineteenth century:

> all children, under the most diverse conditions, speak and understand at about the same age, varying only within a brief time-span.

In the modern era, Chomsky presents a twin-pronged approach to the argument for innate language universals. On the one hand, he stresses what he takes to be the Herculean labour that language learning presents in its complexity, extent and level of abstractness. And on the other, he suggests that children saunter through the task, barely breaking sweat. The problem, though, is that we cannot judge, in any straightforward manner, whether learning is quick or slow. One way might be to compare language acquisition with learning in other cognitive domains during the same developmental period. Thus, we might observe that many four-year-olds lack the fine motor skills and physical co-ordination required to tie their own shoe laces. They also typically lack conservation, the logical ability to judge that, when a ball of clay is rolled out into a sausage, no clay is either lost or gained in the process (Piaget & Inhelder, 1974). And many four-year-olds cannot yet count to 20 (Fluck & Henderson, 1996). At the same time, those same children can produce sentences that approach or surpass 20 words in length with no discernible difficulty.

Alex aged four years:

If any princesses are catched they have to save her and climb up the pole and the king will say 'Thank you' and 'You can marry her'.

Are you looking for the green one who goes at the top of the tree?

It's very good because it's got those things who I've never had before.

Some frogs are like chameleons because they turn to green on leaves and turn to brown on branches.

The contrast between counting and sentence construction is dramatic. The ability to recall 20 number words in the correct sequence seems relatively straightforward. It requires no complex algorithm or rules to place each number name in the correct order. It is more like placing beads on a string, one after the other. Each number name occurs in the same place in the sequence every time. Moreover, children receive a massive amount of practice with this particular sequence of words. Yet many three- and four-year-olds cannot manage this task. In contrast, Alex's sentences (including the first, with 27 words) require a sophisticated understanding of grammatical principles. One cannot just throw the words together in any old order.

Of course, counting is not the only cognitive capacity acquired by children. Other aspects of cognition make language learning look comparatively slow. For example, visual acuity – the ability to see objects clearly – develops rapidly in the first few months of life and has reached near adult levels by the age of two years (Courage & Adams, 1990). Similarly, the child's understanding of object permanence is adult-like within the first two years of life (Ruffman, Slade & Redman, 2005). Thus, toddlers appreciate that an object continues to exist even when it is concealed, and that it remains the same object regardless of which angle it is viewed from or how it is illuminated. Many even argue that a mature knowledge of object permanence is evident within the first few *weeks* of life (Baillargeon, Li, Luo & Wang, 2006). Examples from general cognition demonstrate that there is no straightforward way of judging how quickly a particular mental capacity is acquired. One is left, then, with the rather unsatisfactory conclusion, that 'children *appear* to acquire language quickly' (McGilvray, 2006: 107, my emphasis). To summarize so far, there is something intuitively appealing about Chomsky's observations about language learning. At first blush, it does seem that children acquire language quickly, effortlessly, on limited exposure and with no direct teaching. But on closer examination, none of these assumptions is well supported. We must turn instead to the heavy artillery in the nativist armoury: the argument from the **poverty of the stimulus**.

The poverty of stimulus argument

Plato's problem

The concept of innate knowledge stems back to Ancient Greece and the Socratic Dialogues of Plato (427–347 BC). Socrates leads a slave boy through a series of questions, and demonstrates to the slave's owner, Meno, that the boy understands the basic principles of geometry. Through his questioning,

Socrates guides the boy to produce a square with an area of 8^2 by extending one that is 4^2. Remarkably, the boy achieves this, even though he has never been taught geometry. In consequence, Plato concludes that the boy knows more than can be explained on the basis of experience; the boy's knowledge must be inherent within his soul. Chomsky's central contribution to twentieth-century thought was to argue that the child faces 'Plato's problem' (Chomsky, 1988) within the domain of language acquisition. The argument is that every typical child knows far more about language than could possibly be learned from experience (Chomsky, 1980b; Marcus, 1993; Pinker, 1994; Uriagereka, 1998; Lasnik, 2000). This is because the input (or 'stimulus') is held to be inherently impoverished. In this section, we will consider three aspects of the *poverty of stimulus* argument:

1   Degenerate input: parents provide a poor model for language learning.
2   Negative evidence: parents do not correct their children's errors.
3   Structure dependence: children have knowledge of certain aspects of grammar, despite a lack of evidence for them in the input.

It is not looking good for the input. First, it's degenerate. Then it is poverty-stricken. Next thing we know, it'll be out on the streets, begging. We have covered the first two points in Chapter 4, so we will provide only a brief summary here. The third point, though, on the grammatical property of structure dependence is worth expanding in some detail. With this example, Chomsky provides a modern version of the Socratic dialogues, in which the reader is cast as the slave boy, guided towards a revelation about innate ideas.

Degenerate input

If I wanted to learn the art of soufflé making, I would probably not ask my husband, who did once manage to boil an egg, but then dropped it on the floor. This is true. So I would more naturally turn to a Michelin-starred chef, like Heston Blumenthal, the guiding principle being that if you want to learn something, it makes sense to acquire the best possible model as an example to learn from. What kind of model do children have for language acquisition? You may recall that Chomsky (1965: 31) described what children hear as 'fairly degenerate in quality', further remarking that 'much of the actual speech observed consists of fragments and deviant expressions of a variety of sorts' (ibid.: 201). But who was Chomsky observing? As we saw in Chapter 4, it turns out that these remarks are appropriate when applied to adults interacting with each other. But when adults (and others) address young children the picture is radically different. The description of Child Directed Speech reveals that children are exposed to a remarkably good model of language from which to learn. The input is simplified and clarified in myriad ways, to meet the communicative needs of a linguistically naive conversational partner. The linguistic environment of the child is far from being degenerate.

Negative evidence: Corrective input for grammatical errors

The next plank in the poverty of stimulus argument is the so-called 'no **negative evidence**' assumption. The idea is that parents do not correct their children's grammatical errors. That is, they receive no information about what is, and is not, grammatical. But children must get their knowledge about the bounds of grammar from somewhere. If the environment is lacking, then one can conclude that this knowledge is innate. We will not dwell on the 'no negative evidence' assumption here because we examined it in some depth in Chapter 4. Suffice to say, many authors are reluctant to abandon this assumption (for example, Cowie, 1997; Chomsky, 1999; Crain & Lillo-Martin, 1999; Maratsos, 1999; Marcus, 1999; Rohde & Plaut, 1999; Smith, 2004; Lust, 2006). At the same time, we saw in Chapter 4 that numerous studies now suggest that negative input *is* available, for every grammatical category studied so far, for every individual child on whom data are available, and in every culture that has been studied. So far, then, we have seen that the input is neither degenerate nor lacking in negative input. What, then, of the third part of this argument, the idea that children acquire complex grammatical knowledge without ever being exposed to critical input data. We turn to this idea in the next section.

Knowledge in the absence of experience: The case of structure dependence

Chomsky asserts that children acquire knowledge of grammar in the absence of experience (Berwick, Pietroski, Yankama & Chomsky, 2011). A dramatic example is provided by deaf children who create their own system of manual communication (known as *homesign*). They do this in the absence of exposure to conventional sign language (or any other form of language) (Hunsicker & Goldin-Meadow, 2012). Recall that 90 per cent of parents with deaf children are not deaf themselves, so they are ill-equipped to sign proficiently with their children (Meadow, 1980). It is argued that such children can combine homesigns into recognisable linguistic phrases with hierarchical structure. The absence of experience in this case seems clear. But Chomsky would argue that all children lack the necessary experience to acquire certain aspects of grammar. We can illustrate this idea by considering a property of grammar known as *structure dependence*. Let's start by asking what you know about structure dependence and the rules governing question formation in English. Being asked what you know about grammar might make you squirm, especially if you belong to the lost generation who were not taught anything about grammar at school. But breathe again. We are not concerned with your explicit knowledge of grammatical rules. Rather, the concern is with your *implicit* knowledge, your intuitions about what is grammatical versus ungrammatical. My hunch is that all native English speakers will have the same intuitions about the examples that follow. We will pick up the notion of shared intuitions later on because it bears directly on the poverty of stimulus argument. In the meantime, let's take an innocuous statement and produce the corresponding question:

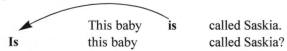

| | This baby | **is** | called Saskia. |
| **Is** | this baby | | called Saskia? |

What is the rule for question formation? Perhaps the simplest rule would be: 'move the 3rd word to the front of the sentence'. But this breaks down very quickly, even for a very similar sentence like: *This newborn baby is called Saskia*. We get linguistic garbage: **Baby this newborn is called Saskia?* Our first conclusion, therefore, is that the linear position of words (1st, 2nd, 3rd, and so on) has no bearing on the issue of question formation. An alternative rule might be: 'Move *is* to the front of the sentence'. Happily, this rule works for both of our examples so far:

> This baby is called Saskia   →   Is this baby called Saskia?
> This newborn baby is called Saskia →   Is this newborn baby called Saskia?

We seem to be up and running, so let's try our rule out on something more complex. Sometimes we find two instances of *is* in a single sentence. Which one do we move? In the next example, we get a well-formed question by moving the first *is*.

| | Saskia | **is** | the only baby who | **is** | named after a cat. |
| **Is** | Saskia | | the only baby who | **is** | named after a cat? |

If we try moving the second *is* in this example, things go badly awry:

| | Saskia | is | the only baby who | **is** | named after a cat. |
| ***Is** | Saskia | is | the only baby who | | named after a cat? |

It looks like we're onto something. Our question rule now is: 'Move the first *is* in a sentence to the front'. But this rule breaks down rather quickly:

| | The baby who | **is** | named after a cat | is | growing whiskers. |
| ***Is** | the baby who | | named after a cat | is | growing whiskers? |

When we move the first *is* in this sentence, the result is ungrammatical. More bothersome still, moving the second *is* produces a well-formed question:

| | The baby who | is | named after a cat | **is** | growing whiskers. |
| **Is** | the baby who | is | named after a cat | | growing whiskers? |

So in some cases we move the first instance of *is*, and in others, we move the second. Again, we see that the question formation rule cannot be based on the linear order of elements (1st *is* versus 2nd *is*). Instead, we need to consider the grammatical structures involved. To construct a grammatical question for our examples, we need the following rule: 'Move the instance of *is* directly following the **subject** of the sentence to the front'. The subject in each of our examples is marked in bold below.

Subject of the sentence:

1   **This baby** is called Saskia.
2   **This newborn baby** is called Saskia.
3   **Saskia** is the only baby who is named after a cat.
4   **The baby who is named after a cat** is growing whiskers.

We can see now where the phrase *structure dependent* comes from. Our rule is based, or rather depends, on the grammatical structure of the subject. The number of words in the subject phrase is irrelevant. The subject might be a single word, as in (3), or a lengthy phrase, as in (4). The critical factor is that the rule applies to the grammatical structure. The following point is also worth emphasizing:

There is no logical reason why languages should use structure-dependent rather than linear rules. Languages can easily be constructed that use computationally simpler linear rules. (Chomsky, 1988: 46)

EXERCISE 8.1
BE AS COPULA OR AUXILIARY

So far, we have avoided talking about which grammatical category *is* belongs to. In fact, it belongs to two different categories: **copula** and **auxiliary verb**. The exercise below helps clarify the difference between them. The verb BE has different forms (*be, am, is, are, was, were, been*). Compare:

We can *be* happy / I *am* happy / You *are* happy / He *was* happy

She *is* happy / They *were* happy / They have *been* happy.

In addition to different forms, BE has two different grammatical functions in English, appearing either as auxiliary verb or copula. Auxiliary verbs are sometimes called 'helping verbs', since they play a supporting role to so-called main verbs, like *talk*, *dance* or *eat*. Compare *I dance like Fred Astaire* with *I can dance like Fred Astaire* or *I could dance like Fred Astaire*. Other auxiliaries include *do, have, must, might, may, shall, will* and *would*. The copula, on the other hand, is used to link a subject to the rest of the sentence, in the absence of any other verb. It is somewhat like the equals sign in X = Y, as in *Saskia is a baby*. In the following examples, identify which forms of BE are an auxiliary verb and which are the copula:

a   Louise **is** a cat lover.
b   Ian must **be** mad to buy so much cat food.

> c   Patricia and Colin **are** having kittens about the fleas in their house.
> d   Saskia **is** wondering what all the interest in cats **is** about.
> e   I **am** wondering what cat would taste like if it **were** roasted.
> f   Cats **were** worshipped in Ancient Egypt.
> g   The cat that **is** stealing my milk has **been** known to steal chicken, too.
> h   **Is** there any reason why cat owners do not look like their pets?
>
> The answers are at the back of the book. Do not be too downhearted if you don't get all of them right first time. Even child language experts sometimes slip up on the copula versus auxiliary BE contrast (e.g., Pinker, 1994: 41; MacWhinney, 2004: 890).

Returning to structure dependence, we can finesse our rule. Questions are formed by moving the copula or auxiliary verb that occurs directly after the subject to the front of the sentence. The auxiliary does not have to be *is* (or other forms of *be*). It could be any auxiliary verb (for example, *shall*, *might*, *will*), as in the example below:

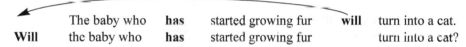

| | The baby who | **has** | started growing fur | **will** | turn into a cat. |
| **Will** | the baby who | **has** | started growing fur | | turn into a cat? |

In fact, we can generalize even further, going beyond the confines of question formation to draw the following broad conclusion: 'all rules in all languages are structure dependent' (Smith, 2004: 50). For this reason, structure dependence is held to be part of Universal Grammar.

Before we move on, it is worth inserting one note of caution. The discussion of question formation is based on the assumption that we start with a statement and convert it into a question by moving an auxiliary or copula. But this kind of movement is not essential and numerous theories of grammar get by quite happily without it (e.g., see Clark & Lappin, 2011: 36). In addition, it has never been shown that this kind of movement corresponds to any kind of mental operation. Many years ago, when Chomsky's ideas first came to prominence, experiments were conducted to see if the number of grammatical operations – transformations – needed to convert one structure into another was reflected in actual processing time. The results were disappointing (Fodor & Garrett, 1967; Watt, 1970). Evidently, there is no straightforward relationship between linguistic theory and psycholinguistic processing. Questions might well be formed *ab initio* with no reference to statements.

The origins of structure dependence

We can now get back to the *poverty of the stimulus*. The first thing to note is how quick and strong our intuitions are about the sentences in the examples above. We know, without prompting, which sentences are grammatical and which ones are ungrammatical. I assume here that all native speakers of English will agree with these judgements. If that is the case, we all have the same tacit knowledge about the grammar of complex questions, and moreover, that knowledge is structure dependent. But where did this knowledge come from? If learning is involved, then Chomsky (1980b) argues that we would need to be exposed to complex questions like *Is Saskia the only baby who is named after a cat?* Simple questions, like *Is this baby called Saskia?*, do not allow us to determine which kind of rule the speaker is following. But Chomsky assumes that the critical evidence 'is not available to the child in terms of direct linguistic experience' (Chomsky, 1980b: 115). That is, children are supposed never to hear complex questions of the type described above. And this time, one of Chomsky's armchair speculations turns out to be accurate. MacWhinney (2004) combed through the CHILDES database looking for evidence of this structure in the speech addressed by adults to children aged up to 5;0. But he uncovered just one single example in something like three million utterances. It looks as though children never (or almost never) hear such sentences. A similar search was conducted on the archives of the *Wall Street Journal* by Pullum & Scholz (2002). The results were slightly more encouraging, since about 1 per cent of sentences conformed to the complex question structure under consideration. But exemplars are still rare. And, more to the point, young children do not read the *Wall Street Journal*. There is, though, another form of input that might help children, namely questions of the following kind (from MacWhinney, 2004: 890):

Where is the dog that you like?

There is only one instance of the copula here (and no auxiliaries). But like our original examples, this question has a complex structure, with one **clause** (*that you like*) embedded inside a **main clause** (*where is the dog...*). To form the question, we must also move the copula from the main clause, as in our previous examples. This kind of question might therefore provide the evidence that children need to learn the structure-dependent question rule. MacWhinney (2004) reports that this kind of structure crops up hundreds of times in the CHILDES corpus. This sounds like a healthy figure, until we do a simple calculation. Even 1,000 such cases over a total of 3,000,000 amounts to just 0.03 per cent of the input, spread over many different children. To all intents and purposes, therefore, the relevant examples of auxiliary or copula movement are seldom, if ever, witnessed by the child.

The imitation of grammatical structures

The preceding discussion highlights an important assumption underpinning the nativist approach to language learning, namely, that the child must hear examples of the 'acquirendum' (the structure to be learned) in order to learn it themselves. As mentioned, non-nativists have extended this idea by looking for structures that are not identical to the acquirendum, but which share critical properties (*Where is the dog that you like?*) (Pullum & Scholz, 2002; MacWhinney, 2004). But there is a confusion here between the acquirendum, which is a grammatical rule, and the output when that rule is applied in a particular instance (a sentence).

When we listen to someone speak, all we hear are the *products* of grammatical rules, not the rules themselves. The child cannot imitate grammar. Imagine how helpful it would be if every word the child heard was tagged in some way, to indicate what grammatical category each word belonged to:

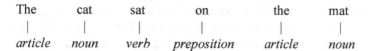

With this kind of tagging, the task of working out the rules of grammar would be greatly ameliorated. Observe, though, that even this system is underdetermined in some ways. That is, it lacks useful information. For example, it would also help to know that the **verb** (*sat*) appears in the past tense, and that **article** and **noun** combine into a grammatical unit (**noun phrase**, or **determiner phrase**, depending on one's theoretical persuasion). And so on. Of course, this kind of help is not available. So how does the child recognize grammatical categories in the input? This is a problem that still taxes language acquisition researchers from both nativist and non-nativist traditions. Either grammatical categories like noun phrase must be constructed by the child, or they are given as part of UG. In either case, these categories must be acquired from a stream of speech that is not tagged in advance. Innate knowledge, by itself, cannot explain language acquisition (cf., Ambridge et al., 2014). This important point is generally glossed over, as revealed in the following remark by Chomsky (1972: 30): 'the idea of "structure-dependent operations" is part of the innate schematism applied by the mind to the data of experience'. As we saw with triggers, the issue that has not been resolved is just how the mind 'applies' its innate knowledge to the input. A bidirectional learning problem persists, therefore: 'how does the child map the words she hears onto the categories she has; how does she map the categories she has onto the words she hears?' (Valian, 2014: 81).

Evidence from children

We have seen that complex questions, of the kind discussed above, are surpassingly rare. This applies not only to Child Directed Speech, but also to sources of formal written English aimed at adults. We might ask, therefore, if such questions are a minority taste. Perhaps only some people acquire this kind of complex structure. But do not forget your own intuitions about the sample sentences above. They should tell you that we all have the same knowledge, regardless of our individual experience. We can tap into an adult's knowledge of grammar by asking directly about their intuitions. But we cannot do this with a very young child. Instead, researchers have to be more ingenious. One approach has been to elicit questions from children by rigging the conversation so that a complex question is called for. If Universal Grammar has endowed children with knowledge of structure dependence, then any questions we can squeeze out of them should be grammatical. Moreover, none of their questions should violate structure dependence.

Unfortunately, very little research has addressed this question directly. In one series of experiments, children aged 3–5 years were presented with a familiar figure, Jabba the Hut from *Star Wars*, and were encouraged to ask him a series of questions (Crain & Nakayama, 1987; Nakayama, 1987). An experimenter showed children various pictures and for each one elicited a question with the frame: *Ask Jabba if _____*, for example, *Ask Jabba if the boy who is being kissed by his mother is happy*. This is not an easy task and children make frequent errors (62 per cent of the time for the younger children). A frequent kind of error was the production of questions with three auxiliary verbs: ***Is** the boy who **is** being kissed by his mother **is** happy?* Nakayama (1987) argues that this task can easily overload the child's processing capacity. But the child's *grammatical* abilities are not overloaded, because children never produced questions that violated the structure-dependent question formation rule (for example, **Is the boy* *who being kissed by his mother is happy?*). In consequence, Crain & Nakayama (1987) conclude that the initial state of the language faculty (Universal Grammar) embodies structure dependence.

There have been some acute criticisms of Crain & Nakayama's methodology (for example, Drozd, 2004; MacWhinney, 2004). But more seriously, the empirical findings of these early studies have been challenged. Ambridge, Rowland & Pine (2008) presented children with a picture that depicted a simple scene, for example, of two boys, one running fast and the other walking. The experimenter then encouraged children to ask a toy dog a question about this scene: *Ask the dog if the boy who is running fast can jump high*. This set-up is rather contrived, but at least children were being asked to pose a real question, that is, one they did not know the answer to. The answer was depicted on the back of the card, 'visible' only to the toy dog. The dog was not only happy to do experiments, but could talk into the bargain, supplying the child with appropriate responses to their questions. See what I mean by contrived? Fortunately, children are very tolerant of adults and do their best to keep them amused. The method adopted by Ambridge et al. (2008) differed from Crain & Nakayama (1987) in two further important ways. First, there were more trials, that is, opportunities to produce a question: 16 per child, compared with a maximum of six. And second, a range of different auxiliary verbs was used. Crain & Nakayama (1987) confined their test questions to copula and auxiliary *is*. But it turns out that children make relatively few errors with these two forms (e.g., Ambridge, Rowland, Theakston & Tomasello, 2006; Rowland, 2007; but see Santelmann, Berk, Austin, Somashekar & Lust, 2002). The low error rates are a sign that children become competent with *is* relatively quickly, and are therefore less likely to produce errors, even with complex questions. To see if children are willing to violate structure dependence, more error-prone auxiliaries are suitable, like *can*, *should* and *do*, or even different forms of *be* (*are* instead of *is*).

With these changes in methodology, Ambridge et al. (2008) report that six-year-old children produce structure dependence errors about 5 per cent of the time:

*Can the boys who run fast can jump high?

*Can the girl who dance can sing?

Can the girl who make cakes can make biscuits?

Can the men that drive cars can drive tractors?

It seems, then, that UG is not acting like a rigid straitjacket, compelling children to observe structure dependence at all times. But why are children willing to produce corrupt sentences for some, but not all structures? Ambridge et al. (2008) suggest that close attention to the input may provide the key. Of special interest are sequences of words that appear side by side in the input, so called bi-grams. For example, sequences like *who unhappy* almost never occur. Try to construct a sentence for yourself that contains this sequence of words. But the child would have to produce this sequence in order to violate structure dependence, as in the following example:

	The boy who	is	unhappy	is	watching Mickey Mouse.
Is	the boy who		unhappy	is	watching Mickey Mouse?

Perhaps children are unwilling to produce bi-grams that they have not actually heard themselves. This so-called conservative approach to learning has often been remarked upon in young children (for example, Snyder, 2007; see also Chapter 9). It would also help explain why some structure dependence errors do occur. For example, the sequence *who dance* is far more likely to occur in a range of sentence types (*People who dance live longer*). This may explain why children are more willing to produce an error like *Can the girl who dance can sing?* This explanation is intriguing, but may suffer from 'Little Englisher' syndrome. As we observed in Chapter 7, the majority of language acquisition research is conducted on (and in) English (see also Wierzbicka, 2011). And this can distort our view, not only of what the child learns, but how. In this vein, it turns out that the solution pursued by Ambridge et al. (2008) may not fare so well beyond the confines of English (Berwick, Pietroski, Yankama & Chomsky, 2011).

If we maintain the focus beyond English, recent evidence from Japanese children provides support for Chomsky's position (Suzuki & Yoshinaga, 2013). These authors examined quantifiers, which modify nouns to express amount (e.g., *several fish, many fish, a few fish*). Japanese has so-called *floating quantifiers*, a phrase which captures the relatively free word order observed in Japanese. Take, for example, the quantifier *nin*, which is used to count people:

San-nin-no	gakusee-ga	koronda.
three	students	fell down
'Three students fell down.'		

Gakusee-ga	san-nin	koronda.
students	three	fell down
'Three students fell down.'		

These examples have been simplified to allow us to focus on the essential point, which is that the quantifier (and the number it attaches to – in this case *three*) can 'float' or appear in different positions without affecting the meaning. Critically, though, quantifiers cannot just float off anywhere.

Their movement is structure dependent and not based on linear order. The input available to children provides almost no information on the syntactic constraint which governs floating quantifiers (Suzuki & Yoshinaga, 2013). At the same time, though, Japanese five- and six-year-olds interpret floating quantifiers correctly, even when they do not occur directly next to the noun they modify. Their interpretation is based on linguistic structure, not on the linear order of words, and there seems to be little help available in the input. We have at least one case, therefore, where learning seems to take place in the absence of experience.

DISCUSSION POINT 8.2

Let's have a heated debate. But first you will need to do some preparatory reading. Organize yourself into groups of three. Everyone should read articles (1) and (5), below. Each person should also take one of the articles (2) to (4). Not as much reading as it might appear (roughly 20 pages each). And worth the effort. In your groups consider the evidence and arguments in favour of each position. How convincing is the empirical evidence offered in the first article (Lidz, Waxman & Freedman, 2003)? How convincing are their arguments, in light of the criticisms which follow?

1   Lidz, J., Waxman, S. & Freedman, J. (2003). What infants know about syntax but couldn't have learned: Experimental evidence for syntactic structure at 18 months. *Cognition, 89(3)*, B65–B73.
2   Tomasello, M. (2004). Syntax or semantics? Response to Lidz et al. *Cognition, 93(2)*, 139–140.
3   Akhtar, N., Callanan, M., Pullum, G.K. & Scholz, B.C. (2004). Learning antecedents for anaphoric one. *Cognition, 93(2)*, 141–145.
4   Regier, T. & Gahl, S. (2004). Learning the unlearnable: The role of missing evidence. *Cognition, 93(2)*, 147–155.
5   Lidz, J. & Waxman, S. (2004). Reaffirming the poverty of the stimulus argument: A reply to the replies. *Cognition, 93(2)*, 157–165.

Poverty of the stimulus: Summary

The poverty of the stimulus argument does not look well supported. We have seen that a number of longstanding assumptions about the input to the child have been refuted. Principal among these are the idea that parents supply degenerate input and also that they do not provide corrective information for grammatical errors. A further observation was that young children receive no direct language teaching. But this is something of a red herring: overt teaching could never be the most efficacious kind of input for a naive language learner. The kind of input they actually receive is more promising in its simplicity, clarity and responsiveness to the child's learning needs. We also considered the idea that language acquisition is quick and effortless.

But defining what these two concepts mean with regard to language learning was problematic. And a survey of other feats in cognitive development revealed that it is not always easy to characterize language as the most rapid achievement of mental development.

We then turned our attention to a specific property of grammar: structure dependence. Chomsky poses a valuable question: Where does our knowledge of structure dependence come from, given that we never hear complex questions of the critical type as we grow up? We observed that despite a lack of input exposure, we, as adults, do seem to share a knowledge of what makes complex questions either grammatical or ungrammatical. In consequence, Chomsky concludes that structure dependence must be part of Universal Grammar. But we also noted that one does not necessarily need to hear a structure in order to acquire it. In this regard, research on machine learning has begun to show that complex questions can be acquired without them appearing in the input to the model (Lewis & Elman, 2001; Reali & Christiansen, 2005; see also Regier & Gahl, 2004). The success of models in this regard suggests that there is no poverty of stimulus problem for the child. At the same time, it remains to explain how the child makes the leap from simple input to complex output.

We also examined the occurrence of structure dependence errors by children. We should first recall that such errors are very rare, even when children are placed under a hot spotlight and offered unusual inducements like talking dogs. We should also note that their violations of UG do not force us to abandon UG as a model of child grammar. We all make mistakes. Unfortunately, though, the mistakes that occur create an empirical headache for UG theory. They make it very difficult to demonstrate, unequivocally, that UG is the guiding force behind child utterances. Errors could arise because child grammars bear no relation to the theoretical description offered by UG theory. Or they could arise because the child does possess UG, but their knowledge of structure dependence is momentarily derailed in the production of a particular question. Distinguishing between these two possibilities may be well nigh impossible. What does remain possible, in principle, is that structure dependence is a property of language that children are born with. But it remains for UG theorists to demonstrate precisely how innate knowledge might assist the child in the acquisition of language (Ambridge et al., 2014).

Let's take our discussion of the poverty of the stimulus back to where we started: the slave boy, whose knowledge of geometry is inherent in his soul. Close examination of this story shows that Socrates suggests most of the answers to the boy and even provides 'negative evidence' in the form of corrections for his errors (Clark & Lappin, 2011). Experience conducive to learning was, in fact, provided. In the case of language acquisition, also, it seems likely that the input available is far richer in information than nativists allow (see Chapter 4).

The contents of UG: What precisely is innate?

We have considered one aspect of grammar – structure dependence – in some detail, because of Chomsky's explicit claim that it constitutes part of Universal Grammar. But what else belongs in UG? Frustratingly, there is no simple answer to this question. One answer seems to be 'anything and everything a UG theorist studies'. In this vein, several book-length treatments have been published which present the theory of Universal Grammar (e.g., Cowper, 1992; Radford, Atkinson, Britain, Clahsen & Spencer, 1999; Adger, 2003). These texts are based on the assumption that the numerous aspects of grammar they describe are all part of UG. For example, Napoli (1993: 4–5) declares that 'the principles developed in [her] book are taken to be universals of human language'. But no attempt is made to justify this assumption. Instead, what we get, if anything, is an appeal to the poverty of stimulus argument: linguistic Principle X is taken to be part of UG because the child's linguistic environment lacks the information required to help them learn this Principle. But this blanket assumption does not get us very far. Linguists (being academics) are likely to disagree on how best to capture the description and explanation of Principle X (for a case in point, see competing accounts of the so-called null-subject phenomenon: Hyams, 1992; Huang, 1995). When competing accounts are advanced, which one should we prefer? Poverty of stimulus arguments cannot help us decide. The reason is that *each and every* account of Principle X can rely on the poverty of stimulus argument to support its claim to UG membership. In other words, poverty of stimulus can never function as an evaluation metric: it cannot be used for choosing among competing explanations to determine the precise constitution of Universal Grammar.

In contrast to the 'anything and everything' approach, the last 15 years has witnessed a much more streamlined approach. First, Hauser et al. (2002) proposed that UG contains just one property of grammar: *recursion*. Recursion occurs where the input to a rule also features as part of its output (see Box 8.2). But is recursion so uniquely privileged? As we pointed out in Chapter 2, it has been argued that songbirds show hierarchical structure and recursive syntactic pattern learning in their songs (Gentner, Fenn, Margoliash & Nusbaum, 2006; Abe & Watanabe, 2011). Meanwhile, some human languages do not appear to show recursion, most notably, the Amazonian language, Pirahã (Everett, 2008). Moreover, recursion is a complex property, and one might argue, for example, that one cannot have recursion without both structure dependence and grammatical categories to apply recursion to. Chomsky's assertion about recursion is regarded by many as a major recantation of his former position on Universal Grammar (Pinker & Jackendoff, 2005). But Chomsky doesn't let the grass grow. While his detractors languish in an overgrown meadow, he has moved on. Currently, Chomsky argues that a much simpler property of language is both biologically endowed and uniquely human (part of the Faculty of Language – Narrow, as discussed in Chapter 2). The property in question is known as Merge, and allows us to combine two linguistic units to create a new kind of unit (Berwick & Chomsky, 2016). We can see these two features at work in the simplest of noun phrases: *electric piano*. The adjective *electric* and the noun *piano* combine to produce a linguistic unit, a noun phrase, which is distinct from both of its constituents. Merge allows for the creation of hierarchical linguistic structures, referred to by Chomsky as the Basic Property of language (ibid., 2016). Once a language is organised in terms of hierarchical phrases, the notion of structure dependence falls out naturally. Undoubtedly, the plausibility of Universal Grammar is enhanced by reducing it to the single, simple property of Merge. As ever, though, there is debate: see Matthews (2007) for a sceptical look at the notion of hierarchy in linguistic phrases.

BOX 8.2 RECURSION

To understand recursion, we first need a few basics concerning the rules of grammar. Words combine to make phrases and phrases combine into sentences in a rule-governed way. In English, I can combine two words like *the* and *hobbit* to produce an acceptable phrase: *the hobbit*. If I switch the order round, the phrase is no longer grammatical: *hobbit the*. Our grammatical phrase (*the hobbit*) can function as a unit: we can move it around as though the two words were glued together and drop it into different positions within a sentence (though not just in any old position): **The hobbit** *in my garden likes toast*. Or *I just met* **the hobbit** *of my dreams*. The important thing about our phrase is that the two words, *the* and *hobbit*, are particular kinds of words. *The* belongs to the category of **determiner** (which also includes *a* and *some*), while *hobbit* belongs to the category of **noun** (to which we can add many thousands of other nouns, like *computer*, *water* and *truth*).

Traditionally, our phrase would be described as a **noun phrase**, and the rule for making noun phrases of this kind would be:

Noun Phrase → Determiner + Noun

More recent treatments argue that our phrase, *the hobbit*, is better described as a **determiner phrase** (Radford et al., 1999; although see Matthews, 2007). But fortunately, our demonstration of syntactic rules is not affected by this twist.

Recursion is a special kind of procedure in which a category (like *noun phrase*) is embedded within itself. For example, in English, we can use recursion to embed one **relative clause** inside another. A relative clause is like a mini-sentence, tucked inside another sentence and is often introduced by *that*, *which* or *who*, as in: *I like the hobbit* **who won the race**. This relative clause is part of a larger noun phrase (*the hobbit who won the race*). We thus have two different kinds of noun phrase. One is fairly simple (*the hobbit*), while the other is more complex (*the hobbit who won the race*). Our complex noun phrase can be captured by the following rule:

Noun Phrase → Noun Phrase + Relative Clause
                the hobbit   + who won the race

Now we get to the nub of recursion. Observe that we have a simple noun phrase, *the race* (determiner + noun), embedded within the relative clause. If we choose, we can

(Continued)

take this latter noun phrase and expand it with our second rule (noun phrase + relative clause). For example: *I like the hobbit who won the race that started in the park.* In principle, we can repeat this process *ad nauseum*, or more properly, *ad infinitum*. Recursion thus allows us to take our limited palette of rules and produce an infinite number of sentences, in a potentially endless cycle. This is because the input to the rule (in our case, noun phrase) also features in the output. Thus, one can always add a new clause: *I like the hobbit who won the race that started in the park that once had a bandstand that …* and so on.

From the outside, the pace of change in UG theory can seem bewildering. The so-called Chomskyan revolution, is, in fact, a series of ongoing revolutions, as the ideas and theories develop over time. We do not need to tussle further with the arguments for and against the idea that UG is restricted to a very limited set of properties. The point here is to highlight the fact that, as yet, there is very little agreement about the precise contents of Universal Grammar. Critically, if we do not know what is, and is not, hypothesized to be innate, we have no way of testing nativist assumptions.

Conclusion

This chapter has introduced the idea of innate knowledge of grammar, characterized by Chomsky as Universal Grammar. We saw that the main source of evidence in support of this idea comes from an analysis of the child's linguistic environment. Chomsky argues that the input is impoverished, in the sense that it lacks the information necessary to permit the acquisition of grammar by a domain-general learning mechanism. We reviewed the so-called argument from the poverty of the stimulus in some detail and found that none of its tenets are especially well supported by available evidence. At the same time, they are not decisively refuted either. The idea that knowledge of grammar might be innate may have seemed rather bizarre at the beginning of this chapter. Perhaps now, though, you may accept that Chomsky's position has an intuitive appeal. All typical children grapple with the obscure complexities of grammar with a speed and facility that can seem quite astonishing. It is therefore natural to predict that genetic factors are implicated. But as we have seen, the arguments for linguistic nativism do not stand up to close empirical scrutiny. The central problem is that Chomsky relies heavily on the argument from the poverty of the stimulus to support his case. And we should emphasize that it *is* largely a matter of argument. Empirical evidence in support of the poverty of the stimulus is thin on the ground. Chomsky (following Koryé, 1968) has often argued that theories are not refuted by data, only by analyses. This situation is unsatisfactory for many psychologists because they are used to testing their hypotheses against substantive data, supported by statistical analyses. Linguistics (still the world's major supplier of Chomskyan nativists) is less steeped in this tradition. Empirical studies by nativists tend to present evidence from very small samples of children (sometimes only one) and adopt a research strategy that, again, psychologists can find frustrating. Typically, these studies report that children of a particular age, say two or three years, demonstrate knowledge of a particular Principle of UG (for example, Hyams, 1986; Radford, 1990; Snyder, 2007). The conclusion that the Principle is innate depends largely on the youth of the children. Two-year-olds, it is argued, cannot have been exposed to the relevant experience to explain their linguistic prowess. But two years is a long time in language acquisition, as we saw in Chapters 5 and 6. And it is very difficult to demonstrate that children lack a particular learning experience with regard to language. In many cases, therefore, the empirical evidence we might require is simply not available. Chomsky himself has recently drawn attention to the limits of our knowledge in this respect:

> I've been working on Universal Grammar for all these years; can anyone tell you precisely how it works [how it develops into a specific language]? It's hopelessly complicated. (Chomsky, 2012: 54)

When we have the wherewithal to understand the workings of the human mind better, we might come closer to discovering what, if any, aspects of linguistic knowledge are genetically determined.

IN A NUTSHELL

- Chomsky asserts that knowledge of grammar is innate, in the form of Universal Grammar.

- UG is the initial state of the language faculty which then develops into knowledge of a particular language, like English or Korean.

- The grammars of the world's languages share many properties; according to nativists, the diversity one sees is either superficial or encompassed within UG as a limited menu of options (parameters).

- Chomsky argues that language acquisition is fast, effortless and achieved on the basis of limited exposure to a poor model of language. None of these claims is well supported.

- The poverty of the stimulus argument is based on the belief that the input for learning lacks the information necessary to explain how the child comes to acquire what they know about grammar.

- Structure dependence is a property of grammar used by Chomsky to demonstrate that even very young children possess an understanding of complex, abstract aspects of grammar despite never having heard anyone use these grammatical structures.

- Children can be induced to produce structure dependence errors in an experimental setting, even though this violates the precepts of Universal Grammar.

- No-one has ever produced a definitive list (or even a working list) of the particular aspects of grammar that are held to be part of UG. This makes it difficult to determine precisely what is, and is not, innate.

- Chomsky's theory of UG is not well supported by empirical evidence. But neither has it been decisively refuted.

FURTHER READING

Botha, R.P. (1989). *Challenging Chomsky: The generative garden game*. Oxford: Basil Blackwell.

In this book, Botha draws crucial distinctions for the reader that help one appreciate the subtlety and precision of Chomsky's work. In the process, Botha provides a very witty analysis of how Chomsky has fended off his critics over the years, written partly in an eighteenth-century style. Not as odd as it sounds. Highly entertaining, in fact.

McGilvray, J. (Ed.) (2005). *The Cambridge companion to Chomsky*. Cambridge: Cambridge University Press.

There have been many books published about Chomsky. This collection covers three Chomskyan themes in depth: language, mind and politics. Several academic heavyweights slug it out in the ring on Chomsky's behalf. This collection is authoritative, up to date and wide-ranging, but do bear in mind the partisan nature of the authors.

Sampson, G. (2005). *The 'language instinct' debate* (revised ed.). London: Continuum.

Also not balanced in its approach, but this time the stance is avowedly anti-nativist. This book overflows with provocative arguments and provides an entertaining, sometimes overheated, attack on the nativist enterprise in child language. Again, read with caution: how well supported, empirically, are Sampson's ideas?

WEBSITES

- **Languages of the World**: www.omniglot.com/

  This site is a treasure trove of basic information on many of the world's languages. Rummage around in this site and marvel at the number and diversity of different languages currently spoken throughout the world. Then consider Chomsky's fundamental claim: the observed differences among languages are, in critical respects, superficial. What matters are the common features that all languages share (Universal Grammar).

- **Chomsky's influence beyond linguistics**: https://chomsky.info/

  You will find sufficient material here to satisfy your curiosity about one of the world's leading intellectuals. The focus is on his political views, but there are also references and links to his academic writings in linguistics, philosophy and (latterly) evolutionary theory.

Still want more? For links to online resources relevant to this chapter and a quiz to test your understanding, visit the companion website at **https://study.sagepub.com/saxton2e**

9

The Usage-based Approach: Making it Up as You Go Along

CONTENTS

OVERVIEW

This chapter deals with the most prominent and most comprehensive non-nativist account of syntax acquisition: usage-based theory.

By the end of this chapter, you should be able to describe some of the critical factors in infant social communication that are said to underpin later language development. These include the child's use of pointing and the emergence of collaborative engagement in pursuit of a shared goal.

You should also be able to discuss and evaluate usage-based research on the child's earliest speech output, with its focus on entire utterances, rather than individual words. The syntactic categories witnessed in adult language are said to emerge only gradually, as the result of the child's experience with language. You should be able to describe the progression towards syntax from early, lexically specific, structures through to broad syntactic generalizations which permit the child to be linguistically productive.

You should gain some appreciation of the challenges facing the usage-based approach. In particular, we will focus on the problems raised in explaining child productivity: (1) how do children acquire general rules, based on mature syntactic categories, that allow them to create their own sentences? And (2) how do children *constrain* their productivity and avoid producing errors? You will gain some appreciation of current usage-based answers to these questions. In the process, it will become apparent that the issue of child productivity continues to present a serious challenge for *all* theories of child syntax acquisition.

Language knowledge from language use

As the name suggests, the usage-based approach rests on the assumption that our knowledge of language is obtained from the *use* of language (Langacker, 1987). There is a natural sympathy, therefore, with functionalism, the belief that 'the forms of natural languages are created, governed, constrained, acquired and used in the service of communicative functions' (Bates & MacWhinney, 1989: 3). In considering how language is used, the overriding question is *What is language for?*, with the answer being some function like requesting, directing or informing. Every utterance is produced with the intention of getting things done or understood. The task of the child is to make the necessary connections between communicative functions and the linguistic forms which are used to express those functions. Take, for example, the **transitive** construction in English:

noun phrase	+	**verb**	+	**noun phrase**
Max		kissed		Anna

The function of transitives is to denote how one participant (*Max*) acts in some way on another (*Anna*). This function maps onto a particular default syntactic form, which in English includes placing the **agent** (*Max*) first, followed by the action (*kiss*) and ending with the **patient** (*Anna*). In the usage-based approach the child must understand the function of this **sentence** first, as a basis for acquisition of the syntactic structure. Generally speaking, 'children acquire language first and foremost by understanding how others use language' (Tomasello, 2009: 86). We will organize our discussion of the usage-based approach around three main themes:

1   Social cognition as a foundation for language learning.
2   Pattern-finding: how the child creates grammatical structures and uses them productively.
3   Constraining productivity: how the child avoids overgeneralization.

In sharp contrast with the nativist approach, usage-based theory does not assume innate knowledge of grammar. Instead, grammar is *learned*. Hence, in the initial stages of language acquisition, the child's knowledge of language is held to be qualitatively different from that of an adult. The child converges gradually on the adult state. Moreover, language is not regarded as a unique cognitive phenomenon that requires specialized (domain-specific) learning mechanisms. Instead, the learning mechanisms required by the child are said to be domain-general. In other words, the learning mechanisms used in the acquisition of language are applied to other, non-linguistic forms of input, including, for example, sequences of auditory tones (Saffran et al., 1999). On this view, language is not considered to be uniquely different, or difficult, as an object of learning. But before we consider how the child tackles the complexities of grammar, let's first examine the social world of the infant and consider how the infant's communication skills might pave the way into language.

Social cognition

Dyadic and triadic interaction

In usage-based theory, the child's understanding of language functions is rooted firmly in the social act of communication. It is argued that certain aspects of social interaction are unique to humans, in particular, the ability to read and share the intentions of others (Tomasello, Carpenter, Call, Behne & Moll, 2005). On this view, the complexities of language, including grammar, derive from this more basic aspect of human interaction. The communication skills of the infant develop over the first year. Very early on, at about 5–6 weeks, infants demonstrate an interest in attending to the mother's face and voice, together with an increase in smiling and cooing. This social awakening in the infant is reciprocated by mothers, with increases in their own vocalizations and displays of interest and affection. Arguably, the adult's ability to capture and then hold the child's attention is critical for language development. By the age of 11–14 months, infants have developed a sophisticated ability to follow changes in the direction of an adult's gaze (Scaife & Bruner, 1975). Critically for language development, the level of shared attention witnessed in adult–child discourse is positively correlated with later vocabulary and syntax level, for both typical children and for those with autistic spectrum disorder (Tomasello, Mannle & Kruger, 1986; Akhtar, Dunham & Dunham, 1991; Rosenthal Rollins & Snow, 1998).

The ability to follow the mother's direction of gaze is just one feature of shared attention. In Chapter 4 we remarked on the adult's use of exaggerated intonation and high pitch to gain an infant's attention. It has also been found that adults *move* differently when interacting with infants, adopting a closer proximity, increased enthusiasm and exaggerated actions. Moreover, infants prefer to look at this special form of infant-directed motion (Brand & Shallcross, 2008). Generally, it has been found that two-year-olds whose mothers indulge in high levels of attention-holding devices score highly on general measures of verbal learning one year later (Schmidt & Lawson, 2002).

Early communication is *dyadic*, in the sense that it involves two participants. Over time, though, the infant becomes increasingly interested in the world of objects and, by three months, is less willing to gaze solely at the mother. In response, mothers adopt a more vigorous, playful approach to interaction, typified by a more excited, arousing mode of speech (Trevarthen, 1983). A *triadic* form of engagement emerges towards the end of the first year, in which adult and infant jointly direct their attention towards a third entity which constitutes a shared goal (Tomasello et al., 2005). This shared goal might manifest in turn-taking games, like rolling a ball back and forth, building a tower from blocks, or book sharing activities. From engagement in triadic activities of this kind, the infant comes to understand that other people have a particular goal in mind which they are trying to achieve through a plan of action. By five months, infants can interpret the goal-directed nature of simple behaviours, such as the act of reaching for an object and grasping it (Woodward, 2009). If an adult reaches for one of two objects, a seven-month-old will typically reach for the same object. But the infant will not do so if the adult directs an *ambiguous* action towards the object, such as making contact with the *back* of their hand (Hamlin, Hallinan & Woodward, 2008). Hence, the infant's response seems to be driven by their interpretation of adult reaching as a form of goal-directed behaviour.

Collaborative engagement and intention-reading

At about 10 months, the uniquely human behaviour of pointing emerges, typically before the child has produced their first word. The act of pointing shares with many words the power to function as an act of reference: they can both pick out entities in the world. But the meaning of pointing is especially underdetermined. To work out what someone is pointing at, I must do more than simply follow the direction in which their index finger is extended. The target is narrowed down in this way, but not precisely specified. Am I pointing at a book? Or the image on the cover? Or at the name of the author? And why am I pointing in the first place? Pointing is underdetermined, both in terms of what is being pointed at, and why. If this seems surprising, then it is because we can take for granted people's intentions and goals. The same pointing behaviour can be interpreted in many different ways according to the shared understanding of the participants.

In a recent study, children aged 14 months were engaged in a game in which the object was to tidy up various toys (Liebal, Behne, Carpenter & Tomasello, 2009). By 14 *years*, as any parent will tell you, this tidying behaviour has ceased altogether. But these tender infants were very co-operative. They engaged in this activity on a one-to-one basis with an adult, before being joined by a second adult. In one experimental condition, the familiar adult pointed at one of the remaining toys, while in a second condition, the unfamiliar adult did the pointing. Infants were far more likely to retrieve the object being pointed at, and tidy it away, if the *familiar* adult was doing the pointing. Hence, the infant only interpreted the pointing as a request to tidy up if it was done by the adult who had been sharing this tidying behaviour previously. Thus, infants use their shared understanding to interpret other people's intentions (cf., Sommerville & Crane (2009) for the influence of prior information on infant behaviour). Joint attention provides a means for picking out objects in the world and labelling them, thus assisting word learning. That said, it should be pointed out (!), that, in some circumstances, even two-year-olds can learn words in the absence of joint attention (Scofield & Behrend, 2011).

Tomasello et al. (2005) argue that the ability to engage in a collaborative activity, with a shared goal, is a uniquely *human* ability. Thus, it is difficult to imagine two chimpanzees co-operating on even simple activities like carrying something together. Chimpanzees are simply not motivated to share intentions, produce a plan of action and divide up the task so that each participant has their own role in achieving a joint goal. Tomasello (2009: 72) underscores the unique nature of human social cognition and argues that it 'paves the way for the acquisition of the "arbitrary" linguistic conventions that infants use'.

At the one-word stage, children sometimes combine a spoken word with a gesture (especially pointing). These gesture–speech combinations are of value because they augment the expressive power of the child considerably. For example, the word *teddy*, by itself, can convey any number of communicative intentions (*I like my teddy*, *My teddy has been out in the rain*, *This teddy isn't mine*, and so on). But if the child points towards a teddy that is out of reach on a shelf, and says 'teddy', then a more specific meaning is conveyed by the gesture–speech combination (*Give me my teddy*, perhaps). The age at which gesture–speech combinations emerge predicts the age at which the first entirely spoken two-word combinations emerge (Iverson & Goldin-Meadow, 2005). Rowe & Goldin-Meadow (2009a) report that parents depict, on average, 26 different meanings per hour through gesture with their 14-month-old children. But, as we saw in Chapter 4, parents differ in their rates of gesturing, which, in turn, affects how often children gesture themselves. These differences are important because 'high-gesture' 18-month-olds develop relatively large vocabularies by 42 months (Rowe & Goldin-Meadow, 2009b). Of interest, these 'high-gesture' children seem to get it from their 'high-gesture' parents. What we see, then, is that progress in language development is associated with an extensive use of gesture.

Collaborative engagement as a basis for language development

The importance of social cognition is emphasized by demonstrating close overlaps between early communication and language. In this vein, we are offered the following argument:

> conversation is an inherently collaborative activity in which the joint goal is to reorient the listener's intentions and attention so that they align with those of the speaker. (Tomasello et al., 2005: 683)

This might seem plausible at first blush, but row back and read that quotation again. You may discover that it rests on some odd assumptions. First, it assumes that the listener has acquiesced somehow in a 'joint goal', the aim of which is to change their own point of view. More problematic still: who is the speaker and who is the listener? In any conversation, these roles alternate with each turn. And of course, we do not always collaborate in conversation. In an argument, each person has an independent and conflicting goal to realign their opponent's views (or intentions). There is no *joint* goal.

Other parallels between collaborative engagement and language seem more straightforward. For example, the intention-reading skill witnessed in non-verbal communication may well be useful in verbal exchanges. Hence, 'if we assume that children are good at working out the intention underlying the verbal utterances of others, they have a head start into the linguistic system' (Behrens, 2009: 396). A component of intention-reading is the ability to take into account prior shared experience. As we have seen, children respond differentially to adult pointing, according to the level of joint prior knowledge shared between adult and child (Liebal et al., 2009). An equivalent within language is our use of **pronouns**. To interpret a pronoun like *she*, as in *She opened another window*, both speaker and hearer must share previous knowledge concerning the identity of *she*. In fact, it takes some time for children to appreciate the anaphoric ('referring back') function of pronouns (Wales, 1986). Pronouns are just one example of so-called *deictic* items that rely on a shared context between speaker and listener for their interpretation. Other examples include **demonstratives** like *here* and *there*, **verbs** of motion like *come* and *go*, and **articles** like *the*. For young children especially, deictic items are crucial, since 73 per cent of all mother–child utterances involve reference to objects and events in the immediate environment (Cross, 1977).

In the usage-based theory, it is predicted that the infant's impressive communication skills function as a precursor to language development. Of particular importance are the emergence of intention-reading skills and an ability to pursue joint goals in a collaborative way. Some authors suggest that intention-reading skills not only precede, but constitute a 'crucial prerequisite for language acquisition' (Diessel, 2004: 38). But arguments in favour of this idea are somewhat speculative. As we have seen, the key social-cognitive skills emerge at about the same time as spoken language. Children start pointing only just in advance of producing their first spoken word. And typically, the first word, at about 12 months, *precedes* signs of truly collaborative social engagement at about 14 months. And we should not forget that both social-cognitive and linguistic skills develop throughout the first year, long before production of the first word. It is difficult, therefore, to construe the ability to engage collaboratively as a necessary *precursor* for language. Rather, it seems that language and early communication share many functional characteristics and develop, to some extent, in tandem.

Early constructions: A route into grammar

In the beginning was the utterance

From the moment of the first word, it seems that children follow an orderly progression from utterances that comprise first one word, then two, three and four words, and more, in progressively longer utterances. The examples below are from Eve (Brown, 1973):

one word →	two words →	three words
pencil	dollie shoe	man taste it
cup	that pencil	lie down stool
hat	finger stuck	drop a cheese

This view of development seduces us into believing that the word is the critical unit in language development. The child simply needs to acquire the capacity to stick more and more words together in the right form and in the right order. But this view may be mistaken. Tomasello (2009) suggests that it is the *utterance*, not the word, that should grab the headlines. On this view, the child is driven to understand the communicative function of whole utterances. To do so, the child must determine the adult's intentions in using a piece of language with them, be it (from an adult perspective) a single word or several. In consequence, the child understands (or tries to understand) a full communicative act, comprising the intentions of the speaker and what they are referring to. In consequence, the child's own early linguistic productions, even when they seem to comprise more than one word, are often best analysed as *holophrases*, that is, indivisible units of language that convey a single, complete communicative intention (Barrett, 1995; Pine, 1995; Tomasello, 2003):

you do it
all gone
here you are
go away
I wanna do it
lemme see it
where the bottle

These phrases may seem like strings of individual words, but close analysis reveals that the child does not use the words independently. By the same token, a single-word utterance might be classified as a holophrase, an idea with a long history in child language research. Thus, Sully (1895: 171) remarks that 'the single-worded utterance of the child is … [a] "sentence-word"'.

Two pieces of evidence support the holophrase hypothesis: (1) the words in a holophrase are pronounced with the **intonation** pattern of whole utterances, be they comprised of one, two or more words; and (2) the words always appear together in the same order. With regard to intonation, three different patterns emerge early on which the child uses for distinct communicative functions: (1) *declarative*, for conveying information; (2) **imperative**, for orders; and (3) *interrogative*, for questions. Each kind of utterance has a characteristic intonation pattern which can be found overlaid on children's holophrases. Utterance-level intonation patterns have been observed in early single-word speech, so it is reasonable to analyse such cases as holophrases also (Dore, 1975). On the second point, consider the phrase *Daddy gone*. If the two words *Daddy* and *gone* do not each appear separately in the child's speech, but do appear consistently together in the same order, then one might reasonably assume that *Daddy gone* is a holophrase. Pine & Lieven (1993) examined the patterns in multi-word speech in children's first 100 words. They found that, on average, 11 per cent of child utterances could be described as holophrases.

On Pine & Lieven's (1993) evidence, holophrases occur only rarely. Admittedly, their figure does not include single-word holophrases, while their sample does include children who are relatively advanced (100 words). But one might still expect a higher incidence rate if the whole utterance were truly dominant in the child's initial speech output. Children who are dominated by the utterance 'do not try to learn words directly; they try to comprehend utterances and in doing so they often must comprehend a word in the sense of determining the functional role it is playing in the utterance' (Tomasello, 2009: 74). If that is the case, we must ask how the child becomes aware of different functional roles within a single utterance (e.g., in the act of giving there is a giver, the thing given, and a recipient). What prompts this segmentation of a communicative act, and, also, a linguistic utterance, into constituent functional parts? Of course, long before any such functional analysis is undertaken, infants are already highly adept at segmenting utterances. They segment the speech stream into individual words using statistical cues (see Chapter 5). Hence, a challenge for the usage-based approach is to integrate what we know about early speech segmentation with the view that the utterance, not the word, is the starting point for the child several months later. Generally speaking, we still need to explain how the child makes the transition from single-unit speech, be it a single word or a single utterance, to multi-unit speech.

From single-unit to multi-unit speech

At about 18 months the child starts going stir crazy and finally breaks out of Holophrase Prison. The child begins to construct utterances from multiple, separate components. Within the usage-based approach, three types of early multi-word construction are recognized:

1   word combinations
2   pivot schemas
3   item-based constructions.

Word combinations comprise two words that each have roughly the same status and which 'partition the experiential scene into multiple symbolizable units' (Tomasello, 2009: 76). A simple example, provided by Tomasello, is the child who sees a ball on a table and says *Ball table*. To do this, the child brings two separate words together. Hence, mastery of individual words, qua words, is a necessary precursor to word combinations. The second construction type, pivot schemas, were first identified by Braine (1963). In a pivot schema, the so-called pivot word is dominant, in the sense that it determines the function of the utterance as a whole. Each schema comprises a pivot and a variable slot that can be filled by a range of different items. The order of pivot and slot is fixed, with the order reflecting that which the child hears in the input. The following three examples are drawn from Braine (1963).

Pivot schemas in children aged 19 and 20 months:

more + _____more cookie, more fish, more high, more hot, more juice, more read
no + _____ no bed, no fix, no home, no mama, no more, no down
other + _____ other bib, other bread, other milk, other pocket, other shirt, other shoe

The 'no' row is especially fascinating: how did a one-year-old write such great blues lyrics? Pivot schemas constitute the first example of linguistic abstraction in the child's progress towards syntax. In each case, the slot is filled by a word that matches the function of the particular pivot word. For example, in the *more* + schema, the pivot word (*more*) seems to function as a way of requesting that an action be repeated or continued. Recall that in the usage-based approach, the function takes priority. What is the child using language *for*? The child's task is to acquire the mapping between particular functions and the particular forms (constructions) used to express those functions. In a pivot schema, the words that fill the slot will therefore conform to the *function* determined by the pivot word. There is no suggestion, in the usage-based approach, that the words in a pivot schema belong to adult syntactic categories, like *noun* or *noun phrase*. Bannard & Lieven (2012) report that for one two-year-old, almost 60 per cent of his utterances involved the insertion of material in a slot, in the manner of a pivot schema.

One step beyond the pivot schema comes the item-based construction (MacWhinney, 2014a). At this point, we detect the stirrings of syntax within the child. Syntactic devices are now used in the construction of multi-word utterances. The systematic use of word order and the emergence of morphological marking provide two examples of this 'syntactic marking' (Tomasello, 2009: 77). We can take word order as an example, having encountered it already in Chapter 1. Compare the following two sentences:

> *Richard introduced Chrissy at the poetry reading.*
> *Chrissy introduced Richard at the poetry reading.*

This simple example shows that, in English, the meaning of a sentence can be fundamentally altered if the words appear in a different order. The ordering of *Richard* and *Chrissy* determines who is the **agent** ('the doer') and who is the **patient** ('the done to'). As it happens, children learning English seem to use word order correctly from the very start (Radford, 1990). Even children as young as two years can act out sentences like *Make the doggie bite the cat*, a sentence which could be ambiguous to a naive child, because both the dog and the cat are capable of being the agent that bites (DeVilliers & DeVilliers, 1973). But why are these early syntactic structures referred to as *item*-based? The answer is fundamental to the usage-based approach: it is assumed that the child's early constructions are tied very closely to specific lexical items.

Item-based constructions are like islands, quite separate from one another, even though, in the adult grammar, they might be governed by the same rules (or *schemas*). This idea was captured in the so-called verb island hypothesis, which predicts that children learn about word order (and other grammatical relations) on a verb-by-verb basis (Tomasello, 1992). The emphasis on verbs arises from their central role in dictating the format of whole sentences. As Tomasello (2003: 122) observes, 'the most abstract constructions characteristic of adult linguistic competence typically revolve around verbs in one way or another'. We shall see this more clearly, below, in our discussion of verb transitivity. The emphasis on verb islands stems, in part, from the assumption that children's own initial use of verbs is predicted to mirror what they hear, with no awareness of the wider world of general syntactic patterns. For example, in a transitive sentence with *take* – *Angela takes aspirin* – the child may know that *Angela* is the 'taker/doer' and *aspirin* is the 'taken/done to'. But on a usage-based approach, the child will not know, initially, that the 'doer' and 'done to' occupy these same positions for all transitive verbs. The child needs to recognize the pattern across multiple verbs to extract the general meaning and the general construction of the transitive. In the early stages, therefore, the child should show no signs of the broad syntactic generalizations that we recognize in the adult grammar. The idea of starting small with lexically specific constructions has considerable mileage. In this vein, one finds that children use low-scope slots in pivot schemas, that is, slots that admit only a small range of lexical items (Cameron-Faulkner, Lieven & Tomasello, 2003). Over development, children extend the range of slots in schemas. They begin to build bridges between verb islands. More broadly, the child begins to form linguistic generalizations as their use of language becomes increasingly schematic (Boyd & Goldberg, 2012).

Does the child go from fully concrete to fully abstract?

An abiding theme in the usage-based approach is that 'constructions vary along a scale of ... abstractness' (Diessel, 2004: 18; see also Lieven, 2016). The child's early constructions are described as concrete because they comprise 'concrete pieces of language, not categories' (Tomasello, 2009: 76). In a similar vein, some aspects of adult linguistic knowledge are also described as concrete, for example, idioms like *kick the bucket*. In contrast, constructions are deemed to be abstract if they consist of grammatical categories like **noun phrase** or **subject**. But the use of the terms *concrete* and *abstract* is problematic. There is nothing concrete about the representation of language in the mind. Even if child utterances have a concrete reality in the physical production of sound, they stem from mental representations, which are abstract. Linguistic representations do not have to be identical to those of the adult grammar in order to be abstract. And Lieven & Tomasello (2008: 170) allow that 'children are capable of abstraction from the beginning'. We need to tread carefully here, because *abstraction* is not the same as *abstract*. Abstraction is a process that can be used in the formation of abstract categories. For example, presented with a set of white objects (a lily, some milk and a wedding dress) we can abstract the quality they have in common, which is their whiteness. Abstraction *is* different from abstract, but its presence from the very start indicates that abstract (not concrete) representations are created by the child. In addition, as mentioned above, Tomasello (2009: 76) suggests that the child's very earliest two-word combinations 'partition the experiential scene into multiple symbolizable units'. Symbols, of course, are the prime example of an abstract object.

Another problem is the projection of a sliding scale from 'totally concrete' (Tomasello, 2009: 76) to 'fully abstract' (Lieven & Tomasello, 2008: 175). The notion of increasingly abstract language is nowhere explained or defined, and is, in fact, difficult to conceive of. What could it mean for something to be more or less abstract? Equally, how can one thing be more concrete than another? If there is a sliding scale from highly concrete through to highly abstract, it would be useful to see examples, with justification, at each point on the scale. In philosophy, phenomena are described as either concrete or abstract (Dummett, 1981). Abstract objects are not accessible to the senses (they cannot be seen, heard or felt); they cannot be causes of change; and they occupy neither space nor time (try explaining the whereabouts of the number 6). While there are problems with each of these three criteria (see Hale, 1987), the distinction between concrete and abstract is clear. Arguably, therefore, usage-based researchers use these terms inappropriately. When they talk about a shift from highly concrete to highly abstract, they are more plausibly talking about a shift in knowledge from linguistically *specific* to linguistically *general*. As Lieven & Tomasello (2008: 170) allow, 'what changes over development is the scope of the abstraction' made by the child. Framed in usage-based terms, this process includes the ability to insert an increasingly wide range of items into a particular slot in an item-based construction. It also includes the ability to connect separate verb islands into a more general schema. A shift from specific to general is not only more plausible, but has a much firmer foundation in the history of child language research (e.g., Kuczaj, 1982).

The productivity puzzle

So far, usage-based theory has taken us on a journey from the child's earliest social skills through to a use of language that includes rudimentary syntactic marking. We now continue on this theoretical path into more complex aspects of syntax. As mentioned, the child must begin to generalize their linguistic knowledge, abstracting patterns which allow for syntactic productivity. A major issue of contention is the point at which children begin to make such generalizations. As we shall see, usage-based theory predicts that it takes some time before we see any productivity that is based on adult-like syntactic categories. By contrast, a substantial body of research, in the so-called *syntactic bootstrapping* framework, suggests that children do, in fact, show signs of productivity at 24 months, or even younger. Efforts have been made to accommodate these findings within the usage-based approach, but it will become apparent that the dust has far from settled on the puzzle of how and when children become syntactically productive.

The transitivity bias

As noted above, usage-based researchers argue that early constructions are lexically specific. It takes some considerable time before the child manifests any understanding of general syntactic categories. In consequence, child speech should lack not only linguistic generalizations, but, logically, there should be no **overgeneralizations** either. If you recall, overgeneralization is the application of a linguistic rule (generalization) beyond its normal confines, with the result that errors are produced. Tomasello (2003: 176) asserts that 'we should expect few overgeneralizations early; such errors should begin only after a certain age – in the domain of syntax perhaps age 3'. But this position has proven to be very difficult to maintain. Others argue that there are numerous signs of early productivity, with concomitant overgeneralizations. In fact, we have only just noted that usage-based researchers themselves now confirm that 'children are capable of abstraction from the beginning' (Lieven & Tomasello, 2008: 170). A basic example is the child's ability to take a linguistic label like *tree* and apply it to trees of different shapes and sizes (see Chapter 6). But we can also find examples in the domain of syntax. Although children as young as 2;1 can successfully interpret transitive sentences, their knowledge is fragile and errors are produced (Brooks & Tomasello, 1999; Goldberg, 2006; Dittmar et al., 2011). To appreciate this research, we need first to examine the notion of **transitivity** in a bit more detail. As will become apparent, a good deal of empirical work has been done on transitivity, both within and beyond the usage-based approach. We can start by observing that the acquisition of each new verb entails working out its particular transitivity status.

transitive	hit	Ashley hit his friend.
	push	Amanda pushed her luck.
intransitive	fall	*Olga fell.*
	sleep	Richard slept.
bitransitive	roll	Kate rolled the ball. / The ball rolled.
	eat	Clare ate a bhaji. / Clare ate.

As you can see, English verbs fall into one of three categories with respect to transitivity: (1) *transitive verbs*, which take an obligatory **direct object** (the **noun phrase** after the verb); (2) *intransitive verbs*, which never take a direct object; and (3) *bitransitive verbs*, which swing both ways, with an optional direct object, which means that they can occur in both transitive and intransitive forms. The majority of verbs are bitransitive. That is, the majority of verbs that can take an object can also appear without one (Huddleston, 1984).

EXERCISE 9.1
VERB TRANSITIVITY

Categorize the following verbs on the basis of their transitivity (transitive, intransitive or bitransitive). The best way of doing this is to make up some sentences for yourself using the verb and some suitable, simple noun phrases. Let's try this with the verb *cook*:

transitive: *The man cooked the steak.* (YES)

intransitive: *The man cooked.* (YES)

Conclusion: *cook* works both ways, so it is bitransitive. Now try these:

want	*wait*	*feel*
jump	*sleep*	*disappear*
leave	*take*	*read*

As mentioned, we witness child productivity in the domain of verb transitivity (Kline & Demuth, 2014). In particular, children sometimes deploy the transitive frame too broadly, applying it to intransitive verbs also, with the result that errors occur: *Don't giggle me* or *Mommy I disappeared my orange juice* or *It won't cough me no more* (Bowerman, 1982;

Figure 9.1 The novel verb '*tam*', depicting a particular manner of motion (adapted from Brooks & Tomasello, 1999)

Brooks & Zizak, 2002). These utterances would sound more natural if they were restored to their normal intransitive status, with no direct object after the verb, possibly something like: *Don't giggle*; *My orange juice disappeared*; and *It won't make me cough no more*. Errors in the other direction are much less common, that is, errors in which a transitive verb is mistakenly used in an intransitive frame (e.g., **Ashley hit*). Children are therefore said to have a *transitivity bias* (Maratsos, Gudeman, Gerard-Ngo & DeHart, 1987). This bias has been observed in experiments that introduce novel verbs to children (Brooks & Tomasello, 1999; Brooks & Zizak, 2002). For example, children were introduced to the novel verb *tam*, as shown in Figure 9.1.

Tam is a so-called 'manner of motion' verb (like *swing*) and can appear in both transitive and intransitive frames (as below). Children were exposed to *tam* in just one of these two frames, in training sessions.

> Transitive: *The girl is tamming the house.*
> Intransitive: *The house is tamming.*

The aim was to determine how willing children are to use a verb with a transitivity status different from the one they have experienced in training. In this regard, Brooks & Zizak (2002) confirmed the transitivity bias in children aged four to six years. If *tam* was modelled as transitive, children used it in a transitive frame themselves on 88 per cent of occasions. But if *tam* was modelled as *intransitive*, then children followed the intransitive pattern only 46 per cent of the time. In this latter condition, children were prone to use *tam* in a transitive frame (the transitivity bias). The transitivity bias has also been observed in children as young as 30 months (Brooks & Tomasello, 1999).

Pattern finding

The transitivity bias suggests that two-year-old children may possess a general schema, or pattern, that guides them in their use of new verbs. The child may no longer be tied to isolated utterances which they have heard other people using. We need to consider, therefore, how the child achieves this linguistic productivity. To this end, a number of possible mechanisms have been suggested in usage-based theory, including: (1) distributional analysis; (2) analogy; and (3) categorization. We will describe the first two briefly here, and explore the third, categorization, in more detail in the next section, in relation to the concept of *type frequency*.

Distributional analysis has been used by linguists for centuries as a method for identifying the members of a syntactic category. It involves finding patterns distributed across a corpus of language. For example, the category of **verb phrase** minimally contains a **verb**, but can take on many different forms. The distribution of verb phrases is such that they often appear after a **noun phrase**. To see how this works, let's first take a simple noun phrase, *our neighbour*. Now consider the phrases below. Only those which can follow *our neighbour* will qualify as verb phrases:

> *Our neighbour ...*
> *ate two profiteroles and a cabbage*
> *a dog*
> *should make less noise late at night*
> *finally lost his marbles*
> *died*
> *friendly*

Eliminating *a dog* and *friendly*, we see that all the other examples qualify as verb phrases because they meet our distributional criterion. It has long been suggested that even young children may perform distributional analyses (for example, Maratsos, 1982). At the same time, it has not proven possible, yet, to demonstrate empirically how children might actually manage this feat. The same empirical problem faces the concept of analogy formation. The idea is that the child can make analogies across isolated constructions, exploiting the commonalities in evidence to extract a productive generalization. For example, consider the following four sentences:

> *Maria dyes her hair.*
> *Cathrine drinks vodka.*
> *Lisa drives a motorbike.*
> *André cures the insane.*

As you will recognize, these are all simple transitive sentences, united both by a similar linguistic structure and by a similar meaning, in which an agent (e.g., *Maria*) causes something to happen to a patient (*her hair*). By analogy, we can perceive the structural similarity that unites these four sentences. The question then is, can the young child detect such analogies and exploit them in the formation of broad linguistic categories? It is assumed that analogizing is a domain-general cognitive skill, *not* one that is tied exclusively to language. Analogies are formed by mapping

248

information from a source entity to a target entity. This mapping is made possible by recognizing some kind of *similarity* between the source and the target. Following Gentner (1983), two kinds of similarity are recognized: 'substantial (or object) similarity, which involves the recognition of shared attributes, and structural similarity, which involves the recognition of shared structures or relationships' (Diessel, 2009: 251). When it comes to syntax, it is this latter kind of analogy that the child must make. Observe that we do not yet know how the child achieves the necessary 'recognition of similarity'. But Diessel & Tomasello (2005) do show that, for children aged four and five years, structural similarity is a key factor in the acquisition of German **relative clauses** (see also Brandt, Diessel & Tomasello, 2008). Analogy formation provides one route to productivity. Another possibility, entertained in usage-based theory, is the exploitation of frequency information in the input. This ability in the child exemplifies the third of our three 'productivity mechanisms' listed above: categorization. We consider the role of frequency in the categorization process next.

Type frequency: A route to productivity

You will be familiar by now with the usage-based credo that knowledge of language emerges from the use, or experience, of language. The *amount* of experience is therefore critical, and is typically measured by the frequency of language forms in the input. Two different kinds of frequency are identified: *token frequency* and *type frequency*. Token frequency is simply the number of times that a given linguistic item appears in a corpus of adult–child speech. The token does not have to be a single word. It could be an entire phrase like *I dunno* (Bybee & Scheibmann, 1999; Tomasello, 2003). Type frequency, meanwhile, refers to the number of times that a linguistic form occurs in a particular slot. In a particular sample of language, we might take a simple frame, *That's* [Noun Phrase], and count how many different noun phrases fill the slot (*That's a teddy*, *That's my book*, and so on). The two kinds of frequency are predicted to have different effects on child productivity. High token frequency protects the child from error (see below), while high type frequency allows the child to generalize their learning (Lieven & Tomasello, 2008). As we shall see, type frequency provides the child with an opportunity to exercise their categorization skills.

The basic idea underlying type frequency is both simple and plausible. When children develop a slot that can be filled by different items, they get an opportunity to form generalizations about grammatical classes of items. A simple example might be the slot in a simple noun phrase that can be filled by different nouns, as in *the* +. This slot can be filled by a range of different words (e.g., *tomato*, *squirrel*, *tarmac*, *hydrangea*). The appearance of these words in the same slot may encourage the child to abstract the features that these words have in common and, eventually, formulate a single category to which they all belong (noun). By increasing type frequency, that is, the number of different words that appear in the slot, the child will have more opportunities to note the commonalities among different items and thus form a broad grammatical category with a range of different members. In this way, we can regard the use of type frequency as an example of the child's categorization abilities.

One study manipulated type frequency by varying the number of different verbs that appeared in the following slot: *It was the cup that the frog* _____ , as in, *It was the cup that the frog*

249

took (Ambridge, Theakston, Lieven & Tomasello, 2006). In one condition, children heard ten different verbs in this slot (including *pull, touch, grab*), compared with just two in a second condition. It was predicted that the greater type frequency in the first condition would help children become more proficient with this complex structure. But this variation in type frequency made no difference for children aged four and five years. The problem might lie in the conception of what type frequency is and how it functions. There seems to be an unwarranted expectation that the child can learn something about syntax – how to put words together correctly into sentences – rather than something much more modest, which is to identify the members of a syntactic category, like noun. To put it another way, the process of filling slots is *paradigmatic* rather than *syntagmatic*. To appreciate the difference, imagine paradigms on a vertical axis, with syntagms on the horizontal. The members of a paradigm occupy the same slot, and therefore belong to the same grammatical category (noun in this case):

> *the   tomato*
> *squirrel*
> *tarmac*
> *hydrangea*

Syntagms, meanwhile, are 'horizontal' in the sense that different categories are brought together, one after the other, to form larger groupings according to the rules of grammar. These larger groupings of categories combine to yield superordinate categories, organized hierarchically, as in the noun phrase shown in Figure 9.2.

As we can see, one could learn something about the members of a syntactic category from the items that fill a particular slot. And once the child is equipped with a category like noun, then further progress could be made in learning how this category combines with others (see Lieven, Behrens, Speares & Tomasello, 2003). But even shifting to the syntax of a simple noun phrase like *the fat squirrel* would represent a substantial advance. In this light, it is perhaps no wonder that the children in Ambridge et al. (2006) did not leap straight into the complexities of the structures underlying *It was the cup that the frog took*. At best, therefore, type frequency could provide only a very partial account of how the child makes linguistic generalizations.

Ambridge et al. (2006) stick closely to the standard definition of type frequency: 'the frequency with which different actual [*sic*] forms occur in the same slot' (Lieven & Tomasello, 2008: 174). In other cases, though, things get rather muddled. Lieven & Tomasello (2008) exemplify the concept of type frequency in two ways: (1) by comparing two forms of the

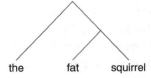

the   fat   squirrel

Figure 9.2 Syntagmatic structure of a noun phrase

German present perfect; and (2) by comparing the regular past and regular plural in English. In both cases, therefore, comparisons are made across different constructions, which takes type frequency at least one step beyond what happens in a single slot in a single construction. Bybee (2008) attempts to salvage this position by broadening out the definition of type frequency to include not only the different contents of a slot, but also 'the number of items that exemplify a pattern' (ibid.: 221). With two kinds of type frequency at large, though, the concept begins to lose its coherence. What, if anything, underpins both kinds of type frequency? At present, we only have a vague formulation to address this issue: 'type frequency measures items that are similar in some way' (Lieven & Tomasello, 2008: 179). But the notion of 'similarity' is not yet well specified. It is perhaps not surprising, therefore, that, as yet, 'we are a long way from understanding all the ways in which similarity is identified and changes with development' (ibid.: 179). Evidently, it has not yet been explained how, in the formation of linguistic categories, the child might recruit some notion of 'similarity' or 'analogy' or 'distribution'. In fact, this is an abiding problem which challenges all child language researchers, not just those within the usage-based approach. The following observation, made in 1982, remains just as true today:

> exactly how the child's diverse analytic abilities and biases combine to result in adult formal categorical organizations remains a central problem. (Maratsos, 1982: 265)

Sounds familiar: The role of frequency

Usage-based theory could not get along without frequency effects. To be fair, *no* theory could, but frequency holds a special place in the usage-based pantheon. Numerous empirical studies in the usage-based tradition underscore the effects of frequency on development (e.g., Rowland, 2007; Abbot-Smith & Tomasello, 2009; Räsänen, Ambridge & Pine, 2014). Intuitively, we can appreciate the importance of frequency. We all know that practice makes perfect. Compare the first soufflé you ever made with your latest effort (what? – you've never made a soufflé?). Exposure to the same input conditions on repeated occasions leads to better learning. But as we have seen, the concept of frequency is not that straightforward. There are different kinds of frequency which at present are not well defined. And the influence of frequency is bound to change if only because the child develops and will be processing input in different ways to different ends over time. In addition, frequency effects are not always observed (MacWhinney, 2014b). Recall the fast mapping children are capable of in learning new words (Chapter 6). A single exposure to a new word can suffice, on occasion, for learning to take place. We should also be clear that – as usage-based theorists allow – frequency by itself explains nothing. Frequency is not a learning mechanism (Ambridge, Kidd, Rowland & Theakston, 2015). We still need an explanation, therefore, for what the child does with input information and why learning is rendered more effective by repeated exposure. That said, it is worth highlighting those areas of development where frequency effects are apparent (Ambridge et al.,ibid.):

1   *Words.* Words which occur frequently in the input are learned sooner than less frequent forms (Fenson et al., 1994).

2   *Inflectional morphology.* High frequency is associated with higher levels of correct usage and, coincidentally, lower levels of error (see the section on Constraining productivity, below). For example, Polish children perform better marking dative, accusative and genitive **case** on novel nouns in cases where input frequency is high (Dąbrowska & Szczerbinski, 2006).

3   *Simple grammar.* Cues which assist in the learning of simple structures – including the transitive – are more abundant in high-frequency structures and are associated with more efficient learning (e.g., Matsuo, Kita, Shinya, Wood & Naigles, 2012).

4   *Complex grammar.* The passive provides an example here. Passive constructions are extremely rare in the input to children (and also rare in Adult Directed Speech) (Gordon & Chafetz, 1991). Accordingly, passives are rare in the speech of young children (Israel, Johnson & Brooks, 2001).

Early productivity: Syntactic bootstrapping

The transitivity bias exposes a fundamental problem for usage-based theory. Early syntactic productivity should not be in evidence, but it seems that child creativity bursts out at an early age, regardless. Early syntactic prowess has been remarked upon most pointedly within an alternative theoretical framework, known as *syntactic bootstrapping* (for example, Naigles, 1990, 1996; Naigles & Kako, 1993; Fisher, Klingler & Song, 2006; Yuan & Fisher, 2009).

> Syntactic bootstrapping is a procedure by which children use the syntax in which a word is placed to narrow down or constrain the meaning of the word. (Naigles & Swenson, 2007: 213)

Before we see how this works, observe that this prediction requires a relatively sophisticated knowledge of syntactic categories in two-year-old children. You may wonder, with some reason, where this knowledge comes from, but since this is not our main focus, see Naigles & Swenson (2007) for further discussion. We can, at least, note a sharp contrast with the usage-based approach.

To illustrate, let's return to the first example in this chapter: *Max kissed Anna*. We first grant the child an understanding of causative verbs in transitive sentence structures. Our task is to consider how the child might use this knowledge of verb transitivity to work out the meaning of a new verb. Imagine, for example, that *kiss* is a new word for the child. Since this word appears in a familiar sentence frame, the child can use this structure to work out something about the meaning and syntactic privileges of *kiss*. The typical meaning conveyed by this structure, as a whole, is causative: an agent (*Max*) causes something to happen to an object or person (*Anna*). In consequence, the child who has never before encountered *kiss* will not be stranded. Its appearance after *Max*, in this particular sentence frame, reveals that *kiss* is a verb. Moreover, it is a causative verb, the precise meaning of which can be inferred from observation of Max and Anna.

We want to know if two-year-olds understand the causative meaning associated with the transitive sentence structure. Several studies suggest that they do. In one study, children were shown

Figure 9.3　24-month-old children prefer to look at a causative event (on the left) when they hear a transitive sentence: '*Look at Cookie Monster squatting Big Bird*' (from Hirsh-Pasek et al., 1996)

videos of two *Sesame Street* characters (Big Bird and Cookie Monster) interacting with each other (Hirsh-Pasek, Golinkoff & Naigles, 1996). Children aged 19–28 months were shown two different scenes simultaneously on a split screen, as shown in Figure 9.3 below.

For children as young as 24 months, when they hear *Look at Cookie Monster squatting Big Bird*, their attention is drawn to the left-hand video. Of course, this is appropriate, because Cookie Monster is actively doing something to Big Bird in this video. In the right-hand video, by contrast, Big Bird and Cookie Monster are just squatting independently, side by side. Neither figure is making the other one do anything. Hirsh-Pasek et al. (1996) conclude that children aged 24 months use syntax (the transitive frame) to guide their interpretation of a verb (*squat*) which was unknown to them. You may think that *squat* sounds odd when used transitively in this way. But if you have no idea what *squat* means, nor how it is used, then you will see that the two-year-old's responses were appropriate. Subsequent work has argued that 21-month-olds appreciate the significance of transitive word order in an abstract, verb-general way (see the brief summary of Gertner et al., 2006, in Chapter 1). By 24 months, children can sometimes repair sentences which are missing a direct object (e.g., *The zebra brings something* rather than *The zebra brings*) (Naigles & Maltempo, 2011). This level of sophistication is not predicted by usage-based theory at such a young age.

Generally, there is a close correspondence between syntax and meaning (semantics) which the child can make use of. Other theories, including usage-based theory, also rest on the assumption that the child can exploit the close links between syntax and semantics. Usage-based theory and syntactic bootstrapping share other basic assumptions, too. For example, they both give prominence to learning about the meanings and constraints on individual lexical items (Fisher, 2002). And they both give priority to the utterance, acknowledging that most of the words children hear are used in sentences, not in isolation. But the two theories part company with respect to the stage at which children are capable of making genuinely syntactic generalizations. Usage-based researchers continue to maintain that the child's early multi-word speech is not based on genuinely syntactic categories (Peter, Chang, Pine, Blything & Rowland, 2015). They shore up their position by highlighting differences in methodology across the two camps. One critical difference is that syntactic bootstrapping studies tend to rely on child comprehension, while usage-based work examines the child's speech output. We have already seen that the level of comprehension shown by a child is typically out of kilter with their productive expertise (see Chapter 6). In essence, children look like syntactic wizards when all we measure is their viewing preferences, but far less competent when they open their mouths to talk.

Two recent studies suggest that two-year-olds may have some grasp of verb transitivity, but that their knowledge is only partial (Dittmar, Abbot-Smith, Lieven & Tomasello, 2008a, 2008b). In English, word order provides an overwhelmingly important cue concerning transitivity. In German, the situation is more complex. Both word order *and* **case** marking provide cues to the identity of the agent. The agent noun bears a special morphological marker (for nominative case) to indicate its status as agent. And, as in English, it often appears first in the sentence. Thus, the two cues of word order and case marking can support each other. But it is possible for them to conflict: an agent with nominative marking does not have to come first in a German sentence. In such cases, case marking takes precedence as the means for identifying the agent. Dittmar et al. (2008a) found that German two-year-olds showed some understanding of verb transitivity, but only when both cues coincided. Five-year-olds, meanwhile, could cope with word order by itself, but not case marking. Only seven-year-olds could cope with both cues, and rely on case marking alone when the two cues were placed in conflict with one another. Dittmar et al. (2008b) also show that two-year-olds require extensive prior training with the specific verbs used in any test of transitivity in order to succeed at all. In consequence, Dittmar et al. (2008b) argue that two-year-olds possess a weak representation of transitivity only. What we need now, of course, is some principled way of measuring the strength of mental representations in young children: what does it mean to have a *weak* representation?

DISCUSSION POINT 9.1
SYNTACTIC PRODUCTIVITY

Assemble in groups of four and then split into two pairs. Each pair should take one of the articles below, and then read it independently:

Dittmar, M., Abbot-Smith, K., Lieven, E. & Tomasello, M. (2008b). Young German children's early syntactic competence: A preferential looking study. *Developmental Science, 11(4)*, 575–582.

Yuan, S. & Fisher, C. (2009). 'Really? She blicked the baby?': Two-year-olds learn combinatorial facts about verbs by listening. *Psychological Science, 20(5)*, 619–626.

Compare notes with your partner and try to resolve any difficulties you may have encountered with the text. Then regroup as a foursome and discuss the different perspectives which the two papers bring to bear on the issue of syntactic productivity.

- Gather together the arguments and evidence both for and against each position. Make notes. The four of you will need to pool resources to get a complete picture.
- At what age do children exploit knowledge of syntax in a productive way?
- What are the limitations of the preferential looking method?
- Which account do you find more convincing? Why?

Generally speaking, child productivity with syntax is a major headache for theories of child language acquisition. Recent research has done much to shed light on the productivity puzzle, but there is still more to learn. The simple usage-based prediction that children are not productive in syntax before the age of three cannot be sustained. In comprehension, at least, children display some grasp of verb transitivity at 24 months. Usage-based researchers have tried to accommodate this early productivity with the idea that comprehension studies tap into 'weak' syntactic representations. This idea lacks refinement at present, but recent usage-based studies *have* shown that, however impressive the two-year-old's syntactic prowess might appear, their knowledge of transitivity is not adult-like until the school years, some time after the child's fifth birthday. It will be interesting to see how different theoretical approaches converge on the solution to the productivity problem in the coming years.

Constraining productivity

As Berko (1958: 150) pointed out: 'the acquisition of language is more than the storing up of rehearsed utterances, since we are all able to say what we have not practiced and what we have never before heard'. But linguistic creativity, encountered in Chapters 2 and 4, presents a problem that taxes every theory of syntax acquisition: how does the child *constrain* productivity? What stops the child from going too wild and producing all manner of sentences that are not, in fact, permissible in the adult grammar? The problem is that the child must become productive, but not too productive. In this section, we review two mechanisms for reining in linguistic generalizations, advanced within the usage-based approach:

1   *Entrenchment:* increasing experience with a particular structure makes it less likely that errors will occur.
2   *Pre-emption:* hearing a verb used in a rare structure may prevent erroneous use of that verb in a more common structure.

Both of these mechanisms rest on the assumption that children are inherently cautious, or *conservative*, in their learning. This assumption underpins pretty much every theoretical approach to syntax acquisition in young children (including the nativist approach considered in Chapter 8). It would be useful, therefore, to set the scene with a brief overview of the conservative child, before we see how this general idea manifests in entrenchment and pre-emption.

Conservative learning

In acquiring a new verb, the child must work out its transitivity status. One way of doing this would be to simply observe what adults do and follow their lead. This approach is known as *conservative learning*, a phrase which denotes a cautious approach in the use of new structures. An entirely conservative learner would never use a verb in a structure that they had not actually witnessed for themselves. This seems like a sensible approach because learning will be error-free. To some extent at least, children must be conservative learners, because they are not rampantly unconstrained in their use of language. We do not hear bizarre sequences like *His hit Ashley friend* or *Bhaji a ate Clare*. For this reason, all language acquisition theories, both nativist and non-nativist, assume a degree of conservatism in the child (Pinker, 1989; Radford, 1990; Tomasello, 2003). In the nativist approach, the child is held in check by Universal Grammar (UG). The child's mind is configured to acquire only certain kinds of syntactic knowledge, those described in UG theory (see Chapter 8). In the usage-based theory, the child's conservatism is ascribed to the influence of the input. In essence, the child sticks closely to what they hear in their own speech output, a theme we elaborate on below. A fundamental challenge for every theory is that children are not confined in a linguistic straitjacket. We have seen numerous examples throughout this book of child errors, cases where children **overgeneralize** the use of linguistic structures beyond their conventional scope. Children are not unfailingly conservative. The abiding challenge is to explain why the child is conservative, but only *partially* conservative.

Entrenchment

In the usage-based approach, frequency is paramount. The frequency of linguistic forms in the input provides a key stimulus for language development. We have already considered type frequency, above, and now turn our attention to *token frequency*. For a given corpus, token frequency is the number of times that a linguistic form occurs in the input to the child. A relationship is assumed between exposure to a linguistic form and the mental representation of that form in the child. In short, the more often a linguistic form occurs in the input, the more often it is experienced by the child, and the stronger the child's representation of it becomes.

On this view, every time a linguistic structure occurs, its mental representation in the child is reinforced or increasingly *entrenched*. An important consequence for the child is that this structure will be activated more easily when using it themselves on subsequent occasions (Diessel, 2009). The actual use of language therefore affects the learning that takes place. On this view, it is predicted that linguistic forms with high token frequency will be learned early and lead to more strongly entrenched linguistic representations (Brooks, Tomasello, Dodson & Lewis, 1999; Theakston & Lieven, 2008). And the more deeply entrenched a structure is, the more likely it becomes that this will form the basis of the child's own speech output. In consequence, the likelihood of the child being diverted into producing an error is diminished. We see, therefore, that high token frequency – as the basis of entrenchment – is predicted to protect the child from error. Confusingly, Lieven contradicts herself on this point, arguing that 'heavily entrenched word sequences compete with the emerging generalizations in production, and this leads to the production of errors' (Bannard & Lieven, 2012: 9). However, the standard usage-based orthodoxy regards entrenchment as a *protection* against error.

If token frequency has a strong influence on child learning, we should expect to see a close relationship between adult input and child output. And, in particular cases, this is exactly what we do see, especially in the early stages. One study of children aged 1;9 to 2;6 found that 45 per cent of all maternal utterances began with one of the following 17 **lexemes**: *what* (most frequent at 8.6 per cent), *that*; *it*; *you*; *are/aren't*; *I*; *do/does/did/don't*; *is*; *shall*; *a*; *can/can't*; *where*; *there*; *who*; *come*; *look*; *let's* (these last three being least frequent at 1 per cent each) (Cameron-Faulkner et al., 2003). In other words, children hear the same few words over and over again. Moreover, these words occur in very specific, item-based frames. For example, *why* occurred in four different frames:

why	don't	_____
	do	_____
	's	_____
	not	_____

We can assess the influence of input frequency by examining which structures children use themselves most often. As predicted, those structures children hear most often are, in certain cases, the ones that they, in turn, use most often themselves. This is true of the **copula**(s) in the following three frames: *There's [NP]*; *That's [NP]*; and *It's [NP]*. As ever, NP stands for *noun phrase* (*a dog, my hat*). The frequency of maternal usage correlates strongly with child usage in all three frames (Cameron-Faulkner et al., 2003). Similar relationships have been found for other structures, too, including uses of the verb *go* and, more generally, the child's first uses of particular verbs (Theakston, Lieven, Pine & Rowland, 2002, 2004; Ambridge et al., 2008).

The evidence so far suggests that high token frequency leads to greater entrenchment. We now need to consider how entrenchment might protect the child from error. Rowland (2007) addresses this question in a study that looked at children's production of different question types. Errors of the following kind were observed in a corpus of ten children aged 2;1 to 5;1:

where does he goes?
where does he does go?
where does you go?
where he does go?
does donuts also have TV?
does her like it?
does he going to the shops?

Don't get the wrong impression from this list. Overall, errors with questions are fairly infrequent, occurring only 7 per cent of the time. But certain kinds of question were more problematic, most notably, WH-questions, those questions that start with a WH- word like *what*, *why* or *where*. One particular kind of WH-question starts with a WH-word and is followed by a modal **auxiliary verb**: **Where will** *you go?* **What can** *you see?* **Who shall** *I invite* (*do/does* is an auxiliary verb, but not a *modal* auxiliary). For this kind of question, the child error rate was relatively high at 18 per cent. Of interest here, the frequency of such questions in the input was relatively low. Hence, errors are more frequent in cases where the child lacks experience. In contrast, high token frequency seems to protect the child from error. Even so, we might point out that the level of protection afforded is not that dramatic. Entrenchment is also in evidence in a study where children were asked to judge the acceptability of structures (e.g., *Daddy giggled the baby*). Children aged five to ten years were more likely to reject ungrammatical sentences which deployed high frequency verbs (Ambridge, Bidgood, Twomey, Pine, Rowland & Freudenthal, 2015). Again, then high frequency protected the children from error.

The concept of entrenchment conjures up an image of doughty toddlers, valiantly digging their way down into a linguistic trench. The deeper they dig themselves in, the more protected they are from enemy fire, in the form of grammatical errors. But this notion of entrenchment raises three problems. First, child grammar *develops*. In usage-based terminology, islands are connected, analogies are drawn, connections between related constructions are made, and schemas become increasingly generalized. But what, in this shifting array, is entrenched? The most obvious answer is that the child's *earliest* linguistic constructions become entrenched (holophrases, early word combinations, pivot schemas, item-based constructions). More complex structures cannot become entrenched early on, because the child has not yet acquired them. And input frequency cannot be put on hold until some convenient moment, later in development, before it starts exerting its effects. But if *early* constructions are entrenched, we need to explain how the child climbs out of the trench and moves on to the next level of syntactic complexity. But how can this be achieved, if initial representations are entrenched? The more entrenched a structure is, the less susceptible it should be to change.

The second problem is related to the first, and also stems from the fact that grammar develops. As the child moves through successive points in development, it seems unlikely that the child's knowledge at each point becomes separately entrenched, in successive turns. But intermediate states of knowledge should each be subject to the same forces of entrenchment. One might seek an exemption for intermediate states and determine that only the endpoint, the equivalent of adult grammatical knowledge, becomes entrenched. But logically, that cannot work. From the child's point of view, a particular state of linguistic knowledge is not intermediate. It does not constitute a staging post on the way to somewhere else (more complex, more adult, more mature). It only looks intermediate from an adult point of view. The general problem, then, is to explain what, in development, becomes entrenched and why. This issue has not yet been broached by usage-based researchers.

The third problem with entrenchment is that, in fact, it does not apply in many cases. Instead, entrenchment is selective. This follows, in part, because child speech is never going to be the mirror image of parental input. For one thing, children younger than two years will not be using any of the more complex structures found in parental speech. And some structures will be avoided for pragmatic reasons. For example, imperatives like *Sit down!* or *Eat up!* are frequent in maternal speech but rare in child speech. Two-year-olds have their *own* ways of bossing their parents about. Dąbrowska (2005: 201) also notes a lack of entrenchment with her observation that, even at the age of four years, Polish children continue to make **case** marking errors with the genitive, despite having heard 'the genitive form of a masculine noun one every two or three minutes' for several years. And Maslen et al. (2004) report that some verbs, like *come*, continue to be overregularized as *comed* (rather than *came*) even after many thousands of exposures to the correct form.

Without doubt, frequency is an important factor in language acquisition. The case of WH-questions, plus several other examples raised in Chapter 4, confirm the significance of input frequency effects. In a handful of cases, there are signs that high input frequency may serve to protect the child somewhat against grammatical errors. But we need to establish why frequency effects are in evidence in some cases, but not in others. Evidently, the frequency of linguistic forms in the input is just one factor at work. Hopefully, therefore, researchers will broaden their palette of enquiry to consider a wider range of factors. As it stands, the child's linguistic environment is characterized in a rather simplistic manner. For example, it neglects any consideration of adult–child interaction (Chapter 4). And research on input frequency does not yet account for how the child's learning mechanisms respond to different kinds of input. For example, it is plausible that, in some instances, rare input events could have a major impact on the child. A relatively large step forward would be made on the basis of relatively little experience. Successful acquisition of different linguistic structures may require different amounts and kinds of both input and interaction, and these will likely exert their effects in complex ways (Goodman, Dale & Li, 2008). We can conclude this section by drawing a careful distinction between frequency effects and entrenchment. In usage-based theory, it is predicted that entrenchment helps explain how input frequency exerts its influence. But there is reason to believe that the concept of entrenchment is flawed. Fundamentally, it does not sit well with the idea that grammar develops, because it suggests that early, immature constructions will become entrenched. In consequence, one is left with the difficult problem of explaining how the child climbs out of the trench and moves on to the next stage. Happily, usage-based theory offers a further mechanism that may help protect the child from error, known as *pre-emption*. We consider pre-emption in what follows.

Pre-emption

We start this section with three verbs, *swing*, *wash* and *play*, that can occur in transitive sentences with an agent as subject:

> *Wilkie swung his golf club.*
> *Lorraine washed her towels.*
> *Phuong played her favourite DVD.*

As noted above, verbs of this kind are causative (the agent causes something to happen). Other verbs, like *disappear*, can also express a causative meaning, but not in this kind of sentence pattern. We cannot say **The magician disappeared the rabbit*. Instead, we have to resort to a rarer construction known as the *periphrastic causative* and say *The magician made the rabbit disappear*.

The idea behind *pre-emption* is that when children hear a verb being used in a rare construction, they will be put off using it in the more common construction available (Goldberg, 1995; 2011). Thus, exposure to *disappear* in a periphrastic causative sentence will pre-empt its use by the child in a simple transitive construction. Potentially, therefore, pre-emption could counteract the effects of input frequency. It allows rarer constructions to exert an influence where necessary. Also, there is no need to panic if errors do crop up from time to time. The child must simply be patient. Eventually, a periphrastic causative will turn up and pre-empt further errors. Of course, periphrastic causatives may well be like the 37 bus. You wait for hours in vain and then two turn up at once. Or worse, none turn up at all.

There have been very few attempts to test the idea that pre-emption may work as an error protection mechanism. With the focus on the periphrastic causative, Brooks & Zizak (2002) introduced children aged four and six years to two novel verbs: our old friend *tam* (see Figure 9.1) and *dack*. The meaning of both verbs involved a particular manner of motion, but one was designated as transitive (*The mouse dacked the block*), with the other being intransitive (*The tree is tamming*). In one condition, children were exposed to pre-emptive uses of *tam* and *dack* by the experimenter, in periphrastic causative sentences like *The rabbit made the car dack*. If pre-emption works, then this experience should discourage the child from using *dack* in simple causative sentences (**The rabbit dacked the car*). As described above, in children's own use of these verbs, the transitivity bias was found. This means that, generally speaking, errors were more likely with the intransitive verb. However, such errors were rarer for children in the pre-emption condition. It seems, therefore, that both four- and six-year-olds were protected from error. Remarkably, it did not take much pre-emption to produce this effect. Children only heard 12 pre-emptive sentences with each verb (see also Brooks & Tomasello, 1999).

Less encouraging results have been reported by Ambridge et al. (2015). No pre-emptive effect was observed for children aged five and nine years when exposed to the rare versions of a **verb argument structure** (e.g., *Lisa made the cup fall*). Children rated the acceptability of sentences on a five-point scale. This provided a measure of their willingness to reject pre-empted sentence constructions (**Lisa fell the cup*). It turned out that children of both ages accepted ungrammatical overgeneralized sentences more readily than adults and that, overall, there was no evidence of pre-emption. We have a conflict, therefore, with the findings of Brooks & Zizak (2002). Ambridge et al. (2015) suggest that pre-emption may only be observed when the pre-empting construction is much more frequent than the erroneous version. The problem is, though, that pre-empting constructions are very rare in Child Directed Speech (0.4 per cent in the case of the periphrastic causative). But recall that Brooks & Zizak not only used novel verbs, they found a pre-emptive effect after only 12 exposures to each verb. What's more, these structures are meant to be rare by definition. It is their very unusualness which is supposed to ring alarm bells in the child, prompting them to reject more conventional forms for particular verbs. Incidentally, this point highlights an intrinsic tension between entrenchment and pre-emption. While pre-emption trades on the rarity of structures, entrenchment depends on frequency to account for conservative learning. Frequency *is* at work with pre-emption, to the extent that the rarity of a pre-emptive structure is established in comparison with its frequent counterpart. But how does the child manage to override the effects of entrenchment, in special cases only, and suddenly be so impressed by a structure precisely because of its scarcity? The outlook for pre-emption as a mechanism in child language does not look entirely secure.

Summary: Reining back on productivity

This section has considered how the child might constrain productivity within the usage-based approach. The two mechanisms we examined were entrenchment and pre-emption. Increasing experience with a structure is supposed to cause it to become entrenched in the child's system. This then protects the child from error, because the structures they have heard most often will be accessed most quickly and easily, reducing the chances that erroneous alternatives will be selected. We saw that frequency effects are present in some, but by no means all, cases. More problematic, though, is the concept of entrenchment. How does the child climb out of the trench and move on to acquire more complex, adult-like structures? Frequency effects are legion in psychology, both within and beyond the confines of child language. What we see, therefore, is that the concept of entrenchment may not be the best way of accounting for them. We have also examined pre-emption, the idea that exposure to a rare structure can stop the child from producing a more obvious, more frequent alternative. Pre-emption is an anti-frequency device that has been demonstrated for at least one structure, the periphrastic causative, in older children aged four years and upwards. Overall, usage-based theory still has some considerable way to go in tackling how the child constrains productivity. We should not be too surprised at this, though. It remains a perennial challenge for all theories of syntax acquisition.

IN A NUTSHELL

- Usage-based theory argues that knowledge of language develops from the use of language. It is a non-nativist theory.

- The social skills of communication which develop in the first year are assumed to provide the precursor for language acquisition. However, language and social cognition seem to develop in tandem.

- In usage-based theory, early child speech lacks adult syntactic categories. The child moves towards syntax via four utterance types:

  - *holophrases*: express a single communicative intention, even if they appear to comprise more than one word.

  - *word combinations*: two-word utterances, where each word has roughly the same status.

- *pivot schemas*: a pivot word and an empty slot filled by words with the same communicative function.

- *item-based schemas*: word combinations which are lexically specific, but which bear the early signs of syntactic marking (for example, via morphological marking or word order).

- Heavy emphasis is placed on input frequency, which means that other aspects of input and interaction are neglected. Two kinds of input frequency are identified:

  - *type frequency*: the number of different items that appear in a particular item-based slot. The concept of type frequency is not yet well specified and, to date, its predicted effects on language learning are not supported empirically.

  - *token frequency*: the number of times that a linguistic item appears in a corpus of adult–child speech (see *entrenchment* below).

- The child develops increasingly general syntactic schemas, by identifying the similarities and patterns across different item-based schemas. *Distributional analysis*, *analogy* and *categorization* are assumed to contribute to this end.

- Two mechanisms are predicted to help children constrain their developing productivity appropriately and avoid overgeneralizations:

  - *entrenchment*: high token frequency is predicted to cause increasingly strong, or entrenched, representations of linguistic structures. But the concept of entrenchment is problematic. It is not clear how the child moves on from an early entrenched structure to acquire more adult-like forms of syntactic knowledge.

  - *pre-emption*: an anti-frequency mechanism. Experience of a verb in a rare construction will cause the child to avoid using that verb in a more common structure. There is conflicting evidence about how sensitive children are to pre-emptive input experience.

FURTHER READING

Tomasello, M. (2009). The usage-based theory of language acquisition. In E.L. Bavin (Ed.), *The Cambridge handbook of child language* (pp. 69–87). Cambridge: Cambridge University Press.

In this chapter, Tomasello sets out the usage-based stall with a broad overview of the theory. You could read this chapter as if it were a manifesto. You end up with a very clear statement of the usage-based position, but you will not get much feel for the substantive challenges that the theory still faces.

Gleitman, L.R. (2014). Syntactic bootstrapping. In P.J. Brooks & V. Kempe (Eds.), *Encyclopedia of language development* (pp. 616–618). London: Sage.

Gleitman provides a succinct overview of syntactic bootstrapping, the alternative to the usage-based approach mentioned here. She argues that children acquire syntactic categories early and exploit this knowledge to infer the meanings of new verbs. See also Naigles & Swenson (2007) for a more comprehensive review.

WEBSITES

- **Michael Tomasello's academic homepage**: www.eva.mpg.de/psycho/staff/tomas/

  You will have gathered by now that the driving force behind the usage-based approach to language development is Michael Tomasello. His homepage provides an excellent source of recent, downloadable research reports on child language. Tomasello has wide research interests, so you will also come across interesting comparative research on communication in chimpanzees (relevant to Chapter 2).

- **Cynthia Fisher's academic homepage**: http://www.psychology.illinois.edu/people/clfishe

  Cynthia Fisher is a leading exponent of syntactic bootstrapping, a theory which ascribes a relatively sophisticated level of syntactic knowledge to children by the age of 24 months. This work therefore provides a direct challenge to the usage-based belief that early child speech is not based on productive, adult-like syntactic generalizations. If the URL defeats you, Google *Cynthia Fisher* and you'll get there quite soon.

Still want more? For links to online resources relevant to this chapter and a quiz to test your understanding, visit the companion website at **https://study.sagepub.com/saxton2e**

10

You Say Nature, I Say Nurture: Better Call the Calling Off Off

CONTENTS

OVERVIEW

This chapter provides a review of facts and ideas presented in the preceding nine chapters. In so doing, the abiding theme of nature and nurture is adopted as a framework for discussion.

At the end of this chapter, you should have a good grasp of some of the basic facts of child language acquisition, having organized them on a timeline. You should also be able to describe some of the fundamental challenges facing both nativist and non-nativist theories of child language. With regard to the non-nativist position, you should be aware of the problems raised by the notion of a domain-general learning mechanism. It is unlikely that any learning mechanism is truly domain general and, moreover, it is likely that several learning mechanisms may be required to help account for language acquisition. In the nativist case, you should be aware that language-learning mechanisms are required, irrespective of whether the child is genetically endowed with Universal Grammar.

A broad overview of methodology is also provided, with a reminder of the variety and ingenuity on display in child language research. Mention is also made of new methods, especially in neuroscience, that promise much for the future. Finally, I ask 40 prominent child language researchers to gaze into my crystal ball and predict the future. No, not the winning lottery numbers (I missed a trick there). But how they view recent achievements in the field and where they envisage the next major advances will come in child language research.

Nature and nurture in the study of child language

The genetic basis of language development

We saw in Chapter 8 that Chomsky's theory of Universal Grammar has not fared well empirically. It is one thing to demonstrate that a particular aspect of syntax, like structure dependence, is a universal property of human language. It is quite another to demonstrate that it is genetically determined. The method Chomsky offers does not seem viable empirically, even though, logically, it makes perfect sense: any aspect of our knowledge of syntax which could not have been attained through experience must be inborn. The empirical problem is to demonstrate the poverty of our experience, relative to the richness of what we come to know. This problem, if we accept it as a genuine problem, has not yet been solved. As we saw in Chapter 4, it is no straightforward matter to demonstrate that the input is impoverished. Meanwhile, an increasing number of authors have mounted demonstrations that syntax *can* be acquired from the information available to the child (see Clark & Lappin, 2011). Chomsky's approach to the 'nature of nature' question is not the only one available. Two prominent alternatives are: (1) twin studies in which the relative contribution of genes to a particular behaviour is estimated; and (2) molecular genetic research which aims to identify specific genes that are implicated in language development. I will make only brief mention of them here, but you can follow them up from the Further Reading section, below.

Twin studies have a long history in the study of intelligence and IQ (Mackintosh, 1998). The two members of any pair of twins share the same environment as they grow up (to a significant degree). But whereas identical twins share 100 per cent of their genes, non-identical twins share only 50 per cent of their genes. Therefore, if a given behaviour is due, even in part, to genes, we would expect identical twins to resemble each other more closely than non-identical twins. This reasoning allows one to calculate a so-called *heritability estimate*, a figure which indicates what proportion of the variance in a behaviour can be attributed to genetic factors. Thus far, twin studies of this kind suggest that two aspects of language-related behaviour may be partly determined by genetic factors: (1) morphology and syntax; and (2) phonological short-term memory (Newbury, Bishop & Monaco, 2005). Molecular genetic research, meanwhile, provides a second method for investigating the genetic contribution to language acquisition. Individual genes which may be important can now be identified. At the same time, the links between cognitive functions (like language) and the action of genes is both indirect and complex. Researchers are only just beginning to think about how to unravel the causal chains between genes and behaviour, but the prospect of being able to do so is at least in sight, somewhere on the horizon. To conclude, Chomsky's method for identifying inherited aspects of language – based on his **poverty of stimulus** argument – has not proven satisfactory empirically. Molecular genetics promises more in this direction, but the following observation provides a cautionary tale:

> Complex traits are not controlled by single genes (Risch, 2000). 'At least 40 loci have been associated with human height, a classic complex trait with an estimated heritability of about 80%, yet they explain only about 5% of phenotypic variance despite studies of tens of thousands of people' (Manolio et al., 2009). (Valian, 2014: 84)

Identifying 40 separate gene loci is one thing. Puzzling out how they actually operate in development is quite another. If human height is so complex – including significant effects of environment – then one can only guess at the task facing researchers when it comes to language acquisition.

Integrating 'nurture' into theories of syntax acquisition

The phrase 'nature–nurture,' with its catchphrase quality and popular appeal, is deceptive. 'Nature–nurture' implies an *opposition* between the learner (nature) and the input to learning (nurture). But this is a false opposition and you will not find any serious researcher willing to subscribe to it. Instead, debate centres on the characteristics of both nature and nurture and the complex ways in which they interact. With respect to nature, we have just seen that non-nativist approaches must appeal to innate learning mechanisms. They are not the sole preserve of linguistic nativists. With respect to nurture, all theories should take into account the linguistic environment and explain how the child makes use of it in the course of language acquisition.

You may have gathered from Chapters 8 and 9 that the child's linguistic environment does not, in fact, feature very prominently in current theories of syntax acquisition. In both nativist and non-nativist theories, the influence of the linguistic environment is downplayed in several ways. First, the emphasis is almost exclusively on input, rather than interaction, as the source of information for learning. And second, within the domain of input, the focus has been on just one feature: frequency of occurrence. On this approach, the critical factor is the sheer number of times the child hears a particular linguistic form. In the nativist approach, very low frequencies (potentially a single exposure) might be all that is required to trigger successful acquisition (Chapter 8). In the non-nativist, usage-based approach, huge input frequencies are implicated as a key factor in explaining how the child achieves deeply 'entrenched' learning. We observed problems with the concept of entrenchment in Chapter 9. And Valian (2014: 82) points out that 'frequency effects are … inconsistent and limited. Children produce structures they have never heard'. Low frequencies or high, in both cases, reference to the child's linguistic environment reduces largely to a matter of input frequency (Saxton, 2009). The richness of interaction and what it can yield for learning are neglected. As we saw in Chapter 4, there are numerous examples of how the *quality* of both input and interaction impact on language acquisition. In the 1970s, there was an explosion of interest in the linguistic 'nurture' of the child, but the numerous discoveries made at that time, and since then, have not yet been fully integrated within a theory of the child's linguistic nature, either nativist or non-nativist. Nurture has not been that well nurtured.

DISCUSSION POINT 10.1
NATURE AND NURTURE IN THE STUDY OF CHILD LANGUAGE

A good deal of research has been motivated by fascination with the ways in which genes and environment influence language acquisition. This is perhaps not surprising, given the massive influence of Chomsky's ideas over the past half century. As another good review exercise, skim each chapter for topics of interest and investigate what is known and/or believed about the genetic basis of the behaviour in question. For instance, you might take categorical perception of phonemes (Chapter 5), or the shape bias in word learning (Chapter 6), or the blocking mechanism in morphology (Chapter 7). Or something else. Try to be specific in your chosen topics (not just *grammar* or *words*, say). If you work in a group, you could split this task and each bring something different to the discussion. In your review, address the following questions, bearing in mind that you'll get a fuller picture if you track down some of the original sources. For each aspect of language:

- What assumptions, if any, do different researchers make about the role of genes? Dig deep: sometimes these assumptions are implicit.
- What empirical evidence do we have concerning the role of genes? How convincing is this evidence?

- Is the chosen language feature assumed to be unique to human development?
- Is it assumed to be both unique to humans *and* to language? The distinction between Faculty of Language Broad versus Narrow – FLB versus FLN – may help out here (Chapter 2).
- What is known about the role of the environment? How convincing is this evidence?

You may well conclude from your discussion that, in many cases, claims concerning the genetic basis of language development are not that well supported empirically. Put another way, almost every assertion concerning the genetic basis of language remains contested, especially when claims are made about the human-specific and/or language-specific nature of genetic influence. As noted, explanations of language acquisition are unfailingly controversial. This can be quite frustrating. Does anyone agree on *anything*? Well, on the basic facts, the answer is, largely, *yes*. On theory and explanation, *no*. But don't be frustrated. Exult, instead, at the richness and diversity of ideas and argument that we get to play with. There is plenty of room for you, Dear Reader, to jump in as a researcher of the future and find answers to the questions: *How?* and *Why?*

Before I shuffle off for a cup of tea, let's give brief consideration to one reason why we do not yet have all the answers. Put simply, psychology is hard. We ask big questions about big topics, like mind, consciousness and development. Research on language acquisition, as a branch of psychology, is not exempt. In fact, it faces the special problems encapsulated by W.C. Fields, a movie star comic from the first half of the twentieth century: 'Never work with children or animals'. Child language researchers do both. To encapsulate the problem: how do we get inside the mind of a child (or animal) and find out what is going on? It is difficult enough with adults, but as we noted in Chapter 1, we cannot simply ask children (or animals) to tell us what they know. You need language – the very thing we are interested in – in order to make this communication. And of course, very young children lack sufficient language to provide us with any workable answers. What can we do instead? Plenty, in fact. Hopefully, you will have been struck already by the ingenuity in the range of different research methods deployed by researchers.

Some basic facts

Dietrich Tiedemann (1787)

The first systematic study we have of child language acquisition was published by a German biologist, Dietrich Tiedemann, in 1787. Tiedemann kept a record of his son's development – including language development – from birth through to the age of almost 30 months (anglophones can refer to the translation by Murchison & Langer, 1927). What we discover in Tiedemann's work is a rich set of observations that are both accurate and a source of perennial research interest. For example, there are notes on imitation, object naming, inflectional morphology, gesture–speech combinations, shared intentionality, grammatical errors and effects of input frequency. Tiedemann was ahead of his time. As you will have noticed, the topics that caught his attention excite the interest of researchers currently, more than two centuries later. Extracts from Tiedemann's work are gathered together in Appendix 1. You will also find reference there to chapters in *this* book where the various topics are discussed from a twenty-first-century perspective. Tiedemann's observations are impressive, but, of course, they do not add up to a complete record of child language. Nothing like. But spooling forward all the way to the 1980s, it was still possible for one commentator to assert that 'what is both desirable and possible in the study of language development at the present time is more facts, more flower-picking natural history' (Campbell, 1986: 30). In other words, at that time it seemed as if many of the basic facts had still not been established. This, at least, is far less true today. We now have a substantial body of evidence to tussle over, following a huge increase in the volume of research over the past 30 years or more. Research on child language has been so prolific, in fact, that no single volume could now contain it all. I have pointed the way to this wider world by throwing the spotlight on some (just some) of the key topics and points of dispute. Hopefully, you now feel better equipped to explore further for yourself.

Child language: A timeline

EXERCISE 10.1
REVIEW OF SOME BASIC FACTS

Inspired by Tiedemann, let's try to get some basic facts together. Copy the timeline below onto the biggest piece of paper you can find and then insert key features of child language according to the age at which they first appear. The space above the line is for *comprehension* – the age at which the child shows initial understanding of some key linguistic feature. And the space below the line is for *production* – the age at which the child actually first produces a particular aspect of language in their own speech. To get started, you might look at the chapter-end summaries and then skim through each chapter in turn, extracting key features as you go. Include features from every aspect of child language: phonology; vocabulary; morphology; grammar; and pragmatics (Chapter 1). I have taken an easy one for myself, by adding the child's first word for you: above the line (comprehension), there are claims that some words can be understood as early as seven months; while below the line (production) 12 months is nearer the mark.

   This exercise will help you create your own survey of child language. But be aware: there are limitations. First, marking an average age of appearance for each feature may create an illusion of specificity. Age of acquisition estimates, when based on spontaneous child speech, are always constrained by the particular sample of language they come from. A child might know and use a particular structure, but simply not display that knowledge in the particular sample taken by the researcher. Second, there are considerable individual differences among children, so a range of ages for each feature would present a more complete (if messier) picture.

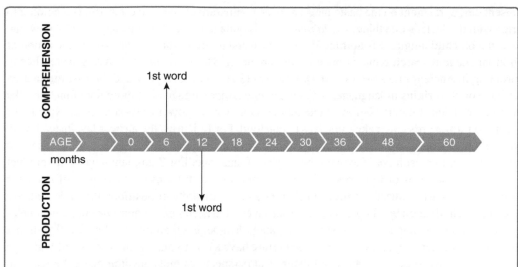

Figure 10.1   Exercise: A child language timeline

And now, a minor revelation: I've had a go at this exercise myself (see Figure 10.3, p. 282). Don't peek until you've tried it yourself. You will find, along with me, that you end up with a rough sketch only of the landmarks in child language. But it does provide a handy, at-a-glance point of reference. You might see this exercise as a work in progress. Add to it as you read beyond the confines of this book and as new discoveries are made. And bear in mind that language acquisition does not cease at 60 months. Vocabulary, morphology, syntax and pragmatics all develop during the school years. What we currently know about development in the school years is probably just a fraction of what remains to be discovered. The relative paucity of research effort focused on older children can be attributed, in part, to the long-held and widespread belief that, for language acquisition, it's all over, bar the shouting, by the age of four or five years (Nippold, 2016, provides a rare exception). As we saw in Chapter 8, some authors even suggest that there is not much left for the child to acquire, apart from vocabulary, past the age of *three* years (McGilvray, 2006). There is, however, no sound empirical basis for this conclusion. If you want to extend your chart into the school years, buy yourself a roll of cheap lining paper (the sort used beneath wallpaper) and make yourself a child language scroll. Then dress up as Psamtik I of Ancient Egypt (Chapter 3) and parade around with your scroll, like a language-mad Pharaoh.

No? Just me then.

The 'nature' in nature–nurture: Something must be innate

Our timeline provides a broad overview of some basic facts of child language. Incidentally, so too does the table summarizing Tiedemann's observations (see Appendix 1). From Tiedemann to the present day, agreement on the basic facts has been comparatively easy to establish. But coming to grips with the facts is one thing. *Explaining* them is quite another. It will be apparent by now that research on child language is nothing if not controversial. Pretty much every fact in the canon of child language research remains open to interpretation. The seeds of controversy were already sprouting in Ancient times (Marx, 1964). Epicurus (341–271 BCE) provided the first rumination we have on the origins of language, with his argument that language is a biological function, like hearing or vision. Epicurus believed that neither God nor the power to reason could explain our ability to form words and make ourselves understood. For Epicurus, the answer lay, instead, with Nature. Of course, a contradictory view soon surfaced. Zeno (333–262 BCE) argued that the human power to reason *could* explain the origins of language. For Zeno, language is the product of learning. The ideas of Epicurus and Zeno are not framed in terms of the origins of language in the *child*. But the questions they considered and the theoretical positions they adopted, are relevant to child language. In particular, we see an emphasis on *either* nature *or* nurture in explanations of how we come to know what we do about language. Of course, we know full well that the issue is not that simple. Both nature *and* nurture have a role to play in any account of language acquisition. If we start with nature, all theoretical perspectives must accommodate the fact that the child brings a genetically determined mind/brain to the task of language development:

> The question is not whether learning presupposes innate structure – of course it does; that has never been in doubt – but rather what those innate structures are in particular domains. (Chomsky, 1975: 13)

This observation entails that *non*-nativist theories of child language depend on 'innate structure' just as surely as nativist theories do. But what is the character of this innate structure? According to the non-nativist view, language does not emerge from the application of domain-*specific* learning mechanisms, dedicated to processing exclusively linguistic input (Ibbotson & Tomasello, 2016). Nor, of course, do non-nativists allow for innate linguistic *knowledge*. But the non-nativist must subscribe to some kind of innately specified learning mechanism. As noted in Chapter 9, this mechanism is typically described as a 'domain-general' learning mechanism.

Learning mechanisms

Domain-general learning: How general?

A domain-general learning mechanism can learn with equal facility from different kinds of input. We encountered one example of domain-general learning – associative learning – in Chapters 6 and 7. This form of learning has been studied in numerous domains within psychology for many decades. We considered its role both in early word learning (Chapter 6) and in the learning of irregular word forms (Chapter 7). Very simply, associative learning takes place when the presence of one cue provides a reliable indication that a second cue is also present. Reliability need not be perfect, a fact which allows for associative learning to be described in probabilistic, or statistical, terms (Chapter 5). Whatever the precise nature of the learning mechanism, the notion of domain-general learning has certainly taken hold within child language research. In Chapters 2 and 5, we considered the argument that infants and tamarin monkeys possess a domain-general capacity to process rapid sequences of discrete acoustic events. These include both the strings of phonemes found in continuous speech and also sequences of pure, non-linguistic tones (Saffran et al., 1999). But just how general is the 'general' in 'domain-general'? Apologies – that's a lot of generals for a book that comes in peace. In the case of tone- and phoneme-strings, the relevant stimuli both reside in the auditory domain. Moreover, they share certain formal characteristics, being: (1) discrete events; (2) organized sequentially; and (3) presented at a consistently high speed. Initial efforts have been made to extend research interest across sensory domains, to include vision (Fiser & Aslin, 2001; Chapter 5). But a truly domain-general learning mechanism would be adapted to process inputs from *any and all* sensory modalities in the course of learning. And the senses we should take into account are numerous. They are not confined to the band of five, familiar to most people: vision, hearing, taste, smell and touch. The following are also considered to be distinct senses, following the differentiation of touch into separate components: vestibular sense (balance and movement); proprioception (the relative position of different body parts); pain; and temperature. We also have a number of internal senses, including, for example, pulmonary stretch receptors for the control of breathing. It seems highly unlikely that a single learning mechanism could take as its input information received from all the human senses. This means that a literal reading of the term 'domain-general learning' appears untenable. Indeed, the term *domain-general* might have to be abandoned for something that is, ironically, more specific.

What is far more plausible is that we possess learning mechanisms which can operate on more than one kind of input, either within, or even across, sensory modalities. The work of Saffran and colleagues supports this position, but as they rightly suggest, even with this scaled down version of 'domain-general' there are serious empirical challenges:

> How does one 'prove' that a learning mechanism is domain-general? Even the clearest cases – where learners show equivalent performance when acquiring materials from two different domains, given the same patterns in the input – could equally well represent two parallel learning mechanisms in lieu of a single domain-general mechanism. (Saffran & Thiessen, 2007: 77)

Evidence already suggests that different kinds of learning mechanism may indeed be required for language learning. In the early stages, we witness the infant segmenting word-like units from a rapid flow of acoustic events. In this case, the input for learning is the uninterrupted strings of phonemes in the speech the infant hears. Later on, these words become, in turn, the input to a different kind of pattern finding – one that involves detecting the principles that bind words together into **sentences** – the acquisition of syntax. Hence, the input that forms the basis for learning is different in each case. Rapid sequences of phonemes are not the same as individual words, and it is entirely possible that the 'pattern-finding' mechanism, which the infant applies to each kind of input is also different in each case (Saffran & Thiessen, 2007). Moreover, the actual kinds of pattern they are finding – word forms versus syntactic rules – also differ in obvious ways. In any event, there may well be more than one learning mechanism at work in the acquisition of language (cf. Lieven, 2016).

The possibility of multiple mechanisms also presents itself in the case of second language learning late in life. In our discussion of critical periods (Chapter 3), we raised the possibility that the way young children acquire their first language differs, qualitatively, from the way adults acquire a second language. While all typical children attain fluent mastery of their native tongue, few adults who embark on a second language attain the child's level of competence. Hence, there may be different learning mechanisms at work at different times of life. While we noted that there are vocal critics of this position (Hakuta et al., 2003), there remains support for the idea that later language development does not rely on the same learning mechanisms exploited by the child. In that case, we should observe that the learning mechanisms brought to bear later in life must be impressive indeed. Adult powers of working memory and long-term memory, together with sophisticated metalinguistic skills, are some of the learning tools which undoubtedly support later second language learning. Although the vast majority of adults do not attain native speaker levels of competence, many such learners nevertheless do very well. The learning mechanisms at their disposal must therefore be relatively powerful. This follows because these adult learners cope fairly well with the complexities of language learning, without the advantage of learning mechanisms specially adapted for the purpose. Of course, these conclusions only follow if one supports the notion of critical periods.

To conclude, it is apparent that non-nativist theories rely on innate learning mechanisms to the same extent as nativist theories do. In the non-nativist case, there remains a lot of work to do in teasing apart the different possibilities and working out how the innate learning machinery, applied by the child in the course of language acquisition, actually works. The concept of domain-general learning undoubtedly needs refinement. It is unlikely that any learning mechanism is truly domain-general, even though some may well apply to more than one form of input, and even to inputs from different sensory modalities. In addition, it is probable that more than one learning mechanism is exploited in the course of language acquisition. It will be fascinating to see how our understanding of domain-general learning develops in the years ahead.

Linguistic nativism: The need for learning mechanisms

Innate mechanisms of learning aside, we should briefly review the concept of innate *ideas*, advanced by Plato and revived by Chomsky. We discovered in Chapter 8 that this concept is surprisingly ethereal. Despite some popular conceptions, no-one seems to suggest that we are born with a knowledge of grammar in our heads. Linguistic nativists do suggest that we possess a *grammar-acquiring capacity*, referred to as Universal Grammar (Jackendoff, 2002; Chapter 8). Moreover, this capacity is domain-specific. It can only acquire human grammar. Hence, our knowledge of grammar is acquired because, when presented with linguistic input, that is all our minds *can* acquire. It seems, therefore, that, even in the nativist approach, we have not quite put learning mechanisms aside. After all, the concept of a 'grammar acquiring capacity' sounds much more like a learning mechanism than a set of innate ideas. This conclusion might not find ready agreement from linguistic nativists. You will recall from Chapters 1 and 8 that the role of learning is downplayed to the point where the concept of learning is actually discarded (Box 1.5). But nativists still need to explain how the categories of Universal Grammar are realized through experience with a particular language. A notable attempt to accommodate learning in a nativist framework is provided by Yang (2004). His reliance on probabilistic learning (Box 5.2) allows for the possibility of domain-general learning without sacrificing a nativist perspective. The point to be made here is that language acquisition *mechanisms* are required in a nativist approach, and these may or may not be domain-general. This holds true regardless of one's beliefs about the genetic underpinnings of grammatical knowledge (Fodor, 2001).

Methodology: Limitations and possibilities

With regard to methodology, we can start by confirming that some of the oldest tools in the box continue to be invaluable. For example, observational data, in the form of video and audio recordings of adult–child interactions, have always been a mainstay of child language research and show no signs of losing their influence as a vital source of information (e.g., Behrens, 2008; see also Box 1.3). Another technique that still earns its keep is the elicited production method, where particular language forms are coaxed out of children (see the studies on structure dependence described in Chapter 8: Crain & Nakayama, 1987; Ambridge, Rowland & Pine, 2008). Add to these both novel word studies (Box 4.2) and the use of grammaticality judgements (Chapter 3) and we get a flavour of the wide range of methods, both old and new, that continue to illuminate the field.

Over the past few decades, there have also been significant steps forward in methodology (Hoff, 2012). For example, in the 1970s, the habituation method first allowed researchers to tap into the way infants perceive human speech. As described in Box 5.1, in this method, a stimulus is presented repeatedly to infants while their attention is gauged in some way (for example, rate of sucking on a dummy). When interest in this initial stimulus wanes (sucking rate declines), a new stimulus is introduced. If sucking rate then revives, it is taken as a sign that the infant has detected that the original stimulus and the new one are different. A range of infant behaviours, not just rate of sucking, are recruited as measures of infant attention, including heart rate and head turning. The habituation method has revealed the power of two-month-old infants to perceive phonemic contrasts categorically, for example, the /p/ – /b/ distinction (Chapter 5). An extension of this method also permitted study of the segmentation problem in the 1990s: the way in which the infant detects the boundaries between individual words in continuous speech (Chapter 5). In this case, the measure taken was the so-called head-turn preference. Given a choice of linguistic stimuli, the infant displays a preference by turning its head towards one of them. In common with other successful methods, a behaviour which is already in the child's repertoire (e.g., head turning or sucking rate) is exploited as a measure of infant attention to language. Incidentally, our friend Tiedemann (1787) observed the reliability of head turning as a measure of infant attention, when his son was four months old: 'the boy, when hearing a sound, always turned his face in the direction whence it came; so he had already learned to tell what he heard through the right ear and what through the left' (Murchison & Langer, 1927: 217). Of course, it took a while to exploit the potential of head turning as a viable research method. But we got there in the end.

Another recent method, also based on infant perceptual preferences, is the so-called inter-modal preferential looking paradigm (mentioned in Chapters 1 and 9). The young child sits on their mother's lap in front of two screens, placed side by side. After a familiarization period, two video events are played at the same time, together with a linguistic stimulus that matches just one of the videos. The 'intermodal' in the title, therefore, refers to the conjunction of two perceptual modes: vision (the video) and sound (the language heard by the infant). The behavioural measure taken is the amount of time the child spends looking at the events on one screen compared with the other. As we saw, inferences can then be made about the child's understanding of language, including verb meanings and grammatical relations. Both preferential listening in infants and preferential looking in young children are ingenious methods that have enriched the repertoire of methods in child language research.

Advances are also being made in brain research, an area touched on in Chapter 3, in our review of critical periods. The ways in which the child's brain responds to linguistic stimuli can be monitored in both time and space. With respect to time, we can chart the course of brain activity as it unfolds over time, using the method of Event Related Potentials (ERP) (e.g., Kaduk,

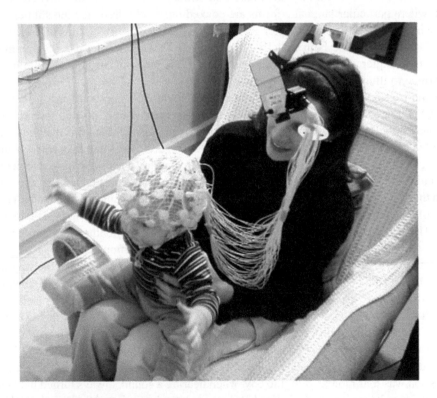

Figure 10.2 An ERP study with a six-month-old child

Source: Benasich, A.A., Choudhury, N., Friedman, J.T., Realpe-Bonilla, T., Chojnowska, C. & Gou, Z.K. (2006). The infant as prelinguistic model for language learning impairments: Predicting from event-related potentials to behavior. *Neuropsychologia, 44(3)*, 396–411, Figure 1, p. 399: Photograph of a 6-month-old child seated on his mother's lap during an ERP testing session using a dense array Geodesic Sensor Net system (Electric Geodesic, Inc., Eugene Oregon, USA).

Bakker, Juvrud, Gredebäck, Westermann, Lunn & Reid, 2016). And with regard to space, we can locate which regions of the brain experience peak activity, following stimulus presentation, using a number of methods, including: (1) *functional Magnetic Resonance Imaging* (fMRI) (Dehaene-Lambertz, Hertz-Pannier, Dubois, Meriaux, Roche, Sigman & Dehaene, 2006; Dubois, Hertz-Pannier, Cachia, Mangin, Le Bihan & Dehaene-Lambertz, 2009; Xiao, Brauer, Lauckner, Zhai, Jia, Margulies & Friederici, 2016); and (2) *near-infrared spectroscopy* (Minagawa-Kawai, Mori, Hebden & Dupoux, 2008). In both cases, measures of brain activity are based on oxygen levels in the blood: active brain regions are characterized by relatively high levels of oxygen use. The scope of this book allows only the briefest mention of neuroscientific methods, but see the Further Reading section if you want to delve further.

There *is* space to make two points about brain research here. First, the ERP method has considerable promise for use in child language research. It is a non-invasive technique that monitors the time course of brain activity via numerous electrodes placed on the scalp (Männel, 2008). As you can see from Figure 10.2, the child looks like some crazy kind of multiple socket, with all the plugs pushed in, and yet, somehow, seems entirely oblivious (maybe it's an outtake from *The Matrix*). ERP research has been valuable in helping confirm findings from other sources, including research on early speech perception (Kuhl & Rivera-Gaxiola, 2008; Chapter 5). ERP has also been used in studies on children who experience significant delays in language acquisition. In one such study, 12-month-olds from families with a history of language problems were monitored, using ERP, until the age of 36 months (Benasich, Choudhury, Friedman, Realpe-Bonilla, Chojnowska & Gou, 2006). Benasich et al. were interested in the infants' ability to process rapid sequences of auditory tones (as found in fluent speech). Infants differ in this respect and these differences can be detected via ERP. Impairment in rapid auditory processing at 12 months is associated with depressed performance on measures of spoken language at 36 months. Put another way, infants who are proficient at processing rapid sound sequences acquire language more quickly and more successfully than less proficient children. We see how measures of brain activity, early in life, can function as predictors of future language learning.

A second point we can make about brain research concerns the use of fMRI scanners to locate regions of peak brain activity. You may know that fMRI scanners require the participant to lie very still in a solid, enclosed tube for an extended period of time. You will not be surprised to learn, therefore, that this method is not yet in use with toddlers. Infants, just a few months old, *have* been placed in scanners, but they have to be asleep at the time (without any form of sedation). Linguistic stimuli are played to the sleeping infant and brain responses can be recorded. Research is in the very early stages in this field (see Further Reading) and has focused on the issue of brain asymmetry, a potential sign of specialization for language: in most people, language is processed in the left brain hemisphere (mentioned in Chapter 3). Observe that, currently, we can only scan infants when they are asleep. Hence, we have no control comparison with the infant brain in the waking state which is, after all, what we are most interested in. While fMRI research on infants is now underway, it is clear that serious empirical challenges remain to be tackled.

Advances in neuroscience, based on the fMRI method, have been phenomenal over the last 20 years or so (e.g., Aslin, Shukla & Emberson, 2015). But the squirming toddler, reluctant (or rather, unable) to lie still in a scanner, presents a significant challenge. Child language researchers cannot always take immediate advantage of advances in technology, a point which brings us back to where we started with respect to methodology: it ain't easy. Methodological advances *have* been made, and will continue to be made. But it is worth reflecting that much of the theoretical disagreements witnessed between child language researchers find their origin in the limitations of their methods. To give just one example, we have seen how the preferential looking method has been used to investigate understanding of transitive sentences in 24-month-olds (Chapter 9). Do infants really understand the role of agent of a causative event? Moreover, do they expect the agent to come first in a simple transitive sentence like *Big Bird is squatting Cookie Monster*? As we discovered, for one group of researchers, the answer is *yes* (Gertner et al., 2006). Others are much more cautious (Dittmar et al., 2008a). These latter, more sceptical researchers, do not want to attribute an extensive degree of syntactic knowledge to very young children on the basis of their looking behaviour. But as Valian (2014: 80) points out:

> Since all experiments impose cognitive and executive function demands on children (e.g. attending to the experimenter, following directions, understanding the task, keeping on task, inhibiting extraneous stimuli), we run the risk of underestimating or mischaracterizing children's syntactic knowledge.

Language acquisition: The state of the art

I first encountered child language at the age of 20, when I went to study psychology at Edinburgh University. As luck would have it, it turned out that I was expected to study more than just straight psychology, so I plumped for linguistics as well (and Japanese and social anthropology, too, as it happens). Hitherto, linguistics was unknown to me as an academic discipline, but it captured my imagination, especially, perhaps, because I studied it alongside psychology. Psycholinguistics combines the heady complexities of linguistics with the even greater complexities of the human mind. Fundamentally, psycholinguistics poses two related questions: how is language acquired and how is language represented in the mind? These are big questions. As someone new to academic life, child language presented itself as an especially fascinating topic within psycholinguistics. My guiding light at the time was a newly published collection, edited by Eric Wanner and Leila Gleitman, entitled *Language acquisition: The state of the art*. The papers in Wanner & Gleitman (1982) collectively asserted the right of child language to be considered as the focus of serious scientific enquiry. The field had already come far since the early days of Jean Berko Gleason's *wugs* and Roger Brown's longitudinal studies of Adam, Eve and Sarah (Berko, 1958; Brown & Bellugi, 1964; see also Chapter 1). By the 1980s, a wealth of imaginative theorising, constrained by a scientific approach, had created a substantial, independent field of enquiry.

But where are we now, more than one third of a century down the line from Wanner & Gleitman (1982)? I thought it would be worthwhile to elicit the views of leaders in the field who are active in research today. This involved the email equivalent of cold-calling a large number of individuals, to canvas their views. My initial cohort was assembled from the editorial boards of three child language journals (*Journal of Child Language*, *First Language* and *Language Acquisition*), plus a number of other likely candidates known to me from their work and/or personal contact.

Gratifyingly, a significant number on my initial list either failed to dump me into their Junk folders or were too slow in hitting the Block button. In fact, something like 40 prominent researchers were generous enough to give their attention to my questions and provide their perspectives on the field. I asked respondents to consider the achievements of the recent past and then cast their minds into the future and predict the next big breakthroughs, in theory, methodology and empirical discovery. The answers were various and fascinating. In what follows, I have identified authors who associated themselves with particular themes (full names can be found in the Acknowledgements at the beginning of the book). Of necessity, I am painting with a broad brush. You should therefore follow up on any particular interests through the published work of authors who catch your eye.

In theoretical terms, the last ten years or so have seen the usage-based theory establish itself as a viable alternative to Chomsky's theory of Universal Grammar (Chapter 8). Numerous alternatives to UG theory have been advanced over the years, but usage-based theory has undoubtedly made the largest impact, both theoretically and empirically (Chapter 9; Tomasello, 2003). Several commentators pointed this out and observed a concomitant expansion of interest in domain-general cognition, as noted above (Berman, Bybee, Guasti, Guerts, Lieven, Pearl, Ravid, Saffran, Shirai, Tomasello, Ullman). On this view, memory (declarative and procedural), theory of mind and even musical cognition (think of intonation) all contribute to language acquisition. The issue of *how* children process input is relevant here, in particular, the influence of input frequency (Chiat, Clark, Phillips, Rowland). In the pursuit of these issues, growing connections to allied disciplines are becoming increasingly important, in particular, experimental psychology and neuroscience (Guasti, Li, Ota, Saffran, Ullman). The rise of usage-based theory has also given rise to the hope that research in future will be less polarised between usage-based and UG-based approaches (Chiat, Marshall, Morgan).

With regard to methodology, two broad themes emerged: (1) the use of modelling; and (2) the rise of methods which tap into online processing. A number of respondents emphasized the importance of computational modelling as a means of examining the interactions between input and learning (Chapter 7 and Becker, Chiat, Clark, Kidd, Li, Lieven, Ota, Pearl, Phillips, van Hout). The value of mathematical models was also raised (Yang). In both cases, the successes of the past 30 years have paved the way for yet more sophisticated use of modelling in the future. The success of models depends in large part on the robustness of the information fed into them. In this respect, a number of authors point to advances in the use of large and/or dense input databases (Berman, Becker, Christophe, Lieven, Pearl). The task of the model is to acquire syntactic categories from the same kinds of input which are available to the child. Hitherto, no model has managed to generate the full complexities of syntax from scratch (Soderstrom, 2014). While this may be possible in the future, one is left with the tantalising possibility that some language-specific, innate machinery will be required to get the learning started. Did anyone say UG? Try as some non-nativists might, they cannot quite shake off the possibility that some form of language-related, innate constraints are needed (cf., Pérez-Leroux & Kahnemuyipour, 2014: e115).

The second aspect of methodology which captures the attention of the child language community is the recent advent of techniques for investigating cognitive processing as it happens in real time (Conti-Ramsden, Kidd, Naigles, Rowland, Saffran). Online processing methods include those mentioned above, such as EEG and MRI, in addition to eye-tracking technology, which provides a sophisticated indication of child attention on a moment-by-moment basis (Oakes, 2012; Odean, Nazareth & Pruden, 2015). These methods allow for the integration of what we know about language processing with what we know about language development, an endeavour which is in its infancy (Chiat, Clark, Pearl). More pointedly, they render the issue of *how* children process linguistic input tractable for the first time. The difficulties of working with very young children notwithstanding, these methods promise much for the future.

At least one (anonymous) contributor voiced disquiet about the empirical clout of child language studies, citing tiny sample sizes, lax statistics and a pervasive failure to replicate key findings. Statistical analyses have undoubtedly become more refined (Ravid), but there is always room for improvement. And the failure to replicate is not confined to child language but is, arguably, the scourge of psychology more widely. What can one do? Thankfully, it is not all doom and gloom. Projects like Stanford University's Metalab tackle this problem, to some extent, by combining the data from numerous related studies and subjecting them to sophisticated statistical techniques (see Websites below). Arguably, meta-analyses should become a standard tool in future child language research (Marshall, Ota). In addition, new tools for automated analyses of large databases are emerging, which complement those already available via CHILDES (Chapter 1). These include LENA (Language Environment Analysis), a set of tools for analysing the language input of young children (e.g., Ko, Seidl, Cristia, Reimchen & Soderstrom, 2016).

In recent years, the empirical storehouse of data on child language has been filling up fast. We now have a more extensive knowledge of the milestones in both initial and more complex syntax (Becker, Clark), semantics (van Hout) and pragmatics (Clark, Naigles) (Chapters 4, 6, 8 and 9). Efforts to tie it all together have also moved forward, in order to understand how syntax, semantics and pragmatics influence each other in development (Lieven, Tomasello). Again, though, there is a lot more to discover on this complex topic.

A final common thread which ran through the responses of many researchers in this *ad hoc* survey was the problem of English (Berman, Becker, Clark, Golinkoff, Guasti, Kidd, Li, Lieven, Pearl, Ravid, van Hout). The English language has been the elephant in the room for decades now, in the sense that the vast majority of research has been conducted on children acquiring English. Yet we live in a multilingual world. Different languages may well present the child with particular challenges, which might easily be neglected if the focus is on just one language. We saw this in Chapter 7, where the notion of regularity, as witnessed in English morphology, looked less universal as soon as one took a short boat trip across the Baltic to nearby Poland. In fact, English can look like a rare beast when looked at from the perspective of certain linguistic features, such as tones. Some 90 per cent of the world's languages – including Mandarin, Cantonese and Thai – are tonal (Golinkoff). This means that the meaning of a word depends in part on its associated intonation contour (e.g., for Mandarin: rise, fall, fall-rise or high level). In Mandarin, the sequence *ma* can mean *mother, hemp, horse* or *scold*, depending on the tone deployed. Imagine saying *My mother scolded the horse for eating the hemp* in Mandarin. Of course, English does not use tones – just one example where our view of the learning problem facing the young child might be impoverished by an exclusive focus on English. There is also the fact that many (probably most) children are bilingual or multilingual. Yet a large proportion of early child language research was conducted on monolingual English speakers. A standard argument in UG theory was that one could study *any* human language in the pursuit of those properties of syntax which are universal (e.g., Chomsky, 1965: 36). This follows from the assertion that *all* languages express the universals embodied in UG. From this it also follows that one can comfortably zoom in on one's own native language, which just happened to be English in the case of many North American (and British) researchers. And in the early days of creating a scientific discipline out of child language studies – the 1960s – the field was dominated by native English speakers. Undoubtedly things have changed. Databases like CHILDES now contain numerous sets of non-English data (Berman, Pearl) and research on bilingual (and multilingual) acquisition has flourished (Behrens, Clark, Guasti, Howe). At the same time, there is still great potential for expanding the horizons of research beyond English.

Finally, several researchers expressed individual hopes and beliefs about the topics which they consider should attract more research attention in the future. These include: language variability, including delay and disorder (Behrens, Naigles); multi-modal learning, as witnessed in speech-gesture interactions (Guasti, Marshall, Naigles and Chapter 4); the need for more longitudinal research (Conti-Ramsden, Chiat) and more individual case studies (Clark); a greater focus on input and interaction (Berman, Behrens, Clark); less focus on input frequency (MacWhinney); and greater attention to practical applications of child language research (Chiat, Golinkoff). This latter point is of particular importance. There are many lessons to be learned from the study of typical language development which can be applied in cases of atypical development, for example, in the development of therapeutic interventions for children with delays and disorders of various kinds (e.g., Paul & Norbury, 2012).

Child language: Acquisition and development

Way back in Chapter 1 (Box 1.5), I suggested that the terms *acquisition* and *development* are somewhat loaded terms. They bear subtle connotations which can reveal which side of the nativist fence a researcher stands on. While acquisition is favoured by nativists, development is more the preserve of non-nativists. I would be the first to admit that this distinction is rather subtle and by no means a foolproof index of an author's theoretical persuasion. At the same time, preferred usage of one term over the other is prevalent and quite often reveals one's bias. The concept of acquisition, very broadly, suggests that possession is taken of a finished product. Development, meanwhile, sits more comfortably with the non-nativist belief that change takes place over time, through learning. But neither *acquisition* nor *development* is so restrictive in scope (check the dictionary to confirm this point). These terms can be used interchangeably without violence, either to their inherent meanings or to the user's theoretical stance. Since the first edition of this book appeared there are signs that the child language community is becoming less sectarian in its use of acquisition versus development (e.g., Rowland, 2014). This can only be a good thing. Both acquisition and development can help describe both nature and nurture at work in the child. Child language is, undoubtedly, a complex topic. I can only urge you to revel in its complexities. There is always something to excite the imagination, always the inspiration of finding oneself at the point where philosophy meets science. Always the simple wonder in observing the acquisition and development of language in the child.

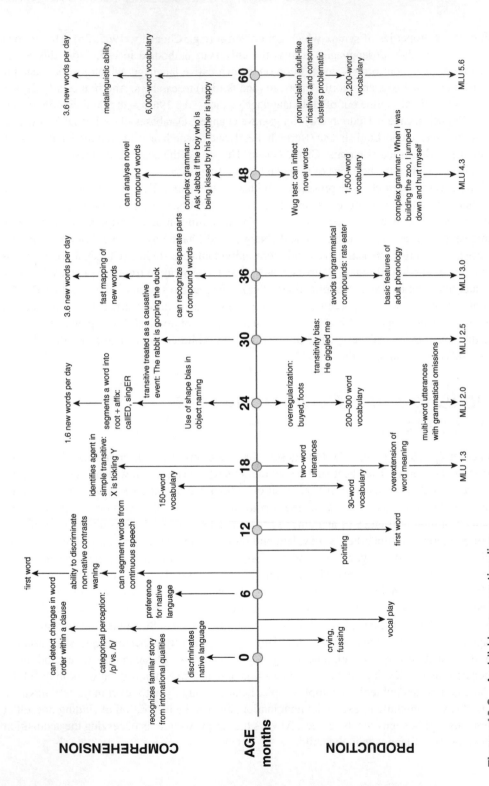

Figure 10.3   A child language timeline

IN A NUTSHELL

- The earliest systematic study of child language was reported by Tiedemann in 1787. Many of his observations remain relevant for current research.

- You can get a good overview of some basic facts in the field by creating your own timeline.

- Both nativist and non-nativist theories depend on innate learning mechanisms to help explain how the child acquires language:

  o Non-nativist theories rely on the idea of a domain-general learning mechanism, one that is not specifically adapted for language. But no learning mechanism can, plausibly, be entirely domain-general, and several learning mechanisms are probably required to explain language acquisition.

  o Nativist theories also require some kind of learning mechanisms, irrespective of the view that the child is innately endowed with Universal Grammar. These learning mechanisms may or may not be domain-general.

- Child language studies make use of a wide range of different methods and much progress has been made in the past 30 years or so. At the same time, the difficulties inherent in studying both infants and young children mean that the interpretation of child language behaviours often remains open. In consequence, the study of child language continues to be both controversial and richly stimulating.

FURTHER READING

Ambridge, B. & Rowland, C.F. (2013). Experimental methods in studying child language acquisition. *WIREs Cognitive Science*. doi: 10.1002/wcs.1215.

This article provides a thorough review of methods in child language research, including the latest methods for exploring the workings of the infant brain. There is also a very useful checklist at the end for researchers planning experimental work with children. Use it when planning your own research project.

Dehaene-Lambertz, G. & Spelke, E.S. (2015). The infancy of the human brain. *Neuron, 88(1)*, 93–109.

A taste of the future. This paper provides a survey of recent research on the infant brain, including discussion of research on language development.

Mueller, K.L., Murray, J.C., Michaelson, J.J., Christiansen, M.H., Reilly, S. & Tomblin, J.B. (2016). Common genetic variants in FOXP2 are not associated with individual differences in language development. *PLoS One*, *11(4)*, pp.e0152576.

Discovery of the gene known as FOXP2 was presented in some media reports as discovery of '*the* gene for language'. But as this paper reveals, the relationship between FOXP2 and language is much more complex (see also Wohlgemuth, Adam & Scharff, 2014, for a songbird twist).

Newbury, D.F., Bishop, D.V.M. & Monaco, A.P. (2005). Genetic influences on language impairment and phonological short-term memory. *Trends in Cognitive Sciences*, *9(11)*, 528–534.

A summary of research on genetic causes of language impairment in children. No specific genes are identified in this kind of research. Instead, different aspects of language behaviour are identified as having a partly genetic basis.

Lidz, J. & Gagliardi, A. (2015). How nature meets nurture: Statistical learning and Universal Grammar. *Annual Review of Linguistics*, *11(1)*, 333–353.

Where does research on Universal Grammar go next? This paper attempts to point the way. While arguing that innate language learning mechanisms are necessary, these authors also concede the need for more general cognitive learning mechanisms.

WEBSITES

- **Metalab at Stanford University**: http://metalab.stanford.edu/

  A research tool for enhancing the statistical power of child language studies. Meta-analyses aggregate the data across numerous related studies to examine how strong the reported effects are. In addition, researchers can plan more rigorously how many participants they will need to produce findings with any real statistical authority. Metalab points the way to a statistically much more sophisticated future for child language research.

- **W.C. Fields in *Pool Sharks* (1915)**

  Search for this in YouTube and enjoy one of the comedy greats from more than 100 years ago. W.C. Fields was the man who first advised: 'never work with children or animals'. Child language researchers do both, of course. In any event, W.C. Fields broke his own rule on several occasions, including in the 1933 version of *Alice in Wonderland* (a poor quality version is available on YouTube). About 45 minutes into the movie, W.C. Fields appears as a querulous Humpty Dumpty, espousing some of Lewis Carroll's observations on word meaning.

- **Fred Astaire and Ginger Rogers in *Let's Call the Whole Thing Off* (1937)**

Search YouTube for *Fred Astaire and Ginger Rogers in Let's Call the Whole Thing Off*. You'll find them tap dancing on roller skates to an old song by George and Ira Gershwin in the movie *Shall We Dance* (see Gershwin, 1959). If you know this song at all, you probably know the 'punch line': *Let's call the whole thing off*. But actually, the real point of the song is expressed in this part of the lyric:

For we know we

Need each other, so we

Better call the calling off off.

When it comes to nature and nurture, this part of the lyric is much more appropriate. Often referred to misleadingly as the nature–nurture controversy, we all know that, in fact, nature and nurture were meant for each other.

Still want more? For links to online resources relevant to this chapter and a quiz to test your understanding, visit the companion website at **https://study.sagepub.com/saxton2e**

Answers to Exercises

Chapter 1: Prelude: Landmarks in the Landscape of Child Language

Exercise 1.2: Grammatical categories

noun	verb	adjective	preposition
dog	eat	hot	in
happiness	inculcate	pusillanimous	by
Somerset	divorce	happy	from
divorce	complete	charming	up
acceptance		complete	

A couple of points to note:

(1) *Divorce* can be both a noun (*her **divorce** came through*) and a verb (*Hillary should've **divorced** Bill*). *Complete* can be both a verb (*I **completed** the puzzle*) and an adjective (*This is a **complete** mess*). Many words can function in more than one grammatical category.

(2) Even if you didn't know that *pusillanimous* means weak-willed or cowardly, you can probably work out that it is an adjective by testing out which sentence slots it fits into most naturally:

He is a pusillanimous (noun)

He pusillanimoused my car yesterday (verb)

He is a pusillanimous man (adjective)

Chapter 3: The Critical Period Hypothesis: Now or Never?

Exercise 3.1: Subject, verb and object

1 The subject of the sentence is marked in **bold**:

   (a) **Gordon's hair** looks like nylon.
   (b) **I** couldn't help noticing the baby elephant in your fridge.
   (c) **The man who lives next door to me** has a fondness for figs.
   (d) **The end of the world** is nigh.
   (e) Have **you** ever seen a Buster Keaton movie?

2 The verb is marked in **bold**:

   (a) Nigella **licked** her spoon in a rather suggestive fashion.
   (b) Now **is** the winter of our discontent.
   (c) Henrietta **scoffed** a big bag of toffees on the bus.
   (d) **Fly** me to the moon.
   (e) **Play** it again, Sam. (I know, I know: Ingrid Bergman doesn't actually say this).

3 The object is marked in **bold**:

   (a) That really takes **the biscuit**.
   (b) Frankly, my dear, I don't give **a damn**.
   (c) I simply adore **champagne**.
   (d) How many **cream buns** can you eat at one sitting?
       (This is a question, which is why the standard S-V-O order has been switched round).
   (e) I'll make him **an offer** he can't refuse.

4 Subject, verb and object in Genie's sentences

   The sentences below, all uttered by Genie, appear in the text of Chapter 3. Check your analyses against my own, below, to see if Genie gets the correct basic English SVO order. Of course, this is only possible in cases where she produces at least two of the three elements, S, V and O. Missing elements have been marked with Ø. Some sentences have material additional to the basic S, V and O (*at hospital* in *like good Harry at hospital*; *no more* in *no more have*).

SUBJECT	VERB	OBJECT
small two cup†	Ø	Ø
Ø	like chew	meat
(no more)	have	Ø
drink		

SUBJECT	VERB	OBJECT	
dentist	say		
	drink	water††	
	tell	door	lock†††
glass	is break	Ø	
Another house	Ø	blue cart††††	
Cookie	sleep	car	
bus	have	big mirror	
Ø	like	good Harry	at hospital
Mama	wash	hair	in sink

† Only one element here, an odd **noun phrase** that could appear as either subject or object, but here it is produced by itself.

†† *Dentist say drink water* is complicated. It seems to have a main **clause** (*dentist say*) and a sub clause (*drink water*), as in *The dentist says 'drink water'*.

††† Also complex, but much more difficult to interpret.

†††† This looks like two separate noun phrases, but my analysis of one as subject and the other as object could well be fanciful.

Chapter 5: Language in the First Year: Breaking the Sound Barrier

Exercise 5.1: Phonological contrasts

The key to this exercise is to find word pairs which differ by one sound only, and then find the phonemic symbol for each contrasting sound from the Pronunciation Guide at the back of the book.

dog	*catch*	*funny*	*ceiling*	*male*
lake	*cheese*	*ship*	*bog*	*chip*
whale	*laze*	*sham*	*peas*	*shack*
been	*feeling*	*cap*	*honey*	*dean*

Minimal Pair	Letters	Contrasting Phonemes
dog – bog	d – b	/d/ – /b/
catch – cap	tch – p	/tʃ/ – /p/

Minimal Pair	Letters	Contrasting Phonemes
funny – honey	f – h	/f/ – /h/
ceiling – feeling	c – f	/s/ – /f/
male – whale	m – wh	/m/ – /w/
lake – laze	k – z	/k/ – /z/
cheese – peas	ch – p	/tʃ/ – /p/
ship – chip	sh – ch	/ʃ/ – /tʃ/
sham – shack	m – ck	/m/ – /k/
been – dean	b – d	/b/ – /d/

Chapter 7: The Acquisition of Morphology: Linguistic Lego

Exercise 7.1: Derived forms

The following symbols are used for grammatical categories: noun (N); verb (V); adjective (A). Answers are given in the form: root → derived form.

obese → obesity	N → N
holy → unholy	A → A
repel → repellent	V → A
London → Londoner	N → N
select → selection	V → N
swim → swimmer	V → N
cure → curable	V → A
black → blacken	A → V
real → realize	A → V
success → successful	N → A
organize → reorganize	V → V
clear → clearance	V → N
play → playful	V → A

special → speciality   A → N

member → membership   N → N

accident → accidental   N → A

Exercise 7.2: Morphological processes

airheads	compound (*air* + *head*) and inflection (plural -*s*)
disgraceful	derivation (*dis-* + *grace* + -*ful*)
hat maker	derivation (*make* + -*er*) and compound (*hat* + *maker*)
monster	simple root form
sampling	inflection (*sample* + -*ing*)
pleased	inflection (*please* + -*ed*)
indefatigable	derivation (*in-* + *de-* + *fatigue* + -*able*)
washing machine	inflection (*wash* + -*ing*) and compounding (*washing* + *machine*)
insider	derivation (*in-* + *side* + -*er*)
coffee table	compound (*coffee* + *table*)
reasserted	derivation (*re-* + *assert*) and inflection (*reassert* + -*ed*)
dressmakers	derivation (*make* + -*er*) and compound (*dress* + *maker*) and inflection (*dressmakers*)
elephant	simple root form
recycles	derivation (*re-* + *cycle*) and inflection (*recycle* + -*s*)
sweetcorn	compound (*sweet* + *corn*)
unhappily	derivation (*un-* + *happy* + -*ily*)

Exercise 7.3: Productivity of derivational suffixes

I provide a few examples below, with the following category abbreviations: Noun (N); verb (V); and Adjective (A). Observe again how the categories of root and derived forms can differ. You will probably have found it especially easy to come up with examples for -*able* and -*er*, a sign (however informal) that they are highly productive affixes in English. Notice how you sometimes have to clear away more than one affix to get at the root form.

Affix	Example	Category of Derived Form	Root Form
pre-	predetermined	A	determine (V)
	premeditated	A	meditate (V)
in-	inedible	A	eat (V)
	inoperable	A	operate (V)
under-	undernourished	A	nourish (V)
	underpaid	A	pay (V)
de-	depopulate	V	populate (V)
	deform	V	form (V)
-cy	frequency	N	frequent (A)
	delinquency	N	delinquent (A)
-able	passable	N	pass (V)
	enjoyable	A	enjoy (V)
-ity	density	N	dense (A)
	acidity	N	acid (A)
-less	speechless	A	speech (N)
	witless	N	wit (N)
-er	farmer	N	farm (N)
	mover	N	move (V)

Chapter 8: Linguistic Nativism: To the Grammar Born

Exercise 8.1: BE as copula or auxiliary

(a) Louise **is** a cat lover.   **copula**

(b) Ian must **be** mad to buy so much cat food.   **copula**

(c) Patricia and Colin **are** having kittens about the fleas in their house.   **auxiliary**

(d) Saskia **is** wondering what all the interest in cats **is** about.
1st *is* = auxiliary; 2nd *is* = copula

(e) I **am** wondering what cat would taste like if it **were** roasted.
am = auxiliary; were = copula

(f) Cats **were** worshipped in Ancient Egypt.   **copula**

(g) The cat that **is** stealing my milk has **been** known to steal chicken, too.
is = auxiliary; been = auxiliary

(h) **Is** there any reason why cat owners do not look like their pets?   **copula**

Chapter 9: The Usage-Based Approach: Making it Up as You Go Along

Exercise 9.1: Verb transitivity

Most verbs in English are bitransitive, because they can appear with or without a direct object (Huddleston, 1984).

transitive	intransitive	bitransitive
want	*sleep*	*leave*
feel	*disappear*	*wait*
take		*jump*
		read

This exercise is not quite as cut and dried as it might seem because people can vary in their use of particular verbs according to the dialect or level of formality being used. For example, I know someone (a native English speaker) who uses *want* in intransitive sentences:

Me: *Do you want a cup of tea?*

Him: *I don't want.*

Appendix 1: Observations on Language Acquisition Made by Dietrich Tiedemann (1787)

Page references are from the translation by Murchison & Langer (1927).

Age (months)	Child behaviour	Tiedemann's notes	Review reading in this book (Chapter)
1 (?)	Early vocal imitation by the child	'infants who have already learned to produce sounds and to employ the vocal organs are involuntarily led to the imitation of sounds' (p. 211)	4
2	Responsiveness to Child Directed Speech	'gentle words and a compassionate voice could hush his passion' (pp. 212–213)	4
4	Preference for speech (singing) over non-speech sounds (accurate if the singing had lyrics)	'Singing always commanded his attention now … Whistling, on the other hand, he did not notice' (p. 216)	5
6	Child attempt to imitate a syllable	'His mother said to him the syllable "Ma"; he gazed attentively at her mouth, and attempted to imitate the syllable' (p. 218)	4
8½	Reduplicated babbling and pointing	'Whenever he met with anything novel or strange he would point his finger at it to call other people's attention to it, and employed the sound, "ha! ha!"' (p. 219)	5, 9
8½	Dyadic interaction / shared intentionality	'deep in human nature lies the desire to reveal ourselves to others, and to feel their participation in anything that strikes our interest' (p. 219)	9

(Continued)

Age (months)	Child behaviour	Tiedemann's notes	Review reading in this book (Chapter)
12	Comprehension of whole utterances	'he knew already what was meant by: "Make a bow", "Swat the fly"' (p. 220)	9
12	Object naming (comprehension)	'certain names of very familiar objects he understood perfectly' (p. 220)	6
15	Single-word speech (production)	'A few words he pronounced clearly … and knew also their meanings exactly; these were "Papa" and "Mama"' (p. 221)	6
15	Word learning as a by-product of shared intentionality	'children begin by learning words for the sake of understanding the intention of others' (p. 221)	9
15	Gesture as a substitute for speech	'Since the speech-organs were not yet sufficiently trained to produce all sorts of articulation, especially long and compound words, he usually denoted the corresponding objects by gestures' (p. 221)	4
15	Gesture + speech combinations	'he was required to say the word "grandmama", and as the word "grand" was too difficult for him to pronounce, he lifted up his hands and at the same time said "mama"' (p. 221)	4
16	Child imitation of adult	'The boy's mania for imitation' (p. 223) 'he attempted … to imitate conversations, to which end he produced a profusion of incomprehensible sounds' (p. 223)	4
16	Comprehension of whole sentences	'he understood a variety of phrases such as: "fetch that", "leave that alone", "put it over there", and so forth' (p. 223)	2, 9
18	Pronunciation: syllable reduction; difficulty with fricatives; mastery of **stops**	'he still found it hard to pronounce words of several syllables. Of these he usually said only the end-syllables or the syllables that was [sic] chiefly accented' (p. 224) 'The consonants z, sch, w [v], st, sp, as also the diphthongs, he could not well pronounce; p, t and k he found the easiest' (p. 224)	6

Age (months)	Child behaviour	Tiedemann's notes	Review reading in this book (Chapter)
21	Short utterances with errors of omission	'he succeeded in saying short sentences, consisting of a noun and a verb, though without correct grammatical form' (p. 225) 'the article was omitted altogether' (p. 225)	2, 3, 4, 9
21	Inflectional morphology	He 'used the nominative in place of all other cases' (p. 225) 'the sense of the other case endings was not clear to him yet' (p. 225)	7
21	Input frequency effects: nominative and infinitive	'Instead of the imperative he always employed the infinitive, and used the nominative in place of all other cases … The nominative he had most frequently heard when things were named for him' (p. 225) 'The infinitive we use most frequently, since the other tenses are often expressed in our dialect by this form' (p. 225)	4, 9
23	Production of grammatical utterances	'he finally succeeded in uttering complete, though short sentences, for example: *There he stands. There he lies.*'	8, 9
26	Symbolic thought as evidence that language is unique to humans	There is 'a voluntary and autonomous association of ideas, the first source of language, in fact of any symbolic expression. Never has anything of the sort been observed in animals …; so the reason why animals have no speech does seem to lie deeper than in the mere lack of adroitness of the speech organs' (p. 228)	2
30	Production of grammatically complex sentences	'he said, when he thought he had acted very cleverly: "People will say, "That is a nice little boy"' (p. 230)	8, 9

Appendix 2: Pronunciation Guide: English Phonemes

The chart below provides a pronunciation guide for the phonemes of English (for more on phonemes, see Box 1.2, Chapter 1). A special set of symbols is used to represent phonemes, written within slash brackets / /. While the symbols for phonemes sometimes correspond to English letters, at other times they do not. You should also bear in mind that this chart holds true only for one variety of English (known as received pronunciation). There is some variation for other dialects, especially among the vowel sounds.

Consonants

p	pale	f	fail	ʃ	sheep
b	bale	v	veil	ʒ	measure
t	tale	s	sail	j	yellow
d	dale	z	zebra	l	leap
k	call	h	hail	ɹ	rail
g	gale	θ	think	w	wail
m	male	ð	this	ʍ	which
n	nail	tʃ	cheap		
ŋ	sing	dʒ	jeep		

Vowels

əʊ	toe	ɪə	deer	eə	hair
ɒ	not	ɜ:	burn	ʊə	moor
i:	feet	ʊ	foot	ʌ	run
ɪ	fit	o	gloat	ə	about
eɪ	wait	ɔ:	more	aɪ	sight
ɛ	wet	æ	mat	aʊ	shout
u:	toot	ɑ:	car	ɔɪ	toy

Glossary of Linguistic Terms

accusative See **case**.

adjective A syntactic category that often denotes states (*happy, dull, quick, disgusting*). Adjectives are used to describe or qualify a **noun** (*a happy banker, a disgusting mess*). They often have comparative (*-er*) and superlative (*-est*) forms (*happier, dullest*), though there are exceptions (*disgustinger). Adjectives also often have **adverb** counterparts ending in *-ly* (*dully, quickly*) and can be turned into nouns with *-ness* (*happiness, quickness*). Again, there are exceptions (*disgustingness).

adverb A syntactic category typically used to denote the manner in which something occurs. English adverbs often end in *-ly* (*sweetly, wonderfully, badly, stupendously*), as in: *Albert is **stupendously** well informed* or *She sings **wonderfully** for a hippo*.

affix A **morpheme** that is added to a word either on the left hand side (**prefix**) or on the right hand side (**suffix**), when reading. In *resealing*, *re-* is a prefix, while *-ing* is a suffix, added to left and right of *seal*.

affricate A sequence of two consonants, **stop** + **fricative**, that often behave as a single **phoneme** in languages (including English). In English there are two affricates: /tʃ/ (the first sound in *cheap*), /dʒ/ (first in *jeep*).

agent Typically, a person who intentionally causes something to happen (*Paul* in *Paul divorced Heather*; *Ziggy* in *Ziggy played guitar*). The agent is one kind of *thematic role*, describing the relationship between a **noun phrase** and a **verb**, in this case, the 'doer of the action'.

article In English, *a* and *the* are articles, words that combine with a **noun** to form a **noun phrase** (*a reptile, the cartoon*). Articles constitute a sub-class of **determiners**.

auxiliary verb A verb that supports the main **verb** of a sentence, hence the traditional description as a 'helping' verb. In English, auxiliaries include so-called modals: *can, could, shall, should, will, may, might, must* (*Sara will enjoy the Red Arrows air show*). Modal auxiliaries express modality, that is, possibility, necessity or futurity. Other auxiliaries include *do, have* and *be* (*The au pair has left again*). It is possible to have more than one auxiliary in a sentence: *Daniel might have eaten another ice-cream*. Further, auxiliaries, but not main verbs, can be inverted when forming questions:

Chris can have a third helping → Can Chris have a third helping?

bitransitive A bitransitive verb can appear in either transitive or intransitive sentence frames (see also **transitivity**). For example, *remember* can be transitive, as in *Lawrence finally remembered my new locker key*, or intransitive, as in *Lawrence finally remembered*.

case The case of a **noun** or **pronoun** marks its grammatical function within a sentence (e.g., **subject**, **object** or possessor). Typically, the form of a noun or pronoun will change according to its case. English has a simple case system with special forms mostly confined to pronouns, in order to mark nominative (subject), accusative (object) or genitive (possessor) case.

nominative	I	you	he	she	it	we	they	who	Colin
accusative	me	you	him	her	it	us	them	who(m)	Colin
genitive	my	your	his	her	its	our	their	whose	Colin's

English has no dative case (for indirect objects), though it is familiar to generations of school children tortured by Latin declensions. Other languages, like Latin, Russian or German, have much more elaborate case systems, marking many more aspects of meaning. Many languages also apply case marking beyond pronouns and nouns, to include **adjectives** and **articles** also.

Child Directed Speech (CDS) The special mode of speech, or register, adopted by adults and older children when speaking with young children. Parents, in particular, simplify and adapt their speech to meet the needs of very young children in a wide variety of ways. **Phonology**, vocabulary and **grammar**, and features of interaction, are all simplified and clarified in various ways.

clause Sentences can comprise a single clause or several clauses, where each clause is a kind of 'mini-sentence'. Each clause contains a **subject** and a **verb**. Simple sentences comprise a single clause, as in *Gary likes chocolate cake* (where *Gary* is the subject and *like* is the verb). You can identify how many clauses there are in a sentence by counting how many main verbs there are. For example, there are two clauses in: *Gary **likes** chocolate cake, but he **hates** anything with cream*. Another example of a multi-clause sentence, with main verbs highlighted, is: *The house that Jack **built** last year has **fallen** down already*. In this example, one clause is embedded within another: *The house [that Jack **built** last year] has **fallen** down*. See also **relative clause**.

common versus proper nouns Common nouns refer to a class of entities. The common noun *chair* does not pick out a particular piece of furniture, but can be used for any and all chairs (a class of entities). Proper nouns are used for *unique* entities, like *London* or *Madonna* or *Batman*. See also **noun**.

competence versus performance The knowledge we have of language (our competence) can be obscured by performance factors, including hesitations, slips of the tongue and faulty retrieval from memory (Chomsky, 1965). Hence, the errors we make in the act of producing language may conceal the fact that our underlying knowledge is perfect.

complement A complement is an expression that combines with a **head** word to form a syntactic phrase. In the **noun phrase**, *the man*, the head of the phrase is the noun, *man,* and the

302

complement is provided by the article, *the*. In *the very tall man*, the complement is *the very tall*. A *sentential* complement, meanwhile, is like a mini-sentence or **clause** embedded within another main clause. Consider *Shiho didn't expect that her mother would marry a woman*. The sentential complement is: *that her mother would marry a woman*.

consonants and vowels   Consonants are produced with some restriction of the airflow through the mouth. There might be a complete blockage of the air, as with /m, p, b/, where the lips are closed at the start (see **stop**). Or there might be a partial restriction, as with /f, v, s, z/, where the articulators are so close that friction can be heard (see **fricative**). Vowels, meanwhile, are produced without any restriction of the air flow through the vocal tract (see also Appendix 2, Pronunciation Guide).

copula   A **verb** that connects a **subject** with the rest of the sentence, in the absence of a main verb. In English the verb BE can be used as a copula, in its various forms (e.g., *am, is, are, were*). The copula can be thought of as the equals sign in the formula X = Y, as in: *Jill is fond of red wine* or *Jill and Wendy are sisters*.

count versus mass nouns   Some languages, including English, distinguish these two kinds of noun. Count nouns are used for objects or entities that can be individuated and counted, like apples, ideas or books. Mass nouns are used for substances that cannot be so readily perceived as anything but an unbounded mass, like wine, or sand, or tarmac. The difference is reflected in the grammar. For example, we can pluralize count nouns and say *three ideas*, but this cannot be done with mass nouns: **three water*.

demonstrative   Terms used to describe a location either relatively close to a speaker (*this, these, here*) or relatively far from them (*that, those, there*). Their interpretation is context-dependent, since their meaning is partly determined by the particular person who is speaking.

derivational morpheme   A **morpheme** added to a stem to produce a new word, which may belong to a different category from the stem. The morpheme *-er* added to the **verb** *believe* produces a **noun**, *believer*. Adding *-ment* to the verb *excite*, produces the noun *excitement*. See also **inflectional morpheme**.

determiner   A syntactic category of words used to modify **nouns**, but with no semantic content (meaning) of their own, including **articles** (*a, the*), **demonstratives** (*this, that*) and quantifiers (*each, every*). Determiners are often used to pick out the particular referent one is talking about (*a prince among men; this apple is rotten; every time we say goodbye*).

determiner phrase   A syntactic phrase comprising (minimally) a **determiner** and a **noun**: *a pickle; this day*. The determiner is described as the **head** of the phrase. Confusingly, phrases like this are also traditionally described as **noun phrases** (with the noun as head). The choice is a matter of dispute among linguists (we'd better leave them to it).

direct object   See **object**.

ecological validity   The extent to which a study reflects conditions in the real world. Laboratory experiments are often accused of having low ecological validity because the things people are

303

asked to do in test cubicles can bear little relation to real-life situations and behaviours. High ecological validity is desirable, because it allows one to generalize the findings of a study more readily and draw conclusions about people in general.

fricative   A class of **consonants** characterized by a hissing quality, caused by air pushing through a very narrow gap in the vocal tract. Consider the word-initial fricatives in the following: /f/ in *fricative*, /θ/ in *think* and /tʃ/ in *champ*. Now have some fricative fun with *She sells sea shells on the seashore.*

genitive   See **case**.

grammar   Traditionally, the grammar (or **syntax**) of a language comprises the rules that determine how words are put together to make sentences. In English, *The cat sat on the mat* is a grammatical sentence because the six words have been placed in a particular order. If I combine the same six words in a different way, the result can be ungrammatical: **Mat the the on sat cat.* In this latter case, the rules (or principles) of grammar have been violated. This traditional interpretation of grammar still has some currency. But you should be aware that grammar, as a term, is quite slippery. In this book I use this word in two ways: (1) to cover both **morphology** and syntax; and (2) as a substitute for syntax. Others use grammar in a very wide sense to embrace syntax, **phonology** and the **lexicon**, that is, the whole language system.

head   A head is an expression that can combine with **modifier** words to form a syntactic phrase. This determines the nature of the overall phrase. A particular head can have one or more modifiers or none at all. In the **noun phrase**, *Queen of Sheba*, the head of the phrase is the noun, *Queen*, and the modifier is provided by *of Sheba*. In the **verb phrase**, *meeting Shirley MacLaine*, the head is the verb, *meeting*, while the modifier is *Shirley MacLaine* (remember me, Shirley?).

heritability   A measure of the contribution of genetic factors to the differences observed between people. One way of estimating heritability is to compare identical twins (who share 100 per cent of their genes) with non-identical twins (who share 50 per cent of their genes). If genes are important for explaining variation in a particular behaviour, then identical twins will be more similar to one another than non-identical twins.

homophone   Two words which are pronounced in the same way, but which have different meanings (and often different spellings), for example, *bear* and *bare*, or *meat* and *meet*.

imperative   In English, the verb form that appears in sentences for giving orders. In *sit down!*, the verb appears as *sit* (not *sits* or *sitting*). In some languages, including Latin and Hungarian, the imperative is marked with its own set of **affixes**.

inflectional morpheme   Inflections are added (in most languages) to the ends of words to denote a particular grammatical function. For example, *-ed* added to the end of a verb indicates that the action took place in the past (compare *walk* and *walked*). Inflections do not change the grammatical category of the word they are attached to (*walk* and *walked* are both **verbs**). English has only eight different inflectional morphemes. Other languages have much richer inflectional morphology (e.g., Finnish and Russian). See also **morphology** and **derivational morpheme**.

Inflectional	Grammatical function	Example morpheme
-ing	progressive	Mary is eat*ing* a pineapple.
-ed	past tense	George call*ed* his mother.
-en	past participle	Brian has fall*en* in the water.
-s	3rd person singular present	Clive witter*s* on remorselessly.
-er	comparative	Mike is tall*er* than Catherine.
-est	superlative	Josephine has the nic*est* garden in Rugby.
-s	plural	Alice has six finger*s* on her left hand.
-'s	possessive	Gary'*s* music is delightful.

innateness (of language)   The property of being inborn or genetically determined. To what extent is language acquisition determined by the action of genes? It is not controversial to suggest that *something* about language development is innate. All typically developing human beings acquire language and so must be endowed with the capacity to do so. The problem is to determine what, precisely, is innate about language acquisition. The degree to which different behaviours are pre-programmed by genes constitutes a central concern within the life sciences generally. When applied to language, a particular interest has been to determine how far knowledge of **grammar** is innate. Those, like Chomsky, who emphasize innate properties are *nativists*.

instrumental   A grammatical **case**, used to mark the instrument or means by which an action is accomplished. English does not have instrumental case, but many other languages do (including Hungarian and Russian).

intonation   The melody of speech. Each utterance has a pitch contour, created by successive rises and falls in pitch. Very often, the end of an utterance is marked by a significant rise or fall in pitch level. Intonation contours can convey semantic or **syntactic** distinctions. Consider *Paula sings loudly when chopping onions.* Produced with a falling intonation at the end, we interpret this utterance as a statement. But produced with rising intonation at the end, it becomes a question. Incidentally, Paula believes that this prevents onions bringing tears to her eyes. I kid you not.

intransitivity   See **transitivity**.

irregular past tense verbs   See **regular and irregular past tense verbs**.

lexeme   Words can appear in different inflected forms: *dance, dances, dancing, danced.* These four **word forms** have, essentially, the same meaning, so they are different versions of a single lexeme, often written in capitals (DANCE). **Derivational morphology** produces new lexemes: DANCE → DANCER. **Inflectional morphology** produces new word forms, not new lexemes: *dance → danced.*

lexicon The mental dictionary comprising a speaker's knowledge of words and **morphemes**. Grammatical information about words is also included in the lexicon, such as **part of speech** (**noun**, **verb**) as well as information on **verb argument structure**.

linguistics The study of language *per se*, rather than the study of *a* language. An adult who succeeds in learning English, French, Warlpiri and Welsh can, legitimately, call themselves a linguist. But in an academic context, a linguist is someone who *studies* language. An academic linguist is interested in explaining what it means to know a language, and what knowledge of language might comprise. Critically, the study of linguistics can encompass *all* languages, in the quest to determine what aspects of language might be universal versus what might be idiosyncratic or particular to individual languages. The major branches of linguistics include: **syntax** (often used as a synonym for **grammar**); semantics (to do with patterns of meaning); and **phonology** (the sound system of a language).

main clause A sentence can comprise a main **clause** – the indispensible core of the sentence – and one or more **subordinate clauses**. In *On her wedding day, Kaoru needed help with her kimono*, the main clause is *Kaoru needed help with her kimono*.

mass nouns See **count versus mass nouns**.

mean length of utterance / MLU The average length of the utterances in a corpus. The MLU of child speech provides a very rough measure of syntactic development, on the assumption that longer utterances are more complex grammatically. However, the relationship between length and complexity breaks down beyond an MLU of about 4.0. An MLU greater than 1.0 indicates that the child has moved from single-word to multi-word speech. Brown (1973) provides a standard method for calculating MLU, based on the average number of **morphemes** (not words) per utterance.

metalinguistic awareness / knowledge / skill Knowledge *about* language and the ability to reflect on it. Metalinguistic awareness does not emerge in any serious way until the child reaches school age (about four or five years). Perhaps the best-known example is the development of so-called *phonological awareness* in children who are learning to read. One aspect of phonological awareness is the ability to recognize explicitly that, for example, the word *cat* has three constituent speech sounds, or **phonemes:** / k æ t /. The child needs metalinguistic awareness in order to analyse the sound structure of words in this way.

modifier See **head**.

morpheme See **morphology** and **inflectional morpheme**.

morphology The study of how words are constituted. *Morphemes* are the smallest units of meaning in a language. Words like *garden* or *swim* each constitute a single morpheme, because they correspond to a single unit of meaning that cannot be decomposed any further: *gar-* in *garden* does not have its own meaning independent of the whole word. *Garden* is a *free morpheme*, because it can stand alone as a word in its own right. *Bound morphemes*, on the other hand, cannot stand alone but are attached to other morphemes within a word. For example, *singing* comprises two morphemes: *sing + ing*, where *-ing* is a bound morpheme, used to denote an action that is ongoing or continuous; *foolishness* has three morphemes: *fool + ish + ness*. See also **inflectional morpheme** and **derivational morpheme**.

nativism   See **innateness**.

negation   A type of grammatical construction used to indicate that a proposition is false. In English, negation can be marked by *not* or *n't*, as in *Lill didn't wear a kimono at the wedding*. Negation can also be marked with *never*, *nobody* and *nothing*.

negative evidence   Information which signals that an utterance is ungrammatical. Parental corrections of child grammatical errors constitute a form of negative evidence.

nominative   See **case**.

noun   A syntactic category which typically denotes some kind of entity (*haggis, mountain, wig*). But many nouns do not refer to an easily identified object in the world (*invasion, sickness, frenzy*). Nouns are therefore defined in grammatical terms. For example, in English, nouns are identified as those words that can co-occur with **articles** in **noun phrases** (*a haggis, a frenzy*). See also **count versus mass nouns** and **common versus proper nouns**.

noun phrase   A syntactic phrase with a **noun** as its **head** (*man* in *a polite young man*; *excesses* in *the excesses of youth*). Noun phrases feature as the **subject** or the **objects** of a sentence. See also **determiner phrase**.

object   A grammatical category which is the **complement** of a **transitive verb** (*the biscuit* in *You ate my last biscuit*). We can distinguish direct and indirect objects. Where verbs take only one object, it is a direct object (*my last biscuit* in our example). Some verbs, like *give*, also have an indirect object:

You gave	my last biscuit	to the dog
	object	indirect object

In English, the object comes after the verb and is marked with objective **case**. *Tim volleyed **it** into the net*, is possible, because *it* has objective case, whereas **Tim volleyed **its** into the net* is disallowed, because *its* does not have objective case.

orthography   The written form of a language as codified in a set of symbols (graphemes). In many languages, graphemes are alphabetic, with each letter in the alphabet corresponding to particular **phonemes**. The grapheme–phoneme correspondence is highly predictable in some languages (like Italian), which means that if you see a particular sequence of letters, you will know how to pronounce it. In other languages, like English, the grapheme–phoneme correspondence is far less regular. For example, the letters *-ough* can be pronounced in several different ways. Compare *tough, through, plough, cough, hiccough, though*. Alphabets represent only one form of

307

writing system. In other systems, graphemes represent a whole syllable (*hiragana* in Japanese) or even whole words (*kanji* in Chinese).

overextension   The use of a word beyond its conventional range. For example, one child used the word *papa* to mean his father, but also used *papa* to denote his grandfather and mother. For the child, the extent of the word's meaning was broader than normal.

overgeneralization   An error in which a grammatical rule is applied beyond its normal range. **Verbs** like *stole* are described as **transitive**, because they require an **object**, as in *Lesley stole our bank book*. Sometimes children overgeneralize the transitive pattern, by applying it to intransitive verbs like *giggle* that do not require an object: *me* in *Don't giggle me*.

overregularization   The misapplication of a grammatical rule to irregular forms. For example, regular plural nouns are formed by adding *-s* to the singular (*one rocket, two rockets*). If *-s* is added to an irregular noun like *sheep*, an overregularized form is produced: *sheeps*. Overregularization is a particular kind of **overgeneralization**.

part of speech   Traditionally, the grammatical category of a word. Traditional grammars identify eight parts of speech in English, as below, though modern linguists offer different analyses (e.g., they generally include **determiners** as a separate part of speech).

noun	*book, truth, clock*
pronoun	*I, she, everyone*
verb	*hope, run, think*
adjective	*green, sloppy, cold*
adverb	*slowly, here, nevertheless*
preposition	*from, by, in*
conjunction	*and, but, because*
interjection	*ouch, alas, oh*

parse   The analysis of language, to establish the structure of words, phrases or sentences. Most frequently used to describe the analysis of sentences to determine their linguistic structure, but one could also parse a word into its constituent **morphemes**.

patient   An **object noun phrase** in a sentence with a thematic role, or meaning, that denotes the recipient of an action. In *Olga swallowed an aspirin*, the patient is *an aspirin*. The patient can also be described as one of a **verb's arguments**.

performance   See **competence**.

person   Traditional grammars of English recognize three persons: first, second and third. First person (*I, we*) includes the speaker. Second person (*you*) excludes the speaker, but includes the addressee. Third person (*he, she, it, they*) refers to neither the speaker nor the addressee, but rather, someone or something else.

phoneme   See **phonology** and Box 2.2.

phonology   The sound system of a language. Each language deploys a repertoire of sounds that are used to convey meaning. The smallest unit of sound is known as the *phoneme* (see Box 2.2) and is written between slash brackets (e.g., /b/). Note that /b/ denotes a meaningful unit of sound, it does not – despite appearances – denote the English letter 'b' (that is a matter of **orthography**, not phonology). If two sounds are *contrastive*, then they will constitute separate phonemes in a language. Consider the words *bat* and *mat*. These two words are identical phonologically, that is, they sound identical, except for the initial sound. The physical difference between the two sounds /b/ and /m/ is sufficient to denote a difference of meaning. Hence, /b/ and /m/ are distinct **phonemes** in English.

pitch   See **intonation**.

possessive   A structure that indicates possession. In English, possession can be marked with a possessive **suffix** which appears in written English as an apostrophe followed by S: *Yvonne's government report*. Having said that, the days of the apostrophe seem to be numbered. If it appears at all, it is often in the wrong place. My favourite is *Mr Cheap Potatoe's*, a shop I used to frequent. Farewell, Apostrophe! Rest in peace.

poverty of the stimulus   The idea that the linguistic environment of the child is impoverished. On this nativist view, the input does not contain sufficient information to allow for the acquisition of grammar. In consequence, **innate** knowledge must be invoked to explain how the child nevertheless manages to acquire language.

pragmatics   The study of how people use language. Pragmatic factors include the context in which an utterance is produced and affect our interpretation of sentences. If I say 'It's cold in here' you are unlikely to believe that I'm making a factual statement about the ambient temperature. You are more likely to interpret it as a request to close the window or turn up the heating.

prefix   A **morpheme** that is added to the left of a word form (as written). In *undo*, the prefix *un-* is added to *do*. In *devalue*, the prefix *de-* is added to *value*.

preposition   A grammatical category typically used to denote location or manner (e.g., *in, of, by, for, under, with, from, at, on*). In English, prepositions can usually be modified by *straight* or *right* (*right under, straight from*). A prepositional phrase has a preposition as its head, as in *over the top, under the wire* or *through the middle*.

pronoun   A word that can be used as a substitute for a **noun**. English pronouns include *I, you, he, she, it, we, they*. In the sentence, *Jane trapped a thief in her car*, we can substitute the pronoun *she* for *Jane*: *She trapped a thief in her car* (well done, Jane). Notice that pronouns do not have an intrinsic meaning. We need to refer to the context (linguistic or social) in order to work out which person *she* refers to.

proper nouns   See **common versus proper nouns**.

regular and irregular past tense verb   Regular verbs follow a default pattern. In English, if I want to talk about past events, I can add *-ed* to the end of a regular verb (*danced, called, wanted*). This allows me to say things about the past, like: *I could've danced all night*. If you consider how *-ed* is pronounced, you will discover that, **phonologically**, there are three possibilities: /t/ as in *danced*; /d/ as in *called*; or /ɪd/ as in *wanted*. Most verbs in English are regular, but some verbs are irregular: they do not follow this simple default pattern: *buy* changes to *bought* (not **buyed*); *go* changes to *went* (not **goed*); and *eat* changes to *ate* (not **eated*).

relative clause   A **clause** that 'relates to' or modifies an expression. In *The neighbours* (*who thought we were out*), the relative clause is bracketed and modifies the noun phrase *the neighbours*. Relative clauses in English can be introduced with a relative pronoun (e.g., *who, that, which*).

segmentation problem   The problem of identifying individual linguistic units, like **phoneme** or word, from continuous speech. This is problematic because, physically, there are often no clear boundaries to mark the beginning or end of individual phonemes or words. The child must nevertheless identify the boundaries between linguistic units.

sentence   A **clause** which can stand by itself and which comprises a **subject noun phrase** followed by a **verb phrase**. In written English, the independence of sentences is marked by starting a new sentence with a capital letter and terminating it with a full stop.

sentential complement   A kind of **subordinate clause**. In *I think that Mo wants to be a burlesque queen*, the sentential complement is *that Mo wants to be a burlesque queen*. See also **complement**.

stop   A consonant sound in which the flow of air leaving the mouth is completely blocked for a very brief period. The stop sounds of English include /b, p, m, t, d, n, g, k/ (see also the Pronunciation Guide).

subject   A grammatical category which takes so-called nominative case marking, which in English can be seen in the choice of **pronouns**: *He* cooks really well. **Him* cooks really well. **His* cooks really well. Only *he* is allowed in subject position, because it carries the correct nominative case. In English, the subject is positioned at the start of a sentence. We can also identify the subject from the fact that it agrees with the **verb**. That is, the ending on the verb is dictated by the properties of the subject. In *Gary reads Private Eye*, we add *-s* to the verb to mark agreement with the singular third person subject *Gary*. In *They read Private Eye*, the uninflected verb form *read* now agrees with the plural subject *they*.

subordinate clause   A **clause** which appears as part of another **main clause**. In *Shiho wanted to go shopping in London*, the subordinate clause is *to go shopping in London*.

suffix   A **morpheme** that is added to the right of a word form (when written). In *walked*, the suffix *-ed* is added to *walk* (see **inflectional morpheme**). In *madness*, the suffix *-ness* is added to *mad* (see **derivational morpheme**).

syllable   A phonological unit of speech, whose nucleus is usually a **vowel**. There can be optional consonants both before (onset) and after (coda) the nucleus. The word *eye* comprises a single syllable with just a vowel nucleus (no onset or coda). *Pie* has both an onset, /p/ and a nucleus, while *ape* has both a vowel and coda, /p/ (ignore spellings of *eye*, *pie* and *ape* and focus on how they sound). *Cat* meanwhile has it all: onset–nucleus–coda: /kæt/. There are typically ten syllables in each line of a Shakespeare sonnet. Try counting them in the first line of Sonnet 18: *Shall I compare thee to a summer's day?*

syntax   The rules that determine how words are put together to make sentences. If you think this sounds like grammar, you'd be right. But linguists sometimes use grammar as an umbrella term for other aspects of language. See the entry under **grammar** to discover how these two terms differ.

transitivity   Verbs like *take*, *eat* or *kick*, which require a direct **object**, are transitive. Compare *Diana watered her garden* with the odd *Diana watered. The verb *water* implies that something is *watered* (the object). Other verbs describe states or activities which are not directed towards anything, and which therefore do not need an object. These verbs are intransitive. Compare *Sally slept* with **Sally slept the bed*. The verb *sleep* is intransitive and so does not require an object (*the bed*).

verb   Verbs are a syntactic category, often described as 'doing words' or 'actions', as in: *Sue* ***cooks*** *really well* or *Jim* ***cleaned*** *the brass door plate*. But verbs are not confined to observable actions. For example, they can also be used to denote states (*believe*) and sensations (*feel*). What unites all verbs is that they can take inflections, like *-ed*, *-s* or *-ing* (*governed*, *governs*, *governing*). In essence, verbs constitute the heart of a sentence. **Subject** and **object** are **complements** of the verb in a sentence.

verb argument structure   The arguments in a sentence describe the different roles played by the participants. The sentence, *André lost some weight at last*, comprises a predicate (the verb *lose*) and two arguments (*André* and *some weight at last*). The argument structure of a verb dictates how many arguments are required, and what roles they fulfil. For example, the verb *sleep* requires only one argument (the person sleeping), as in *Richard slept* (**Richard slept the bed* is not possible). Other verbs require three arguments, for example, *give*, as in *Martha's voice gives me the creeps*. We need three arguments: the giver (*Martha*), the given (*the creeps*) and a recipient (*me*).

verb phrase   A syntactic phrase which is **headed** by a **verb**. The verb phrase is bracketed in the following: *Dante* (*has an unusual name*) or *Isaac* (*plays computer games all day*). The verb phrase can comprise a verb plus its arguments (see **verb argument structure**). For example, the verb *hold* requires one argument: *hold* (*the fort*). *Deliver* requires two arguments, as in *deliver* (*the pizza*) (*to Gabriel*).

voiced and voiceless sounds   A voiced sound is produced when the vocal cords (located in your Adam's apple) are vibrating. Voiceless sounds are produced without vocal cord vibration. Place your fingers on your Adam's apple and try alternating between the voiceless /f/ and the voiced /v/.

vowel   See **consonants and vowels**.

word form   See **lexeme**.

References

Abbot-Smith, K., Imai, M., Durrant, S. & Nurmsoo, E. (2017). The role of timing and prototypical causality on how preschoolers fast-map novel verb meanings. *First Language, 37(2)*, 186–204.

Abbot-Smith, K. & Tomasello, M. (2009). The influence of frequency and semantic similarity on how children learn grammar. *First Language, 30(1)*, 1–23.

Abe, K. & Watanabe, D. (2011). Songbirds possess the spontaneous ability to discriminate syntactic rules. *Nature Neuroscience, 14(8)*, 1067–1074.

Adams, A.M. & Gathercole, S.E. (2000). Limitations in working memory: Implications for language development. *International Journal of Language and Communication Disorders, 35(1)*, 95–116.

Adger, D. (2003). *Core syntax: A minimalist approach.* Oxford: Oxford University Press.

Aitchison, J. (1998). *The articulate mammal: An introduction to psycholinguistics* (4th ed.). London: Routledge.

Aitchison, J. (2010). *Teach yourself linguistics* (7th ed.). London: Hodder Headline.

Akhtar, N. (2005). The robustness of learning through overhearing. *Developmental Science, 8(2)*, 199–209.

Akhtar, N., Callanan, M., Pullum, G.K. & Scholz, B.C. (2004). Learning antecedents for anaphoric one. *Cognition, 93(2)*, 141–145.

Akhtar, N., Dunham, F. & Dunham, P.J. (1991). Directive interactions and early vocabulary development: The role of joint attentional focus. *Journal of Child Language, 18*, 41–49.

Aksu-Koç, A. (1997). Verb inflection in Turkish: A preliminary analysis of the early stage. In W.U. Dressler (Ed.), *Studies in pre- and proto morphology* (pp. 127–139). Vienna: Verlag Der Österreichischen Akademie der Wissenschaften.

Aksu-Koç, A. & Slobin, D.I. (1985). The acquisition of Turkish. In D.I. Slobin (Ed.), *The cross-linguistic study of language acquisition (Vol. 1)* (pp. 839–878). Hillsdale, NJ: Erlbaum.

Albin, D.D. & Echols, C.H. (1996). Stressed and word-final syllables in infant-directed speech. *Infant Behavior & Development, 19(4)*, 401–418.

Albirini, A. (2015). Factors affecting the acquisition of plural morphology in Jordanian Arabic. *Journal of Child Language, 42(4)*, 734–762.

Albright, A. & Hayes, B. (2003). Rules vs. analogy in English past tenses: A computational/experimental study. *Cognition, 90(2)*, 119–161.

Ambridge, B. (2010). Children's judgments of regular and irregular novel past-tense forms: New data on the English past-tense debate. *Developmental Psychology, 46(6)*, 1497–1504.

Ambridge, B. (2013). How do children restrict their linguistic generalizations?: An (un-) grammaticality judgment study. *Cognitive Science, 37(3)*, 508–543.

Ambridge, B., Bidgood, A., Twomey, K.E., Pine, J.M., Rowland, C.F. & Freudenthal, D. (2015). Preemption versus entrenchment: Towards a construction-general solution to the problem of the retreat from verb argument structure overgeneralization. *PLoS One, 10(4)*, e0123723.

Ambridge, B., Kidd, E., Rowland, C.F. & Theakston, A.L. (2015). The ubiquity of frequency effects in first language acquisition. *Journal of Child Language, 42(2)*, 239–273.

Ambridge, B., Pine, J.M. & Lieven, E.V.M. (2014). Child language acquisition: Why universal grammar doesn't help. *Language, 90(3)*, e53–e90.

Ambridge, B., Pine, J.M., Rowland, C.F. & Young, C.R. (2008). The effect of verb semantic class and verb frequency (entrenchment) on children's and adults' graded judgements of argument-structure overgeneralization errors. *Cognition, 106(1)*, 87–129.

Ambridge, B. & Rowland, C.F. (2013). Experimental methods in studying child language acquisition. *WIREs Cognitive Science*. doi: 10.1002/wcs.1215.

Ambridge, B., Rowland C.F. & Pine, J.M. (2008). Is structure dependence an innate constraint? New experimental evidence from children's complex-question production. *Cognitive Science, 32(1)*, 222–255.

Ambridge, B., Rowland, C.F., Theakston, A. & Tomasello, M. (2006). Comparing different accounts of children's non-inversion errors in object wh-questions: What experimental data can tell us? *Journal of Child Language, 30(3)*, 519–557.

Ambridge, B., Theakston, A.L., Lieven, E.V.M & Tomasello, M. (2006). The distributed learning effect for children's acquisition of an abstract syntactic construction. *Cognitive Development, 21(2)*, 174–193.

Anderson, D.R. & Pempek, T.A. (2005). Television and very young children. *American Behavioral Scientist, 48(5)*, 505–522.

Anderson, J. (1983). *The architecture of cognition*. Cambridge, MA: Harvard University Press.

Anglin, J.M. (1993). Knowing versus learning words. *Monographs of the Society for Research in Child Development, 58*, 176–186.

Archer, S.L., Zamunerb, T., Engel, K., Fais, L. & Curtin, S. (2016). Infants' discrimination of consonants: Interplay between word position and acoustic saliency. *Language Learning and Development, 12(1)*, 60–78.

Archibald, L.M.D. & Gathercole, S.E. (2007). Nonword repetition and serial recall: Equivalent measures of verbal short-term memory? *Applied Psycholinguistics, 28(4)*, 587–606.

Argus, R., Laalo, J. & Johansen Ijäs, K. (2014). Acquisition of compound nouns in Estonian, Finnish and Sami: Similarities and differences. *The Central and Eastern European Online Library, 08–09*, 648–669.

Arunachalam, S. (2013). Two-year-olds can begin to acquire verb meanings in socially impoverished contexts. *Cognition, 129*, 569–573.

Asano, T., Kojima, T., Matsuzawa, T., Kubota, K. & Murofushi, K. (1982). Object and colour naming in chimpanzees (Pan troglodytes). *Proceedings of the Japan Academy Series B – Physical and Biological Sciences, 58(5)*, 118–122.

314

Aslin, R.N., Shukla, M. & Emberson, L.L. (2015). Hemodynamic correlates of cognition in human infants. *Annual Review of Psychology, 66,* 349–379.

Au, T.K.F., Dapretto, M. & Song, Y.K. (1994). Input versus constraints: Early word acquisition in Korean and English. *Journal of Memory and Language, 33(5),* 567–582.

Bachelard, G. (1960/1971). *The poetics of reverie: Childhood, language, and the cosmos* (translated by D. Russell). Boston, MA: Beacon Press.

Baillargeon, R. (1987). Object permanence in 3½-month-old and 4½-month-old infants. *Developmental Psychology, 23(5),* 655–664.

Baillargeon, R., Li, J., Luo, Y.Y. & Wang, S.H. (2006). Under what conditions do infants detect continuity violations? *Attention and Performance, 20,* 163–188.

Baker, P. & Eversley, J. (Eds.) (2000). *Multilingual capital: The languages of London's schoolchildren and their relevance to economic, social and educational policies.* London: Battlebridge.

Bakker, I., MacGregor, L.J., Pulvermüller, F. & Shtyrov, Y. (2013). Past tense in the brain's time: Neurophysiological evidence for dual-route processing of past-tense verbs. *NeuroImage, 71,* 187–195.

Bannard, C. & Lieven, E. (2012). Formulaic language in L1 acquisition. *Annual Review of Applied Linguistics, 32,* 3–16.

Barnes, S., Gutfreund, M., Satterly, D. & Wells, G. (1983). Characteristics of adult speech which predict children's language development. *Journal of Child Language, 10(1),* 65–84.

Barr, R. & Wyss, N. (2008). Reenactment of televised content by 2-year olds: Toddlers use language learned from television to solve a difficult imitation problem. *Infant Behavior and Development, 31(4),* 696–703.

Barrett, M. (1995). Early lexical development. In P. Fletcher & B. MacWhinney (Eds.), *The handbook of child language* (pp. 362–392). Oxford: Blackwell.

Bates, E., Dale, P.S. & Thal, D. (1995). Individual differences and their implications for theories of language development. In P. Fletcher & B. MacWhinney (Eds.), *The emergence of language* (pp. 29–79). Mahwah, NJ: Lawrence Erlbaum.

Bates, E. & Goodman, J.C. (1997). On the inseparability of grammar and the lexicon: Evidence from acquisition, aphasia and real-time processing. *Language and Cognitive Processes, 12(5–6),* 507–584.

Bates, E. & Goodman, J.C. (1999). On the emergence of grammar from the lexicon. In B. MacWhinney (Ed.), *The emergence of language.* Mahwah, NJ: Lawrence Erlbaum.

Bates, E. & MacWhinney, B. (1989). Functionalism and the competition model. In B. MacWhinney & E. Bates (Eds.), *The crosslinguistic study of sentence processing* (pp. 3–76). Cambridge: Cambridge University Press.

Bates, E., Marchman, V.A., Thal, D., Fenson, L., Dale, P., Reznick, J.S., Reilly, J. & Hartung, J. (1994). Developmental and stylistic variation in the composition of early vocabulary. *Journal of Child Language, 21(1),* 85–123.

Bavin, E.L. (1992). The acquisition of Warlpiri. In D.I. Slobin (Ed.), *The crosslinguistic study of language acquisition (Vol. 3).* Hillsdale, NJ: Lawrence Erlbaum.

Becker, J.A. (1994). 'Sneak-shoes', 'sworders', and 'nose-beards': A case study of lexical innovation. *First Language, 14(2),* 195–211.

Beckers, G.J.L. (2011). Bird speech perception and vocal production: A comparison with humans. *Human Biology*, *83(2)*, 191–212.

Behrens, H. (Ed.) (2008). *Corpora in language acquisition research: History, methods, perspectives.* Amsterdam: John Benjamins.

Behrens, H. (2009). Usage-based and emergentist approaches to language acquisition. *Linguistics*, *47(2)*, 383–411.

Bekoff, M. (2013). We are animals and therein lies hope for a better future. Blog post. *Psychology Today*. www.psychologytoday.com/blog/animal–emotions/201312/we–are–animals–and–therein–lies–hope–better–future. Accessed December 1, 2015.

Benasich, A.A., Choudhury, N., Friedman, J.T., Realpe-Bonilla, T., Chojnowska, C. & Gou, Z. (2006). The infant as a prelinguistic model for language learning impairments: Predicting from event-related potentials to behavior. *Neuropsychologia*, *44(3)*, 396–411.

Berent, I. & Pinker, S. (2008). Compound formation is constrained by morphology: A reply to Seidenberg, MacDonald & Haskell. *The Mental Lexicon*, *3(2)*, 176–187.

Berko, J. (1958). The child's learning of English morphology. *Word*, *14*, 150–177.

Berman, R. (1985). The acquisition of Hebrew. In D.I. Slobin (Ed.), *The crosslinguistic study of language acquisition (Vol. 1)*. Hillsdale, NJ: Lawrence Erlbaum.

Berman, R. (1987). A developmental route: Learning about the form and use of complex nominals in Hebrew. *Linguistics*, *25*, 1057–1085.

Berman, R. & Clark, E.V. (1989). Learning to use compounds for contrast: Data from Hebrew. *First Language*, *9(3)*, 247–270.

Berwick, R.C. & Chomsky, N. (2016). *Why only us: Language and evolution*. Cambridge, MA: MIT Press.

Berwick, R.C., Okanoya, K., Beckers, G.J.L., Bolhuis, J.J. (2011). Songs to syntax: The linguistics of birdsong. *Trends in Cognitive Science*, *15*, 113–121.

Berwick, R.C., Pietroski, P., Yankama, B. & Chomsky, N. (2011). Poverty of the stimulus revisited. *Cognitive Science*, *35(7)*, 1207–1242.

Best, C.T. & McRoberts, G.W. (1989). Phonological influences on the perception of native and non-native speech contrasts. Paper presented at the biennial meeting of the Society for Research in Child Development.

Best, C.T. & McRoberts, G.W. (2003). Infant perception of non-native consonant contrasts that adults assimilate in different ways. *Language and Speech*, *46*, 183–216.

Best, C.T., McRoberts, G.W., Lafleur, R. & Silverisenstadt, J. (1995). Divergent developmental patterns for infants' perception of two nonnative consonant contrasts. *Infant Behavior & Development*, *18(3)*, 339–350.

Best, C.T., McRoberts, G.W. & Sithole, N.M. (1988). Examination of perceptual reorganization for nonnative speech contrasts: Zulu click discrimination by English-speaking adults and infants. *Journal of Experimental Psychology*, *14(3)*, 345–360.

Bialystok, E. (1997). The structure of age: In search of barriers to second language acquisition. *Second Language Research*, *13*, 116–137.

Bialystok, E. & Hakuta, K. (1994). *In other words: The science and psychology of second language acquisition.* New York: Basic Books.

Bialystok, E. & Hakuta, K. (1999). Confounded age: Linguistic and cognitive factors in age differences for second language acquisition. In D. Birdsong (Ed.), *Second language acquisition and the critical period hypothesis.* Mahwah, NJ: Lawrence Erlbaum.

Bialystok, E. & Miller, B. (1999). The problem of age in second language acquisition: Influences from language, task, and structure. *Bilingualism: Language and Cognition, 2(2),* 127–145.

Birdsong, D. (1992). Ultimate attainment in second language acquisition. *Language, 68,* 706–755.

Birjandi, P. & Nasrolahi, A. (2012). Negative evidence in Iranian children: How do Iranian parents correct their children's errors? *Journal of Language Teaching and Research, 3(4),* 700–706.

Bishop, D.V.M., Adams, C.V. & Norbury, C.F. (2006). Distinct genetic influences on grammar and phonological short-term memory deficits: Evidence from 6-year-old twins. *Genes Brain and Behavior, 5(2),* 158–169.

Blom, E. & Paradis, J. (2016). Introduction: Special issue on age effects in child language acquisition. *Journal of Child Language, 43(3),* 473–478.

Bloom, L. (1973). *One word at a time: The use of single-word utterances before syntax.* The Hague: Mouton.

Bloom, L., Hood, L. & Lightbown, P.M. (1974). Imitation in language development: If, when, and why. *Cognitive Psychology, 6(3),* 380–420.

Bloom, L., Tinker, E. & Margulis, C. (1993). The words children learn: Evidence against a noun bias in early vocabularies. *Cognitive Development, 8,* 431–450.

Bloom, P. (2000). *How children learn the meanings of words.* Cambridge, MA: MIT Press.

Bloom, P. (2004). Can a dog learn a word? *Science, 304(5677),* 1605–1606.

Bloom, P. & Markson, L. (1998). Capacities underlying word learning. *Trends in Cognitive Sciences, 2,* 67–73.

Bohannon, J.N., Padgett, R.J., Nelson, K.E. & Mark, M. (1996). Useful evidence on negative evidence. *Developmental Psychology, 32(3),* 551–555.

Bohannon, J.N. & Stanowicz, L. (1988). The issue of negative evidence: Adult responses to children's language errors. *Developmental Psychology, 24,* 684–689.

Bohannon, J.N. & Warren-Leubecker, A. (1985). Theoretical approaches to language acquisition. In J. Berko Gleason (Ed.), *The development of language* (pp. 173–226). Columbus, OH: C.E. Merrill.

Bongaerts, T., Planken, B. & Schils, E. (1995). Can late starters attain a native accent in a foreign language? A test of the critical period hypothesis. In D. Singleton & Z. Lengyel (Eds.), *The age factor in second language acquisition: A critical look at the critical period hypothesis.* Clevedon: Multilingual Matters.

Booth, A.E. & Waxman, S.R. (2008). Taking stock as theories of word learning take shape. *Developmental Science, 11(2),* 186–194.

Booth, A.E. & Waxman, S.R. (2009). A horse of a different color: Specifying with precision infants' mappings of novel nouns and adjectives. *Child Development, 80(1),* 15–22.

Borgström, K., Torkildsen, J. von Koss & Lindgren, M. (2015). Substantial gains in word learning ability between 20 and 24 months: A longitudinal ERP study. *Brain and Language, 149,* 33–45.

Bornstein, M.H., Cote, L.R., Maital, S., Painter, K., Park, S.Y., Pascual, L., Venuti, P. & Vyt, A. (2004). Cross-linguistic analysis of vocabulary in young children: Spanish, Dutch, French, Hebrew, Italian, Korean, and American English. *Child Development, 75(4)*, 1115–1139.

Botha, R.P. (1989). *Challenging Chomsky: The generative garden game.* Oxford: Basil Blackwell.

Bowerman, M. (1982). Reorganizational processes in lexical and syntactic development. In E. Wanner & L.R. Gleitman (Eds.), *Language acquisition: The state of the art.* Cambridge: Cambridge University Press.

Bowey, J.A. (2005). Grammatical sensitivity: Its origins and potential contribution to early word reading skill. *Journal of Experimental Child Psychology, 90(4)*, 318–343.

Boyd, J.K. & Goldberg, A.E. (2012). Young children fail to fully generalize a novel argument structure construction when exposed to the same input as older learners. *Journal of Child Language, 39(3)*, 457–481.

Braine, M.D.S. (1963). The ontogeny of English phrase structure: The first phase. *Language, 39(1)*, 1–13.

Braine, M.D.S., Brooks, P.J., Cowan, N., Samuels, M.C. & Tamis-LeMonda, C.S. (1993). The development of categories at the semantics syntax interface. *Cognitive Development, 8(4)*, 465–494.

Brand, R.J. & Shallcross, W.L. (2008). Infants prefer motionese to adult-directed action. *Developmental Science, 11(6)*, 853–861.

Brandt, S., Diessel, H. & Tomasello, M. (2008). The acquisition of German relative clauses: A case study. *Journal of Child Language, 35(2)*, 325–348.

Broca, P. (1865). Sur le siège de la faculté du langage articulé suivies d'une observation d'aphémie, *Bulletin de la Société Anatomique de Paris, 6*, 330.

Broen, P.A. (1972). The verbal environment of the language-learning child. *Monograph of the American Speech and Hearing Association, 17.*

Brooks, P.J. & Kempe, V. (2012). *Language development.* Chichester: BPS Blackwell.

Brooks, P.J. & Tomasello, M. (1999). How children constrain their argument structure constructions. *Language, 75(4)*, 720–738.

Brooks, P.J., Tomasello, M., Dodson, K. & Lewis, L.B. (1999). Young children's overgeneralizations with fixed transitivity verbs. *Child Development, 70(6)*, 1325–1337.

Brooks, P.J. & Zizak, O. (2002). Does pre-emption help children learn verb transitivity? *Journal of Child Language, 29(4)*, 759–781.

Brown, G.D.A. & Watson, F.L. (1987). First in, first out: Word learning age and spoken word frequency as predictors of word familiarity and word naming latency. *Memory and Cognition, 15(3)*, 208–216.

Brown, R. (1958). *Words and things: An introduction to language.* New York: Free Press.

Brown, R. (1973). *A first language.* London: George Allen & Unwin.

Brown, R. & Bellugi, U. (1964). Three processes in the child's acquisition of syntax. *Harvard Educational Review, 34*, 133–151.

Brown, R. & Hanlon, C. (1970). Derivational complexity and order of acquisition in child speech. In R. Brown (Ed.), *Psycholinguistics.* New York: Free Press.

Bruer, J.T. (2001). A critical and sensitive period primer. In D.B. Bailey, J.T. Bruer, F.J. Symons & J.W. Lichtman (Eds.), *Critical thinking about critical periods*. Baltimore, MD: Paul Brookes.

Buchan, H. & Jones, C. (2014). Phonological reduction in maternal speech in northern Australian English: Change over time. *Journal of Child Language, 41(4)*, 725–755.

Buck-Gengler, C.J., Menn, L. & Healy, A.F. (2004). What 'Mice Trap' tells us about the mental lexicon. *Brain and Language, 90(1–3)*, 453–464.

Buttelmann, D., Carpenter, M., Call, J. & Tomasello, M. (2007). Enculturated chimpanzees imitate rationally. *Developmental Science, 10(4)*, F31–F38.

Bybee, J. (2008). Usage-based grammar and second language acquisition. In P. Robinson & N.C. Ellis (Eds.), *Handbook of cognitive linguistics and second language acquisition* (pp. 216–236). New York: Routledge.

Bybee, J.L. & Scheibmann, J. (1999). The effect of usage on degrees of constituency: The reduction of *don't* in English. *Linguistics, 37(4)*, 575–596.

Čadková, L. (2015). Do they speak language? *Biosemiotics, 8(1)*, 9–27.

Cameron-Faulkner, T. (2012). A functional account of verb use in the early stages of English multiword development. *Journal of Child Language, 39(4)*, 885–897.

Cameron-Faulkner, T., Lieven, E. & Tomasello, M. (2003). A construction based analysis of child directed speech. *Cognitive Science, 27(6)*, 843–873.

Cameron-Faulkner, T. & Noble, C. (2013). A comparison of book text and Child Directed Speech. *First Language, 33(3)*, 268–279.

Campbell, R.N. (1986). Language acquisition and cognition. In P. Fletcher & M. Garman (Eds.), *Language acquisition* (2nd ed.). (pp. 30–48). Cambridge: Cambridge University Press.

Campbell, R.N. & Grieve, R. (1982). Royal investigations of the origin of language. *Historiographia Linguistica IX, 1(2)*, 43–74.

Caramazza, A. & Yeni-Komshian, G.H. (1974). Voice onset time in two French dialects. *Journal of Phonetics, 2*, 239–245.

Carey, S. (1978). The child as word learner. In M. Halle, G. Miller & J. Bresnan (Eds.), *Linguistic theory and psychological reality*. Cambridge, MA: MIT Press.

Carey, S. (1985). *Conceptual change in childhood*. Cambridge, MA: MIT Press.

Carey, S. & Bartlett, E. (1978). Acquiring a single new word. *Papers and Reports on Child Language Development, 15*, 17–29.

Cattell, R. (2000). *Children's language: Consensus and controversy*. London: Cassell.

Cazden, C.B. (1965). Environmental assistance to the child's acquisition of grammar. Unpublished PhD thesis, Harvard University, Cambridge, MA.

Cerri, G., Cabinio, M., Blasi, V., Borroni, P., Iadanza, A., Fava, E., Fornia, L., Ferpozzi, V., Riva, M., Casarotti, A., Boneschi, F.M., Falini, A. & Bello, L. (2015). The Mirror Neuron System and the strange case of Broca's Area. *Human Brain Mapping, 36*, 1010–1027.

Chater, N. & Manning, C.D. (2006). Probabilistic models of language processing and acquisition. *Trends in Cognitive Sciences, 10(7)*, 335–344.

Chater, N., Tenenbaum, J.B. & Yuille, A. (2006). Probabilistic models of cognition: Conceptual foundations. *Trends in Cognitive Sciences, 10(7)*, 287–291.

Chen, J., Rossum, D. & ten Cate, C. (2015). Artificial grammar learning in zebra finches and human adults: XYX versus XXY. *Animal Cognition, 18(1)*, 151–164.

Cheshire, J. (1982). *Variation in an English dialect: A sociolinguistic study.* Cambridge: Cambridge University Press.

Choi, S. (1998). Verbs in early lexical and syntactic development in Korean. *Linguistics, 36(4)*, 755–780.

Cholewiak, D.M., Sousa-Lima, R.S. & Cerchio, S. (2013). Humpback whale song hierarchical structure: Historical context and discussion of current classification issues. *Marine Mammal Science, 29(3)*, E312–E332.

Chomsky, N. (1957). *Syntactic structures.* The Hague: Mouton.

Chomsky, N. (1959). Review of *Verbal behavior* by B.F. Skinner, *Language, 35(1)*, 26–58.

Chomsky, N. (1965). *Aspects of the theory of syntax.* Cambridge, MA: MIT Press.

Chomsky, N. (1966). *Cartesian linguistics: A chapter in the history of rationalist thought.* New York: Harper & Row.

Chomsky, N. (1972). *Problems of knowledge and freedom.* London: Fontana.

Chomsky, N. (1975). *Reflections on language.* London: Temple Smith.

Chomsky, N. (1980a). *Rules and representations.* Oxford: Blackwell.

Chomsky, N. (1980b). Initial states and steady states. In M. Piattelli-Palmarini (Ed.), *Language and learning: The debate between Jean Piaget and Noam Chomsky.* Cambridge, MA: Harvard University Press.

Chomsky, N. (1981). *Lectures on government and binding.* Dordrecht: Foris.

Chomsky, N. (1985). *Turning the tide: U.S. intervention in Central America and the struggle for peace.* London: Pluto Press.

Chomsky, N. (1988). *Language and problems of knowledge: The Managua lectures.* Cambridge, MA: MIT Press.

Chomsky, N. (1995). *The minimalist program.* Cambridge, MA: MIT Press.

Chomsky, N. (1999). On the nature, use, and acquisition of language. In W.C. Ritchie & T.K. Bhatia (Eds.), *Handbook of child language acquisition* (pp. 33–54). San Diego, CA: Academic Press.

Chomsky, N. (2005). *Imperial ambitions: Conversations with Noam Chomsky on the post 9/11 world: Interviews with David Barsamian.* London: Hamish Hamilton.

Chomsky, N. (2011). Language and other cognitive systems: What is special about language? *Language Learning and Development, 7(4)*, 263–278.

Chomsky, N. (2012). *The science of language.* Cambridge: Cambridge University Press.

Chouinard, M.M. & Clark, E.V. (2003). Adult reformulations of child errors as negative evidence. *Journal of Child Language, 30(3)*, 637–669.

Chow, K.L. & Stewart, D.L. (1972). Reversal of structural and functional effects of long-term visual deprivation in cats. *Experimental Neurobiology, 34*, 409–433.

Christensen, J.B. (1984). The perception of voice-onset-time: A cross-language study of American English and Danish. *Annual Report of the Institute of Phonetics University of Copenhagen, 18*, 163–184.

Cimpian, A. & Markman, E.M. (2005). The absence of a shape bias in children's word learning. *Developmental Psychology, 41(6)*, 1003–1019.

Clahsen, H., Hadler, M. & Weyerts, H. (2004). Speeded production of inflected words in children and adults. *Journal of Child Language, 31(3)*, 683–712.

Clancy, P. (1985). The acquisition of Japanese. In D.I. Slobin (Ed.), *The crosslinguistic study of language acquisition (Vol. 1)*. Hillsdale, NJ: Lawrence Erlbaum.

Clancy, P. (1989). A case study in language socialisation: Korean wh-questions. *Discourse Processes, 12*, 169–191.

Clark, A. & Lappin, S. (2011). *Linguistic nativism and the poverty of the stimulus*. Oxford: Wiley Blackwell.

Clark, E.V. (1973). What's in a word? On the child's acquisition of semantics in his first language. In T.E. Moore (Ed.), *Cognitive development and the acquisition of language* (pp. 65–110). New York: Academic Press.

Clark, E.V. (1979). Building a vocabulary: Words for objects, actions, and relations. In P. Fletcher & M. Garman (Eds.), *Language acquisition* (pp. 149–160). Cambridge: Cambridge University Press.

Clark, E.V. (1981). Lexical innovations: How children learn to create new words. In W. Deutsch (Ed.), *The child's construction of language* (pp. 299–328). London: Academic Press.

Clark, E.V. (1993). *The lexicon in acquisition*. Cambridge: Cambridge University Press.

Clark, E.V. (2003). *First language acquisition*. Cambridge: Cambridge University Press.

Clark, E.V. & Bernicot, J. (2008). Repetition as ratification: How parents and children place information in common ground. *Journal of Child Language, 35(2)*, 349–371.

Clark, E.V., Gelman, S.A. & Lane, N.M. (1985). Compound nouns and category structure in young children. *Child Development, 56(1)*, 84–94.

Clark, E.V. & Hecht, B.F. (1982). Learning to coin agent and instrument nouns. *Cognition, 12(1)*, 1–24.

Clark, E.V., Hecht, B.F. & Mulford, R.C. (1986). Acquiring complex compounds: Affixes and word order in English. *Linguistics, 24*, 7–29.

Clark, R. (1977). What's the use of imitation? *Journal of Child Language, 4(3)*, 341–359.

Clarke, E., Reichard, U.H. & Zuberbühler, K. (2006). The syntax and meaning of wild gibbon songs. *PLoS One, 1*, e73.

Cleave, P., Becker, S., Curran, M., Van Horne, A. & Fey, M.E. (2015). The efficacy of recasts in language intervention: A systematic review and meta-analysis. *American Journal of Speech-Language Pathology, 24(2)*, 237–255.

Cole, E.B. & St. Clair-Stokes, J. (1984). Caregiver-child interactive behaviours – a videotape analysis procedure. *Volta Review, 86(4)*, 200–216.

Colunga, E. & Smith, L.B. (2008). Knowledge embedded in process: The self-organization of skilled noun learning. *Developmental Science, 11(2)*, 195–203.

Conley, J.J. (1984). Not Galton, but Shakespeare: A note on the origin of the term 'nature and nurture'. *Journal of the History of the Behavioral Sciences, 20*, 184–185.

Cook, R., Bird, G., Catmur, C. Press, C. & Heyes, C. (2014). Mirror neurons: From origin to function. *Behavioral and Brain Sciences, 37*, 177–241.

Cook, V.J. (1988). *Chomsky's Universal Grammar: An introduction*. Oxford: Basil Blackwell.

Cooper, R.P. & Aslin, R.N. (1990). Preference for infant-directed speech in the first month after birth. *Child Development, 61(5)*, 1584–1595.

321

Coppieters, R. (1987). Competence differences between native and near-native speakers. *Language, 63*, 544–573.

Courage, M.L. & Adams, R.J. (1990). Visual acuity assessment from birth to three years using the acuity card procedures: Cross-sectional and longitudinal samples. *Optometry and Vision Science, 67*, 713–718.

Cowie, F. (1997). The logical problem of language acquisition. *Synthese, 111*, 17–51.

Cowper, E.A. (1992). *A concise introduction to syntactic theory: The Government-binding approach*. Chicago, IL: University of Chicago Press.

Crain, S. & Lillo-Martin, D. (1999). *An introduction to linguistic theory and language acquisition*. Oxford: Blackwell.

Crain, S. & Nakayama, M. (1987). Structure dependence in grammar formation. *Language, 63(3)*, 522–543.

Cross, T.G. (1977). Mothers' speech adjustments: The contribution of selected child listener variables. In C.E. Snow & C.A. Ferguson (Eds.), *Talking to children: Language input and acquisition* (pp. 151–188). Cambridge: Cambridge University Press.

Csibra, G. (2008). Goal attribution to inanimate agents by 6.5-month-old infants. *Cognition, 107(2)*, 705–717.

Curtiss, S. (1977). *Genie: A psycholinguistic study of a modern-day 'wild child'*. New York: Academic Press.

Curtiss, S. (1988). Abnormal language acquisition and the modularity of language. In F.J. Newmeyer (Ed.), *Linguistics: The Cambridge survey (Vol. 2)*. Cambridge: Cambridge University Press.

Curtiss, S., Fromkin, V., Krashen, S., Rigler, D. & Rigler, M. (1974). The linguistic development of Genie. *Language, 50(3)*, 528–554.

Dąbrowska, E. (2004). *Language, mind and brain: Some psychological and neurological constraints on theories of grammar*. Edinburgh: Edinburgh University Press.

Dąbrowska, E. (2005). Productivity and beyond: Mastering the Polish genitive inflection. *Journal of Child Language, 32(1)*, 191–205.

Dąbrowska, E. & Szczerbinski, M. (2006). Polish children's productivity with case marking: The role of regularity, type frequency, and phonological diversity. *Journal of Child Language, 33(3)*, 559–597.

Danko, S., Boytsova, J., Solovjeva, M., Chernigovskaya, T. & Medvedev, S. (2014). Event-related brain potentials when conjugating Russian verbs: The modularity of language procedures. *Human Physiology, 40(3)*, 237–243.

Dapretto, M. & Bjork, E.L. (2000). The development of word retrieval abilities in the second year and its relation to early vocabulary growth. *Child Development, 71(3)*, 635–648.

Davidson, D. & Tell, D. (2005). Monolingual and bilingual children's use of mutual exclusivity in the naming of whole objects. *Journal of Experimental Child Psychology, 92(1)*, 25–45.

de la Mora, D.M. & Toro, J.M. (2013). Rule learning over consonants and vowels in a non-human animal. *Cognition, 126(2)*, 307–312.

de Saussure, F. (1916/1974). *Course in general linguistics*. London: Fontana/Collins.

de Waal, F.B.M. (1995). Bonobo, sex and society. *Scientific American*, March, 58–64.

DeCasper, A.J. & Spence, M.J. (1986). Prenatal maternal speech influences newborns' perception of speech sounds. *Infant Behavior and Development, 9(2)*, 133–150.

Dehaene-Lambertz, G., Hertz-Pannier, L., Dubois, J., Meriaux, S., Roche, A., Sigman, M. & Dehaene, S. (2006). Functional organization of perisylvian activation during presentation of sentences in preverbal infants. *Proceedings of the National Academy of Sciences of the United States of America, 103(38)*, 14240–14245.

Dehaene-Lambertz, G. & Spelke, E.S. (2015). The infancy of the human brain. *Neuron, 88(1)*, 93–109.

DeHart, G.B., Sroufe, L.A. & Cooper, R.G. (2000). *Child development: Its nature and course* (4th ed.). Boston, MA: McGraw-Hill.

DeKeyser, R.M. (2000). The robustness of critical period effects in second language acquisition. *Studies in Second Language Acquisition, 22*, 499–533.

Demetras, M.J., Post, K.N. & Snow, C.E. (1986). Feedback to first language learners: The role of repetitions and clarification questions. *Journal of Child Language, 13*, 275–292.

Depaolis, R.A., Vihman, M.M. & Keren-Portnoy, T. (2014). When do infants begin recognizing familiar words in sentences? *Journal of Child Language, 41(1)*, 226–239.

DeVilliers, J. & DeVilliers, P. (1973). Development of the use of word order in comprehension. *Journal of Psycholinguistic Research, 2(4)*, 331–341.

Diesendruck, G. (2007). Mechanisms of word learning. In E. Hoff & M. Shatz (Eds.), *Blackwell handbook of language development* (pp. 257–276). Malden, MA: Blackwell.

Diessel, H. (2004). *The acquisition of complex sentences.* Cambridge: Cambridge University Press.

Diessel, H. (2009). On the role of frequency and similarity in the acquisition of subject and non-subject relative clauses. In T. Givón & M. Shibatani (Eds.), *Syntactic complexity* (pp. 251–276). Amsterdam: John Benjamins.

Diessel, H. & Tomasello, M. (2005). A new look at the acquisition of relative clauses. *Language, 81(4)*, 882–906.

Dilley, L.C., Millett, A.L., Devin McAuley, J. & Bergeson, T.R. (2014). Phonetic variation in consonants in infant-directed and adult-directed speech: The case of regressive place assimilation in word-final alveolar stops. *Journal of Child Language, 41(1)*, 155–175.

Dispaldro, M. & Benelli, B. (2012). Putting singular and plural morphology in context. *Journal of Child Language, 39(4)*, 863–884.

Dittmar, M., Abbot-Smith, K., Lieven, E. & Tomasello, M. (2008a). German children's comprehension of word order and case marking in causative sentences. *Child Development, 79(4)*, 1152–1167.

Dittmar, M., Abbot-Smith, K., Lieven, E. & Tomasello, M. (2008b). Young German children's early syntactic competence: A preferential looking study. *Developmental Science, 11(4)*, 575–582.

Dittmar, M., Abbot-Smith, K., Lieven, E. & Tomasello, M. (2011). Children aged 2;1 use transitive syntax to make a semantic-role interpretation in a pointing task. *Journal of Child Language, 38(5)*, 1109–1123.

Dooling, R.J. & Brown, S.D. (1990). Speech perception by budgerigars (Melopsittacus undulatus): Spoken vowels. *Perception and Psychophysics, 47*, 568–574.

Dore, J. (1975). Holophrases, speech acts and language universals. *Journal of Child Language*, *2(1)*, 21–40.

Dromi, E. (1987). *Early lexical development.* Cambridge: Cambridge University Press.

Drozd, K.F. (2004). Learnability and linguistic performance. *Journal of Child Language*, *31(2)*, 431–458.

Dubois, J., Hertz-Pannier, L., Cachia, A., Mangin, J.F., Le Bihan, D. & Dehaene-Lambertz, G. (2009). Structural asymmetries in the infant language and sensori-motor networks. *Cerebral Cortex*, *19(2)*, 414–423.

Dummett, M. (1981). *Frege: Philosophy of language* (2nd ed.). London: Duckworth.

Dye, C.D., Walenski, M., Prado, E.L., Mostofsky, S. & Ullman, M.T. (2013). Children's computation of complex linguistic forms: A study of frequency and imageability effects. *PLoS One*, *8(9)*, e74683.

Eadie, P.A., Fey, M.E., Douglas, J.M. & Parsons, C.L. (2002). Profiles of grammatical morphology and sentence imitation in children with Specific Language Impairment and Down syndrome. *Journal of Speech, Language, and Hearing Research*, *45*, 720–732.

Eimas, P.D. (1974). Auditory and linguistic processing of cues for place of articulation by infants. *Perception and Psychophysics*, *16*, 513–521.

Eimas, P.D. (1975). Auditory and phonetic coding of cues for speech: Discrimination of [r-l] distinction by young infants. *Perception & Psychophysics*, *18(5)*, 341–347.

Eimas, P.D. & Miller, J.L. (1980a). Contextual effects in infant speech perception. *Science*, *209*, 1140–1141.

Eimas, P.D. & Miller, J.L. (1980b). Discrimination of the information for manner of articulation. *Infant Behavior and Development*, *3*, 367–375.

Eimas, P.D., Siqueland, E.R., Jusczyk, P.W. & Vigorito, J. (1971). Speech perception in infants. *Science*, *209*, 1140–1141.

Elman, J.L. (2008). The shape bias: An important piece in a bigger puzzle. *Developmental Science*, *11(2)*, 219–222.

Elsabbagh, M., Hohenberger, A., Campos, R., Van Herwegen, J., Serres, J., De Schonen, S., Aschersleben, G. & Karmiloff-Smith, A. (2013). Narrowing perceptual sensitivity to the native language in infancy: Exogenous influences on developmental timing. *Behavioral Science*, *3(1)*, 120–132.

Emmorey, K., Bellugi, U., Friederici, A. & Horn, P. (1995). Effects of age of acquisition on grammatical sensitivity: Evidence from on-line & off-line tasks. *Applied Psycholinguistics*, *16*, 1–23.

Erbaugh, M.S. (1992). The acquisition of Mandarin. In D.I. Slobin (Ed.), *The crosslinguistic study of language acquisition (Vol. 3).* Hillsdale, NJ: Lawrence Erlbaum.

Estes, K.G., Evans, J.L., Alibali, M.W. & Saffran, J.R. (2007). Can infants map meaning to newly segmented words? Statistical segmentation and word learning. *Psychological Science*, *18(3)*, 254–260.

Evans, N. & Levinson, S.C. (2009). The myth of language universals: Language diversity and its importance for cognitive science. *Behavioral and Brain Sciences*, *32(5)*, 429–448.

Everett, D. (2008). *Don't sleep, there are snakes: Life and language in the Amazonian jungle.* London: Profile.

Eysenck, M.W. & Keane, M.T. (2005). *Cognitive psychology: A student's handbook* (5th ed.). Hove: Psychology Press.

Fancher, R.E. (1979). A note on the origin of the term 'nature and nurture'. *Journal of the History of the Behavioral Sciences, 15,* 321–322.

Fantz, R.L. (1961). The origin of form perception. *Scientific American, 204(5),* 66–72.

Farrant, B.M. & Zubrick, S.R. (2013). Parent–child book reading across early childhood and child vocabulary in the early school years: Findings from the Longitudinal Study of Australian Children. *First Language, 33(3),* 280–293.

Farrar, M.J. (1992). Negative evidence and grammatical morpheme acquisition. *Developmental Psychology, 28(1),* 90–98.

Fenson, L., Dale, P.S., Reznick, J.S., Bates, E., Thal, D.J. & Pethick, S.J. (1994). Variability in early communicative development. *Monographs of the Society for Research in Child Development, 59(5).*

Ferguson, C.A. (1977). Baby talk as a simplified register. In C.E. Snow & C.A. Ferguson (Eds.), *Talking to children.* Cambridge: Cambridge University Press.

Ferguson, C.A. & Debose, C.E. (1977). Simplified registers, broken language, and pidginization. In A. Valdman (Ed.), *Pidgin and creole linguistics.* Bloomington, IN: Indiana University Press.

Fernald, A. (1989). Intonation and communicative intent in mothers' speech to infants: Is the melody the message? *Child Development, 60,* 1497–1510.

Fernald, A. & Mazzie, C. (1991). Prosody and focus in speech to infants and adults. *Developmental Psychology, 27,* 209–221.

Fernald, A. & Simon, T. (1984). Expanded intonation contours in mothers' speech to newborns. *Developmental Psychology, 20(1),* 104–113.

Fernald, A., Taeschner, T., Dunn, J., Papousek, M., Deboysson-Bardies, B. & Fukui, I. (1989). A cross-language study of prosodic modifications in mothers' and fathers' speech to preverbal infants. *Journal of Child Language, 16(3),* 477–501.

Fernald, A. & Weisleder, A. (2015). Twenty years after 'meaningful differences,' it's time to reframe the 'deficit' debate about the importance of children's early language experience. *Human Development, 58(1),* 1–4.

Finn, A.S. & Kam, C.L.H. (2008). The curse of knowledge: First language knowledge impairs adult learners' use of novel statistics for word segmentation. *Cognition, 108(2),* 477–499.

Fiser, J. & Aslin, R.N. (2001). Unsupervised statistical learning of higher-order spatial structures from visual scenes. *Psychological Science, 12,* 499–504.

Fisher, C. (2002). The role of abstract syntactic knowledge in language acquisition: A reply to Tomasello (2000). *Cognition, 82(3),* 259–278.

Fisher, C., Klingler, S.L. & Song, H.J. (2006). What does syntax say about space? 2-year-olds use sentence structure to learn new prepositions. *Cognition, 101(1),* B19–B29.

Flege, J.E., Takagi, N. & Mann, V. (1995). Japanese adults can learn to produce English /r/ and /l/ accurately. *Language and Speech, 38(1),* 25–55.

Flege, J.E., Takagi, N. & Mann, V. (1996). Lexical familiarity and English-language experience affect Japanese adults' perception of j and l. *Journal of the Acoustical Society of America, 99(2)*, 1161–1173.

Floccia, C., Keren-Portnoy, T., Depaolis, R., Duffy, H., Delle Luche, C., Durrant, S., White, L., Goslin, J. & Vihman, M. (2016). British English infants segment words only with exaggerated infant-directed speech stimuli. *Cognition, 148*, 1–9.

Floor, P. & Akhtar, N. (2006). Can 18-month-old infants learn words by listening in on conversations? *Infancy, 9(3)*, 327–339.

Fluck, M. & Henderson, L. (1996). Counting and cardinality in English nursery pupils. *British Journal of Educational Psychology, 66*, 501–517.

Fodor, J.A. (2001). Doing without *What's within*: Fiona Cowie's criticism of nativism. *Mind, 110*, 99–148.

Fodor, J.A. & Garrett, M. (1967). Some syntactic determinants of sentential complexity. *Perception and Psychophysics, 2*, 289–296.

Forrest, K. & Elbert, M. (2001). Treatment for phonologically disordered children with variable substitution patterns. *Clinical Linguistics and Phonetics, 15(1)*, 41–45.

Fougeron, C. & Keating, P. (1997). Articulatory strengthening at edges of prosodic domains. *Journal of the Acoustical Society of America, 101*, 3728–3740.

Fouts, R.S. & Fouts, D.H. (2004). Primate language. In R.L. Gregory (Ed.), *The Oxford companion to the mind* (pp. 631–633). Oxford: Oxford University Press.

Frank, M.C., Braginsky, M., Yurovsky, D. & Marchman, V.A. (2016). Wordbank: An open repository for developmental vocabulary data. *Journal of Child Language*. Published online: 18 May 2016, pp. 1–18.

Freedman, R.D. (1979). *Developmental neurobiology of vision*. New York: Plenum Press.

Freyd, P. & Baron, J. (1982). Individual differences in acquisition of derivational morphology. *Journal of Verbal Learning and Verbal Behavior, 21(3)*, 282–295.

Fry, D.B. (1955). Duration and intensity as physical correlates of linguistic stress. *Journal of the Acoustical Society of America, 27*, 765–768.

Furrow, D., Baillie, C., McLaren, J. & Moore, C. (1993). Differential responding to two- and three-year-olds' utterances: The role of grammaticality and ambiguity. *Journal of Child Language, 20*, 363–375.

Gallese, V., Fadiga, L., Fogassi, L. & Rizzolatti, G. (1996). Action recognition in the premotor cortex. *Brain, 119(2)*, 593–609.

Gampe, A., Brauer, J. & Daum, M.M. (2016). Imitation is beneficial for verb learning in toddlers. *European Journal of Developmental Psychology*. Published online: 3 February 2016, pp. 1–20.

Gampe, A., Liebal, K. & Tomasello, M. (2012). Eighteen-month-olds learn novel words through overhearing. *First Language, 32(3)*, 385–397.

Ganger, J. & Brent, M.R. (2004). Reexamining the vocabulary spurt. *Developmental Psychology, 40(4)*, 621–632.

Gardner, B.T. & Gardner, R.A. (1991). Chimp-language wars. *Science, 252(5009)*, 1046.

Gardner, R.A. & Gardner, B.T. (1969). Teaching sign language to a chimpanzee. *Science, 165*, 664–673.

326

Garnica, O.K. (1977). Some prosodic and paralinguistic features of speech to young children. In C.E. Snow & C.A. Ferguson (Eds.), *Talking to children* (pp. 63–88). Cambridge: Cambridge University Press.

Gathercole, S.E. (2006). Nonword repetition and word learning: The nature of the relationship. *Applied Psycholinguistics, 27(4)*, 513–543.

Gathercole, S.E., Willis, C., Emslie, H. & Baddeley, A.D. (1992). Phonological memory and vocabulary development during the early school years: A longitudinal study. *Developmental Psychology, 28(5)*, 887–898.

Gelman, S., Croft, W., Fu, P., Clausner, T.C. & Gottfried, G. (1998). Why is a pomegranate an *apple?* The role of shape, taxonomic relatedness, and prior lexical knowledge in children's overextensions. *Journal of Child Language, 25(2)*, 267–291.

Gentner, D. (1982). Why nouns are learned before verbs: Linguistic relativity versus natural partitioning. In S.A. Kuczaj (Ed.), *Language development, Vol. 2: Language, thought, and culture* (pp. 301–334). Hillsdale, NJ: Lawrence Erlbaum.

Gentner, D. (1983). Structure-mapping: A theoretical framework for analogy. *Cognitive Science, 7(2)*, 155–170.

Gentner, D. (2006). Why verbs are hard to learn. In K. Hirsh-Pasek & R.M. Golinkoff (Eds.), *Action meets word: How children learn verbs* (pp. 544–564). Oxford: Oxford University Press.

Gentner, D. & Boroditsky, L. (2001). Individuation, relativity, and early word learning. In M. Bowerman & S.C. Levinson (Eds.), *Language acquisition and conceptual development* (pp. 215–256). Cambridge: Cambridge University Press.

Gentner, T.Q., Fenn, K.M., Margoliash, D. & Nusbaum, H.C. (2006). Recursive syntactic pattern learning by songbirds. *Nature, 440(7088)*, 1204–1207.

Gershkoff-Stowe, L. (2001). The course of children's naming errors in early word learning. *Journal of Cognition and Development, 2(2)*, 131–155.

Gershkoff-Stowe, L. (2002). Object naming, vocabulary growth, and the development of word retrieval abilities. *Journal of Memory and Language, 46(4)*, 665–687.

Gershkoff-Stowe, L., Connell, B. & Smith, L. (2006). Priming overgeneralizations in two- and four-year-old children. *Journal of Child Language, 33(3)*, 461–486.

Gershkoff-Stowe, L. & Hahn, E.R. (2007). Fast mapping skills in the developing lexicon. *Journal of Speech Language and Hearing Research, 50(3)*, 682–697.

Gershkoff-Stowe, L. & Hahn, E.R. (2013). Word comprehension and production asymmetries in children and adults. *Journal of Experimental Child Psychology, 114(4)*, 489–509.

Gershkoff-Stowe, L. & Smith, L. (2004). Shape and the first hundred nouns. *Child Development, 75(4)*, 1098–1114.

Gershwin, I. (1959). *Lyrics on several occasions.* New York: Knopf.

Gertner, Y., Fisher, C. & Eisengart, J. (2006). Learning words and rules: Abstract knowledge of word order in early sentence comprehension. *Psychological Science, 17(8)*, 684–691.

Gervain, J. & Werker, J.F. (2013). Learning non-adjacent regularities at age 0;7. *Journal of Child Language, 40(4)*, 860–872.

Gibson, D.J., Congdon, E.L. & Levine, S.C. (2015). The effects of word-learning biases on children's concept of angle. *Child Development, 86(1)*, 319–326.

Gibson, E. & Wexler, K. (1994). Triggers. *Linguistic Inquiry, 25*, 407–454.

Gillette, J., Gleitman, H., Gleitman, L.R. & Lederer, A. (1999). Human simulations of vocabulary learning. *Cognition, 73(2)*, 135–176.

Gillis, S. & Ravid, D. (2006). Typological effects on spelling development: A crosslinguistic study of Hebrew and Dutch. *Journal of Child Language, 33(3)*, 621–659.

Gleitman, L.R. (2014). Syntactic bootstrapping. In P.J. Brooks & V. Kempe (Eds.), *Encyclopedia of language development* (pp. 616–618). London: Sage.

Goldberg, A.E. (1995). *Constructions: A construction grammar approach to argument structure.* Chicago, IL: University of Chicago Press.

Goldberg, A.E. (2006). *Constructions at work: The nature of generalization in language.* Oxford: Oxford University Press.

Goldberg, A.E. (2011). Corpus evidence of the viability of statistical preemption. *Cognitive Linguistics, 22(1)*, 131–153.

Goldfield, B.A. & Reznick, J.S. (1992). Rapid change in lexical development in comprehension and production. *Developmental Psychology, 28*, 406–413.

Goldman, H.I. (2001). Parental reports of 'MAMA' sounds in infants: An exploratory study. *Journal of Child Language, 28*, 497–506.

Golinkoff, R. (1986). 'I beg your pardon?': The preverbal negotiation of failed messages. *Journal of Child Language, 13*, 455–476.

Golinkoff, R.M., Can, D.D., Soderstrom, M. & Hirsh-Pasek, K. (2015). (Baby) talk to me: The social context of infant-directed speech and its effects on early language acquisition. *Current Directions in Psychological Science, 24(5)*, 339–344.

Golinkoff, R.M. & Hirsh-Pasek, K. (2008). How toddlers begin to learn verbs. *Trends in Cognitive Sciences, 12(10)*, 397–403.

Gombert, J.E. (1992). *Metalinguistic development* (translated by T. Pownall). New York: Harvester Wheatsheaf.

Goodman, J.C., Dale, P.S. & Li, P. (2008). Does frequency count? Parental input and the acquisition of vocabulary. *Journal of Child Language, 35(3)*, 515–531.

Gopnik, A. & Meltzoff, A.N. (1986). Words, plans, things, and locations: Interactions between semantic and cognitive development in the one-word stage. In S. Kuczaj & M. Barrett (Eds.), *The development of word meaning.* New York: Springer-Verlag.

Gordon, P. (1985). Level-ordering in lexical development. *Cognition, 21(2)*, 73–93.

Gordon, P. & Chafetz, J. (1991). Verb-based vs. class-based accounts of actionality effects in children's comprehension of the passive. *Cognition, 36(3)*, 227–254.

Gordon, R.G. (Ed.) (2005). *Ethnologue: Languages of the world* (15th ed.). Dallas, TX: SIL International.

Graf Estes, K. (2012). Infants generalize representations of statistically segmented words. *Frontiers in Psychology, 3.* Published online: 29 October 2012.

Gravetter, F.J. & Walnau, L.B. (1992). *Statistics for the behavioral sciences: A first course for students of psychology and education* (3rd ed.). St Paul, MN: West.

Greenberg, J.H. (1966). *Language universals: With special reference to feature hierarchies.* The Hague: Mouton.

Greer, R. & Du, L. (2015). Experience and the onset of the ability to name objects incidentally by exclusion. *The Psychological Record, 65(2)*, 355–373.

Griffiths, P. (1986). Early vocabulary. In P. Fletcher & M. Garman (Eds.), *Language acquisition: Studies in first language development* (2nd ed.) (pp. 279–306). Cambridge: Cambridge University Press.

Grimshaw, G.M., Adelstein, A., Bryden, M.P. & MacKinnon, G.E. (1998). First-language acquisition in adolescence: Evidence for a critical period for verbal language development. *Brain & Language, 63*, 237–255.

Gropen, J., Pinker, S., Hollander, M. & Goldberg, R. (1991). Syntax and semantics in the acquisition of locative verbs. *Journal of Child Language, 18(1)*, 115–151.

Haggan, M. (2002). Self-reports and self-delusion regarding the use of Motherese: Implications from Kuwaiti adults. *Language Sciences, 24(1)*, 17–28.

Hahn, E.R. & Cantrell, L. (2012). The shape-bias in Spanish-speaking children and its relationship to vocabulary. *Journal of Child Language, 39(2)*, 443–455.

Hakuta, K. (2001). A critical period for second language acquisition? In D.B. Bailey, J.T. Bruer, F.J. Symons & J.W. Lichtman (Eds.), *Critical thinking about critical periods.* Baltimore, MD: Paul Brookes.

Hakuta, K., Bialystok, E. & Wiley, E. (2003). Critical evidence: A test of the critical-period hypothesis for second-language acquisition. *Psychological Science, 14(1)*, 31–38.

Hale, B. (1987). *Abstract objects.* Oxford: Basil Blackwell.

Hall, D.G. & Waxman, S.R. (Eds.) (2004), *Weaving a lexicon.* Cambridge, MA: MIT Press.

Hall, D.G., Williams, S. & Bélanger, J. (2015). Learning count nouns and adjectives: Understanding the contributions of lexical form class and social-pragmatic cues. *Journal of Cognition and Development, 11(1)*, 86–120.

Hall, S., Rumney, L., Holler, J. & Kidd, E. (2013). Associations among play, gesture and early spoken language acquisition. *First Language, 33(3)*, 294–312.

Hamilton, M. (1999). Ethnography for classrooms: Constructing a reflective curriculum for literacy. *Pedagogy, Culture and Society, 7(3)*, 429–444.

Hamlin, J.K., Hallinan, E.V. & Woodward, A.L. (2008). Do as I do: 7-month-old infants selectively reproduce others' goals. *Developmental Science, 11(4)*, 487–494.

Hampton, J.A. (2007). Typicality, graded membership, and vagueness. *Cognitive Science, 31(3)*, 355–384.

Hanna, J. & Pulvermüller, F. (2014). Neurophysiological evidence for whole form retrieval of complex derived words: A mismatch negativity study. *Frontiers in Human Neuroscience, 8.*

Hao, M., Liu, Y., Shu, H., Xing, A., Jiang, Y. & Li, P. (2015). Developmental changes in the early child lexicon in Mandarin Chinese. *Journal of Child Language, 42(3)*, 505–537.

Happé, F. (1994). *Autism: An introduction to psychological theory.* London: UCL Press.

Hare, B., Rosati, A., Kaminski, J., Bräuer, J., Call, J. & Tomasello, M. (2010). The domestication hypothesis for dogs' skills with human communication: A response to Udell et al. (2008) and Wynne et al. (2008). *Animal Behavior, 79(2)*, e1–e6.

Harley, B. & Hart, D. (1997). Language aptitude and second language proficiency in classroom learning of different starting ages. *Studies in Second Language Acquisition, 19*, 379–400.

Harris, L. & Humphreys, G. (2015). Semantic impairment and past tense verb production: Neighbourhood and frequency modulation of irregular past tense production. *Aphasiology, 29(7)*, 799–825.

Harris, M., Yeeles, C., Chasin, J. & Oakley, Y. (1995). Symmetries and asymmetries in early lexical comprehension and production. *Journal of Child Language, 22(1)*, 1–18.

Hart, B. & Risley, T.R. (1995). *Meaningful differences in the everyday experiences of young American children*. Baltimore, MD: Paul Brookes.

Harweth, R.S., Smith III, E.L., Crawford, M.J.L. & van Noorden, G.K. (1989). The effects of reverse monocular deprivation in monkeys. I. Psychophysical experiments. *Experimental Brain Research, 74*, 327–337.

Haskell, T.R., MacDonald, M.C. & Seidenberg, M.S. (2003). Language learning and innateness: Some implications of Compounds Research. *Cognitive Psychology, 47(2)*, 119–163.

Hauser, M., Chomsky, N. & Fitch, T. (2002). The faculty of language: What is it, who has it, and how did it evolve? *Science, 298(5598)*, 1569–1579.

Hauser, M.D., Newport, E.L. & Aslin, R.N. (2001). Segmentation of the speech stream in a non-human primate: Statistical learning in cotton-top tamarins. *Cognition, 78(3)*, B53–B64.

Hay, J.F., Pelucchi, B., Graf Estes, K. & Saffran, J.R. (2011). Linking sounds to meanings: Infant statistical learning in a natural language. *Cognitive Psychology, 63(2)*, 93–106.

Hayes, K.J. & Hayes, C. (1951). The intellectual development of a home-raised chimpanzee. *Proceedings of the American Philosophical Society, 95(2)*, 105–109.

Heath, S.B. (1983). *Ways with words*. Cambridge: Cambridge University Press.

Heibeck, T.H. & Markman, E.M. (1987). Word learning in children: An examination of fast mapping. *Child Development, 58*, 1021–1034.

Herman, L.M., Kuczaj, S.A. & Holder, M.D. (1993). Responses to anomalous gestural sequences by a language-trained dolphin: Evidence for processing of semantic relations and syntactic information. *Journal of Experimental Psychology: General, 122(2)*, 184–194.

Herman, L.M., Richards, D.G. & Wolz, J.P. (1984). Comprehension of sentences by bottlenosed dolphins. *Cognition, 16*, 129–219.

Hernandez, A.E. & Li, P. (2007). Age of acquisition: Its neural and computational mechanisms. *Psychological Bulletin,* 133(4), 638–650.

Herrnstein, R.J. & Murray, C. (1994). *The bell curve: Intelligence and class structure in American life*. New York: Free Press.

Herschensohn, J.R. (2007). *Language development and age*. Cambridge: Cambridge University Press.

Hillenbrand, J.M., Minifie, F.D. & Edwards, T.J. (1979). Tempo of spectrum change as a cue in speech sound discrimination by infants. *Journal of Speech and Hearing Research, 22*, 147–165.

Hills, T. (2013). The company that words keep: Comparing the statistical structure of child- versus adult-directed language. *Journal of Child Language, 40(3)*, 586–604.

Hirsh-Pasek, K. & Golinkoff, R.M. (Eds.) (1996). *The origins of grammar: Evidence from early language comprehension*. Cambridge, MA: MIT Press.

Hirsh-Pasek, K. & Golinkoff, R.M. (Eds.) (2006). *Action meets word: How children learn verbs*. Oxford: Oxford University Press.

Hirsh-Pasek, K., Golinkoff, R.M. & Naigles, L. (1996). Young children's use of syntactic frames to derive meaning. In K. Hirsh-Pasek & R.M. Golinkoff (Eds.), *The origins of grammar: Evidence from early language comprehension* (pp. 123–158). Cambridge, MA: MIT Press.

Hirsh-Pasek, K., Kemler Nelson, D.G., Jusczyk, P.W., Cassidy, K.W., Druss, B. & Kennedy, L. (1987). Clauses are perceptual units for young infants. *Cognition, 26(3)*, 269–286.

Hirsh-Pasek, K., Treiman, R. & Schneiderman, M. (1984). Brown & Hanlon revisited: Mothers' sensitivity to ungrammatical forms. *Journal of Child Language, 11*, 81–88.

Hockett, C.F. (1963). The problem of universals in language. In J.H. Greenberg (Ed.), *Universals of language* (pp. 1–29). Cambridge, MA: MIT Press.

Hockett, C.F. & Altmann, S. (1968). A note on design features. In T. Sebeok (Ed.), *Animal communication: Techniques of study and results of research.* (pp. 61–72). Bloomington, IN: Indiana University Press.

Hoff, E. (2001). *Language development* (2nd ed.). Belmont, CA: Wadsworth.

Hoff, E. (2004). Progress, but not a full solution to the logical problem of language acquisition. *Journal of Child Language, 31(4)*, 923–926.

Hoff, E. (2006). How social contexts support and shape language development. *Developmental Review, 26(1)*, 55–88.

Hoff, E. (2012). *Guide to research methods in child language.* London: Blackwell-Wiley.

Hoff, E., Core, C. & Bridges, K. (2008). Non-word repetition assesses phonological memory and is related to vocabulary development in 20- to 24-month-olds. *Journal of Child Language, 35(4)*, 903–916.

Hoff, E. & Naigles, L. (2002). How children use input to acquire a lexicon. *Child Development, 73(2)*, 418–433.

Hoff, E. & Shatz, M. (Eds.) (2007). *Blackwell handbook of language development.* Oxford: Blackwell.

Hoff-Ginsberg, E. (1985). Some contributions of mothers' speech to their children's syntactic growth. *Journal of Child Language, 12(2)*, 367–385.

Holland, A., Simpson, A. & Riggs, K.J. (2015). Young children retain fast mapped object labels better than shape, color, and texture words. *Journal of Experimental Child Psychology, 134*, 1–11.

Hollich, G. & Golinkoff, R.M. (2007). Young children associate novel words with complex objects rather than salient parts. *Developmental Psychology, 43(5)*, 1051–1061.

Holtheuer, C. & Rendle-Short, J. (2013). *Ser* and *estar*: Corrective input to children's errors of the Spanish copula verbs. *First Language, 33(2)*, 155–167.

Horst, J.S. & Samuelson, L.K. (2008). Fast mapping but poor retention by 24-month-old infants. *Infancy, 13(2)*, 128–157.

Huang, B.H. (2014). The effects of age on second language grammar and speech production. *Journal of Psycholinguist Research, 43*, 397–420.

Huang, B.H. (2015). A synthesis of empirical research on the linguistic outcomes of early foreign language instruction. *International Journal of Multilingualism*, doi:10.1080/14790718.2015.1066792.

Huang, Y. (1995). On null subjects and null objects in generative grammar. *Linguistics, 33(6)*, 1081–1123.

Hubel, D.H. & Wiesel, T.N. (1963). Receptive fields of cells in striate cortex of very young, visually inexperienced kittens. *Journal of Neurophysiology, 26(6)*, 994–1002.

Hubel, D.H. & Wiesel, T.N. (1970). The period of susceptibility to the physiological effects of unilateral eye closure in kittens. *Journal of Physiology, 206(2)*, 419–436.

Huddleston, R. (1984). *Introduction to the grammar of English.* Cambridge: Cambridge University Press.

Hunsicker, D. & Goldin-Meadow, S. (2012). Hierarchical structure in a self-created communication system: Building nominal constituents in homesign. *Language, 88(4),* 732–763.

Hupp, J.M. (2008). Demonstration of the shape bias without label extension. *Infant Behavior and Development, 31(3),* 511–517.

Hupp, J.M. (2015). Development of the shape bias during the second year. *The Journal of Genetic Psychology, 176(2),* 82–92.

Hurry, J., Nunes, T., Bryant, P., Pretzlik, U., Parker, M., Curno, T. & Midgley, L. (2005). Transforming research on morphology into teacher practice. *Research Papers in Education, 20(2),* 187–206.

Hurtado, N., Marchman, V.A. & Fernald, A. (2008). Does input influence uptake? Links between maternal talk, processing speed and vocabulary size in Spanish-learning children. *Developmental Science, 11(6),* F31–F39.

Huttenlocher, J. (1974). The origin of language comprehension. In R.L. Solso (Ed.), *Theories in cognitive psychology: The Loyola Symposium.* Potomac, MD: Lawrence Erlbaum.

Hyams, N. (1986). *Language acquisition and the theory of parameters.* Dordrecht: Reidel.

Hyams, N. (1992). A reanalysis of null subjects in child language. In J. Weissenborn, H. Goodluck & T. Roeper (Eds.), *Theoretical issues in language acquisition: Continuity and change in development.* (pp. 249–267). Hillsdale, NJ: Lawrence Erlbaum.

Hyltenstam, K. & Abrahamsson, N. (2000). Who can become native-like in a second language? All, some, or none? *Studia Linguistica, 54(2),* 150–166.

Ibbotson, P. & Tomasello, M. (2016). What's universal grammar? Evidence rebuts Chomsky's theory of language learning. [Online]. Available at: www.salon.com/2016/09/10/what-will-universal-grammar-evidence-rebuts-chomskys-theory-of-language-learning_partner/. Accessed 17 October 2016.

Imai, M. & Haryu, E. (2004). Word-learning biases and lexical development. In D.G. Hall & S. Waxman (Eds.), *Weaving a lexicon* (pp. 411–444). Cambridge, MA: MIT Press.

Imai, M., Haryu, E. & Okada, H. (2005). Mapping novel nouns and verbs onto dynamic action events: Are verb meanings easier to learn than noun meanings for Japanese children. *Child Development, 76(2),* 340–355.

Imai, M., Li, L.J., Haryu, E., Okada, H., Hirsh-Pasek, K., Golinkoff, R.M. & Shigematsu, J. (2008). Novel noun and verb learning in Chinese-, English-, and Japanese-speaking children. *Child Development, 79(4),* 979–1000.

Immelmann, K. & Suomi, S.J. (1981). Sensitive phases in development. In K. Immelmann, G.W. Barlow, L. Petrinovich & M. Main (Eds.), *Behavioral development: The Bielefeld interdisciplinary project.* (pp. 395–431). Cambridge: Cambridge University Press.

Ioup, G., Boustagui, E., El Tigi, M. & Moselle, M. (1994). Reexamining the Critical Period Hypothesis: A case study of successful adult SLA in a naturalistic environment. *Studies in Second Language Acquisition, 16(1),* 73–98.

Israel, M., Johnson, C. & Brooks, P.J. (2001). From states to events: The acquisition of English passive participles. *Cognitive Linguistics, 11(1–2),* 103–129.

Iverson, J.M. & Goldin-Meadow, S. (2005). Gesture paves the way for language development. *Psychological Science, 16(5)*, 367–371.

Jackendoff, R. (1993). *Patterns in the mind: Language and human nature.* New York: Harvester Wheatsheaf.

Jackendoff, R. (1997). *The architecture of the language faculty.* Cambridge, MA: MIT Press.

Jackendoff, R. (2002). *Foundations of language: Brain, meaning, grammar, evolution.* Oxford: Oxford University Press.

Jaeger, J.J., Lockwood, A.H., Kemmerer, D.L., Van Valin, R.D., Murphy, B.W. & Khalak, H.G. (1996). A positron emission tomographic study of regular and irregular verb morphology in English. *Language, 72*, 451–497.

Jakobson, R. (1941/1968). *Child language, aphasia and phonological universals.* The Hague: Mouton.

Jaswal, V.K. (2010). Explaining the disambiguation effect: Don't exclude mutual exclusivity. *Journal of Child Language, 37(1)*, 95–113.

Jespersen, O. (1922). *Language: Its nature, development and origin.* London: George Allen and Unwin.

Johnson, C.J., Paivio, A. & Clark, J.M. (1996). Cognitive components of picture naming. *Psychological Bulletin, 120(1)*, 113–139.

Johnson, E.K. & Jusczyk, P.W. (2001). Word segmentation by 8-month-olds: When speech cues count more than statistics. *Journal of Memory and Language, 44(4)*, 548–567.

Johnson, J.S. & Newport, E.L. (1989). Critical period effects in second language learning: The influence of maturational state on the acquisition of English as a second language. *Cognitive Psychology, 21(1)*, 60–99.

Johnson, J.S. & Newport, E.L. (1991). Critical period effects on universal properties of language: The status of subjacency in the acquisition of a second language. *Cognition, 39*, 215–258.

Jolly, H.R. & Plunkett, K. (2008). Inflectional bootstrapping in 2-year-olds. *Language and Speech, 51(1&2)*, 45–59.

Jones, S.S., Smith, L.B. & Landau, B. (1991). Object properties and knowledge in early lexical learning. *Child Development, 62(3)*, 499–516.

Joyce, J. (1922/1960). *Ulysses.* Harmondsworth: Penguin.

Juffs, A. & Harrington, M. (1995). Parsing effects in L2 sentence processing: Subject and object asymmetries in WH-extraction. *Studies in Second Language Acquisition, 17(4)*, 483–516.

Jusczyk, P.W. (1989). Perception of cues to clausal units in native and non-native languages. Paper presented at the biennial meeting of the Society for Research in Child Development, Kansas City.

Jusczyk, P.W. (1997). *The discovery of spoken language.* Cambridge, MA: MIT Press.

Jusczyk, P.W. (2002). How infants adapt speech-processing capacities to native language structure. *Current Directions in Psychological Science, 11(1)*, 15–18.

Jusczyk, P.W. & Aslin, R.N. (1995). Infants' detection of sound patterns of words in fluent speech. *Cognitive Psychology, 29(1)*, 1–23.

Jusczyk, P.W., Copan, H. & Thompson, E. (1978). Perception by two-month-olds of glide contrasts in multisyllabic utterances. *Perception and Psychophysics, 24(6)*, 515–520.

Jusczyk, P.W., Houston, D. & Newsome, M. (1999). The beginnings of word segmentation in English-learning infants. *Cognitive Psychology, 39(3–4)*, 159–207.

Kaduk, K., Bakker, M., Juvrud, J., Gredebäck, G., Westermann, G., Lunn, J. & Reid, V.M. (2016). Semantic processing of actions at 9 months is linked to language proficiency at 9 and 18 months. *Journal of Experimental Child Psychology, 151*, 96–108.

Kail, R. (1990). *The development of memory in children* (3rd ed.). New York: W.H. Freeman.

Kaminski, J., Call, J. & Fischer, J. (2004). Word learning in a domestic dog: Evidence for 'fast mapping'. *Science, 304(5677)*, 1682–1683.

Kaminski, J., Shulz, L. & Tomasello, M. (2012). How dogs know when communication is intended for them. *Developmental Science, 15(2)*, 222–232.

Karlsson, F. & Koskenniemi, K. (1985). A process model of morphology and lexicon. *Folia Linguistica, 29*, 207–231.

Karmiloff, K. & Karmiloff-Smith, A. (2001). *Pathways to language: From fetus to adolescent.* Cambridge, MA: Harvard University Press.

Kaschak, M.P., Loney, R.A. & Borreggine, K.L. (2006). Recent experience affects the strength of structural priming. *Cognition, 99(3)*, B73–B82.

Kauschke, C. & Hofmeister, C. (2002). Early lexical development in German: A study on vocabulary growth and vocabulary composition during the second and third year of life. *Journal of Child Language, 29(4)*, 735–757.

Kellog, W.N. & Kellog, L.A. (1933). *The ape and the child: A study of environmental influence upon early behavior.* New York: McGraw-Hill.

Kemler Nelson, D.G., Frankenfield, A., Morris, C. & Blair, E. (2000). Young children's use of functional information to categorize artifacts: Three factors that matter. *Cognition, 77(2)*, 133–168.

Kemler Nelson, D.G., Hirsh-Pasek, K., Jusczyk, P.W. & Cassidy, K.W. (1989). How the prosodic cues in motherese might assist language learning. *Journal of Child Language, 16(1)*, 55–68.

Kempe, V., Brooks, P.J., Mironova, N., Pershukova, A. & Fedorova, O. (2007). Playing with word endings: Morphological variation in the learning of Russian noun inflections. *British Journal of Developmental Psychology, 25(1)*, 55–77.

Kessel, F.S. (Ed.) (1988). *The development of language and language researchers: Essays in honor of Roger Brown.* Hillsdale, NJ: Lawrence Erlbaum.

Ketrez, F.N. (2014). Harmonic cues for speech segmentation: A cross-linguistic corpus study on child-directed speech. *Journal of Child Language, 41(2)*, 439–461.

Key, A.P.F., Lambert, E.W., Aschner, J.L. & Maitre, N.L. (2012). Influence of gestational age and postnatal age on speech sound processing in NICU infants. *Psychophysiology, 49(5)*, 720–731.

King, S.L. & Janik, V.M. (2013). Bottlenose dolphins can use learned vocal labels to address each other. *Proceedings of the National Academy of Sciences of the United States of America, 110(32)*, 13216–13221.

Kintsch, W. (1981). Semantic memory: A tutorial. In R.S. Nickerson (Ed.), *Attention and Performance (Vol. VIII)*. Hillsdale, NJ: Lawrence Erlbaum.

Kiparsky, P. (1983). Word-formation and the lexicon. In F. Ingemann (Ed.), *Proceedings of the 1981 Mid-America linguistics conference* (pp. 3–29). Lawrence, KS: University of Kansas Press.

Kirjavainen, M., Nikolaev, A. & Kidd, E. (2012). The effect of frequency and phonological neighbourhood density on the acquisition of past tense verbs by Finnish children. *Cognitive Linguistics, 23(2)*, 273–315.

Kisilevsky, B.S., Hains, S.M.J., Lee, K., Xie, X., Huang, H.F., Ye, H.H., Zhang, K. & Wang, Z.P. (2003). Effects of experience on fetal voice recognition. *Psychological Science, 14(3)*, 220–224.

Kitamura, C. & Lam, C. (2009). Age-specific preferences for infant-directed affective intent. *Infancy, 14(1)*, 77–100.

Klatt, D.H. & Stefanski, R.A. (1974). How does a mynah bird imitate human speech? *The Journal of the Acoustical Society of America, 55(4)*, 822–832.

Kline, M. & Demuth, K. (2014). Syntactic generalization with novel intransitive verbs. *Journal of Child Language, 41(3)*, 543–574.

Kluender, K. (1991). Effects of first formant onset properties on voicing judgments result from processes not specific to humans. *Journal of the Acoustical Society of America, 90(1)*, 83–96.

Ko, E.-S., Seidl, A., Cristia, A., Reimchen, M. & Soderstrom, M. (2016). Entrainment of prosody in the interaction of mothers with their young children. *Journal of Child Language, 43(2)*, 284–309.

Koryé, A. (1968). *Metaphysics and measurement: Essays in scientific revolution.* London: Chapman and Hall.

Krcmar, M., Grela, B. & Lin, K. (2007). Can toddlers learn vocabulary from television? An experimental approach. *Media Psychology, 10(1)*, 41–63.

Krott, A., Gagné, C.L. & Nicoladis, E. (2009). How the parts relate to the whole: Frequency effects on children's interpretations of novel compounds. *Journal of Child Language, 36(1)*, 85–112.

Krott, A. & Nicoladis, E. (2005). Large constituent families help children parse compounds. *Journal of Child Language, 32(1)*, 139–158.

Kučera, H. (1992). The mathematics of language. In *The American heritage dictionary of the English language* (3rd ed.) (pp. xxxi–xxxiii). Boston, MA: Houghton Mifflin.

Kučera, H. & Francis, W.M. (1967). *Computational analysis of present day American English.* Providence, RI: Brown University Press.

Kuczaj, S.A. (1982). On the nature of syntactic development. In S.A. Kuczaj (Ed.), *Language development. Volume 1: Syntax and semantics* (pp. 37–71). Hillsdale, NJ: Lawrence Erlbaum.

Kuhl, P.K. (2004). Early language acquisition: Cracking the speech code. *Nature Reviews Neuroscience, 5(11)*, 831–843.

Kuhl, P.K., Conboy, B.T., Coffey-Corina, S., Padden, D., Rivera-Gaxiola, M. & Nelson, T. (2008). Phonetic learning as a pathway to language: New data and native language magnet theory expanded (NLM-e). *Philosophical Transactions of the Royal Society B – Biological Sciences, 363(1493)*, 979–1000.

Kuhl, P.K., Conboy, B.T., Padden, D., Nelson, T. & Pruitt, J. (2005). Early speech perception and later language development: Implications for the 'critical period'. *Language Learning and Development, 1*, 237–264.

Kuhl, P.K. & Miller, J.D. (1975). Speech perception by the chinchilla: Voiced–voiceless distinction in alveolar plosive consonants. *Science, 190*, 69–72.

Kuhl, P.K. & Padden, D.M. (1983). Enhanced discriminability at the phonetic boundaries for the place feature in macaques. *Journal of the Acoustical Society of America, 73*, 1003–1010.

Kuhl, P.K. & Rivera-Gaxiola, M. (2008). Neural substrates of language acquisition. *Annual Review of Neuroscience, 31(1)*, 511–534.

Kuhl, P.K., Stevens, E., Hayashi, A., Deguchi, T., Kiritani, S. & Iverson, P. (2006). Infants show a facilitation effect for native language phonetic perception between 6 and 12 months. *Developmental Science, 9(2)*, F13–F21.

Kuhl, P.K., Tsao, F. & Liu, H. (2003). Foreign language experience in infancy: Effects of short term exposure and interaction on phonetic learning. *Proceedings of the National Academy of Sciences, 100*, 9096–9101.

Laakso, M. & Soininen, M. (2010). Mother-initiated repair sequences in interactions of 3-year-old children. *First Language, 30(3–4)*, 329–353.

Ladefoged, P. (2004). *Vowels and consonants: An introduction to the sounds of language* (2nd ed.). Oxford: Blackwell.

Ladefoged, P. (2006). *A course in phonetics* (5th ed.). Boston, MA: Thomas Wadsworth.

Landau, B., Smith, L.B. & Jones, S.S. (1988). The importance of shape in early lexical learning. *Cognitive Development, 3(3)*, 299–321.

Lane, H. (1976). *The wild boy of Aveyron.* Cambridge, MA: Harvard University Press.

Langacker, R.W. (1987). *Foundations of cognitive grammar (Vol. 1): Theoretical prerequisites.* Stanford, CA: Stanford University Press.

Lanter, J.A. & Basche, R.A. (2014). Effect of number and similarity on children's plural comprehension. *First Language, 34(6)*, 519–536.

Larsen-Freeman, D. (2015). Saying what we mean: Making a case for 'language acquisition' to become 'language development'. *Language Teaching, 48(4)*, 491–505.

Lasnik, H. (2000). *Syntactic Structures revisited: Contemporary lectures on transformational theory.* Cambridge, MA: MIT Press.

Lee, D. (1992). Universal Grammar, learnability, and the acquisition of English reflexive binding by L1 Korean speakers. Unpublished doctoral dissertation, University of Southern California, Los Angeles.

Lehrman, D.S. (1970). Semantic and conceptual issues in the nature–nurture problem. In L. Aronson, E. Tobech, D.S. Lehrman & J. Rosenblatt (Eds.), *Development and evolution of behavior: Essays in memory of T.C. Schneirla.* San Francisco, CA: W.H. Freeman.

Lenneberg, E.H. (1967). *Biological foundations of language.* New York: Wiley.

Leopold, W.F. (1939). *Speech development of a bilingual child: A linguist's record. Vol. I: Vocabulary growth in the first two years.* Evanston, IL: Northwestern University Press.

Leopold, W.F. (1949). *Speech development of a bilingual child: A linguist's record. Vol. III: Grammar and general problems in the first two years.* Evanston, IL: Northwestern University Press.

Leopold, W.F. (1952). *Bibliography of child language.* Evanston, IL: Northwestern University Press.

Levin, I., Ravid, D. & Rapaport, S. (2001). Morphology and spelling among Hebrew-speaking children. *Journal of Child Language, 28(3)*, 741–769.

Levitt, A., Jusczyk, P.W., Murray, J. & Carden, G. (1988). The perception of place of articulation contrasts in voiced and voiceless fricatives by two-month-old infants. *Journal of Experimental Psychology: Human Perception and Performance, 14*, 361–368.

Lew-Williams, C., Pelucchi, B. & Saffran, J.R. (2011). Isolated words enhance statistical language learning in infancy. *Developmental Science, 14(6)*, 1323–1329.

Lew-Williams, C. & Saffran, J.R. (2012). All words are not created equal: Expectations about word length guide infant statistical learning. *Cognition, 122(2)*, 241–246.

Lewis, J.D. & Elman, J.L. (2001). Learnability and the statistical structure of language: Poverty of stimulus arguments revisited. In *Proceedings of the 26th annual Boston University Conference on language development* (pp. 359–370). Somerville, MA: Cascadilla.

Lidz, J. & Gagliardi, A. (2015). How nature meets nurture: Statistical learning and Universal Grammar. *Annual Review of Linguistics, 11(1)*, 333–353.

Lidz, J. & Waxman, S. (2004). Reaffirming the poverty of the stimulus argument: A reply to the replies. *Cognition, 93(2)*, 157–165.

Lidz, J., Waxman, S. & Freedman, J. (2003). What infants know about syntax but couldn't have learned: Experimental evidence for syntactic structure at 18 months. *Cognition, 89(3)*, B65–B73.

Liebal, K., Behne, T., Carpenter, M. & Tomasello, M. (2009). Infants use shared experience to interpret pointing gestures. *Developmental Science, 12(2)*, 264–271.

Lieberman, A.M., Borovsky, A., Hatrak, M. & Mayberry, R.I. (2015). Real-time processing of ASL signs: Delayed first language acquisition affects organization of the mental lexicon. *Journal of Experimental Psychology: Learning, Memory, and Cognition, 41(4)*, 1130–1139.

Lieberman, P. (1993). An untrustworthy guide to ape-language research. *Current Anthropology, 34(3)*, 327–328.

Lieven, E.V.M. (1994). Crosslinguistic and crosscultural aspects of language addressed to children. In C. Gallaway & B. Richards (Eds.), *Input and interaction in language acquisition* (pp. 56–73). Cambridge: Cambridge University Press.

Lieven, E.V.M. (2016). Usage-based approaches to language development: Where do we go from here? *Language and Cognition, 8(3)*, 346–368.

Lieven, E.V.M., Behrens, H., Speares, J. & Tomasello, M. (2003). Early syntactic creativity: A usage-based approach. *Journal of Child Language, 30(2)*, 333–370.

Lieven, E.V.M. & Tomasello, M. (2008). Children's first language acquisition from a usage-based perspective. In P. Robinson & N.C. Ellis (Eds.), *Handbook of cognitive linguistics and second language acquisition* (pp. 168–196). New York: Routledge.

Lightfoot, D. (1989). The child's trigger experience: Degree-0 learnability. *Behavioral and Brain Sciences, 12*, 321–375.

Lightfoot, D. (2005). Plato's problem, UG, and the language organ. In J. McGilvray (Ed.), *The Cambridge companion to Chomsky* (pp. 42–59). Cambridge: Cambridge University Press.

Linebarger, D.L. & Walker, D. (2005). Infants' and toddlers' television viewing and language outcomes. *American Behavioral Scientist, 48(5)*, 624–645.

Long, M.H. (2005). Problems with supposed counter-evidence to the critical period hypothesis. *International Review of Applied Linguistics, 43(4)*, 287–317.

Lukens, H.T. (1894). Preliminary report on the learning of language. *Pedagogical Seminary, 3,* 424–460.

Lust, B. (2006). *Child language: Acquisition and growth.* Cambridge: Cambridge University Press.

Lyn, H. & Savage-Rumbaugh, E.S. (2000). Observational word learning in two bonobos (Pan paniscus): Ostensive and non-ostensive contexts. *Language & Communication, 20(3),* 255–273.

Lyytinen, P. & Lyytinen, H. (2004). Growth and predictive relations of vocabulary and inflectional morphology in children with and without familial risk for dyslexia. *Applied Psycholinguistics, 25(3),* 397–411.

Mackintosh, N.J. (1998). *IQ and human intelligence.* Oxford: Oxford University Press.

MacWhinney, B. (1985). Hungarian language acquisition as an exemplification of a general model of grammatical development. In D.I. Slobin (Ed.), *The crosslinguistic study of language acquisition (Vol. II)* (pp. 1069–1155). Hillsdale, NJ: Lawrence Erlbaum.

MacWhinney, B. (2000). *The CHILDES project: Tools for analyzing talk. Vol. 2: The database* (3rd ed.). Mahwah, NJ: Lawrence Erlbaum.

MacWhinney, B. (2004). A multiple process solution to the logical problem of language acquisition. *Journal of Child Language, 31(4),* 883–914.

MacWhinney, B. (2014a). Item-based patterns in early syntactic development. In T. Herbst, H.-J. Schmid & S. Faulhaber (Eds.), *Valency relations* (pp. 33–70). Berlin: Springer.

MacWhinney, B. (2014b). What we have learned. *Journal of Child Language, 41(S1),* 124–131.

MacWhinney, B. & O'Grady, W. (Eds.) (2015). *The handbook of language emergence.* New York: Wiley.

Magen, H.S. (2014). A behavioral study of regularity, irregularity and rules in the English past tense. *Journal of Psycholinguistic Research, 43(6),* 791–814.

Mameli, M. & Bateson, P. (2006). Innateness and the sciences. *Biology & Philosophy, 21(2),* 155–188.

Mandalaywala, T., Fleener, C. & Maestripieri, D. (2015). Intelligence in nonhuman primates. In S. Goldstein, D. Princiotta & J.A. Naglieri (Eds.), *Handbook of intelligence: Evolutionary theory, historical perspective, and current concepts* (pp. 27–46). Berlin: Springer.

Mandel, D.R., Kemler Nelson, D.G. & Jusczyk, P.W. (1996). Infants remember the order of words in a spoken sentence. *Cognitive Development, 11(2),* 181–196.

Männel, C. (2008). The method of event-related brain potentials in the study of cognitive processes: A tutorial. In A.D. Friederici & G. Thierry (Eds.), *Early language development: Bridging brain and behaviour* (pp. 1–22). Amsterdam: John Benjamins.

Manolio, T.A., Collins, F.S., Cox, N.J., Goldstein, D.B., Hindorff, L.A., Hunter, D.J. & Visscher, P. M. (2009). Finding the missing heritability of complex diseases. *Nature, 461(7265),* 747–753.

Maratsos, M. (1982). The child's construction of grammatical categories. In E. Wanner & L.R. Gleitman (Eds.), *Language acquisition: The state of the art* (pp. 240–265). Cambridge: Cambridge University Press.

Maratsos, M. (1999). Some aspects of innateness and complexity in grammatical acquisition. In M. Barrett (Ed.), *The development of language* (pp. 191–228). Hove: Psychology Press.

Maratsos, M. (2000). More overregularisations after all: New data and discussion on Marcus, Pinker, Ullman, Hollander, Rosen & Xu. *Journal of Child Language*, *27(1)*, 183–212.

Maratsos, M., Gudeman, R., Gerard-Ngo, P. & DeHart, G. (1987). A study in novel word learning: The productivity of the causative. In B. MacWhinney (Ed.), *Mechanisms of language acquisition* (pp. 89–113). Hillsdale, NJ: Lawrence Erlbaum.

Marchetto, E. & Bonatti, L.L. (2015). Finding words and word structure in artificial speech: The development of infants' sensitivity to morphosyntactic regularities. *Journal of Child Language*, *42(4)*, 873–902.

Marcus, G.F. (1993). Negative evidence in language acquisition. *Cognition*, *46*, 53–85.

Marcus, G.F. (1995). Children's overregularization of English plurals: A quantitative analysis. *Journal of Child Language*, *22(2)*, 447–460.

Marcus, G.F. (1999). Language acquisition in the absence of explicit negative evidence: Can simple recurrent networks obviate the need for domain-specific learning devices? *Cognition*, *73(3)*, 293–296.

Marcus, G.F. (2001). *The algebraic mind: Integrating connectionism and cognitive science.* Cambridge, MA: MIT Press.

Marcus, G.F., Fernandes, K.J. & Johnson, S.P. (2007). Infant rule learning facilitated by speech. *Psychological Science*, *18(5)*, 387–391.

Marcus, G.F., Pinker, S., Ullman, M., Hollander, M., Rosen, T.J. & Xu, F. (1992). Overregularization in language acquisition. *Monographs of the Society for Research in Child Development*, Serial no. 228.

Marcus, G.F., Vijayan, S., Rao, S.B. & Vishton, P.M. (1999). Rule learning by seven-month-old infants. *Science*, *283(5398)*, 77–80.

Markman, E.M. (1990). Constraints children place on word meanings. *Cognitive Science*, *14(1)*, 57–77.

Markman, E.M. & Abelev, M. (2004). Word learning in dogs? *Trends in Cognitive Sciences*, *8(11)*, 479–481.

Markman, E.M. & Hutchinson, J.E. (1984). Children's sensitivity to constraints on word meaning: Taxonomic versus thematic relations. *Cognitive Psychology*, *16(1)*, 1–27.

Markman, E.M. & Wachtel, G.F. (1988). Children's use of mutual exclusivity to constrain the meanings of words. *Cognitive Psychology*, *20(2)*, 121–157.

Marsden, R.E. (1902). Record from a parent note-book. *Paidologist*, *4*, 97–100.

Marsh, H.L., Vining, A.Q., Levendoski, E.K., Judge, P.G. & Call, J. (2015). Inference by exclusion in lion-tailed macaques (Macaca silenus), a hamadryas baboon (Papio hamadryas), capuchins (Sapajus apella), and squirrel monkeys (Saimiri sciureus). *Journal of Comparative Psychology*, *129(3)*, 256–267.

Marshall, P.J. & Meltzoff, A.N. (2014). Neural mirroring mechanisms and imitation in human infants. *Philosophical Transactions of the Royal Society of London. Series B, Biological Sciences*, *369(1644)*, 20130620.

Martin, N., Weisberg, R.W. & Saffran, E.M. (1989). Variables influencing the occurrence of naming errors: Implications for models of lexical retrieval. *Journal of Memory and Language*, *28(4)*, 462–485.

Marx, O. (1964). The history of the biological basis of language. In E.H. Lenneberg (Ed.), *New directions in the study of language* (pp. 443–469). Cambridge, MA: MIT Press.

Maslen, R.J.C., Theakston, A.L., Lieven, E.V.M. & Tomasello, M. (2004). A dense corpus study of past tense and plural overregularization in English. *Journal of Speech, Language, and Hearing Research, 47(6)*, 1319–1333.

Masur, E.F. & Flynn, V. (2008). Infant and mother-infant play and the presence of the television. *Journal of Applied Developmental Psychology, 29(1)*, 76–83.

Masur, E.F., Flynn, V. & Olson, J. (2016). Infants' background television exposure during play: Negative relations to the quantity and quality of mothers' speech and infants' vocabulary acquisition. *First Language, 36(2)*, 109–123.

Masur, E.F. & Olson, J. (2008). Mothers' and infants' responses to their partners' spontaneous action and vocal/verbal imitation. *Infant Behavior & Development, 31(4)*, 704–715.

Matsuo, A., Kita, S., Shinya, Y., Wood, G.C. & Naigles, L. (2012). Japanese two-year-olds use morphosyntax to learn novel verb meanings. *Journal of Child Language, 39(3)*, 637–663.

Matthews, D. (Ed.) (2014). *Pragmatic development in first language acquisition.* Amsterdam: John Benjamins.

Matthews, P.H. (2007). *Syntactic relations: A critical survey.* Cambridge: Cambridge University Press.

May, L., Byers-Heinlein, K., Gervain, J. & Werker, J.F. (2011). Language and the newborn brain: Does prenatal language experience shape the neonate neural response to speech? *Frontiers in Psychology, 2.* Published online: 21 September 2011.

Mayberry, R.I. & Eichen, E.B. (1991). The long-lasting advantage of learning sign language in childhood: Another look at the critical period for language acquisition. *Journal of Memory & Language, 30*, 486–512.

Maye, J., Weiss, D.J. & Aslin, R.N. (2008). Statistical phonetic learning in infants: Facilitation and feature generalization. *Developmental Science, 11(1)*, 122–134.

Maye, J., Werker, J.F. & Gerken, L. (2002). Infant sensitivity to distributional information can affect phonetic discrimination. *Cognition, 82(3)*, B101–B111.

McBride-Chang, C., Tardif, T., Cho, J.R., Shu, H., Fletcher, P., Stokes, S.F., Wong, A. & Leung, K. (2008). What's in a word? Morphological awareness and vocabulary knowledge in three languages. *Applied Psycholinguistics, 29(3)*, 437–462.

McClelland, J.L. & Patterson, K. (2002). Rules or connections in past-tense inflections: What does the evidence rule out? *Trends in Cognitive Sciences, 6(11)*, 465–472.

McComb, K., Shannon, G., Sayialel, K.N. & Moss, C. (2014). Elephants can determine ethnicity, gender and age from acoustic cues in human voices. *Proceedings of the National Academy of Sciences of the United States, 111(114)*, 5433–5438.

McDonough, L. (2002). Basic-level nouns: First learned but misunderstood. *Journal of Child Language, 29(2)*, 357–377.

McEwen, F., Happé, F., Bolton, P., Rijsdijk, F., Ronald, A., Dworzynski, K. & Plomin, R. (2007). Origins of individual differences in imitation: Links with language, pretend play, and socially insightful behavior in two-year-old twins. *Child Development, 78(2)*, 474–492.

McGilvray, J. (Ed.) (2005). *The Cambridge companion to Chomsky.* Cambridge: Cambridge University Press.

McGilvray, J. (2006). On the innateness of language. In R. Stainton (Ed.), *Contemporary debates in cognitive science* (pp. 97–112). Oxford: Blackwell.

McMurray, B. & Aslin, R.N. (2005). Infants are sensitive to within-category variation in speech perception. *Cognition, 95(2),* B15–B26.

Mead, M. (1930). *Growing up in New Guinea: A study of adolescence and sex in primitive societies.* Harmondsworth: Penguin.

Meadow, K.P. (1980). *Deafness and child development.* London: Edward Arnold.

Medawar, P.B. (1967). *The art of the soluble.* London: Methuen.

Mehler, J., Bertoncini, J., Barrière, M. & Jassik-Gerschenfeld, D. (1978). Infant recognition of mother's voice. *Perception, 7,* 491–497.

Meltzoff, A.N. (1988). Infant imitation and memory: Nine-month-olds in immediate and deferred tests. *Child Development, 59,* 217–225.

Meltzoff, A.N. (2002). Elements of a developmental theory of imitation. In A.N. Meltzoff & W. Prinz (Eds.), *The imitative mind: Development, evolution, and brain bases* (pp. 19–41). Cambridge: Cambridge University Press.

Meltzoff, A.N. & Moore, M.K. (1983). Newborn infants imitate adult facial gestures. *Child Development, 54,* 702–709.

Meltzoff, A.N. & Moore, M.K. (1997). Explaining facial imitation: A theoretical model. *Early Development and Parenting, 6(3 4),* 179–192.

Menn, L. & Stoel-Gammon, C. (2005). Phonological development: Learning sounds and sound patterns. In J. Berko Gleason (Ed.), *The development of language* (6th ed.) (pp. 62–111). Boston, MA: Pearson.

Mervis, C.B. (1987). Child-basic object categories and early lexical development. In U. Neisser (Ed.), *Concepts and conceptual development: Ecological and intellectual factors in categorization* (pp. 201–233). New York: Cambridge University Press.

Mervis, C.B. & Bertrand, J. (1995). Acquisition of the novel name-nameless category. *Child Development, 65,* 1646–1663.

Mervis, C.B., Catlin, J. & Rosch, E. (1976). Relationships amongst goodness-of-example, category norms, and word frequency. *Bulletin of the Psychonomic Society, 7(3),* 283–284.

Messer, D.J. (1981). The identification of names in maternal speech to infants. *Journal of Psycholinguistic Research, 10(1),* 69–77.

Miles, L.H. (1983). Apes and language: The search for communicative competence. In J. de Luce & H.T. Wilder (Eds.), *Language in primates: Perspectives and implications.* New York: Springer.

Miller, K.L. & Schmitt, C. (2012). Variable input and the acquisition of plural morphology, *Language Acquisition, 19(3),* 223–261.

Minagawa-Kawai, Y., Mori, K., Hebden, J.C. & Dupoux, E. (2008). Optical imaging of infants' neurocognitive development: Recent advances and perspectives. *Developmental Neurobiology, 68(6),* 712–728.

Mintz, T.H. (2005). Linguistic and conceptual influences on adjective acquisition in 24- and 36-month-olds. *Developmental Psychology, 41(1),* 17–29.

Moerk, E.L. (1991). Positive evidence for negative evidence. *First Language, 11(2),* 219–251.

Moerk, E.L. & Moerk, C. (1979). Quotations, imitations and generalizations: Factual and methodological analyses. *International Journal of Behavioral Development, 2(1),* 43–72.

Moon, C., Cooper, R.P. & Fifer, W.P. (1993). Two-day-olds prefer their native language. *Infant Behavior and Development, 16,* 495–500.

Morgan, J.L., Bonamo, K.M. & Travis, L.L. (1995). Negative evidence on negative evidence. *Developmental Psychology, 31(2),* 180–197.

Morgan, J.L. & Travis, L.L. (1989). Limits on negative information in language input. *Journal of Child Language, 16,* 531–552.

Morrison, C.M. & Ellis, A.W. (2000). Real age of acquisition effects in word naming and lexical decision. *British Journal of Psychology, 91,* 167–180.

Mueller, K.L., Murray, J.C., Michaelson, J.J., Christiansen, M.H., Reilly, S. & Tomblin, J.B. (2016). Common genetic variants in FOXP2 are not associated with individual differences in language development. *PLoS One, 11(4),* pp.e0152576.

Mulcaster, R. (1582). *The first part of the Elementarie, which entreateth chefelie of the right writing of our English tung.* London: T. Vautraillier.

Mumme, D.L. & Fernald, A. (2003). The infant as onlooker: Learning from emotional reactions observed in a television scenario. *Child Development, 74,* 221–237.

Muncer, S.J. & Ettlinger, G. (1981). Communication by a chimpanzee: First-trial mastery of word order that is critical for meaning, but failure to negate conjunctions. *Neuropsychologia, 19(1),* 73–78.

Murchison, C. & Langer, S. (1927). Tiedemann's observations on the development of the mental faculties of children. *Pedagogical Seminary and Journal of Genetic Psychology, 34,* 205–230.

Murphy, R.A., Mondragon, E. & Murphy, V.A. (2008). Rule learning by rats. *Science, 319(5871),* 1849–1851.

Murphy, V.A. (2000). Compounding and the representation of L2 inflectional morphology. *Language Learning, 50(1),* 153–197.

Murphy, V.A. (2010). The relationship between age of learning and exposure to the second language in L2 children. In E. Macaro (Ed.), *Continuum companion to second language acquisition.* London: Continuum.

Nagy, E., Pal, A. & Orvos, H. (2014). Learning to imitate individual finger movements by the human neonate. *Developmental Science, 17(6),* 841–857.

Nagy, W.E. & Anderson, R.C. (1984). How many words are there in printed school English? *Reading Research Quarterly, 19(3),* 304–330.

Naigles, L. (1990). Children use syntax to learn verb meanings. *Journal of Child Language, 17(2),* 357–374.

Naigles, L.R. (1996). The use of multiple frames in verb learning via syntactic bootstrapping. *Cognition, 58(2),* 221–251.

Naigles, L.G. & Gelman, S. (1995). Overextensions in comprehension and production revisited: Preferential-looking in a study of dog, cat, and cow. *Journal of Child Language, 22(1),* 19–46.

Naigles, L.G. & Kako, E.T. (1993). First contact in verb acquisition: Defining a role for syntax. *Child Development, 64(6)*, 1665–1687.

Naigles, L.R. & Maltempo, A. (2011). Verb argument structure acquisition in young children: Defining a role for discourse. *Journal of Child Language, 38(3)*, 662–674.

Naigles, L.R. & Mayeux, L. (2000). Television as an incidental teacher. In D. Singer & J. Singer (Eds.), *Handbook of children and the media* (pp. 135–153). New York: Sage.

Naigles, L.R. & Swensen, L.D. (2007). Syntactic supports for word learning. In E. Hoff & M. Shatz (Eds.), *Blackwell handbook of language development* (pp. 212–231). Malden, MA: Blackwell.

Nakayama, M. (1987). Performance factors in subject-auxiliary inversion by children. *Journal of Child Language, 14(1)*, 113–125.

Napoli, D.J. (1993). *Syntax: Theory and problems.* Oxford: Oxford University Press.

Nash, H. & Snowling, M. (2006). Teaching new words to children with poor existing vocabulary knowledge: A controlled evaluation of the definition and context methods. *International Journal of Language and Communication Disorders, 41(3)*, 335–354.

Nazzi, T., Bertoncini, J. & Mehler, J. (1998). Language discrimination by newborns: Towards an understanding of the role of rhythm. *Journal of Experimental Psychology: Human Perception and Performance, 24*, 756–766.

Nazzi, T., Dilley, L.C., Jusczyk, A.M., Shattuck-Hufnagel, S. & Jusczyk, P.W. (2005). English-learning infants' segmentation of verbs from fluent speech. *Language and Speech, 48*, 279–298.

Nazzi, T., Jusczyk, P.W. & Johnson, E.K. (2000). Language discrimination by English-learning 5-month-olds: Effects of rhythm and familiarity. *Journal of Memory and Language, 43*, 1–19.

Neiworth, J.J. (2013). Chasing sounds. *Behavioural Processes, 93*, 111–115.

Nelson, K.E., Denninger, M.M., Bonvillian, J.D., Kaplan, B.J. & Baker, N. (1984). Maternal input adjustments and non-adjustments as related to children's linguistic advances and to language acquisition theories. In A.D. Pellegrini & T.D. Yawkey (Eds.), *The development of oral and written language in social contexts.* Norwood, NJ: Ablex.

Nemeth, D., Janacsek, K., Turi, Z., Lukacs, A., Peckham, D., Szanka, S., Gazso, D., Lovassy, N. & Ullman, M.T. (2015). The production of nominal and verbal inflection in an agglutinative language: Evidence from Hungarian. *PLoS One, 10(3)*, e0119003.

Neville, H.J. & Bruer, J.T. (2001). Language processing: How experience affects brain organization. In D.B. Bailey, J.T. Bruer, F.J. Symons & J.W. Lichtman (Eds.), *Critical thinking about critical periods* (pp. 173–192). Baltimore, MD: Paul Brookes.

Neville, H.J., Coffey, S.A., Lawson, D.S., Fischer, A., Emmorey, K. & Bellugi, U. (1997). Neural systems mediating American Sign Language: Effects of sensory experience & age of acquisition. *Brain & Language, 57*, 285–308.

Newbury, D.F., Bishop, D.V.M. & Monaco, A.P. (2005). Genetic influences on language impairment and phonological short-term memory. *Trends in Cognitive Sciences, 9(11)*, 528–534.

Newman, A.J., Bavelier, D., Corina, D., Jezzard, P. & Neville, H.J. (2002). A critical period for right hemisphere recruitment in American Sign Language processing. *Nature Neuroscience, 5(1)*, 76–80.

Newman, R., Ratner, N.B., Jusczyk, A.M., Jusczyk, P.W. & Dow, K.A. (2006). Infants' early ability to segment the conversational speech signal predicts later language development: A retrospective analysis. *Developmental Psychology, 42(4)*, 643–655.

Newman, R., Rowe, M.L. & Ratner, N.B. (2015). Input and uptake at 7 months predicts toddler vocabulary: The role of child-directed-speech and infant processing skills in language development. *Journal of Child Language, 43(5)*, 1158–1173.

Newport, E.L. (1975) Motherese: The speech of mothers to young children. Unpublished doctoral dissertation, University of Pennsylvania, Philadelphia, PA.

Newport, E.L. (1988). Constraints on learning and their role in language acquisition: Studies of the acquisition of American Sign Language. *Language Sciences, 10*, 147–172.

Newport, E.L. (1990). Maturational constraints on language learning. *Cognitive Science, 14*, 11–28.

Newport, E.L., Bavelier, D. & Neville, H.J. (2001). Critical thinking about critical periods: Perspectives on a critical period for language acquisition. In E. Dupoux (Ed.), *Language, brain and cognitive development: Essays in honor of Jacques Mehler* (pp. 481–502). Cambridge, MA: MIT Press.

Newport, E.L., Gleitman, H. & Gleitman, L.R. (1977). Mother, I'd rather do it myself: Some effects and non-effects of maternal speech style. In C.E. Snow & C.A. Ferguson (Eds.), *Talking to children* (pp. 101–149). Cambridge: Cambridge University Press.

Newport, E.L., Hauser, M.D., Spaepen, G. & Aslin, R.N. (2004). Learning at a distance II: Statistical learning of non-adjacent dependencies in a non-human primate. *Cognitive Psychology, 49(2)*, 85–117.

Nicoladis, E. (2003). What compound nouns mean to preschool children. *Brain and Language, 84(1)*, 38–49.

Nicoladis, E. & Murphy, V.A. (2004). Level-ordering does not constrain children's ungrammatical compounds. *Brain and Language, 90(1–3)*, 487–494.

Nicoladis, E. & Paradis, J. (2012). Acquiring regular and irregular past tense morphemes in English and French: Evidence from bilingual children. *Language Learning, 62(1)*, 170–197.

Ninio, A. (1986). The direct mapping of function to form in children's early language. *Journal of Psycholinguistic Research, 15*, 559 (Abstract).

Ninio, A. (2004). Young children's difficulty with adjectives modifying nouns. *Journal of Child Language, 31(2)*, 255–285.

Nippold, M.A. (2016). *Later language development: The school-age and adolescent years* (4th ed.). Austin, TX: Pro-Ed.

Nishimura, T. (2005). Developmental changes in the shape of the supralaryngeal vocal tract in chimpanzees. *American Journal of Physical Anthropology, 126(2)*, 193–204.

Oakes, L.M. (2012). Advances in eye tracking in infancy research. *Infancy, 17*, 1–8.

Obler, L.K. & Gjerlow, K. (1999). *Language and the brain.* Cambridge: Cambridge University Press.

Ochs, E. (1982). Talking to children in Western Samoa. *Language in Society, 11*, 77–104.

Odean, R., Nazareth, A. & Pruden, S.M. (2015). Novel methodology to examine cognitive and experiential factors in language development: Combining eye-tracking and LENA technology. *Frontiers in Psychology, 6*, 1266.

O'Doherty, K., Troseth, G., Shimpi, P.M., Goldberg, E., Akhtar, N. & Saylor, M.M. (2011). Third-party social interaction and word learning from video. *Child Development, 82(3)*, 902–915.

Ohms, V.R., Beckers, G.J.L., ten Cate, C. & Suthers, R.A. (2012). Vocal tract articulation revisited: The case of the monk parakeet. *The Journal of Experimental Biology, 215(1)*, 85–92.

Olson, J. & Masur, E.F. (2012). Mothers respond differently to infants' familiar versus non-familiar verbal imitations. *Journal of Child Language, 39(4)*, 731–752.

Olson, J. & Masur, E.F. (2015). Mothers' labeling responses to infants' gestures predict vocabulary outcomes. *Journal of Child Language, 42(6)*, 1289–1311.

Owens, R.E. (2008). *Language development: An introduction* (7th ed.). Boston, MA: Pearson.

Pacton, S. & Deacon, S.H. (2008). The timing and mechanism of children's use of morphological information in spelling: A review of evidence from English and French. *Cognitive Development, 23(3)*, 339–359.

Pallier, C., Bosch, L. & Sebastián-Gallés, N. (1997). A limit on behavioral plasticity in speech perception. *Cognition, 64(3)*, B9–B17.

Pallier, C., Dehaene, S., Poline, J.-B., Le Bihan, D., Argenti, A.M., Dupoux, E. & Mehler, J. (2003). Brain imaging of language plasticity in adopted adults: Can a second language replace the first? *Cerebral Cortex, 13(2)*, 155–161.

Pan, B.A. (2005). Semantic development: Learning the meanings of words. In J. Berko Gleason (Ed.), *The development of language* (6th ed.) (pp. 112–147). Boston, MA: Pearson.

Patterson, F.G. (1978). The gestures of a gorilla: Language acquisition in another pongid. *Brain and Language, 5*, 72–97.

Patterson, F.G., Tanner, J. & Mayer, N. (1988). Pragmatic analysis of gorilla utterances: Early communicative development in the gorilla Koko. *Journal of Pragmatics, 12*, 35–54.

Patterson, J.L. (2002). Relationships of expressive vocabulary to frequency of reading and television experience among bilingual toddlers. *Applied Psycholinguistics, 23(4)*, 493–508.

Patterson, M.D., Bly, B.M., Porcelli, A.J. & Rypma, B. (2007). Visual working memory for global, object, and part-based information. *Memory & Cognition, 35(4)*, 738–751.

Paul, R. & Norbury, C.F. (2012). *Language disorders from infancy through adolescence: Listening, speaking, reading, writing, and communicating* (4th ed.). St Louis, MO: Elsevier.

Pearl, L. (2014). Evaluating learning-strategy components: Being fair. (Commentary on Ambridge, Pine, & Lieven). *Language, 90(3)*, e107–e114.

Peña, M., Maki, A., Kovačič, D., Dehaene-Lambertz, G., Koizumi, H., Bouquet, F. & Mehler, J. (2003). Sounds and silence: An optical topography study of language recognition at birth. *Proceedings of the National Academy of Sciences, 100(20)*, 11702–11705.

Penner, S.G. (1987). Parental responses to grammatical and ungrammatical child utterances. *Child Development, 58*, 376–384.

Pepperberg, I.M. (2006). Cognitive and communicative abilities of Grey Parrots. *Applied Animal Behavior Science, 100*, 77–86.

Pepperberg, I.M. (2010). Vocal learning in Grey Parrots: A brief review of perception, production, and cross-species comparisons. *Brain and Language, 115*, 81–91.

Pepperberg, I.M. & Carey, S. (2012). Grey Parrot number acquisition: The inference of cardinal value from ordinal position on the numeral list. *Cognition, 125(2)*, 219–232.

Pepperberg, I.M., Koepke, A., Livingston, P., Girard, M. & Leigh, A.H. (2013). Reasoning by inference: Further studies on exclusion in Grey Parrots (Psittacus erithacus). *Journal of Comparative Psychology, 127(3)*, 272–281.

Perani, D., Paulesu, E., Galles, N.S., Dupoux, E., Dehaene, S., Bettinardi, V., Cappa, S.F., Fazio, F. & Mehler, J. (1998). The bilingual brain: Proficiency and age of acquisition of the second language. *Brain, 121,* 1841–1852.

Pérez-Leroux, A.T. & Kahnemuyipour, A. (2014). News, somewhat exaggerated: Commentary on Ambridge, Pine, & Lieven. *Language, 90(3)*, e115–e125.

Peter, M., Chang, F., Pine, J.M., Blything, R. & Rowland, C.F. (2015). When and how do children develop knowledge of verb argument structure? Evidence from verb bias effects in a structural priming task. *Journal of Memory and Language, 81*, 1–15.

Philippon, A.C., Cherryman, J., Bull, R. & Vrij, A. (2007). Earwitness identification performance: The effect of language, target, deliberate strategies and indirect measures. *Applied Cognitive Psychology, 21(4)*, 539–550.

Phillips, J.R. (1973). Syntax and vocabulary of mothers' speech to young children: Age and sex comparisons. *Child Development, 44*, 182–185.

Piaget, J. & Inhelder, B. (1974). *The child's construction of quantities: Conservation and atomism.* London: Routledge & Kegan Paul.

Piattelli-Palmarini, M. (Ed.) (1980). *Language and learning: The debate between Jean Piaget and Noam Chomsky.* Cambridge, MA: Harvard University Press.

Pierotti, R. & Annett, C. (1994). Patterns of aggression in gulls: Asymmetries and tactics in different social categories. *The Condor, 96(3)*, 590–599.

Pilley, J.W. (2013). Border collie comprehends sentences containing a prepositional object, verb, and direct object. *Learning and Motivation, 44(4)*, 229–240.

Pilley, J.W. & Reid, A.K. (2011). Border collie comprehends object names as verbal referents. *Behavioural Processes, 86(2)*, 184–195.

Pine, J.M. (1995). Variation in vocabulary development as a function of birth order. *Child Development, 66(1)*, 272–281.

Pine, J.M. & Lieven, E.V.M. (1993). Reanalyzing rote-learned phrases: Individual differences in the transition to multi-word speech. *Journal of Child Language, 20(3)*, 551–571.

Pinker, S. (1984). *Language learnability and language development.* Cambridge, MA: Harvard University Press.

Pinker, S. (1989). *Learnability and cognition: The acquisition of argument structure.* Cambridge, MA: MIT Press.

Pinker, S. (1994). *The language instinct: The new science of language and mind.* London: Penguin.

Pinker, S. (1999). *Words and rules: The ingredients of language.* New York: Perennial.

Pinker, S. & Jackendoff, R. (2005). The faculty of language: What's special about it? *Cognition, 95(2)*, 201–236.

Pinker, S. & Prince, A. (1988). On language and connectionism: Analysis of a parallel distributed processing model of language acquisition. *Cognition, 28(1–2)*, 73–193.

Pinker, S. & Ullman, M.T. (2002). The past and future of the past tense. *Trends in Cognitive Sciences, 6(11)*, 456–463.

Plomin, R. (1990). *Nature and nurture: An introduction to human behavioral genetics.* Pacific Grove, CA: Brooks/Cole.

Plunkett, K. & Wood, C. (2004). The development of children's understanding of grammar. In J. Oates & A. Grayson (Eds.), *Cognitive and language development in children* (pp. 163–204). Milton Keynes: Open University Press.

Polka, L., Jusczyk, P.W. & Ravchev, S. (1995). Methods for studying speech perception in infants and children. In W. Strange (Ed.), *Speech perception and linguistic experience: Theoretical and methodological issues in cross-language speech research.* Timonium, MD: York Press.

Poremba, A., Malloy, M., Saunders, R.C., Carson, R.E., Herscovitch, P. & Mishkin, M. (2004). Species-specific calls evoke asymmetric activity in the monkey's temporal poles. *Nature, 427,* 448–451.

Post, K. (1994). Negative evidence in the language learning environment of laterborns in a rural Florida community. In J.L. Sokolov & C.E. Snow (Eds.), *Handbook of research in language development using CHILDES* (pp. 132–173). Hillsdale, NJ: Lawrence Erlbaum.

Poulin-Dubois, D. & Graham, S.A. (2007). Cognitive processes in early word learning. In E. Hoff & M. Shatz (Eds.), *Blackwell handbook of language development* (pp. 191–211). Malden, MA: Blackwell.

Premack, D. & Woodruff, G. (1978). Does the chimpanzee have a theory of mind? *Behavioral and Brain Sciences, 1(4),* 515–526.

Price, P.J., Ostendorf, M., Shattuck-Hufnagel, S. & Fong, C. (1991). The use of prosody in syntactic disambiguation. *Journal of the Acoustical Society of America, 90(6),* 2956–2970.

Pullum, G.K. & Scholz, B.C. (2002). Empirical assessment of stimulus poverty arguments. *Linguistic Review, 19,* 9–50.

Purver, M., Ginzburg, J. & Healey, P. (2001). On the means for clarification in dialogue. In J. van Kuppevelt & R. Smith (Eds.), *Current and new directions in discourse and dialogue* (pp. 235–256). Dordrecht: Kluwer.

Pye, C. (1986). Quiché Mayan speech to children. *Journal of Child Language, 13(1),* 85–100.

Quine, W.V.O. (1960). *Word and object.* Cambridge, MA: MIT Press.

Rabin, J. & Deacon, H. (2008). The representation of morphologically complex words in the developing lexicon. *Journal of Child Language, 35(2),* 453–465.

Radford, A. (1990). *Syntactic theory and the acquisition of English syntax: The nature of early child grammars of English.* Oxford: Basil Blackwell.

Radford, A., Atkinson, M., Britain, D., Clahsen, H. & Spencer, A. (1999). *Linguistics: An introduction.* Cambridge: Cambridge University Press.

Raffaele, P. (2006). Speaking bonobo. *Smithsonian, 37(8),* 74.

Ramirez, N.F., Leonard, M.K., Torres, C., Hatrak, M., Halgren, E. & Mayberry, R.I. (2014). Neural language processing in adolescent first-language learners. *Cerebral Cortex, 24(10),* 2772–2783.

Ramirez, N.F., Liebermann, A.M. & Mayberry, R.I. (2013). The initial stages of first-language acquisition begun in adolescence: When late looks early. *Journal of Child Language, 40(2),* 391–414.

Ramírez-Esparza, N., García-Sierra, A. & Kuhl, P.K. (2014). Look who's talking: Speech style and social context in language input to infants are linked to concurrent and future speech development. *Developmental Science, 17(6)*, 880–891.

Ramscar, M., Dye, M. & Hübner, M. (2013). When the fly flied and when the fly flew: How semantics affect the processing of inflected verbs. *Language and Cognitive Processes, 28(4)*, 468–497.

Räsänen, S.H.M., Ambridge, B. & Pine, J.M. (2014). Infinitives or bare stems? Are English-speaking children defaulting to the highest-frequency form? *Journal of Child Language, 41(4)*, 756–779.

Ravid, D. & Geiger, V. (2009). Promoting morphological awareness in Hebrew-speaking grade-schoolers: An intervention using linguistic humor. *First Language, 29(1)*, 81–112.

Reali, F. & Christiansen, M.H. (2005). Uncovering the richness of the stimulus: Structure dependence and indirect statistical evidence. *Cognitive Science, 29*, 1007–1028.

Regel, S., Opitz, A., Müller, G. & Friederici, A.D. (2015). The past tense debate revisited: Electrophysiological evidence for subregularities of irregular verb inflection. *Journal of Cognitive Neuroscience, 27(9)*, 1870–1885.

Regier, T. & Gahl, S. (2004). Learning the unlearnable: The role of missing evidence. *Cognition, 93*, 147–155.

Rensink, R.A., O'Regan, J.K. & Clark, J.J. (2000). On the failure to detect changes in scenes across brief interruptions. *Visual Cognition, 7(1–3)*, 127–145.

Rescorla, L.A. (1980). Overextension in early language development. *Journal of Child Language, 7*, 321–335.

Rescorla, L.A., Lee, Y., Oh, K. & Kim, Y. (2013). Lexical development in Korean: Vocabulary size, lexical composition, and late talking. *Journal of Speech, Language, and Hearing Research, 56(2)*, 735–747.

Ribeiro, L.A., Zachrisson, H.D., Gustavson, K. & Schjølberg, S. (2016). Maternal distress during pregnancy and language development in preschool age: A population-based cohort study. *European Journal of Developmental Psychology, 13(1)*, 20–39.

Rice, M.L., Huston, A.C., Truglio, R. & Wright, J. (1990). Words from Sesame Street: Learning vocabulary while viewing. *Developmental Psychology, 26(3)*, 421–428.

Rice, M.L. & Woodsmall, L. (1988). Lessons from television: Children's word learning when viewing. *Child Development, 59(2)*, 420–429.

Risch, N.J. (2000). Searching for genetic determinants in the new millennium. *Nature, 405(6788)*, 847–856.

Rivas, E. (2005). Recent use of signs by chimpanzees (Pan Troglodytes) in interactions with humans. *Journal of Comparative Psychology, 119(4)*, 401–417.

Rivera-Gaxiola, M., Silva-Pereyra, J. & Kuhl, P.K. (2005). Brain potentials to native and non-native speech contrasts in 7- and 11-month-old American infants. *Developmental Science, 8(2)*, 162–172.

Rizzolatti, G. & Arbib, M.A. (1998). Language within our grasp. *Trends in Neurosciences, 21(5)*, 188–194.

Rochat, P. (2001). *The infant's world.* Cambridge, MA: Harvard University Press.

Rogers, T.T. & Patterson, K. (2007). Object categorization: Reversals and explanations of the basic-level advantage. *Journal of Experimental Psychology: General, 136(3)*, 451–469.

348

Rohde, D.L.T. & Plaut, D.C. (1999). Language acquisition in the absence of explicit negative evidence: How important is starting small? *Cognition, 72(1)*, 67–109.

Romberg, A. & Saffran, J.R. (2010). Statistical learning and language acquisition. *Advanced Review WIREs Cognitive Science*. Published online: 26 July 2010.

Rondal, J. & Cession, A. (1990). Input evidence regarding the semantic bootstrapping hypothesis. *Journal of Child Language, 17*, 711–717.

Rosch, E.H. (1973). Natural categories. *Cognitive Psychology, 4(3)*, 328–350.

Rosen, S. & Iverson, P. (2007). Constructing adequate non-speech analogues: What is special about speech anyway? *Developmental Science, 10(2)*, 165–168.

Rosenthal Rollins, P. & Snow, C.E. (1998). Shared attention and grammatical development in typical children and children with autism. *Journal of Child Language, 25(3)*, 653–673.

Rowe, M.L. (2008). Child-directed speech: Relation to socioeconomic status, knowledge of child development and child vocabulary skill. *Journal of Child Language, 35(1)*, 185–205.

Rowe, M.L. (2012). A longitudinal investigation of the role of quantity and quality of child-directed speech in vocabulary development. *Child Development, 83(5)*, 1762–1774.

Rowe, M.L. & Goldin-Meadow, S. (2009a). Early gesture selectively predicts later language learning. *Developmental Science, 12(1)*, 182–187.

Rowe, M.L. & Goldin-Meadow, S. (2009b). Differences in early gesture explain SES disparities in child vocabulary size at school entry. *Science, 323(5916)*, 951–953.

Rowland, C.F. (2007). Explaining errors in children's questions. *Cognition, 104(1)*, 106–134.

Rowland, C.F. (2014). *Understanding language acquisition*. Abingdon: Routledge.

Ruffman, T., Slade, L. & Redman, J. (2005). Young infants' expectations about hidden objects. *Cognition, 97(2)*, B35–B43.

Rumelhart, D.E. & McClelland, J.L. (1986). On learning the past tenses of English verbs. In J.L. McClelland, D.E. Rumelhart & the PDP Research Group (Eds.), *Parallel distributed processing: Explorations in the microstructure of cognition. Vol. 2: Psychological and biological models*. Cambridge, MA: Bradford Books/MIT Press.

Rymer, R. (1993). *Genie: A scientific tragedy*. Harmondsworth: Penguin.

Sachs, J., Bard, B. & Johnson, M.L. (1981). Language learning with restricted input: Case studies of two hearing children of deaf parents. *Applied Psycholinguistics, 2*, 33–54.

Sachs, J., Brown, R. & Salerno, R. (1976). Adult's speech to children. In W. von Raffler Engel & Y. Lebrun (Eds.), *Baby talk and infant speech* (pp. 240–245). Lisse: Peter de Ridder Press.

Saffran, J.R. (2003). Statistical language learning: Mechanisms and constraints. *Current Directions in Psychological Science, 12(4)*, 110–114.

Saffran, J.R., Aslin, R.N. & Newport, E.L. (1996). Statistical learning by 8-month-old infants. *Science, 274(5294)*, 1926–1928.

Saffran, J.R., Hauser, M., Seibel, R.L., Kapfhamer, J., Tsao, F. & Cushman, F. (2008). Grammatical pattern learning by infants and cotton-top tamarin monkeys. *Cognition, 107*, 479–500.

Saffran, J.R., Johnson, E.K., Aslin, R.N. & Newport, E.L. (1999). Statistical learning of tone sequences by human infants and adults. *Cognition, 70*, 27–52.

Saffran, J.R., Newport, E.L. & Aslin, R.N. (1996). Word segmentation: The role of distributional cues. *Journal of Memory and Language, 35*, 606–621.

Saffran, J.R., Pollak, S.D., Seibel, R.L. & Shkolnik, A. (2007). Dog is a dog is a dog: Infant rule learning is not specific to language. *Cognition, 105(3)*, 669–680.

Saffran, J.R. & Thiessen, E.D. (2003). Pattern induction by infant language learners. *Developmental Psychology, 39*, 484–494.

Saffran, J.R. & Thiessen, E.D. (2007). Domain-general learning capacities. In E. Hoff & M. Shatz (Eds.), *Blackwell handbook of language development* (pp. 68–86). Malden, MA: Blackwell.

Saito, A. & Shinozuka, K. (2013). Vocal recognition of owners by domestic cats (Felis catus). *Animal Cognition, 16(4)*, 685–690.

Salkie, R. (1990). *The Chomsky update: Linguistics and politics.* London: Unwin Hyman.

Sampson, G. (2005). *The 'language instinct' debate* (revised ed.). London: Continuum.

Samuelson, L.K., Horst, J.S., Schutte, A.R. & Dobbertin, B.N. (2008). Rigid thinking about deformables: Do children sometimes overgeneralize the shape bias? *Journal of Child Language, 35(3)*, 559–589.

Samuelson, L.K. & Smith, L.B. (2005). They call it like they see it: Spontaneous naming and attention to shape. *Developmental Science, 8*, 182–198.

Santelmann, L., Berk, S., Austin, J., Somashekar, S. & Lust, B. (2002). Continuity and development in the acquisition of inversion in yes/no questions: Dissociating movement and inflection. *Journal of Child Language, 29(4)*, 813–842.

Sarnecka, B.W., Kamenskaya, T.O., Yamana, Y. & Yudovina, J.B. (2004). *Language as lens: Plural marking and numeral learning in English, Japanese, and Russian.* Somerville, MA: Cascadilla Press.

Savage-Rumbaugh, E.S., Murphy, J., Sevcik, R.A., Brakke, K.E., Williams, S.L. & Rumbaugh, D.M. (1993). Language comprehension in ape and child. *Monographs of the Society for Research in Child Development. Serial 233, 58*, 3–4.

Saxton, M. (1995). Negative evidence versus negative feedback: A study of corrective input in child language acquisition. Unpublished doctoral dissertation, University of Oxford.

Saxton, M. (1997). The Contrast theory of negative input. *Journal of Child Language, 24*, 139–161.

Saxton, M. (2000). Negative evidence and negative feedback: Immediate effects on the grammaticality of child speech. *First Language, 20(2)*, 221–252.

Saxton, M. (2008). What's in a name? Coming to terms with the child's linguistic environment. *Journal of Child Language, 35(3)*, 677–686.

Saxton, M. (2009). The inevitability of Child Directed Speech. In S. Foster-Cohen (Ed.), *Advances in language acquisition* (pp. 62–86). London: Palgrave Macmillan.

Saxton, M., Backley, P. & Gallaway, C. (2005). Negative input for grammatical errors: Effects after a lag of 12 weeks. *Journal of Child Language, 32*, 643–672.

Saxton, M., Houston-Price, C. & Dawson, N. (2005). The Prompt hypothesis: Clarification requests as corrective input for grammatical errors. *Applied Psycholinguistics, 26(3)*, 393–414.

Saxton, M., Kulcsar, B., Marshall, G. & Rupra, M. (1998). Longer-term effects of corrective input: An experimental approach. *Journal of Child Language, 25*, 701–721.

Scaife, M. & Bruner, J. (1975). The capacity for joint visual attention in infants. *Nature, 253*, 265–266.

Schachter, F.F., Fosha, D., Stemp, S., Brotman, N. & Ganger, S. (1976). Everyday caretaker talk to toddlers vs. 3s and 4s. *Journal of Child Language, 3(2)*, 221–245.

Schachter, J. (1990). On the issue of completeness in second language acquisition. *Second Language Research, 6*, 93–124.

Schlesinger, I.M. (1977). Role of cognitive development and linguistic input in language acquisition. *Journal of Child Language, 4(2)*, 153–169.

Schmidt, A., Oliveira, F.M., Santos Lotério, L. & Gomes, G. (2016). Learning name–object relations after a single exclusion trial in 18- to 48-month-old children. *The Psychological Record, 66(1)*, 53–63.

Schmidt, C.L. (1996). Scrutinizing reference: How gesture and speech are coordinated in mother–child interaction. *Journal of Child Language, 23(2)*, 279–305.

Schmidt, C.L. & Lawson, K.R. (2002). Caregiver attention-focusing and children's attention-sharing behaviours as predictors of later verbal IQ in very low birthweight children. *Journal of Child Language, 29(1)*, 3–22.

Scholz, B.C. & Pullum, G.K. (2006). Irrational nativist exuberance. In R.J. Stainton (Ed.), *Contemporary debates in cognitive science* (pp. 59–80). Oxford: Basil Blackwell.

Schoner, G. & Thelen, E. (2006). Using dynamic field theory to rethink infant habituation. *Psychological Review, 113(2)*, 273–299.

Schouten, B., Gerrits, E. & van Hessen, A. (2003). The end of categorical perception as we know it. *Speech Communication, 41*, 71–80.

Scofield, J. & Behrend, D.A. (2011). Clarifying the role of joint attention in early word learning. *First Language, 31(3)*, 326–341.

Scovel, T. (1988). *A time to speak: A psycholinguistic inquiry into the critical period for human speech*. Cambridge, MA: Newbury House.

Seidenberg, M.S. (1992). Connectionism without tears. In S. Davis (Ed.), *Connectionism: Theory and practice* (pp. 84–122). New York: Oxford University Press.

Seidenberg, M.S., MacDonald, M.C. & Saffran, J.R. (2002). Does grammar start where statistics stop? *Science, 298(5593)*, 553–554.

Seidenberg, M.S. & Petitto, L.A. (1979). Signing behavior in apes: A critical review. *Cognition, 7*, 177–215.

Seidl, A. & Johnson, E.K. (2006). Infant word segmentation revisited: Edge alignment facilitates target extraction. *Developmental Science, 9(6)*, 565–573.

Seidl, A. & Johnson, E.K. (2008). Boundary alignment enables 11-month-olds to segment vowel initial words from speech. *Journal of Child Language, 35(1)*, 1–24.

Seifert, K.L., Hoffnung, R.J. & Hoffnung, M. (2000). *Lifespan development* (2nd ed.). Boston, MA: Houghton Mifflin.

Seitz, S. & Stewart, C. (1975). Imitations and expansions: Some developmental aspects of mother–child communication. *Developmental Psychology, 11(6)*, 763–768.

Seuss, Dr (1958). *The cat in the hat.* London: Collins.

Seyfarth, R.M. & Cheney, D.L. (2003). Signalers and receivers in animal communication. *Annual Review of Psychology, 54*, 145–173.

Shady, M. & Gerken, L. (1999). Grammatical and caregiver cues in early sentence comprehension. *Journal of Child Language, 26(1)*, 163–175.

Shankweiler, D., Palumbo, L.C., Fulbright, R.K., Mencl, W.E., Van Dyke, J., Kollia, B., et al. (2010). Testing the limits of language production in long-term survivors of major stroke: A psycholinguistic and anatomic study. *Aphasiology, 24(11)*, 1455–1485.

Shatz, M. & Gelman, R. (1973). The development of communication skills: Modifications in the speech of young children as a function of the listener. *Monographs of the Society for Research in Child Development*, serial no. 5, 38.

Shaw, G.B. (1911). *The doctor's dilemma, getting married, and the shewing-up of Blanco Posnet*. London: Constable.

Shneidman, L.A., Arroyo, M.E., Levine, S.C. & Goldin-Meadow, S. (2013). What counts as effective input for word learning? *Journal of Child Language, 40(3)*, 672–686.

Shultz, S. & Vouloumanos, A. (2010). Three-month-olds prefer speech to other naturally occurring signals. *Language Learning and Development, 6(4)*, 241–257.

Siegel, L.S. (2008). Morphological awareness skills of English language learners and children with dyslexia. *Topics in Language Disorders, 28(1)*, 15–27.

Singh, L., Liederman, J., Mierzejewski, R. & Barnes, J. (2011). Rapid reacquisition of native phoneme contrasts after disuse: You do not always lose what you do not use. *Developmental Science, 14(5)*, 949–959.

Singh, L., Reznick, J.S. & Xuehua, L. (2012). Infant word segmentation and childhood vocabulary development: A longitudinal analysis. *Developmental Science, 15(4)*, 482–495.

Sinnott, J.M. (1998). Comparative phoneme boundaries. *Current Topics in Acoustical Research, 2*, 135–138.

Skinner, B.F. (1957). *Verbal behavior*. New York: Appleton-Century-Crofts.

Slobin, D.I. (1973). Cognitive prerequisites for the development of grammar. In C.A. Ferguson & D.I. Slobin (Eds.), *Studies of child language development*. New York: Holt, Rinehart & Winston.

Slobin, D.I. (1978). A case study of early language awareness. In A. Sinclair, R.J. Jarvella & W.J.M. Levelt (Eds.), *The child's conception of language* (pp. 45–54). New York: Springer.

Smith, L.B. (1999). Children's noun learning: How general learning processes make specialized learning mechanisms. In B. MacWhinney (Ed.), *The emergence of language* (pp. 277–303). Mahwah, NJ: Lawrence Erlbaum.

Smith, L.B. (2000). Learning how to learn words: An associative crane. In R.M. Golinkoff, K. Hirsh-Pasek, L. Bloom, L.B. Smith, A.L. Woodward, N. Akhtar, M. Tomasello & G. Hollich (Eds.), *Becoming a word learner: A debate on lexical acquisition* (pp. 51–80). Oxford: Oxford University Press.

Smith, L.B. (2001). How domain-general processes may create domain-specific biases. In M. Bowerman & S.C. Levinson (Eds.), *Language acquisition and conceptual development* (pp. 101–131). Cambridge: Cambridge University Press.

Smith, N. (2004). *Chomsky: Ideas and ideals* (2nd ed.). Cambridge: Cambridge University Press.

Smith, N.A. & Trainor, L. (2008). Infant-directed speech is modulated by infant feedback. *Infancy, 13(4)*, 410–420.

Smith-Lock, K.M. (2015). Rule-based learning of regular past tense in children with specific language impairment. *Cognitive Neuropsychology*, *32(3–4)*, 221–242.

Snow, C.E. (1972). Mothers' speech to children learning language. *Child Development*, *43(2)*, 549–566.

Snow, C.E. (1981). The uses of imitation. *Journal of Child Language*, *8(1)*, 205–212.

Snow, C.E. (1987). Relevance of a critical period to language acquisition. In M.H. Bornstein (Ed.), *Sensitive periods in development: Interdisciplinary perspectives* (pp. 183–210). Hillsdale, NJ: Lawrence Erlbaum.

Snow, C.E. (1995). Issues in the study of input: Finetuning, universality, individual and developmental differences and necessary causes. In P. Fletcher & B. MacWhinney (Eds.), *The handbook of child language* (pp. 180–193). Oxford: Basil Blackwell.

Snow, C.E., Arlman-Rupp, A., Hassing, Y., Jobse, J., Joosten, J. & Vorster, J. (1976). Mothers' speech in three social classes. *Journal of Psycholinguistic Research*, *5*, 1–20.

Snyder, W. (2007). *Child language: The parametric approach.* Oxford: Oxford University Press.

Soderstrom, M. (2007). Beyond babytalk: Re-evaluating the nature and content of speech input to preverbal infants. *Developmental Review*, *27(4)*, 501–532.

Soderstrom, M. (2014). All hands on deck: In defense of the prosodic bootstrapping hypothesis and multiple theoretical approaches. (Commentary on Ambridge, Pine, & Lieven.) *Language*, *90(3)*, e126–e130.

Soderstrom, M., Blossom, M., Foygel, R. & Morgan, J.L. (2008). Acoustical cues and grammatical units in speech to two preverbal infants. *Journal of Child Language*, *35(4)*, 869–902.

Soja, N.N., Carey, S. & Spelke, E.S. (1991). Ontological categories guide young children's inductions of word meaning – object terms and substance terms. *Cognition*, *38(2)*, 179–211.

Sommerville, J.A. & Crane, C.C. (2009). Ten-month-old infants use prior information to identify an actor's goal. *Developmental Science*, *12(2)*, 314–325.

Song, L., Spier, E.T. & Tamis-LeMonda, C.S. (2014). Reciprocal influences between maternal language and children's language and cognitive development in low-income families. *Journal of Child Language*, *41(2)*, 305–326.

Song, S., Su, M., Kang, C., Liu, H., Zhang, Y., McBride-Chang, C., Tardif, T., Li, H., Liang, W., Zhang, Z. & Shu, H. (2015). Tracing children's vocabulary development from preschool through the school-age years: An 8-year longitudinal study. *Developmental Science*, *18(1)*, 119–131.

Sontag, L.W. & Wallace, R.I. (1936). Changes in the heart rate of the human fetal heart in response to vibratory stimuli. *American Journal of Diseases*, *51*, 583–589.

Sorace, A. (1993). Incomplete vs. divergent representations of unaccusativity in non-native grammars of Italian. *Second Language Research*, *9*, 22–47.

Spaai, G.W.G., Derksen, E.S., Hermes, D.J. & Kaufholz, P.A.P. (1996). Teaching intonation to young deaf children with the intonation meter. *Folia Phoniatrica et Logopaedica*, *48*, 22–34.

Spaepen, E. & Spelke, E. (2007). Will any doll do? 12-month-olds' reasoning about goal objects. *Cognitive Psychology*, *54(2)*, 133–154.

Spelke, E.S. (1994). Initial knowledge: Six suggestions. *Cognition*, *50*, 443–447.

Spelke, E.S. & Kinzler, K.D. (2007). Core knowledge. *Developmental Science*, *10(1)*, 89–96.

Spence, M.J. & DeCasper, A.J. (1987). Prenatal experience with low-frequency maternal-voice sounds influences neonatal perception of maternal voice samples. *Infant Behavior and Development, 10*, 133–142.

Srinivasan, M. & Snedeker, J. (2014). Polysemy and the taxonomic constraint: Children's representation of words that label multiple kinds. *Language Learning and Development, 10(2)*, 97–128.

Stanfield, C., Williamson, R. & Özçalişkan, Ş. (2014). How early do children understand gesture–speech combinations with iconic gestures? *Journal of Child Language, 41(2)*, 462–471.

Stark, R.E. (1986). Prespeech segmental feature development. In P. Fletcher & M. Garman (Eds.), *Language acquisition: Studies in first language development* (2nd ed.) (pp. 149–173). Cambridge: Cambridge University Press.

Stern, D.N., Spieker, S., Barnett, R.K. & MacKain, K. (1983). The prosody of maternal speech: Infant age and context related changes. *Journal of Child Language, 10(1)*, 1–15.

Stern, W. (1924). *Psychology of early childhood up to the sixth year of age.* New York: Holt.

Stich, S. (1975). *Innate ideas.* Berkeley, CA: University of California Press.

Stilwell-Peccei, J. (2006). *Child language: A resource book for students.* Abingdon: Routledge.

Stoel-Gammon, C. & Sosa, A.V. (2007). Phonological development. In E. Hoff & M. Shatz (Eds.), *Blackwell handbook of language development* (pp. 238–256). Malden, MA: Blackwell.

Stoeger, A., Mietchen, D., Oh, S., De Silva, S., Herbst, C., Kwon, S. & Fitch, W.T. (2012). An Asian elephant imitates human speech. *Current Biology, 22(22)*, 2144–2148.

Strapp, C.M. (1999). Mothers', fathers', and siblings' responses to children's language errors: Comparing sources of negative evidence. *Journal of Child Language, 26*, 373–391.

Strapp, C.M., Bleakney, D.M., Helmick, A.L. & Tonkovich, H.M. (2008). Developmental differences in the effects of negative and positive evidence. *First Language, 28(1)*, 35–53.

Strapp, C.M. & Federico, A. (2000). Imitations and repetitions: What do children say following recasts? *First Language, 20(3)*, 273–290.

Streeter, L.A. (1976). Language perception of 2-month-old infants shows effects of both innate mechanisms and experience. *Nature, 259*, 39–41.

Sully, J. (1895). *Studies of childhood.* London: Longmans Green.

Sumner, M. & Samuel, A.G. (2007). Lexical inhibition and sublexical facilitation are surprisingly long lasting. *Journal of Experimental Psychology – Learning Memory and Cognition, 33(4)*, 769–790.

Suzuki, T. & Yoshinaga, N. (2013). Children's knowledge of hierarchical phrase structure: Quantifier floating in Japanese. *Journal of Child Language, 40(3)*, 628–655.

Swensen, L.D., Naigles, L.R. & Fein, D. (2007). Does maternal input affect the language of children with autism? In H. Caunt-Nolan, S. Kulatilake & I. Woo (Eds.), *Proceedings of the 30th Annual Boston University conference on language development.* Somerville, MA: Cascadilla Press.

Szagun, G. (2001). Learning different regularities: The acquisition of noun plurals by German-speaking children. *First Language, 21(2)*, 109–141.

Taha, H. & Saiegh-Haddad, E. (2016). The role of phonological versus morphological skills in the development of Arabic spelling: An intervention study. *Journal of Psycholinguist Research, 45(3)*, 507–535.

Taine, H. (1877). On the acquisition of language by children. *Mind, 2*, 252–259.

Tamis-LeMonda, C.S., Bornstein, M., Kahana-Kalman, R., Baumwell, L. & Cyphers, L. (1998). Predicting variation in the timing of language milestones in the second year: An events history approach. *Journal of Child Language, 25,* 675–700.

Tamis-LeMonda, C.S., Kuchirko, Y. & Song, L. (2014). Why is infant language learning facilitated by parental responsiveness? *Current Directions in Psychological Science, 23(2),* 121–126.

Tardif, T. (1996). Nouns are not always learned before verbs: Evidence from Mandarin speakers' early vocabularies. *Developmental Psychology, 32(3),* 492–504.

Tardif, T., Gelman, S.A. & Xu, F. (1999). Putting the 'noun bias' in context: A comparison of English and Mandarin. *Child Development, 70(3),* 620–635.

Taylor, N., Donovan, W., Miles, S. & Leavitt, L. (2009). Maternal control strategies, maternal language usage and children's language usage at two years. *Journal of Child Language, 36(2),* 381–404.

Teigen, K.H. (1984). Note on the origin of the term nature and nurture – not Shakespeare and Galton, but Mulcaster. *Journal of the History of the Behavioral Sciences, 20(4),* 363–364.

ten Cate, C. (2014). On the phonetic and syntactic processing abilities of birds: From songs to speech and artificial grammars. *Current Opinion in Neurobiology, 28,* 157–164.

Tenenbaum, E.J., Sobel, D.M., Sheinkopf, S.J., Malle, B.F. & Morgan, J.L. (2015). Attention to the mouth and gaze following in infancy predict language development. *Journal of Child Language, 42(6),* 1173–1190.

Terrace, H. (1979). *Nim.* New York: Knopf.

Theakston, A.L. & Lieven, E.V.M. (2008). The influence of discourse context on children's provision of auxiliary BE. *Journal of Child Language, 35(1),* 129–158.

Theakston, A.L., Lieven, E.V.M., Pine, J.M. & Rowland, C.F. (2002). Going, going, gone: The acquisition of the verb 'go'. *Journal of Child Language, 29(4),* 783–811.

Theakston, A.L., Lieven, E.V.M., Pine, J.M. & Rowland, C.F. (2004). Semantic generality, input frequency and the acquisition of syntax. *Journal of Child Language, 31(1),* 61–99.

Thiessen, E.D., Hill, E.A. & Saffran, J.R. (2005). Infant-directed speech facilitates word segmentation. *Infancy, 7(1),* 53–71.

Thiessen, E.D. & Saffran, J.R. (2003). When cues collide: Use of stress and statistical cues to word boundaries by 7- to 9-month-old infants. *Developmental Psychology, 39(4),* 706–716.

Thiessen, E.D. & Saffran, J.R. (2004). Spectral tilt as a cue to word segmentation in infancy and adulthood. *Perception and Psychophysics, 66(5),* 779–791.

Thurm, A., Lord, C., Lee, L.C. & Newschaffer, C. (2007). Predictors of language acquisition in preschool children with autism spectrum disorders. *Journal of Autism and Developmental Disorders, 37(9),* 1721–1734.

Tomasello, M. (1992). *First verbs: A case study of early grammatical development.* New York: Cambridge University Press.

Tomasello, M. (2003). *Constructing a language: A usage-based theory of language acquisition.* Cambridge, MA: Harvard University Press.

Tomasello, M. (2004). Syntax or semantics? Response to Lidz et al. *Cognition, 93(2),* 139–140.

Tomasello, M. (2005). Beyond formalities: The case of language acquisition. *The Linguistic Review, 22(2–4),* 183–197.

Tomasello, M. (2009). The usage-based theory of language acquisition. In E.L. Bavin (Ed.), *The Cambridge handbook of child language* (pp. 69–87). Cambridge: Cambridge University Press.

Tomasello, M. & Carpenter, M. (2007). Shared intentionality. *Developmental Science, 10(1)*, 121–125.

Tomasello, M., Carpenter, M., Call, J., Behne, T. & Moll, H. (2005). Understanding and sharing intentions: The origins of cultural cognition. *Behavioral and Brain Sciences, 28(5)*, 675–691.

Tomasello, M. & Kaminski, J. (2009). Like infant, like dog. *Science, 325(5945)*, 1213–1214.

Tomasello, M., Mannle, S. & Kruger, A.C. (1986). Linguistic environment of 1- to 2-year-old twins. *Developmental Psychology, 22*, 169–176.

Tomasello, M. & Stahl, D. (2004). Sampling children's spontaneous speech: How much is enough? *Journal of Child Language, 31(1)*, 101–121.

Trehub, S.E. (1976). The discrimination of foreign speech contrasts by infants and adults. *Child Development, 47*, 466–472.

Trevarthen, C. (1983). Interpersonal abilities of infants as generators for transmission of language and culture. In A. Oliverio & M. Zapella (Eds.), *The behaviour of human infants*. London: Plenum.

Tsao, F.M., Liu, H.M. & Kuhl, P.K. (2004). Speech perception in infancy predicts language development in the second year of life: A longitudinal study. *Child Development, 75(4)*, 1067–1084.

Tsao, F.M., Liu, H.M. & Kuhl, P.K. (2006). Perception of native and non-native affricate-fricative contrasts: Cross-language tests on adults and infants. *Journal of the Acoustical Society of America, 120(4)*, 2285–2294.

Tsushima, T., Takizawa, O., Sasaki, M., Nishi, K., Kohno, M., Menyuk, P. & Best, C.T. (1994). Discrimination of English /r-l/ and /w-y/ by Japanese infants at 6–12 months: Language specific developmental changes in speech perception abilities. Paper presented at International Conference on Spoken Language Processing, 4. Yokohama, Japan.

Uchikoshi, Y. (2005). Narrative development in bilingual kindergartners: Can Arthur help? *Developmental Psychology, 41(3)*, 464–478.

Ullman, M.T., Pancheva, R., Love, T., Yee, E., Swinney, D. & Hickok, G. (2005). Neural correlates of lexicon and grammar: Evidence from the production, reading and judgment of inflection in aphasia. *Brain and Language, 93(2)*, 185–238.

Uriagereka, J. (1998). *Rhyme and reason: An introduction to minimalist syntax*. Cambridge, MA: MIT Press.

Valian, V. (2014). Arguing about innateness. *Journal of Child Language, 41(S1)*, 78–92.

Vasilyeva, M., Waterfall, H. & Huttenlocher, J. (2008). Emergence of syntax: Commonalities and differences across children. *Developmental Science, 11(1)*, 84–97.

Vihman, M.M. (2014). *Phonological development: The first two years* (2nd ed.). Malden, MA: Wiley-Blackwell.

Vivanti, G., Nadig, A., Ozonoff, S. & Rogers, S.J. (2008). What do children with autism attend to during imitation tasks? *Journal of Experimental Child Psychology, 101(3)*, 186–205.

von Frisch, K. (1954). *The dancing bees: An account of the life and senses of the honey bee* (translated by D. Ilse). London: Methuen.

von Humboldt, W. (1836/1988). *Über die Verschiedenheit des menschlichen Sprachbaues und ihren Einfluss auf die geistige Entwickelung des Menschengeschlechts*. English translation by P. Heath. Cambridge: Cambridge University Press.

Vouloumanos, A. & Curtin, S. (2014). Foundational tuning: How infants' attention to speech predicts language development. *Cognitive Science, 38(8)*, 1675–1686.

Vouloumanos, A., Hauser, M.D., Werker, J.F. & Martin, A. (2010). The tuning of human neonates' preference for speech. *Child Development, 81(2)*, 517–527.

Vouloumanos, A., Kiehl, K.A., Werker, J.F. & Liddle, P.F. (2001). Detection of sounds in the auditory stream: Event-related fMRI evidence for differential activation to speech and non-speech. *Journal of Cognitive Neuroscience, 13(7)*, 994–1005.

Vouloumanos, A. & Werker, J.F. (2007). Listening to language at birth: Evidence for a bias for speech in neonates. *Developmental Science, 10(2)*, 159–171.

Vygotsky, L.S. (1934/1962). *Thought and language.* Cambridge, MA: MIT Press.

Wade, T. (1992). *A comprehensive Russian grammar.* Oxford: Blackwell.

Wales, R. (1986). Deixis. In P. Fletcher & M. Garman (Eds.), *Language acquisition* (2nd ed.). (pp. 401–428). Cambridge: Cambridge University Press.

Walle, E.A. & Campos, J.J. (2014). Infant language development is related to the acquisition of walking. *Developmental Psychology, 50(2)*, 336–348.

Wallman, J. (1992). *Aping language.* Cambridge: Cambridge University Press.

Wallman, J. (1993). On *Aping language*: Reply to Lieberman. *Current Anthropology, 34(4)*, 431–432.

Wanner, E. & Gleitman, L.R. (Eds.) (1982). *Language acquisition: The state of the art.* Cambridge: Cambridge University Press.

Warlaumont, A.S. & Jarmulowicz, L. (2012). Caregivers' suffix frequencies and suffix acquisition by language impaired, late talking, and typically developing children. *Journal of Child Language, 39(5)*, 1017–1042.

Warren-Leubecker, A. & Bohannon, J.N. (1984). Intonation patterns in child-directed speech – mother–father differences. *Child Development, 55(4)*, 1379–1385.

Wartenburger, I., Heekeren, H.R., Abutalebi, J., Cappa, S.F., Villringer, A. & Perani, D. (2003). Early setting of grammatical processing in the bilingual brain. *Neuron, 37(1)*, 159–170.

Wasserman, E.A., Brooks, D.I. & McMurray, B. (2015). Pigeons acquire multiple categories in parallel via associative learning: A parallel to human word learning? *Cognition, 136*, 99–122.

Watt, W.C. (1970). On two hypotheses concerning psycholinguistics. In J.R. Hayes (Ed.), *Cognition and the development of language.* New York: Wiley.

Waxman, S.R. & Markow, D.B. (1995). Words as invitations to form categories: Evidence from twelve- to thirteen-month-old infants. *Cognitive Psychology, 29*, 257–302.

Weisleder, A. & Fernald, A. (2013). Talking to children matters: Early language experience strengthens processing and builds vocabulary. *Psychological Science, 24(11)*, 2143–2152.

Weisleder, A., Otero, N., Marchman, V.A. & Fernald, A. (2015). Child-directed speech mediates SES differences in language-processing skill and vocabulary in Spanish-learning children. Paper presented at the Biennial Meeting of the Society for Research in Child Development, Philadelphia, PA.

Weiss, D.J. & Newport, E.L. (2006). Mechanisms underlying language acquisition: Benefits from a comparative approach. *Infancy, 9(2)*, 241–257.

Weissenborn, J., Goodluck, H. & Roeper, T. (1992). Introduction: Old and new problems in the study of language acquisition. In J. Weissenborn, H. Goodluck & T. Roeper (Eds.), *Theoretical issues in language acquisition: Continuity and change in development.* (pp. 1–23). Hillsdale, NJ: Lawrence Erlbaum.

Weppelman, T.L., Bostow, A., Schiffer, R., Elbert-Perez, E. & Newman, R.S. (2003). Children's use of the prosodic characteristics of infant-directed speech. *Language and Communication, 23(1)*, 63–80.

Werker, J.F. & Hensch, T.K. (2015). Critical periods in speech perception: New directions. *Annual Review of Psychology, 66*, 173–196.

Werker, J.F. & Lalonde, C. (1988). Cross-language speech perception: Initial capabilities and developmental change. *Developmental Psychology, 24*, 672–683.

Werker, J.F. & McLeod, P.J. (1989). Infant preference for both male and female infant-directed talk: A developmental study of attentional and affective responsiveness. *Canadian Journal of Psychology-Revue Canadienne De Psychologie, 43(2)*, 230–246.

Werker, J.F. & Tees, R.C. (1984). Cross-language speech perception: Evidence for perceptual reorganization during the first year of life. *Infant Behavior and Development, 7*, 49–63.

Werker, J.F. & Yeung, H.H. (2005). Infant speech perception bootstraps word learning. *Trends in Cognitive Sciences, 9(11)*, 519–527.

White, L. & Genesee, F. (1996). How native is near-native? The issue of ultimate attainment in adult second language acquisition. *Second Language Research, 12*, 233–365.

Widen, S.C. & Russell, J.A. (2008). Children acquire emotion categories gradually. *Cognitive Development, 23(2)*, 291–312.

Wierzbicka, A. (2011). Bilingualism and cognition: The perspective from semantics. In V. Cook & B. Bassetti (Eds.), *Language and bilingual cognition* (pp. 191–218). New York: Psychology Press.

Willits, J.A., Seidenberg, M.S. & Saffran, J.R. (2015). Distributional structure in language: Contributions to noun-verb difficulty differences in infant word recognition. *Cognition, 132(3)*, 429–436.

Wilson, B., Smith, K. & Petkov, C.I. (2015). Mixed-complexity artificial grammar learning in humans and macaque monkeys: Evaluating learning strategies. *European Journal of Neuroscience, 41(5)*, 568–578.

Winters, B.D., Saksida, L.M. & Bussey, T.J. (2008). Object recognition memory: Neurobiological mechanisms of encoding, consolidation and retrieval. *Neuroscience and Biobehavioral Reviews, 32(5)*, 1055–1070.

Wohlgemuth, S., Adam, I. & Scharff, C. (2014). FoxP2 in songbirds. *Current Opinion in Neurobiology, 28*, 86–93.

Woodward, A.L. (2009). Infants' grasp of others' intentions. *Current Directions in Psychological Science, 18(1)*, 53–57.

Wuillemin, D., Richardson, B. & Lynch, J. (1994). Right hemisphere involvement in processing later-learned languages in multilinguals. *Brain & Language, 46*, 620–636.

Xanthos, A., Laaha, S., Gillis, S., et al. (2011). On the role of morphological richness in the early development of noun and verb inflection. *First Language, 31(4)*, 461–479.

Xiao, Y., Brauer, J., Lauckner, M., Zhai, H., Jia, F., Margulies, D.S. & Friederici, A.D. (2016). Development of the intrinsic language network in preschool children from ages 3 to 5 years. *PLoS One, 11(11)*, e0165802.

Xu, F. & Tenenbaum, J.B. (2007). Word learning as Bayesian inference. *Psychological Review*, *114(2)*, 245–272.

Yang, C.D. (2004). Universal grammar, statistics or both? *Trends in Cognitive Sciences*, *8(10)*, 451–456.

Yang, C.D. (2013). Ontogeny and phylogeny of language. *Proceedings of the National Academy of Sciences of the United States of America*, *110(16)*, 6324–6327.

Yeni-Komshian, G.H., Flege, J.E. & Liu, S. (2000). Pronunciation proficiency in the first and second languages of Korean-English. *Bilingualism: Language and Cognition*, *3(2)*, 131–149.

Yoshinaga-Itano, C. (2003). From screening to early identification & intervention: Discovering predictors to successful outcomes for children with significant hearing loss. *Journal of Deaf Studies and Deaf Education*, *8(1)*, 11–30.

Yu, A.C. & Margoliash, D. (1996). Temporal hierarchical control of singing in birds. *Science*, *273(5283)*, 1871–1875.

Yuan, S. & Fisher, C. (2009). 'Really? She blicked the baby?': Two-year-olds learn combinatorial facts about verbs by listening. *Psychological Science*, *20(5)*, 619–626.

Zhang, Y., Kuhl, P.K., Imada, T., Kotani, M. & Tohkura, Y. (2005). Effects of language experience: Neural commitment to language-specific auditory patterns. *Neuroimage*, *26(3)*, 703–720.

Zhang, Y.W., Jin, X.M., Shen, X.M., Zhang, J.M. & Hoff, E. (2008). Correlates of early language development in Chinese children. *International Journal of Behavioral Development*, *32(2)*, 145–151.

Author Index

Subject Index